"Andrew Wilson's book is extraordinary in every way: extraordinary in the breadth of research; extraordinary in the multitude of world-significant events that Wilson identifies for 1776; extraordinary in the depth of his insight on what those events meant (and continue to mean); extraordinary in the verve with which he makes his arguments; and, not least, extraordinary in the persuasive Christian framework in which he sets the book. *Remaking the World* is a triumph of both creative historical analysis and winsome Christian interpretation."

Mark Noll, Research Professor of History, Regent College; author, *America's Book: The Rise and Decline of a Bible Civilization, 1794–1911*

"Andrew Wilson is a wise and witty guide through the eventful year 1776 (eventful in, as he shows, sometimes surprising ways). He convincingly demonstrates that we're still living in the wake of that historical moment—and offers shrewd suggestions for how Christians might navigate those rough waters."

Alan Jacobs, Distinguished Professor of Humanities, Baylor University

"Andrew Wilson's extraordinary *Remaking the World* delivers a gripping history of how the seeds of the post-Christian West were sown in the late eighteenth century. It is an intellectual tour de force and a model of Christian scholarship."

Thomas S. Kidd, Research Professor of Church History, Midwestern Baptist Theological Seminary; author, *Thomas Jefferson: A Biography of Spirit and Flesh*

"The eighteenth century is one of the most fascinating and important periods in human history, and in this book, Andrew Wilson shows exactly why. *Remaking the World* isn't just a history book, however. It's a wide-ranging examination and exploration of the past that makes sense of our present and shines a light on the future. Few books offer as compelling, rich, and insightful cultural analysis that covers so much ground as this one. It's history for history lovers—and for the rest of us."

Karen Swallow Prior, author, *The Evangelical Imagination: How Stories, Images, and Metaphors Created a Culture in Crisis*

"Brilliantly conceived, carefully researched, and written with verve, this book shows how one single year—1776—made the world all of us inhabit. Bringing together historical drama and specific events told in granular detail, this is history as it should be recounted—provocative, engaging, and consequential. Heartedly recommended!"

Timothy George, Distinguished Professor of Divinity, Beeson Divinity School, Samford University

"When Americans see '1776' in the subtitle of a book written by an Englishman, they likely think they know what to expect—an apologia for monarchy. That's not this book. Instead, *Remaking the World* offers an insightful and trenchant intellectual history of how the ideas and figures of a single year catapulted us into the present. A book like this should make Christians more discerning and critical about the taken-for-granted assumptions that we all believe are routine but are really the product of forces outside our control. Toward the end, Wilson gives Christians a pathway to witness to a world that thinks it has eclipsed the claims of Christianity but remains unable to explain itself apart from it."

Andrew T. Walker, Associate Professor of Christian Ethics, The Southern Baptist Theological Seminary; Fellow, The Ethics and Public Policy Center

"This is an arresting book. Even though Andrew Wilson is a vocational pastor and not a professional historian, his historical judgment and modesty are exemplary. His narrative is sensitive to the many complex causes of 'modernity,' never gets bogged down in details, and is written with elegant and lively prose. I can think of no better book to help Christians understand how our world has (and has not) become post-Christian. In *Remaking the World*, Wilson has established himself among contemporary Christianity's most subtle and interesting thinkers."

Matthew Lee Anderson, Assistant Research Professor of Ethics and Theology, Institute for Studies of Religion, Baylor University; Cohost, *Mere Fidelity*

Remaking the World

Remaking the World

How 1776 Created the Post-Christian West

Andrew Wilson

WHEATON, ILLINOIS

Library of Congress Cataloging-in-Publication Data

Names: Wilson, Andrew, 1978- author.
Title: Remaking the world : how 1776 created the post-Christian West / Andrew Wilson.
Other titles: How 1776 created the post-Christian West
Description: Wheaton, Illinois : Crossway, 2023. | Includes bibliographical references and index.
Identifiers: LCCN 2022058032 (print) | LCCN 2022058033 (ebook) | ISBN 9781433580536 (hardcover) | ISBN 9781433580543 (pdf) | ISBN 9781433580567 (epub)
Subjects: LCSH: Civilization, Western—18th century. | Seventeen seventy-six, A.D. | Secularism—Western countries. | Social values—Western countries.
Classification: LCC CB411 .W55 2023 (print) | LCC CB411 (ebook) | DDC 909/.0982109033—dc23/eng/20230130
LC record available at https://lccn.loc.gov/2022058032
LC ebook record available at https://lccn.loc.gov/2022058033

For Mum, Dad, Annie, Sarah, and David,
in abundance

*We have it in our power
to begin the world over again.*
THOMAS PAINE, *COMMON SENSE*

*The modern world is full
of the old Christian virtues
gone mad.*
G. K. CHESTERTON, *ORTHODOXY*

Contents

Illustrations

Tables

Figures

Author's Note

EIGHTEENTH-CENTURY SPELLING and punctuation can be erratic. In general, I have tidied up the sources to make them more readable; occasionally, I have left them unchanged for effect, even though I know that makes me inconsistent. I have also tended to use each person's most familiar name or title throughout their lives (Johann Wolfgang von Goethe, Rebecca Protten, Captain James Cook, and so forth), rather than varying it in order to be strictly accurate. Translations are my own unless otherwise stated.

PART 1

CHANGES

1

Roots

The Presence of the Past

Who controls the past controls the future.
GEORGE ORWELL

We are our history.
JAMES BALDWIN

IN 1776, AT WEYANOKE on the James River in Virginia, Mary Marot Armistead married her fiancé, John. With all that was going on in America that year, it didn't make headlines. She was only fifteen, and John was nearly thirty, but age gaps like that were fairly normal in the thirteen colonies. In many ways, they were a classic example of rich Virginians at the time: Mary was the only daughter of wealthy parents and stood to inherit the beautiful family estate on the edge of Chesapeake Bay, while John had attended William and Mary College, shared a room with Thomas Jefferson, started practicing as a lawyer, and then served a stint in the Continental Army before being appointed as a judge.

Together they had eight children. Unusually, in an age of high infant mortality, all eight of them survived into adulthood. Although John became Governor of Virginia, the chances are that most of us would never have heard of the family were it not for their sixth child, born in 1790 and also named John. He was a frail boy, wafer thin and prone to bouts of diarrhea with which he struggled his whole life. But he followed his father into law and local politics and gradually climbed through the ranks until on April 4, 1841, John Tyler became the tenth president of the United States. Four years later, he signed into law the annexation of Texas.

Curiously, that is only the fourth most remarkable thing about him. The third is that he served the longest presidential term in history without being elected, stepping into the role after William Henry Harrison died just a month into his term. The second is that he got married in office, the first of only two presidents to do so, after his first wife suffered a stroke and died in the White House. And the first—which sounds like it cannot possibly be true for someone who predated the metric system and whose parents were courting during the Battle of Lexington—is that as of 2022, one of his grandsons is still alive.

Not Even Past

Harrison Ruffin Tyler still lives in Charles County, Virginia, where his great-grandparents were married in 1776. He is well into his nineties. Born in 1928, just before the Jazz Age and the Roaring Twenties gave way to the Wall Street Crash and the Great Depression, Harrison was in elementary school when Hitler came to power and secondary school when the Japanese attacked Pearl Harbor. Like anyone of his generation, he has seen astonishing change, both technologically (televisions, atom bombs, the moon landing, the Internet) and politically (World War II, Indian independence, the Chinese Revolution, decolonization). But the social changes he has witnessed are even more dramatic. Just one year older than Martin Luther King, Harrison lived to see the election of Barack Obama and the emergence of the Black Lives Matter movement, despite having had a father who defended the Confederacy and a grandfather who owned seventy slaves.

Harrison's father, Lyon Gardiner Tyler (1853–1935), lived through an even more seismic period of world history. He learned to read and write before the US Civil War, in a state where people owned slaves but not light bulbs. China was in the midst of the Taiping Rebellion, in which thirty million people died. Japan was a feudal society under the *shogun* and the *samurai*. Karl Marx was working on *Das Kapital* in the reading room of the British Museum, and David Livingstone was exploring the Zambezi River. Charles Darwin published *The Origin of Species* when Lyon was six.

The vast majority of the world's population worked on the land, with an average life expectancy of twenty-nine. By the time Lyon died, the Second Industrial Revolution had swept across the world, bringing electricity and indoor plumbing, telephones and movies, factories and skyscrapers, planes, trains, and automobiles. Global life expectancy was above forty and rising rapidly. Women in dozens of countries were going to university, gaining equality under the law, and voting.

Lyon's father, John (1790–1862), would have struggled to cope with the world of his children, let alone his grandchildren. They, and we, would have struggled to live in his. John came into the world on a slave plantation, a few weeks after George Washington's first State of the Union, and nine months into the French Revolution. He was a toddler when Beethoven was first commissioned to write music and when Mary Wollstonecraft published *A Vindication of the Rights of Woman*. As John grew up, his days were continually punctuated by revolution—from the Reign of Terror in France (1793–1794) to the Latin American wars of independence (1808–1833) to the overthrow of nearly all European governments in 1848—not to mention the even more significant "revolution" which was emanating from the mines and mills of Northern England. The speed of transformation was dizzying, as we can tell from the rapid evolution of the English language. Dozens of terms that we cannot imagine a world without—including *industry, factory, scientist, journalism, nationality, railway, working class, middle class, statistics, capitalism, socialism*, and *photograph*—were coined during John's lifetime.[1]

The world in which John Tyler's parents were married in 1776 seems almost unimaginably different from ours. It feels more like a period drama or a theme park than a place where our ancestors actually lived: a land of duels and harpsichords, where people took snuff and talked about "Providence" and "victuals," wearing wigs on their heads, frock coats on their backs, and smallpox scars on their faces.

Yet we are separated from it by only a couple of generations.* The legacy of that world lives on in our ideas and institutions, our race relations and

---

* The British Prime Minister H. H. Asquith (1852–1928) was born during the life of Eliza Hamilton (1757–1854) and yet lived to see the birth of the future Queen Elizabeth II (1926–2022). More astonishingly, a giant tortoise named Adwaita, who once belonged to Robert Clive of India, was born in the Seychelles before the Seven Years War started (ca. 1750) and died during the American occupation of Iraq in 2006. The past is closer than we think.

sexual relations, our ambitions and maps. Grandparents are like that. Their influence lingers on in the lives of their grandchildren, shaping their prospects and their values long after they are gone. "The past is never dead," wrote Faulkner. "It's not even past."[2]

A Forgetful Age

Ours is a forgetful age, though. Lots of us do not remember the names of our great-grandparents; perhaps it is unsurprising that we do not remember their world either. The rate of change in the last two centuries makes the past feel much further away than it actually is, which inclines us to fawn over the future, and either patronize the past or ignore it altogether.

Our technology does not help us here. We spend much of our lives on devices that are designed to need replacing every three years, accessing social media platforms that amplify the sense of a continuous present and an absent past. A huge number of well-educated people, for example, marked the end of 2016 by lamenting it (quite unironically) as "the worst year ever," despite having marked the one-hundredth anniversary of The Battle of the Somme just six months before. Mainstream media outlets are no different. The Coronavirus pandemic of 2020 was repeatedly described as unprecedented in its impact, despite the Spanish flu (or for that matter, the Black Death). More amusingly, I think of the European correspondent for Reuters in the 1970s who, apparently unaware of World War II, claimed that "Relations between Britain and Germany fell to an all-time low today over potato quotas."[3] In an era of instant news, amnesia is baked in. And amnesia has consequences.

One is confusion. The dizzying number of social changes in the anglophone West from 2014 to 2017 alone—gay marriage, Brexit, Trump, #BlackLivesMatter, transgender rights, Antifa, #MeToo, and so forth—left many people reeling, punch-drunk, even fearful about what would happen next. For obvious reasons, periods of social upheaval are always disorienting. But they can be particularly distressing when we do not know our history. Everything feels unexpected, as if it is coming out of nowhere. Developments appear unconnected to the past, and indeed to each other. In the absence of a plausible historical narrative, people retreat into tribalism or conspiracy theories (perhaps both) to help them make sense of the pace of change, because the deeper currents that shape society over decades and centuries—what James Davison Hunter calls the cultural "climate," as opposed to the "weather"—are invisible to them.[4] The results can be painful.

Another result of amnesia is arrogance, and it is available in both conservative and progressive flavors. In the progressive version, our current mores are self-evidently correct, which means that anyone who thought differently a hundred years ago, or even ten years ago, must have been either stupid or evil (or both). In the conservative version, the only reasons for a person's success are their own ability and effort, which means that anyone who highlights the importance of historical privileges, or oppression, must be either jealous or lazy (or both). Memory, in contrast, should generate humility: the acknowledgment of our past, with all its strengths and weaknesses, and the recognition that the reason we have the moral convictions we do, and the material advantages we do, is because of our ancestors. As James Baldwin relentlessly pointed out, we are our history.[5]

Remaking the World

The big idea of this book is that 1776, more than any other year in the last millennium, is the year that made us who we are.[6] We cannot understand ourselves without it. It was a year that witnessed seven transformations taking place—globalization, the Enlightenment, the Industrial Revolution, the Great Enrichment, the American Revolution, the rise of post-Christianity, and the dawn of Romanticism—which have remade the world and profoundly influenced the way we think about God, life, the universe, and everything.[†]

These transformations—some call them "revolutions"—explain all kinds of apparently unrelated features of our culture. They reveal why we believe in human rights, free trade, liberal democracy, and religious pluralism; they ground our preference for authenticity over authority, choice over duty, and self-expression over self-denial; and they account for all kinds of phenomena that our great-grandparents would have found incomprehensible, from intersectionality to bitcoin. 1776 provides us with an origin story for the post-Christian West.

That involves a combination of two claims. One relates to the world we live in today, and one to the world of two and a half centuries ago.

---

† Needless to say, none of these transformations springs up out of nowhere in 1776. For the larger stories within which each development makes sense, see chapters 3–9.

The first claim, which will be the focus of chapter 2, is that the most help-ful way of identifying what is distinctive about our society, relative to others past and present, is that it is WEIRDER: Western, Educated, Industrialized, Rich, Democratic, Ex-Christian, and Romantic.[7] Those seven features make us outliers. The vast majority of people in human history have not shared our views of work, family, government, religion, sex, identity, or morality, no matter how universal or self-evident we may think they are. We are the WEIRDER ones.[‡]

The second claim is that all seven of those things are true because of things that happened in 1776. Telling that story will occupy most of this book, but we can see it in outline by considering just ten prominent events from that year.

In January, Thomas Paine released his pamphlet *Common Sense* in Philadelphia, arguing that the American colonies should pursue indepen-dence from British rule; it caused an immediate sensation and became one of the fastest-selling and most influential books in American history. In February, Edward Gibbon published the first volume of *The History of the Decline and Fall of the Roman Empire*, which set new standards in history writing, while also challenging the established church and providing a skeptical narrative of early Christianity that endures to this day. James Watt's steam engine, probably the single most important in-vention in industrial history, started running at the Bloomfield colliery in Staffordshire on March 8. The very next day, Adam Smith released the foundational text of modern economics, *An Inquiry into the Nature and Causes of the Wealth of Nations*.

‡   There are numerous other ways of referring to this world, but all of them suffer from significant limitations. Some—*the First World* or *the civilized world* or *the free world*—are patronizing and inaccurate. Geographical descriptors like *the Western hemisphere* make little or no sense to anyone who has consulted a globe and seen where "Western" countries actually are. Chrono-logical terms like *modern, late modern,* or *postmodern* are complicated by heated disagreements over what exactly "modernity" is and whether we are still in it. Some terms highlight ideas and values (*secular, liberal,* or *pluralist*), or institutions and systems (*capitalist, democratic*), to the exclusion of material circumstances. Others do the reverse and focus on material or technological development, like *industrialized, rich, developed, urban, bourgeois, postindustrial,* or *digital,* although these terms are too broad to stand on their own, since they apply just as much to Shanghai and Dubai as they do to Paris or Chicago. By contrast the term WEIRDER, in bundling seven adjectives into one, combines geographical, material, ideological, historical, and even emotional features of the world it describes, which gives it a range and nuance that other terms lack.

The most famous transformations of the year took place in the American summer, with the establishing of a nation that would play an increasingly dominant role in the next two centuries: the ratification of the Declaration of Independence (July 4), the Battle of Long Island and the taking of Brooklyn by the British (August 27), and the formal adoption of the name United States (September 9). On the other side of the Atlantic, Captain James Cook was sailing southward in the *Resolution* in the last of his three voyages to the South Seas, the impact of which can still be felt throughout the Pacific Islands, New Zealand, and Australia. Immanuel Kant was in Königsberg, writing the outline for his *Critique of Pure Reason*, which would bring about a so-called Copernican Revolution in philosophy. In Edinburgh, David Hume finally completed his *Dialogues concerning Natural Religion*, one of the greatest arguments against Christian theism ever written, before dying on August 25. The autumn saw Friedrich Klinger write his play *Sturm und Drang* ("Storm and Stress"), which soon gave its name to the proto-Romantic movement in German music and literature, just as Jean-Jacques Rousseau was writing his extraordinary *Reveries of a Solitary Walker*. And in December, as Washington and his army were crossing the Delaware to surprise the British at Trenton, Benjamin Franklin arrived in Paris on a diplomatic mission to bring France into the war against Britain. It would eventually prove successful, and lead ultimately to the American victory at Yorktown (1781), and the collapse of the French *ancien régime* into bankruptcy and revolution (1789).

Between them, those ten events represent a series of transformations that inaugurated the WEIRDER world. Some are so prominent that they have passed into everyday speech. People freely refer to the Industrial Revolution, the American Revolution and the Enlightenment. Others are less recognized but no less significant. You could argue that the long-term impact of globalization or post-Christianity or Romanticism or the Great Enrichment has been just as "revolutionary" as American independence, if not more so.

As such, it is only fair to my American readers to point out that much of this book is not about America at all. For obvious reasons, people who look back to 1776 as the start of their nation are inclined to see it as a year in which only one significant event occurred; in the immortal words of Ron Swanson, "History began on July 4th 1776. Everything before that was a mistake."[8] But many of the momentous events that took place in this remarkable year had nothing to do with independence or war with Britain, and instead were occurring in French salons, Italian cafés, German theaters, Scottish pubs, and English factories.

It was a year in which the things that were done—battles, retreats, river crossings, and so forth—were not nearly as important as the things that were said and written. Indeed, it is hard to think of a year in which more quotable, seminal remarks were made than this one. Some of them, of course, have passed into folklore in America because of their rhetorical power in the context of the revolutionary war: Thomas Paine's "These are the times that try men's souls,"[9] and Washington's "Are these the men with which I am to defend America?"[10] Others are noteworthy for how well they articulated the implications of the revolution: Lemuel Haynes for his fellow African-Americans ("Liberty is equally as precious to a black man as it is to a white one, and bondage equally as intolerable to the one as it is to the other"),[11] Abigail Adams for women ("In the new Code of Laws which I suppose it will be necessary for you to make I desire you would Remember the Ladies")[12], and Edmund Burke for Britain ("I can hardly believe, from the tranquillity of everything about me, that we are a people who have just lost an empire. But it is so").[13] John Wesley, eager to defend his own loyalty to the Crown and his willingness to pay taxes, explained his radical commitment to simple living: "I have a silver teaspoon at London and two at Bristol. This is all the plate I have at present, and I shall not buy any more while so many round me lack bread."[14]

Other statements are famous because they encapsulate the spirit of an age: a spirit of confidence in human reason and potential that was almost tangible in the late eighteenth century, and the aftershocks of which can still be felt today. "We have it in our power to begin the world over again," declared Paine in one of the most audacious sentences ever written.[15] Matthew Boulton, revealing his phalanx of steam machines to James Boswell, drew his optimism from the possibilities of technology: "I sell here, Sir, what all the world desires to have—POWER."[16] Jeremy Bentham took the opportunity to reframe human ethics ("It is the greatest happiness of the greatest number that is the measure of right and wrong"),[17] and Adam Smith did the same with economics ("He intends only his own gain, and he is in this, as in many other cases, led by an invisible hand to promote an end which was no part of his intention").[18] Horace Walpole captured the ambiguity of the age of enlightenment and sentiment with his trademark wit: "This world is a comedy to those that think, a tragedy to those that feel."[19] James Madison, making adjustments to the Virginia Declaration of Rights, insisted that the final section include the phrase, "All men are equally entitled to the free exercise of religion, according to the dictates of conscience."[20] Most influentially of all, the Declaration of Independence proclaimed it "self-evident, that all men are created equal, that they are endowed by their Creator with certain unalienable rights, that among these are life, liberty and the pursuit of happiness."[21]

These ideas—and the individuals, institutions, and inventions with which they are associated—made us WEIRDER. We are who we are because of them. That is the argument of chapters 3–9.

Table 1.1   1776 and the WEIRDER world

	Feature	Development	Key Events in 1776
W	Western	Globalization	Captain James Cook's third voyage begins
			Endeavour / *Lord Sandwich* sails for New York
			Mai returns to Tahiti on the *Resolution*
			Georg Forster writes his *Voyage Around the World*
E	Educated	Enlightenment	Immanuel Kant drafts his *Critique of Pure Reason*
			Edward Gibbon publishes his *Decline and Fall*
			Carl Linnaeus retires
			Baron d'Holbach's salon, The Club, Poker Club, etc.
I	Industrialized	Industrial Revolution	James Watt's steam engine
			Richard Arkwright's mill at Cromford
			Bridgewater canal opens
			Lunar Society begins meeting
R	Rich	Great Enrichment	Beginning of dramatic rise in GDP
			Adam Smith publishes *Wealth of Nations*
			American Revolution
			Raynal's *Histoire* released in English

(Table 1.1 continued)

	Feature	Development	Key Events in 1776
D	Democratic	American Revolution	Declaration of Independence Virginia Declaration of Rights Benjamin Franklin's diplomatic mission Washington's crossing
E	Ex-Christian	Rejection of Christianity	David Hume completes his *Dialogues*, then dies Franklin's edit to the Declaration of Independence Diderot's *Interview* Sade's ex-Christian morality
R	Romantic	Romantic Revolution	Rousseau writes his *Reveries of a Solitary Walker* Klinger writes *Sturm und Drang* Herder, Goethe and friends all in Weimar First sexual revolution in London

So What?

The final two chapters address the question: So what?

I am writing as a Christian pastor. I find history fascinating, and I am convinced that it can help us become wiser, humbler, and more loving neighbors. But my primary motive in writing this is to help the church thrive in a WEIRDER world. What challenges and opportunities emerge from Westernization or Romanticism or Industrialization, and what should we do about them? How should Christians act in an Ex-Christian culture? What does faithful Christianity look like in the shadow of 1776? And here, I believe, we can draw a great deal of wisdom from an obvious source: faithful Christianity in 1776. How did believers in this turbulent and transformative era respond to what was happening around them? And what can we learn?

As it happens, several strands within the contemporary church look back to 1776 as an especially formative year. It was a crucial period in the development of early Methodism. John Wesley secured, and began fundraising for, a site on which to build a new headquarters in London. John Fletcher, whom most people assumed would succeed Wesley as the next leader, caught tuberculosis, which prompted a complete rethink of how the movement would be led in the next generation. The American Revolution began a chain of events that would lead the Methodists to ordain their own ministers and finally separate from the Anglican church. The need for new premises, new leadership, and a new denomination would prove catalytic for the rapid growth of Methodism in the following century.

It was a landmark year in other denominations as well. American dissenters, as we have just seen, saw the crucial words "free exercise of religion" appear in the Virginia Declaration of Rights and subsequently in the first amendment of the US Constitution. San Francisco was founded by Catholic missionaries. Former slave trader John Newton was working on the Olney Hymns, which would be published in 1779 and include his "Amazing Grace" and William Cowper's "God Moves in a Mysterious Way." Lemuel Haynes wrote his antislavery manuscript *Liberty Further Extended.* The fifteen year-old William Carey, who would grow up to become the father of modern missions and translate the Bible into six Indian languages, had the experience that led to his conversion. Marie Durand, the French Huguenot famous for scratching the word "RESISTER" on the wall of her cell during an imprisonment that lasted thirty-eight years, died at the age of sixty-five. Calvinist vicar Augustus Toplady published "Rock of Ages." Holy Trinity Church Clapham, later attended by members of the Clapham Sect including William Wilberforce, Granville Sharp, and Hannah More, opened for worship.

Most of these people would be widely known within Christian circles today, and often outside them. Their institutions, hymns, missionary exploits, and abolitionism are part of the mythology of evangelicalism. But we will also reflect on some individuals whose contributions are less recognized: Rebecca Protten, the former slave who became a Moravian missionary; Johann Georg Hamann, the first postsecular philosopher;[22] Olaudah Equiano, whose *Interesting Narrative* would become so important in the battle to end the slave trade. Though miles apart in their experiences and writings, each of these people have a great deal to teach us about living as Christians in a WEIRDER world.

The Need for Roots

A few years ago, I noticed how many of my favorite authors were writing during or immediately after World War II. It had not occurred to me before, and I wondered why it might be the case. There are probably some stylistic reasons. Their language is near enough to our own day not to sound arcane, and the crispness, simplicity, and visual quality of their prose was shaped by the advent of the cinema. Their works are also marked by a deep awareness of radical evil, which is hardly surprising given the times in which they lived. It gives their essays an urgency, and their poetry and fiction a cosmic drama that few writers before or since have achieved: think of Big Brother and Room 101, Sauron and Saruman, *Lord of the Flies*, the White Witch, *Animal Farm*, and the role of sin and the devil in Graham Greene's novels.

So it is fascinating how often their responses to radical evil involve an appeal to history. Sometimes this comes as a direct address to the reader, like James Baldwin's writings on race, Hannah Arendt's on revolution, Leszek Kołakowski's on communism, Isaiah Berlin's on liberalism, or Dorothy Sayers's *Creed or Chaos*. T. S. Eliot and W. H. Auden do it through their numerous references and allusions. Greene and Flannery O'Connor draw on their Catholicism. C. S. Lewis makes the point through essays on why we should read old books and by skewering chronological snobbery at every opportunity, from *That Hideous Strength* to the fates of Uncle Andrew and King Miraz in the Narnia stories.

J. R. R. Tolkien does it through his medieval language and setting, his complex prehistories, and his plot: remember Sam on the edge of Mount Doom, reminiscing about the Shire and reminding Frodo of the old stories long before totalitarian evil seized the world. Simone Weil's greatest work is entitled *L'Enracinement*, usually translated *The Need for Roots*. Most powerfully of all, George Orwell creates worlds where nobody remembers the past, and where those in power, from the pigs in *Animal Farm* to the Party in *1984*, are free to manipulate it for their own purposes, throwing unwanted recollections down the memory hole. "History has stopped. Nothing exists except an endless present in which the Party is always right."[23] All of these writers had witnessed the near-collapse of the West in recent memory, and they knew the dangers of losing their history, as well as the importance of not allowing it.

We do not have to look too hard for contemporary equivalents. History is the most contested of subject areas, now as then, because (as Orwell pointed out) those who control the past control the future. If you want to prevent twenty-first century Christians from preaching the gospel, pursuing social reform and holding fast to orthodox faith, then history is your friend: just cast eighteenth-century missionaries as rapacious villains, nineteenth-century reformers as patrician moralists, and the defense of biblical authority in the twentieth century as a thinly disguised power play, and browbeaten believers will flee the public square like rabbits in the field when the fox arrives. Conversely, if you want to ensure that the divisions and injustices of the eighteenth-century church continue into the present, then give people a triumphalist historical narrative of evangelistic breakthrough, social transformation, and spiritual revival, while carefully omitting the egregious racial, sexual, and political failures of their heroes. Paint goodies and baddies in lurid color, and make all historical context a vague, indecipherable pastille gray. Rinse, wash, repeat.

We are storytelling creatures, so narrating origin stories is inevitable. Indeed, since it is impossible to be theologically neutral when it comes to history, narrating *theological* origin stories is probably inevitable. The only question is whether those origin stories are true, good, and beautiful: whether they reflect what really happened and why; whether they nudge us toward courageous humility and love; whether they recount the wondrous deeds of the Lord alongside the successes and failures of human beings. The arrogance of amnesia is always a threat, not least in periods of great technological and economic change, and so is the defeatism born of weary cynicism about flawed ancestors.

So it is vital, as the Psalms and the Prophets remind us, to remember: remember the deeds of our fathers and mothers, remember the rock from which we were hewn, and the quarry from which we were dug. It can help us understand why our world is the way it is—how it became Western, Educated, Industrialized, Rich, Democratic, Ex-Christian, and Romantic, not least through the transformations of 1776—and how to love, live, and thrive in it.

2

Quirks

The WEIRDER World

Once the world of ideas has been transformed,
reality cannot hold out for long.
G. W. F. HEGEL

With most people, unbelief in one thing springs
from blind belief in something else.
GEORG CHRISTOPH LICHTENBERG

THE WORLD YOU LIVE IN IS WEIRDER. I am too. So are you. Let me tell you about yourself.

Start with the obvious: you can read. You have been literate since you were a small child. The way you process information is marked by that fact in countless ways, including the manner and scope of your education, the things you remember and forget, the length and shape of your sentences, the way you solve problems, and your approaches to tradition, law, religion, and social hierarchy. Not only can you read, and almost certainly write; in a sense, you cannot *not* read. If you tried to look at the characters on this page simply as swirls of ink, without any semantic content, your brain would find it impossible not to retrieve the information. If you have ever tried the Stroop test, in which a color's name is written in ink of a different color (like the word *red* written in blue ink), you will know how difficult it is to stop yourself from reading, even if you are desperately trying not to. Literacy has rewired your brain.

Specifically, you can read in English. This Germanic language, a curious amalgam of Frisian, Latin, Saxon, Old Norse, and French, was spoken only by about four million people when Geoffrey Chaucer was writing it down in the late fourteenth century. Today, English is used by at least two billion people worldwide, three quarters of whom do not speak it at home. This five-hundredfold increase is not the result of unusually high fertility levels in the British Isles. Rather, it is the result of the widespread commercial, political, and cultural influence of English-speaking people over the last three centuries in particular.

As such, your ability to read this page is striking evidence of Westernization. Granted, there are a number of different ways of defining "the West." We might see it through the lens of geography (those who live in Western Eurasia) or demography (those descended from the West Asian population core, whom we will meet in chapter 3). We might trace it back to its historical origins in the political division between the Eastern and Western Roman empires or the subsequent religious one between the Eastern (Greek, Orthodox) and Western (Latin, Catholic) parts of Christendom. We could define "the West" based on the history of colonization (the North Atlantic maritime empires and their American and Antipodean settlements), or based on economic ideology during the Cold War (the capitalist and communist systems on either side of the Berlin Wall). Or we might use a combination of these. But the fact that you speak English means that you have certainly been Westernized in at least one of these senses, and probably in all of them, even if you live thousands of miles away from the land of Shakespeare.

You have been educated in a wide variety of subjects that make very little difference to your day-to-day life. For at least ten years, and probably longer, it is likely that the state paid for you to be taught various subjects (like history, chemistry, literature, and so on) that are of no vocational value to the vast majority of its citizens. The state saw education as a public good in itself, a basic privilege that we expect all children to receive. So did your teachers. So do you. You might believe that state-funded education should become entirely skills-based at age sixteen. You might believe that taxpayers should fund doctoral studies for arts graduates. But you almost certainly believe that some measure of vocational irrelevance—learning things simply because they interest us and expand our horizons—is important to our intellectual and personal development and that we should all pay taxes in order to fund it.

This point is made powerfully in Tara Westover's bestselling memoir, *Educated*.[1] Born into a family of Mormon survivalists, she develops plenty of technical skills in her father's junkyard but receives no formal schooling and arrives at university aged seventeen knowing nothing of Western art, and without having heard of the Holocaust. Her classmates, and we as readers, regard her as both inexplicable and tragically impoverished for her ignorance, and root for her to become educated, which she eventually does. In the process, we come to realize just how important we think education is, and how far we see learning for its own sake as integral to human flourishing.

You see academic qualifications as a key indicator of social status: more important than noble blood, land, class, family connections, and perhaps even wealth. You want your own children, if you have them, to be educated to the highest level possible. Because you are literate, you will continue to learn superfluous information throughout your life without thinking you are wasting your time (which includes reading books just like this one). Whatever your political views, you almost certainly regard the education of all children—not just unusually well-born, gifted, or affluent ones—as a social and moral imperative, not least because it has the capacity to promote social equality by enabling bright children from poor backgrounds to succeed.

The room in which you are reading this is a microcosm of industrialization and economic prosperity, however wealthy (or not) you are in relative terms. You are sitting or lying on a piece of furniture that was not built in your house, and perhaps not even in your country. You bought it because it was the best available item at the cheapest available price. Numerous products within a few feet of you were designed in one country, built in another, sold in yet another, and have reached you by means of a complex web of container ships, railways, delivery vans, and retail outlets. The room has at least one window and a door. It has electric lighting, mobile phone signal, and perhaps Wi-Fi. The building you are in contains more timepieces than the average medieval country. The presence of central heating and air conditioning means that you are neither too hot nor too cold at the moment. There is a toilet within thirty seconds' walk of you. You are wearing at least one piece of clothing made of cotton, and probably several. There is a device nearby, no larger than a human hand, that gives you instant access to more information than has been printed in the history of the world.

Equally striking are the things that you are not experiencing. You are not at war. You cannot smell livestock or their excrement from where you are sitting. You are not hungry or thirsty. You almost certainly do not work on the land, and even if you do, your produce will not generate the vast majority of the calories you consume in a day. The clothes you are currently wearing were not made by you, and they do not express a particular regional or cultural identity; the shirt, trousers, and shoes you have on look roughly equivalent to what people your age are wearing in Beijing, São Paolo, Istanbul, Mumbai, and Los Angeles. You do not owe a proportion of your labor to a master, lord, or family member (unless you count taxation, on which see the next paragraph). You do not barter, and you do not store most of your available wealth in physical form. You may never have seen a dead body. You have never offered an animal sacrifice. You are not married to one of your blood relatives, and you do not personally know anyone who is.

By law, you have the right to vote. You take it for granted that your governments have the right to tax you, and that you have the right to boot out your officials if you disapprove of them. This conviction extends to all sorts of other institutions as well: it seems natural to you that businesses, charities, voluntary organizations, religious groups, and unions should take into account the views of the people they represent, whether expressed through formal elections or informal consent—and that if they do not, the appropriate response is to withhold your support from them. It also extends into your private life (a category that you almost certainly believe in). Fundamental to your understanding of human freedom is the capacity to make choices. From breakfast cereals to career paths, fabric softeners to family size, marriage partners to religious commitments, you expect to be able to choose for yourself rather than acting out of legal compulsion or familial obligation. Remarkably, all of these things are true regardless of whether you are male or female.

Your view of the world is Ex-Christian in a variety of ways, even if (like me) you believe in God and go to church every week. You doubt. Some days it is harder to believe than not to believe: in miracles, in the goodness of God, in the idea that he can hear your prayers, even in his existence. You distinguish sharply between the sacred and the secular, even when trying not to. You probably regard the language of faith as inappropriate in certain contexts: in meetings with clients, in political broadcasts, during sexual intercourse, or whatever it is. You struggle with mystery at both intellectual and emotional levels. You spend a substantial portion of your leisure time consuming media—articles, songs, newspapers, websites, television shows—whose ideology is either post- or anti-Christian.

You accept religious pluralism as a reality in your society. Even when pressing for Christian ethical commitments in the public square, you would be careful not to articulate them using biblical arguments alone. You operate on a secular rather than a religious calendar: your year starts in January and/or September rather than Advent, and your week starts on Monday rather than Sunday. You think religious commitment is a choice that each person should make for themselves. You reject theocracy, believing in the separation of church and state. You see lightning bolts as atmospheric phenomena rather than acts of God. In Charles Taylor's language, you see the self as "buffered" rather than porous or vulnerable, and naturally view this world, rather than the next, as the location of ultimacy and meaning.[2] You live in a universe rather than a cosmos: a disenchanted world of impersonal laws (even if they are occasionally broken) rather than a divinely indwelt temple.

At the same time, you hold all sorts of Christian assumptions about the world, even if you do *not* believe in God.[3] It is clear to you that there are such things as human rights, such that a certain level of dignity belongs to all people simply because they are members of the human race, and laws and customs should reflect this in practice. You reject polygamy. You believe in limitations on the power of the state and that the rule of law is essential to a healthy society, whereby the *rex* (king) is always subject to the *lex* (law). You think those with much should provide for those with little, whether this is expressed through a redistributive state, charitable giving, or both. You affirm the fundamental equality of all people before the law. You abhor slavery. You do not seek to justify inequalities in wealth or status as part of the natural order of things, and to a greater or lesser degree you seek to reduce them.

You think the central unit in human relations is the self, the sovereign individual, rather than the group to which the self belongs. You think all people are equally endowed with free will, reason, and moral agency. Humility in others is more attractive to you than pride. Love is more appealing to you than honor. You think colonialism is morally problematic, and that those who have benefited from it have obligations (however defined) to those who did not. You think of time as an arrow rather than a wheel: you believe that we are gradually making progress toward a better world rather than declining from a previous Golden Age or recurring in an endless series of cycles, and as such you would think "behind the times" is an insult and "ahead of her time" is a compliment. You admire people who forgive their enemies. You long for transcendence and are likely to describe yourself as spiritual, open to the supernatural, and even as praying sometimes. Even if the God of Abraham is dead to you, your language, legal framework, moral imagination, and sense of self are all haunted by his ghost.[4]

Finally, you see your identity as something you choose and construct for yourself rather than something you are given. The true "you" is not imposed on you from the outside, by your ancestors or your community; it is something internal, and only you get to say exactly what it is, even if you describe it using categories strikingly similar to the ones your peers use. You may choose different self-definitions in different contexts (so your Facebook, Twitter, Instagram, and LinkedIn profiles may vary from one another, and indeed from what they each said five years ago, depending on what aspects of yourself you want to emphasize). Authenticity is far more valuable to you than conformity. You shudder at the thought of being in an arranged marriage. It might seem natural to you that people can choose their sexual orientation, gender, and pronouns, or it might seem absurd— but either way, you almost certainly see your own sexuality as an integral part of what it is to be you, and regard sexual intercourse as a context for self-expression, not just procreation or marital union.

You make all kinds of decisions based on your gut feeling. You used to watch Disney movies where the lead characters had to "find themselves," "follow their hearts," or "be true to themselves," and perhaps you still do. You have taken at least one personality test. You see dancing as an opportunity for expressing individuality rather than aligning yourself with what everyone else is doing; in Roger Scruton's phrase, you dance "at" other people rather than "with" them.[5] Many of your contemporaries wear tattoos, with designs they chose themselves. You believe that great art, music, and literature come from within and involve creation and imagination rather than representation and imitation. The artwork in your office likely contains far more abstract shapes than religious or mythical figures. You find wild and remote landscapes more beautiful than meticulously manicured gardens and would use words like "inspiring" or "breathtaking" to describe them. More of the songs on your playlist are about romantic relationships than anything else.

I have just made over a hundred generalizations about you, and you have probably worked out which ones (e.g., "your room has electric lighting," or "you have taken at least one personality test") relate to which development (e.g., industrialization or Romanticism). The vast majority of these statements are presumably true in your case. And the vast majority of them are *not* true of most people in history.

That insight is not new to you. If you have read much history, traveled a bit, lived in a diverse area, or even watched television, you already know how different you are from a great many of your fellow humans. But it hopefully makes the point nonetheless. You are WEIRDER, and you know it.

Weirder Psychology

But being WEIRDER affects our behavior, and even our brains, in ways that are much less obvious. The moral psychologist Jonathan Haidt gives a host of examples in his superb book *The Righteous Mind*.[6] For instance, we are unique in regarding certain actions as morally permissible even if we find them personally disgusting. Haidt gives the example of a man who purchases a raw chicken from a supermarket and then has sex with it. Most people throughout history would regard that as morally wrong; WEIRDER people will usually say that it is gross, but it cannot be immoral if it does not harm anyone.

We see the world in terms of discrete, separate objects rather than the relationships between them. If asked to define ourselves using the phrase "I am _____," we are much more likely to self-identify using our interests, achievements, and personal characteristics than using genealogies or relationships to other people. We think analytically, based on abstractions, more than holistically, based on context. There is data for all of this.

It runs so deep that it affects our visual perception. In the framed-line test, a group of Western and East Asian participants are shown a vertical line inside a square frame. They are then shown another square frame of a different size and asked to draw a line that is identical to the first line, either in absolute terms or relative to the size of the frame.[7] Western people excel at the absolute test because they remember the line as a distinct object. East Asians excel at the relative test because they remember the line in relation to the square. Our brains have become WEIRDER.

Haidt's most important observation is that we evaluate morality in a far narrower range of ways than most societies do because we value autonomy far more than tradition or solidarity. In a WEIRDER culture, actions are assessed as right or wrong based on two key questions: whether they cause harm to another person and whether they are fair to everybody. These two questions are used to evaluate morality in almost all cultures, but most societies will add several others. Is this action loyal, or does it reflect betrayal or treason? Does it express appropriate submission to authority, or is it subversive? Does it demonstrate sanctity, purity, and cleanness, or is it filthy, prompting repugnance and disgust?

Because we are unfamiliar with these moral frameworks, by and large, we struggle to understand the way many people in the world appraise right and wrong. A dramatic example of this was played out in 2006, in front of hundreds of millions of people. When Zinedine Zidane headbutted Marco Materazzi during the World Cup final, after Materazzi had insulted his sister, the WEIRDER world was baffled that anyone could be so foolish as to get sent off at the pinnacle moment of his sporting career, and lose his country the biggest trophy in sport, over something so trivial. Much of the worldwide audience, for whom a sister's honor would matter far more than prize money or national prestige, did not see things that way. Many were baffled that anyone could do anything else.

For Haidt, our narrowness of moral vision—evaluating morality along two axes rather than five or six, and with a disproportionate emphasis on the question of whether something is demonstrably harmful—helps to explain why our political and cultural disagreements are so heated. Many citizens are appealing to moral frameworks that many others simply do not recognize. In a subsequent book, he goes on to show how the reduction of all moral reasoning to accusations of harm, and the gradual morphing of what constitutes "harm" in the first place, has contributed to various other modern pathologies including safetyism, trigger warnings, cancel culture, tribalism, safe spaces, microaggressions, and the dismissal of dissenting views as oppressive.[8] Being WEIRDER, without realizing that we are, is making us angrier and increasingly divided.

The anthropologist Joseph Henrich, who first coined the term WEIRD, takes things in a slightly different direction.[9] Psychologically speaking, he argues, we are "highly individualistic, self-obsessed, control-oriented, non-conformist and analytical" when compared with the rest of humanity. We look for universal patterns to structure our information. We project trends. We break down complex phenomena into manageable chunks and assign them abstract properties, meticulously analyzing trees but often missing the forest. We are patient, hardworking, trusting, and overconfident. We are unusually impartial, often treating strangers very much the same way as we treat our family members, and deploring nepotism. Moral transgressions cause us guilt rather than shame; we are more likely to lose sleep than lose face. Our intuitions and institutions are strikingly individualistic. We value self-esteem more than other-esteem. We tend to see people as acting consistently based on innate personal traits rather than varying widely depending on social context. As a result, we are more likely than most to suffer from cognitive dissonance.

The effects of this in daily life are far-reaching. Statistically speaking, we are unusually comfortable with delayed gratification, and likely to wait significantly longer before receiving a payoff for something we have done. Our honesty toward people we do not personally know is high. If WEIRDER people are given diplomatic immunity, such that we can park wherever we want without receiving a ticket, we will stick to the rules anyway; perhaps unsurprisingly, the propensity to stick to the rules in situations like this is closely correlated with the lack of corruption in a country. (In a natural experiment among UN diplomats in New York City, from 1997–2002, the delegations from Sweden, Canada, Australia, and the UK got no parking tickets at all. The delegations from Egypt, Chad, and Bulgaria accumulated one hundred tickets *per member*.)[10] When appraising people's choices, we place a large amount of weight on their intentions, not just their actions or their consequences. We are much less likely than most people to testify falsely in order to save a friend. We are much more likely to voluntarily give blood. There is data for all of this too.

The main cause of all this, in Henrich's view, is the Western church.[11] (This is one of the reasons I refer to the WEIRDER world as Ex-Christian, even though Henrich does not.) His story goes roughly like this: Ever since the advent of farming, human beings have functioned in intensive kin-based institutions involving extended families, clans, and tribes. That is still how much of the world works. But the Western church, beginning with Pope Gregory the Great in 597, gradually dismantled kinship-based relations in medieval Europe by introducing a number of new norms.*

The cumulative effect of those changes, across the next thousand years or more, was huge. Polygamy and cousin marriage all but vanished. Women got married and had children later. Families got smaller. Europeans began choosing their relational networks rather than being born into them, and began forming voluntary associations like charter towns, guilds, universities, monasteries, and convents. Artisans and merchants traded on the basis of their reputation, not their family connections, which incentivized impartiality, cooperation with strangers, precision, punctuality, and diligence. By the High Middle Ages, Europe was experiencing urbanization, a rise in trade, commerce and credit, renewed interest in law, improving transport connections, and even a craze for towns having their own clocks. The implications of all this would ultimately feed into the Protestant Reformation, all the transformations of 1776, and what we now refer to as the "modern world"—including what sits between your ears.

It does not matter much whether you agree with all the details of Henrich's narrative (or Haidt's, come to that). I do not agree with all of them myself. The point I am making here is that your psychology and your behavior, not just your environment and your culture, are WEIRDER, including in all sorts of ways that you may never have noticed. And there is an impressive amount of experimental research to back that up.

---

* Namely (a) monogamy, (b) taboos against cousin marriage, (c) bilateral as opposed to patrilineal descent, (d) nuclear families, and (e) neolocal residence, whereby newly married couples form a separate household from their parents'.

Weirder Art

If you really want to feel WEIRDER, then consider the art you admire. I have already mentioned Disney films and popular music, which might seem like a bit of a cheap shot. But it is true of more serious art as well. Stop for a moment and ask yourself: If you had to make a list of the greatest pieces of art produced in the twenty-first century so far—novels, movies, paintings, plays, sculptures, television shows, music, dance, poetry—what would make up your top ten? And could any of them have been created in a society that was not WEIRDER from top to bottom?

Take an obvious example. In 2015, Michelle Obama went to the Public Theater in New York City to watch an off-Broadway musical. It had been receiving rave reviews, and she wanted to see what all the fuss was about; within minutes, she found out. In the next few months, the musical transferred to Broadway, and by the following March she and the president were hosting a performance by the entire cast at the White House. The show went on to break records at the Tony Awards, win a Grammy and a Pulitzer Prize, become a Disney film, transfer to the West End and take home seven Olivier Awards, and generate over one billion dollars in revenue. The former First Lady now describes *Hamilton* as "simply the best piece of art in any form that I have ever seen in my life."[12]

If you haven't seen it, here is the one sentence summary: An impoverished immigrant arrives in a new land with nothing but his wits, joins the revolution, writes his way to recognition, fights his way to victory, works his way up to become treasury secretary, designs the nation's financial system, founds a newspaper and a political party, antagonizes nearly everybody, cheats on his wife, loses his son, decides an election, gets shot and killed by the vice president, and ends up on the ten dollar bill.[13] If it were not true, you would never believe it.†

But Alexander Hamilton is not the only bright, scrappy, upstart immigrant who fights his way to the top in *Hamilton*. It is a story of multiple clashes between old and new worlds, in which young, brash, loquacious energy collides with stuffy, patrician traditionalism and comes out on top.

---

† There are so many extraordinary details to Alexander Hamilton's life that one show cannot possibly cover them all. A less well-known example is that Hamilton very nearly ended up in a duel with future President James Monroe over the Reynolds affair, and that the "second" chosen by Monroe (who eventually diffused the situation) was none other than Aaron Burr.

At the personal level, Hamilton takes on Aaron Burr and Thomas Jefferson. At the national level, New York City and its banks struggle for supremacy with Virginia and its plantations. At the international level, America goes to war with Britain. In each case, the new kid on the block is derided for its big mouth, garish fashions, immigrant ways, and obsession with money, but wins anyway. The world is turned upside down.[14] You can sneer at them if you like, and dismiss them as "obnoxious, arrogant, loud-mouthed bother[s]"[15] but the future belongs to Hamilton, New York City, and America, not the slaveowners of the south, or the flowery, crown-wearing buffoons on the other side of the Atlantic.

In that sense, *Hamilton*—which also begins in 1776—is the story of the WEIRDER world. The commercial, industrial North is convinced that the traditional, agricultural South is unprepared for the century ahead. They think this for both economic and moral reasons: economically because of the possibilities of urbanization and shared capital, and morally because of slavery. So the North, at Hamilton's urging and to Jefferson's horror, forges a new path of centralized finance and then industrialization, which upsets a lot of Southern apple carts but generates a lot of money and power. This is the tussle that dominates the second half of *Hamilton*. It also dominates American history until the Civil War and beyond.

It has interesting parallels elsewhere. In nineteenth-century Europe, the bankers and manufacturers in the Protestant North (Britain, Germany, Holland) pull ahead of the farmers in the Catholic South (Italy, Spain, Portugal), creating an economic imbalance that continues to this day. A similar contrast can be seen between North American capitalists and Latin American *encomenderos* in the same period: an industrial and mostly Protestant North rapidly surges ahead of an agricultural and mostly Catholic South, with all sorts of geopolitical implications from the Monroe Doctrine onward. Commercial societies overcome agrarian ones, whether we like it or not.

As viewers of *Hamilton*, we all know this. Whether we rejoice in it as a death blow to slavery, or lament it as the loss of an older more genteel way of life, or even both, the fact remains: Hamilton is destined to win. The world will inexorably become WEIRDER. America will be Industrialized, Rich, and Democratic. New York City, the upwardly mobile and polyglot city of immigrants, will become the embodiment of what it is to be Western, right through to 9/11 and the years following.

The reason Hamilton prevails, in his rap battles as well as in his political and military ones, has nothing to do with land, nobility, or moral character. It is simply that he is clever, and he works hard. He gets to New York in the first place by being smarter and working than everyone else,[16] gets a scholarship to King's College (now Colombia University), rises to the top through long hours and sheer brainpower, and writes his way out of trouble time and time again,[17] a strategy that eventually proves to be his undoing. Several of his monologues (in "My Shot," "Non-Stop" and "Hurricane") revolve around how bright and articulate he is, and his speeches are deliberately written with a lyrical dexterity and wit that the other characters cannot reach. Like Lin-Manuel Miranda himself (*Hamilton's* creator), Alexander Hamilton is an advert for the power of intelligence, diligence, and being Educated.

He is also a Romantic icon. This is not just because he is at the center of a love triangle, or even quadrangle, which drives several of the most powerful numbers in the show ("Helpless," "Satisfied," "It's Quiet Uptown"). He is also an exhausted genius who follows his heart into a destructive sexual relationship ("Take a Break," "Say No to This"). He is a fount of creative inspiration and imagination, able to build "palaces out of paragraphs"[18] for his wife ("Burn") and his president ("One Last Time"), and invent constitutional arguments and financial systems out of thin air ("Non-Stop," "Hurricane"). He is impulsive in contrast to the caution of Aaron Burr ("Wait for It," "The Room Where It Happens") and incorrigibly passionate in contrast to Thomas Jefferson, the stereotypical man of reason ("Cabinet Battle #1," "Washington on Your Side"). And he dies tragically—in a duel, of all things—before being hailed as a genius by everybody, including his enemies ("The World Was Wide Enough," "Who Lives, Who Dies"). Few heroes express the ideals of Romanticism more impeccably than he does.

Perhaps the most interesting way in which *Hamilton* is WEIRDER is in its treatment of Christianity. For much of the show, Christianity plays a minimal role, despite its importance to much of the plot and many of the characters. Christian themes do occasionally appear. We hear about providence and prayer, homilies and hymns, the sinners and the saints. Aaron Burr tells us obliquely that his grandfather was the Puritan theologian Jonathan Edwards. But watching the show, you would never know how large a role Christianity played in the American Revolution or the battles over slavery, or that Eliza Hamilton was a devout Christian for her ninety-seven years, or that Thomas Jefferson was decidedly not. There are a limited number of things you can explore in a stage show, and for most of *Hamilton*, Christianity is not one of them.

Then suddenly, when Hamilton's son dies in a duel, it all comes pouring out. "It's Quiet Uptown" is the most moving song in the musical, and it brings the emotional catharsis we need after watching a teenage boy bleed out in front of his parents. We witness Hamilton's spiritual renewal. He takes the children to church on Sunday, making the sign of the cross on the way in. He begins to pray, admitting that this has not been his practice until now. We hear about the grace that is too powerful to name. And then we see Eliza forgive him, not just for his infidelity but for failing to stop his son from getting himself killed.

It might as well be a parable of the Ex-Christian West. Religion is firmly in the background while things are going well and we are winning wars and making money, and even while we are doing shady deals and having affairs and getting away with it. Although Christianity still shapes our history, ethics, architecture, and psychology, when times are good we rarely think about it. But when things fall apart—when we lose our children or our partners, when we face death ourselves, when we have done something unimaginable and need forgiveness, when what we need more than anything else is *grace*—we know there is only one place we will find it. We may head to church for the first time in years. We might start praying or reading the Scriptures. Spirituality returns.

My point is not that Lin-Manuel Miranda deliberately wrote all of these themes into Hamilton (although much of it is clearly intentional). In some ways, my case is stronger if he didn't. Our best art is WEIRDER because we are, and that is true whether we recognize it or not.

The same is true of the television show from which Miranda drew so much inspiration: Aaron Sorkin's *The West Wing*. This award-winning political drama, set in a fictional White House, is quintessentially WEIRDER. Western norms and values are lauded patriotically and unashamedly, and regularly contrasted with those in other parts of the world (Russian secrecy, Chinese disdain for human rights, Islamic attitudes toward women, Mexican economic policy, African ethnic warfare, Iranian medical research, and so on). Education is the highest good in the show. It is the subject of more policy discussions than any other, and the silver bullet that can solve almost any social problem. The main characters all went to top universities, are absurdly articulate, and work eighteen-hour days. On the rare occasions when they leave their Rich, Industrialized environment, they are visibly uncomfortable and frequently condescending, which depending on the situation can either be humorous ("20 Hours in America") or deeply moving ("In Excelsis Deo"). Democracy is celebrated, not only in practice but in principle, even when the results go against the protagonists ("The Midterms," "Guns Not Butter").

The legacies of Christianity and Romanticism collide with remarkable effect in "Two Cathedrals," one of the great television episodes of the modern era. The president, played by Martin Sheen, is weighing up whether to run for reelection. It has emerged that he concealed a major health condition from the public. His longtime assistant has just died in a car crash. We already know him as a conflicted yet devout Catholic, characterized by an internal struggle between idealistic conviction and political ambition. But in this episode, we witness his childhood for the first time, caught between a Catholic mother and a violent Protestant father, whose school (and church) he attends. In a pivotal scene, the president walks down the nave of the Washington Cathedral, lambasting God as a feckless thug and issuing a visceral tirade of abuse in Latin, at the end of which he announces he will not be standing for a second term. We can see him conflating God with his abusive father, blaming the former for the sins of the latter and blurring together the two cathedrals. But he does not recognize the distinction until a later scene, when his dead assistant appears to him in the Oval Office. She corrects him, and the Ex-Christian West along with him: you cannot project your experience of abusive authority onto God. He listens, and decides to run again. The final montage is a magnificent Gothic swirl, like something out of *Wuthering Heights*: rain, darkness, howling winds, a banging door, a ghost, an empty cathedral, a drenched hero defying all convention, and the haunting sound of *Brothers in Arms*.

This fusion of Christian and Romantic influences is even clearer in by far the most popular piece of art produced this century. *Harry Potter* is a thoroughly Romantic story. It is a tale of childhood innocence confronting the desire to have power over the world, and emerging victorious. The setting is a dark castle filled with ghosts and suits of armor. Our heroes are adolescents discovering themselves. People drink potions to escape, dig deep into historic myths, and resist evil by projecting their happiest memories. Spells work only if they are cast with sufficient levels of feeling. The most odious characters in the story are the thoroughly sensible, rationalist, antimagical Dursleys. Harry, Snape, and Dumbledore all die for love; Snape in particular is a Gothic antihero, dressed in a long dark cloak and plagued by unrequited desire. The entire series is an exercise in magical realism, mingling wonder and reality, familiarity and strangeness: studying for exams in herbology, writing lines in your own blood, house competitions with flying dragons.

It is also a thoroughly Christian story. This becomes very obvious in the final volume, as Harry lays down his life for his friends, passes into another world at King's Cross station, and then rises from the dead to defeat the powers of darkness. But Christian themes are present throughout the series: the conflict between the House of the Lion and the House of the Snake, the references to Scripture at key moments, the frequent sacramental allusions, the eschatology, the sevenfold structure, the portrayal of good as substitutionary sacrifice, the depiction of evil as the desire to be godlike and master of death, and the Gethsemanesque scene in which Dumbledore drinks the cup of suffering so that Harry does not have to. There is plenty of debate over whether J. K. Rowling was deliberately writing a Christian allegory here, but this is somewhat beside the point. The pervasive influence of Christianity on WEIRDER culture is even more obvious if she wasn't.

Or consider Sam Mendes's Oscar-winning war movie, *1917*. As a film about the Great War, we would expect it to tell a very Western and Industrialized story, which it does. But it also offers a fundamentally Christian and Romantic picture of the world through its emphasis on trees, which throughout the movie represent the life, variety, and hope of creation in the face of human destruction.[19] "Keep your eyes on the trees," Blake tells Schofield (and us). "Not another bloody tree," says Private Cooke.[20] The single shot for which the film is famous begins and ends with Schofield resting on a tree, in parallel moments of peace and calm. Much of the plot in between centers on Schofield's search for a pinewood, where he eventually finds what he is looking for. The landscape is scattered with trees that have been felled by the mindless violence, sometimes lone oaks, sometimes entire groves. On more than one occasion they block the road or a river, stopping soldiers in their tracks or forming a dam for Schofield to cross. Yet in the end, we are assured that the trees will recover from the ravages of war to become even more numerous than they were—and so will creation, and so will we. "Jesus," says Blake as he enters an orchard with blossoms swimming in the wind. "They chopped them all down. Cherries. Lamberts." Schofield asks him if that means they are all goners. "Oh no," Blake responds. "They'll grow again when the stones rot. You'll end up with more trees than before." The metaphor is hard to miss.

Blake is the aesthetic voice in the film, the champion of beauty and hope, teaching Schofield that there is more to the world than matter and machinery. Schofield sees dead wood, while Blake sees the trees they used to be: "Cuthberts, Queen Annes, Montmorencys, sweet ones, sour ones." Schofield sees a "bit of tin," whereas Blake sees a medal, "and it's got a ribbon on it." Blake pulls Schofield out of the rubble that the war has created, both physically and metaphorically. His death wakes Schofield up: it revitalizes and reenchants him, releasing new layers of feeling and urgency and enabling him to look at the landscape, and even the pictures of his family, with fresh eyes. Once more, it is unclear how much of the Christianity, and even the Romanticism, in the film is intentional. But the fact that the characters are named after William Blake (whose art and poetry combined Romanticism and Christianity in such original ways) and John Schofield (a soldier who accused Blake of treason after being evicted from his garden for being drunk) should make us wonder.[21]

For a final example, take Hilary Mantel's masterful trilogy on the rise and fall of Thomas Cromwell. It might seem odd that three long novels about a Tudor minister five centuries ago have become such a commercial and critical success. The books contain a wealth of detail about legal and ecclesiastical developments that are hard for modern people to follow, let alone find interesting. There is a fiendishly large cast of characters, only a tiny minority of whom are relatable or admirable. There are no lurid sex scenes, shocking twists, or sudden explosions. There aren't even any unexpected developments, since we essentially know how the stories will end. But Mantel's genius is to turn our knowledge to her advantage. Heavy dramatic irony drives the plot. We know which of Henry's wives will lose their position, or their head, and which of his children will survive. We know which Reformers will get caught. Each book builds toward a beheading—of Thomas More (*Wolf Hall*), Anne Boleyn (*Bring Up the Bodies*), and Cromwell himself (*The Mirror and the Light*)—and even though we know it's coming, we aren't quite sure why, or how. Much of the tension derives from trying to work it out.

More subtly, the same thing happens at a macro level. The novels are set as the late medieval world is giving way to the early modern one. Cromwell lives in a world of knights, monks, and phantoms, where heretics are burned and traitors are killed gruesomely—and in public. Henry's marital decisions are not presented as lecherous whims but as genuine attempts (however misguided) to respect the will of God and produce a male heir. The world of late Christendom is unsettling and strange to modern readers. Yet we also find it intriguing, precisely because we know that it will eventually become WEIRDER. Dramatic irony overshadows our perception of the culture as a whole, as well as the characters: we know that monarchs will eventually yield to Parliament, that England will become Protestant, and that the day will come when people will marry for love and read the Scriptures for themselves. We know that Christendom will become Europe and that God's providential control of all things will change from a conviction to an assumption, and then to an implausibility. We know, as Cromwell sees in a moment of clarity, that "chivalry's day is over. One day soon moss will grow in the tilt yard. The days of the moneylender have arrived, and the days of the swaggering privateer; banker sits down with banker, and kings are their waiting boys."[22] And we relate to Cromwell because we see him encapsulating this new, WEIRDER world as it rises up against the old: the skeptical Protestant against the doctrinaire Catholics, the meritocratic minister versus the aristocratic nobles, the streetwise blacksmith's son and the hereditary monarch, the mirror and the light.

You get the idea. I have deliberately avoided pieces that are more explicitly Western and Romantic—like Pixar and Disney movies, airport paperbacks, and romantic comedies—as well as those that are more explicitly Christian, like Peter Jackson's *The Lord of the Rings*, Beyoncé's *Lemonade*, Martin Scorsese's *Silence*, or Marilynne Robinson's *Gilead*. I have not included my two favorite movies of the century so far, Alejandro González Iñárritu's *The Revenant* or Christopher Nolan's *Inception*, in which (like several of the works I have mentioned) ghosts and resurrections play a starring role. In an earlier draft of this chapter, I included Adele's *21*, Vince Gilligan's five-act tragedy *Breaking Bad*, Ryan Coogler's *Black Panther*, and Paul Thomas Anderson's *There Will Be Blood*, which features an astonishing pair of scenes in which a pastor is forcibly baptized in oil and the oil man is forcibly baptized by the pastor, symbolizing the tussle between riches and Christianity in industrializing America. If you were so inclined, you could probably do a similar exercise with your top ten as well. From prizewinning artists to children's television and chart music, our art is WEIRDER. So are we.

Weirder Culture

The fusion of Ex-Christianity and Romanticism has been culturally fertile, like the mingling of two great oceans. The inescapable tensions between the two value systems—self-sacrifice versus self-actualization, the worship of Creator versus the worship of creature, and so forth—fuel much of our greatest art, as we have seen. They drive our philosophy of education, with its blend of instruction and imagination, "putting in" to a child and "drawing out" what is already there. You can see them in our slogans ("don't be evil" versus "just do it"), and in fascinating ways in sport.

But they also make us culturally unstable. There are certain key questions for which this tension is not creative but divisive, and that generates instability. Sexuality is an obvious example. A Christian ethic of chastity, in which sex has a transcendent meaning defined by God, will obviously conflict with a Romantic ethic in which sex is about desire, self-expression, and the transgression of boundaries.

Politics is another. There is a clear thread from Christian ethical teaching to contemporary social democracy. There is another clear thread from the Romantic ideals of authenticity and self-reliant individualism to modern libertarianism, and indeed nationalist populism. Our recent history shows how difficult it is to reconcile the two threads. (One of the paradoxes of American political affiliation, at least from a European perspective, is that those with a Romantic vision of sexuality are more likely to share an Ex-Christian vision of politics, and vice versa.)

In the last decade or so, traditional political alignments have been reshaped by a new phenomenon, the name of which is still to be decided. Depending on whether people like it, and why, they might call it the successor ideology, intersectionality, wokeness, identity politics, cultural Marxism, social justice, or something else. Essentially, it uses a number of axes (sex, race, wealth, sexuality, class, disability, age, and so on) to distinguish between those with more privilege and those with less. It has proved controversial. Its proponents see it as an important tool for addressing injustices, past and present, and furthering opportunity for those who have been disadvantaged or oppressed. Its critics see it as a socially divisive fad conjured up by wealthy elites trying to assuage their own guilt.

Whatever you think of it, it is undeniably WEIRDER. It could never have emerged in a society that was not trying to come to terms with its uniquely Western privileges, including how Industrialized and Rich it is. It owes both its development and its influence to the prestige of Higher Education. It follows a satisfyingly Democratic logic: people should have the same opportunities, and if they do not, then we should do something to fix it. Ideologically, it draws heavily from the Christian moral imperative to exalt the humble and humble the exalted, as reflected in Christ's teaching ("the last will be first, and the first last," Matt. 20:16), his incarnation ("he has brought down the mighty from their thrones and exalted those of humble estate," Luke 1:52), and above all his crucifixion ("he humbled himself by becoming obedient to the point of death, even death on a cross," Phil. 2:8).[23] And it reflects deeply Romantic convictions—channeled and reinterpreted through Marx and Freud in particular—about innocence, pity, freedom, and the corrupting effects of society.

We could say the same of the change in attitudes toward transgender identities in the last decade or so. How has the idea that a woman could be trapped inside a man's body, to the point of being able to compete as a woman in the Olympics despite every cell in his body having XY chromosomes, changed so quickly from being obviously false to obviously true? Romanticism is clearly a key factor. The "inward turn" of the Romantic movement, as we will see in chapter 8, saw the self increasingly defined by the inner life, as opposed to external actions or realities. Ethics became shaped by aesthetic categories like sympathy, feeling, and sentiment, and individual authenticity displaced social conformity (let alone religious authority) as a criterion for human flourishing.[24] The therapeutic categories of psychology moved from marginality to respectability, then popularity, then dominance.[25] Expressive individualism became the "habit of the heart" in Western culture.[26] Meaning was made an interior and private matter, as declared famously by Supreme Court Justice Anthony Kennedy: "At the heart of liberty is the right to define one's own concept of existence, of meaning, of the universe, and of the mystery of human life."[27] By the time Bruce/Caitlyn Jenner appeared on the cover of *Vogue* in 2015, an apparently sudden transformation had been two and a half centuries in the making. Society was individualized; the individual was psychologized; psychology was sexualized; sexuality was politicized.[28]

Romanticism is only part of this story, though. The Democratic assumption, that things are good only if they are chosen by an autonomous individual, is also critical. So is Industrialization, not just because transitioning genders requires medical and surgical treatments that would be impossible without industrialized technology, but also because industrialization has changed our attitude to the natural world (including biological sex): we no longer believe in what Marilynne Robinson calls "the givenness of things" and instead see nature as something to be manipulated through technique until it suits our purpose.[29] So is Ex-Christianity, for the conviction that those who are marginalized or victimized (as those with gender dysphoria almost always have been) should be treated with dignity and given whatever help is available.[30] So is the fact that we are Rich. One of the reasons why trans rights have been enthusiastically embraced by big capitalism, as Slavoj Žižek points out, is that doing so gives the impression of supporting revolutionary social change without actually doing anything to sacrifice profitability.[31] The *trans*formation is WEIRDER through and through.

We could go on. We could analyze the changes in our language: from the *soul* to the *self*, from *creation* to *nature*, from *passions* and *affections* to *emotions* and *feelings*. We could reflect on the catchphrases that appear in songs and on T-shirts, which manage to encapsulate the entire WEIRDER world in just a handful of words. "You do you" is a perfect distillation of expressive individualism. "I am mine" sums up metaphysical capitalism: the view that, as Alan Jacobs puts it, "I am a commodity owned solely by myself; I may do with this property whatever I want and call it whatever I want; any suggestion that my rights over myself are limited in any way I regard as an intolerable tyranny."[32] "Love means love," which if taken at face value means nothing at all, is really a statement of untrammeled sexual freedom: I can have sex with whomever I want, and neither the state nor any religious tradition can stop me. "What's next?" evokes what Zygmunt

Bauman called liquid modernity, with its restless transience and its obsession with becoming rather than being.[33] And so forth.

All of which is to say that our culture is WEIRDER all the way down. Our environment, possessions, moral frameworks, psychology, art, political disagreements, and language all tell the same story. Relative to most people in history, and many across the world today, we are conspicuously Western, Educated, Industrialized, Rich, Democratic, Ex-Christian, and Romantic. We may celebrate that. We may lament it. We may have mixed feelings about it. But hopefully we can all recognize it.

For the next seven chapters, we will be addressing the very simple question: Why?[‡] And the answer, to reduce an extraordinarily complex process to a single number, is: 1776.

---

‡   In order to keep the story moving, the next seven chapters will not follow the WEIRDER acronym directly. WDEEIRR does not have the same ring to it, sadly.

PART 2

ORIGINS

3

Maps

Becoming Western

No man will ever venture farther than I have done.

JAMES COOK

Tata meitai, fenua ino.

MAHINE OF BORA BORA

TWO FORMER COAL SHIPS LEFT the south coast of England in the summer of 1776, headed for virtually opposite destinations. Physically, the only real difference between them was their size. They were both built in the same docks in the Yorkshire port of Whitby, by the same man, for the same purpose: that of carrying coal down the east coast from Newcastle to London.

Both had since diversified somewhat. The smaller one was sailing west for Newfoundland, as part of a battle fleet that would eventually anchor in New York harbor in August. The larger one sailed alone, running south from Plymouth toward the Cape of Good Hope, which she reached in mid-September. From there she turned eastward, crossing the Indian Ocean in the southern summer and making landfall in Van Diemen's Land in January.

Neither vessel was much to look at. In an age of sophisticated naval warfare, dominated by elegant ships-of-the-line with sixty guns or more, a Whitby bark—flat-bottomed and often dirty, with a rounded bow, rein-forced hull, and maximum speed of eight knots—would have seemed hardy and practical but rather dull, even dumpy. If you didn't already know, you would never guess the roles that these unglamorous colliers had played in world history, or the fact that both of them had rounded Cape Horn, visited Tahiti, and circumnavigated the globe. Nor would you imagine that frag-ments of the larger one, long believed to be fragments of the smaller one, would end up orbiting the earth and landing on the moon.[1]

Between them, these two ships saw more of the world than any before them, and a good many after. In doing so, they raised a fascinating question and provided an even more fascinating answer. The question was why there are such disparities between different peoples—economically, materially, technologically, and so forth—and particularly why Western nations seemed to have such an advantage by 1776.

The answer was provided by a young Polynesian man whom history has almost forgotten.

The *Endeavour's* Question

The smaller ship was sailing under a new name. Previously, when she had sailed to the South Seas under Captain James Cook, she had been known as the *Endeavour*. This was the name by which she would be known to posterity, and she bequeathed it to a host of other enterprises and individu-als, from Inspector Morse to the Space Shuttle *Endeavour* (which NASA, in memory of her, graciously spelled with a "u"). By the time she sailed toward America in May 1776, she had been repurposed and rebranded. She was now a transport vessel, carrying 206 Hessian soldiers ready to take on George Washington, and she bore the name of the only person alive whose surname would become more famous than the future President's. On August 12, surrounded by the largest British armada ever assembled until the D-Day landings, the *Lord Sandwich* dropped anchor off Staten Island.

But it is for her first circumnavigation (1768–1771), as HMS *Endeavour*, that she will always be known. The original purpose of the trip was to ob-serve the transit of Venus: a rare astronomical event that would enable the scientists of the Royal Society to calculate the distance between the earth and the sun. Once this was achieved, she was to pursue the quest for a southern continent, the *Terra Australis Incognita* ("unknown southern land"), which was believed to exist but had never been seen. The theory was that a large southern landmass was needed to counterbalance the continents in the northern hemisphere, and there was great excitement about the biodiversity and "spectacles" it might contain.

She was also something of a floating laboratory. Besides Cook and his crew, the ship's company of ninety-four included an official astronomer, a scientific secretary, two artists, two slaves, and three botanists: the Finnish naturalist Herman Spöring Jr., a Swedish apostle of Carl Linnaeus named Daniel Solander, and the raffish young Englishman Joseph Banks. These last three took with them a vast assortment of books, nets, trawls, hooks, telescopes, microscopes, bottles, tools, chemicals, storage chests, and other contraptions for the purpose of catching and cataloguing new species. Today, their most famous legacy is Botany Bay in Sydney, flanked by the twin headlands of Cape Solander and Cape Banks. But their achievement as naturalists was nothing short of astonishing. In the course of the voyage, they collected a staggering 30,000 dried specimens, which led to the identification of over a hundred new genera and thirteen hundred new species, and increased by a quarter the total number of known flora in the world.

The three-year voyage was a journey of firsts, at least for the ship's company, and not only when it came to lands or species. No Europeans had ever witnessed the Polynesian practice of surfing until May 29, 1769, when Joseph Banks "stood admiring this very wonderful scene for full half an hour, in which time no one of the actors attempted to come ashore but all seemed most highly entertained with their strange diversion."[2] They had never learned the name of an Aboriginal Australian until they met Yaparico, one of the Guugu Yimithirr people in what is now Queensland. Nor had they seen a *kanguru* before June 23, 1770, and they had no idea what to make of it when they did: "to compare it to any European animal would be impossible, as it has not the least resemblance of any one I have seen."[3] More surprising still was the response of the Aboriginal Australians, who had never seen white people, to their first encounter with *Endeavour* ("entirely unmoved by the neighbourhood of so remarkable an object as a ship")[4] and all who sailed in her ("Mr Hicks, who was the officer ashore, did all in his power to entice them to him by offering them presents etc, but it was to no purpose; all they seemed to want was for us to be gone.").[5] The Aboriginals may have been onto something, given some of the more tragic firsts of the voyage. Until 1769, no Maori had ever been shot with a gun. No Tahitian had witnessed a flogging.

But *Endeavour's* travels also raised some big anthropological questions. Were the Maori related to the Tahitians? It certainly looked like they were, given the obvious physical and linguistic similarities between them, their shared use of earth ovens, and the customs they had in common, most strikingly the marking of the skin with the Maori spiral *moko* or the elaborate Tahitian *tatau*. But if so, then why did the Maori sometimes eat their enemies, a practice which horrified the Tahitians? And how was it even possible, given that they were separated by thousands of miles of open ocean? As one French officer had asked in exasperation: "Who the devil went and placed them on a small sandbank like this one and as far from the continent as they are?"*

Even more inexplicably: Why were there so many linguistic connections between Polynesia, Java, Malaysia, and even Madagascar, lands that were (quite literally) half a world away from each other? How was it that the Maori were so much more advanced, in their technology and social structure, than the Aboriginal Australians? Why were the Tahitians so much more developed than the Haush people of the Tierra del Fuego, whom Cook described as "perhaps as miserable a set of people as are this day upon earth"?[6] Why were their responses to the arrival of Europeans so different, such that some immediately began exchanging goods (and sexual partners), some defended their territory by force, and some ignored the new arrivals altogether?

The clear differences between the Pacific peoples, in terms of their social, economic, and technological development, invites a more fundamental question. What about the equally clear differences between the people on

---

* This mystery continued to bamboozle Europeans well into the twentieth century. They simply could not believe that the Polynesians could navigate with such extraordinary accuracy without modern scientific equipment, using just the stars and their experience. Yet they could, and did. One schooner captain, after losing his compass overboard, marveled that his Polynesian crew were able to take him straight to his destination without one and asked them how they knew where the island was. Their reply was delightfully matter-of-fact: "It has always been there." See Lincoln Paine, *Sea and Civilization* (New York: Vintage, 2013), 14; David Lewis, *The Voyaging Stars: Secrets of the Pacific Island Navigators* (New York: Norton, 1978), 19.

the *Endeavour* and the lands they visited? Why was it that Europeans had sent a ship to the Pacific islands, carrying guns and botanists and telescopes, rather than the other way around? Why was James Cook at the helm of a three-hundred-ton ship full of books and provisions, while the Haush didn't have canoes, the Maori didn't read or write, and the Aboriginals were still hunter-gatherers? And why, as a result of these differences, would the inhabitants of the South Pacific end up adopting European languages, technology, religion, and even sport, rather than seeing the Polynesian way of life spread across Europe? Why, in short, would so much of the world become Western?

It is a question with profound implications. Very few people today will give the explicitly racist answer that many Europeans gave in the nineteenth century—namely, that Western people are biologically or genetically superior to people from other parts of the world. But some alternatives are equally likely to foster disunity and ethnic pride. Perhaps it is not Western biology but Western culture that is fundamentally superior—creatively, philosophically, scientifically, religiously—thanks to the unique fusion of Greco-Roman and Judeo-Christian values.[7] If so, then perhaps Western people should be unashamed about spreading it, and if that comes across as arrogant and dismissive toward other cultures, then so be it.

Versions of this argument can be found in books, and tragically churches, across the Western world today. Needless to say, I do not subscribe to it myself. But it is not enough to dismiss an explanation because its implications are distasteful. Unless we can articulate a better alternative, provocateurs will continue to make this sort of case, and people who feel their culture is under attack will continue to swallow it.

Nor is interest in the subject limited to WEIRDER people. Jared Diamond starts his Pulitzer Prize winning *Guns, Germs, and Steel* with a question he was asked by a New Guinean friend named Yali: "Why is it that you white people developed so much cargo and brought it to New Guinea, but we black people had little cargo of our own?"[8] The Ottoman writer Ibrahim Müteferrika had a similar query: "Why do Christian nations, which were so weak in the past compared with Muslim nations, begin to dominate so many lands in modern times?"[9] Malaysian lawyer Shad Saleem Faruqi put it this way in conversation with the British journalist Martin Jacques: "I am wearing your clothes, I speak your language, I watch your films, and today is whatever date it is because you say so."[10] Even Samuel Johnson, writing two and a half centuries ago, had the Abyssinian Prince Rasselas ask simply, "By what means are the Europeans thus powerful? Or why, since they can so easily visit Asia and Africa for trade or conquest, cannot the Asiatics and the Africans invade their coasts, plant colonies in their ports, and give laws to their natural princes?"[11] It is a question that the *Endeavour*'s circumnavigation raises in a particularly acute form. Why indeed?

Mahine's Answer

For the answer, we need to turn our attention to the other former coal ship from Whitby that sailed from southern England in the summer of 1776. She was the larger of the two. Like the *Endeavour*, she had spent three years circumnavigating the world under James Cook (1772–1775), mainly in the south Pacific, looking for new lands and encountering new peoples. She also, like the *Endeavour*, set sail that summer with a new mission—a mission that would ultimately lead to the death of her captain. Her name was HMS *Resolution*.

The official purpose of her first voyage was to find the southern continent. This would take them farther south than anyone had ever been, and for much longer. Cook knew what lay ahead of him. "When I think of the inhospitable parts I am going to," he wrote when he reached Cape Town, "I think the voyage dangerous."[12] Whereas the *Endeavour* had stayed mostly in lower latitudes, visiting sedentary peoples on tropical islands, the *Resolution* was headed more for ice than sunshine, and was more likely to encounter nomads than farmers. Her company was also diminished by the loss of Banks and Solander, after a bizarre dispute over the design of the ship and the size of their party (which had risen to fourteen, including six servants and two French horn players). They were hurriedly replaced by the German naturalist Johann Forster and his son Georg, who would write a description of the journey in 1776.

It is hard to say whether the expedition was a success or a failure. The *Resolution* never found the temperate, habitable continent it was looking for. And Cook increasingly saw that the impact of the voyage upon the local Pacific peoples was at best morally ambiguous, and at times clearly destructive.[†] Yet Cook clearly thought the expedition had succeeded. "I flatter myself," he wrote, "that the intention of the voyage has in every respect been fully answered, the southern hemisphere sufficiently explored, and a final end put to the searching after a southern continent. . . . No man will ever venture farther than I have done."[13] Admittedly, he had not found the habitable landmass that was the purpose of the trip. But he had demonstrated beyond reasonable doubt that it did not exist, while travelling farther south than anyone ever had—"not only farther than any other man has been before me, but as far as I think it possible for man to go"[14]—and correctly deduced that "there is a tract of land near the Pole, which is the source of most of the ice which is spread across this vast southern ocean."[15] And the voyage included plenty of discovery. As well as returning to New Zealand and the Society Islands, the *Resolution* and the *Adventure* landed on Tonga, Easter Island, the Marquesas, Niue, Vanuatu, New Caledonia, and Norfolk Island, in each case learning things that no previous Europeans had known. They also discovered the Cook Islands and several small islands in the Atlantic.

For much of this time, they were accompanied by two young Polynesian guests, who joined them in 1773. Mahine was from Bora Bora, and he sailed on the *Resolution* for just under a year before returning to Tahiti, to something of a hero's welcome. Mai, the son of a Ra'iatean landowner, took the *Adventure* the whole way back to London, where he would remain until 1776. Of the two of them, Mai was by far the more famous in his lifetime, thanks to the year he spent in Britain. Joseph Banks introduced him to

---

† At Meretoto in New Zealand, for example, Cook noted in his diary that "we debauch their morals, already too prone to vice, and we interduce among them wants and perhaps diseases which they never before knew, and which serves only to disturb that happy tranquillity they and their forefathers had injoyed" (June 4, 1773). He acknowledged that Europeans had dramatically exaggerated the sexual exoticism of Polynesian women: "Great injustice has been done the women of Tahiti and the Society Isles, by those who have represented them without exception as ready to grant the last favour to any man who will come up to their price" (September 17, 1773). He also recognized "how liable we are to mistake these peoples' meaning and to ascribe to them customs they never knew" (June 3, 1773), a point which was to have fatal consequences for Cook in Hawaii a few years later. Local symbols were not always ambiguous, however. After firing over the heads of a group in Vanuatu, Cook recalled, "One fellow showed us his backside in such a manner that it was not necessary to have an interpreter to explain his meaning" (August 6, 1774). All Cook's journal entries for this voyage can be accessed online at https://www.gutenberg.org/cache/epub/15777/pg15777.html and https://www.gutenberg.org/cache/epub/15869/pg15869.html, accessed December 21, 2022.

everybody who was anybody; Mai learned to read and write English, and he took up a number of British hobbies including chess, ice skating, and shooting. He even met King George III and Queen Charlotte.

But it was Mahine who, while leaving Easter Island on board the *Resolution*, summarized the answer to the question raised by the *Endeavour*. The puzzle of Cook's first voyage—not just why the Europeans were so different from the Pacific islanders but also why the Javans were so much more developed than the Haush, and the Polynesians were more apparently advanced than the Aboriginals—had emerged again on his second. It was brought into particularly sharp focus at Easter Island. Here were a people clearly related to Tongans, Maori, and Tahitians (given their appearance, weapons, tattoos and language) yet who were also substantially poorer, lower in number, and more basic in their housing and farming than any Polynesians they had encountered elsewhere.

More strangely still, they seemed poorer and less developed than their own ancestors had been a few generations before. The giant statues for which the island is famous were inexplicable; they seemed far beyond any technology the islanders had available (a point that would prompt plenty of conspiracy theories in the following century). Johann Forster, who was the first European to sketch them, was astonished: "It was incomprehensible to me how such great masses could be formed by a set of people among whom we saw no tools, or raised or erected by them without machinery."[16]

Forster's solution to the mystery was that "these people were formerly more numerous, opulent and happy" but that more recently their nation had been "degraded to its present indigence" by a "general catastrophe which seems to have happened."[17] Subsequent archaeology would show this guess to be essentially correct. For around eight hundred years, from 800 to 1600, the Rapa Nui were very like the Tahitians in their social structures and technology. They had built the magnificent statues to commemorate their ancestral chiefs. But at some point in the previous century, a combination of soil erosion and overcultivation had caused a significant drop in agricultural productivity. Increasingly thin soils led to poor harvests, a lack of timber, and a sharp fall in population. The island's small size and remoteness meant that there was no easy way of replenishing the supplies of wood, food, technology, or even humans, and the result was plain to see: an impoverished people, surrounded by the glories of their recent past yet painfully unable to emulate them. Mahine, leaving Easter Island on the *Resolution*, summarized the situation in just four words: *tata meitai, fenua ino*. It was a profound comment, recorded in the book Georg Forster wrote during 1776. It means: "good people, bad land."[18]

To this day, it is hard to explain the disparities in human development more succinctly than that. Mahine, of course, was not trying to do anything of the sort. He was trying to make sense of a very specific phenomenon—namely, the vast differences in scale, culture, and technology between two groups of people (the Rapa Nui and the Tahitians) who were clearly related. But in the process, he also provided an explanation for the differences between all kinds of other societies. Without realizing it, he was offering an answer to the questions raised by Yali, Ibrahim Müteferrika, Prince Rasselas, Jared Diamond, and the *Endeavour*.

Why, as of 1776, had the Europeans developed further and faster than the Tahitians and the Maori, who had in turn developed further and faster than the Aboriginals and the Haush? Why, as a result, was the world of the next two centuries set to become increasingly Western? It was not down to any fundamental differences between the abilities of the *tata*, the people; it was primarily a result of the *fenua*, the land, in which those people lived. The most significant factor in the rate and extent of human development was not biology (as suggested in racist theories then and now), or even philosophy (whether religious or pagan). It was geography.

Why Mahine Was Right

To explain why Mahine was right, not just about the Rapa Nui but about the rise of the West, we have to leave 1776 for a moment and go back twelve thousand years.

It is 10,000 BC. The earth is warming up after the last ice age, and plants and animals are spreading into areas that were previously too cold to survive in. So are human beings. Africa and Eurasia have been inhabited since the beginning of humanity, but in the last few millennia people have crossed the land bridge between Siberia and Alaska and spread south through the Americas. The ancestors of the Haush have just reached Tierra del Fuego.

The world will not remain connected for long. Rising sea levels are about to separate America from Eurasia altogether. They are also separating Yaparico's ancestors in Australia from nearby New Guinea. Soon there will be three distinct land masses on earth—Afro-Eurasia, America, and Australia—with virtually no contact between each other. Cook's ancestors in Europe could theoretically interact with Mahine's ancestors, who still live in southern China. But neither of them could interact with the ancestors of the Haush, or the Aboriginals. For all intents and purposes, these three land masses are different worlds.

The total population of the world is around one million. It is entirely comprised of peoples who feed themselves and their families by killing animals; foraging for berries, fruits, and nuts; and fishing.[19] To some, it will seem like an appealingly simple way to live. To others, it will sound like a nightmare. Thomas Hobbes famously described it as "solitary, poor, nasty, brutish and short": a life without industry or commerce, art, or books, and haunted by the continual fear of violent death.[20] Cook, who (unlike Hobbes) actually met hunter-gatherers firsthand, felt differently: "they may appear to some to be the most wretched people upon earth, but in reality they are far more happy than we Europeans . . . they live in a tranquillity which is not disturbed by the inequality of condition."[21]

Whichever view we take, it is undeniable that groups of foragers and hunter-gatherers face limitations when it comes to generating food surpluses, population growth, specialization, and all that flows from it. In order to get beyond the level our ancestors reached in 10,000 BC— to develop law codes, cities, bureaucracy, government, and so forth—you first need to produce enough food to generate a surplus, so that some people can give their time to other things. (This surplus also needs to be storable, for obvious reasons, which gives societies that grow wheat or rice a significant advantage over those that grow yams, cassava, or tubers.) If 80 percent of the people are producing enough food for everybody, then the other 20 percent can become artisans, merchants, priests, scribes, and bureaucrats, and eventually teachers and philosophers, actors and football players, doctors and scientists. And for that, you need farming.

So it would not be surprising if the first groups of human beings to develop farming were also the first to develop other key technologies, like writing, wheels, money, stonemasonry, and seafaring.[22] We might expect these groups of farmers to have more advanced weapons and more elaborate buildings than the groups around them. We might also expect to find some of them increasing in number, expanding, and gradually displacing any groups of hunter-gatherers nearby, whether by force or by assimilation.

Which is exactly what we do find. West Asian farmers, with their complex societies and advanced technology, gradually spread through Europe and took over from local hunter-gatherers (which is why all Europe's languages, with the exception of Basque, originated in West Asia).[23] Chinese farmers filled southeast Asia. The agricultural Bantu displaced the nomadic Khoisan in southern Africa. For a striking recent example, we need only go back to 1835, when nine hundred Maori—the grandchildren of those who encountered the *Endeavour* and the *Resolution*—landed on the Chatham Islands, home of the Moriori. Both groups were Polynesians. But the Maori were food producers, who had formed a large, socially stratified and technologically sophisticated society, and the Moriori were hunter-gatherers with limited weaponry and no central leadership. The result was a massacre. Hundreds of Moriori were killed, and the Maori enslaved the rest.

Food production, in the long term, gives a society a tremendous developmental advantage. It enables food surpluses, higher birth rates, larger population centers, and more specialization—and all of these drive social, economic, and technological development. An additional advantage—unpleasant but hugely significant historically—is that farmers spend a lot of time around domestic animals, catching their diseases and developing immunity to them.[24] So when a group of farmers arrives in a new land, bringing all their germs with them, the consequences for the local people can be catastrophic. Ask the Incas.

With all that in mind, we can go back to 10,000 BC and run a thought experiment. The world is about to be divided into three great land masses: Afro-Eurasia, America, and Australia. Everyone on earth is a hunter-gatherer, including you. But you know in advance that the people who develop farming first will have a huge head start when it comes to social and technological development, and you want to maximize your chance of that happening to you. You also know everything there is to know about geography at that time. You are given a choice: on which of the three continents do you want to live, and why?

Even if we did not know any of the subsequent history, there would be good reasons for choosing Afro-Eurasia. In fact, there would be good reasons for being more specific: our best chances of developing farming would come if we lived in Asia, somewhere in the temperate zone between 20° and 35° north, and ideally at the western or eastern end of the continent rather than in the middle. That would put us in one of two places. One is in eastern China, somewhere in the vicinity of the Yangtze and Yellow rivers. The other is in the Fertile Crescent in West Asia, between the Mediterranean Sea and the Euphrates.

Over the next ten thousand years, food production would emerge in a dozen different areas around the world. But it happened far more comprehensively and successfully in these two places than anywhere else. And the reasons for that, as Mahine would say, have nothing to do with the intelligence or creativity of the people (the "chaps"), and everything to do with their environment (the "maps"). We could summarize them under six *w*'s: weather, width, water, wood, wheat, and wildlife. Together, they provide a powerful explanation for the rise of the West.

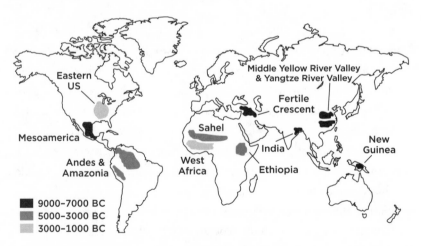

Figure 3.1   The origins of food production. (Adapted from Seshat: Global History Databank, https://seshatdatabank.info/.)

Weather. Faced with a map of the world, and the choice of where to try and start food production, the first factor most of us would consider is climate. We would want to avoid areas that were too dry (like Australia and much of northern Africa), or too cold (like most places beyond the forty-second parallel north or south). Areas where tropical diseases are common, or where the seasons are too unpredictable from year to year, would also pose problems. Without thinking too hard, we could quickly narrow our search to about a quarter of the earth's surface, most of it in the temperate zone of Eurasia, the central part of America, or southern Africa.

With a bit more reflection, we could zero in further. It would be much easier to start farming in an area with a consistent pattern of long, dry summers and mild, wet winters (what we now call a Mediterranean climate), for instance, than in one governed by the monsoon or an erratic pattern like the El Niño in the Pacific. Globally, there are only five such areas, each of them found to the western end of a major continent: California, central Chile, Southwest Australia, the Western Cape, and the Mediterranean basin itself. Of these, the Mediterranean is by far the largest and therefore the most promising place to start farming.

Width. All other things being equal, a larger continent has advantages over a smaller one. That much is probably obvious: it has more land, more plant and animal species, more varieties of habitat, and more people. So it is no great surprise that Eurasia developed farming and Australia did not. What is less obvious, but also very significant, is that a wide continent has advantages over a tall one. Continents that run largely east to west, like Eurasia, have a geographical privilege that continents that run largely north to south, like America or Africa, do not. That is because environmental conditions—like temperature, rainfall, day length, seasonal variations, habitats, and diseases—change far less when you move east-west than when you move north-south. So it is far easier for animal species, plant species, and even human beings to move horizontally than vertically.

Think of it this way: You can walk from Hungary in central Europe to Manchuria in eastern China, a distance of some five thousand miles, and hardly leave one kind of habitat—the grassy plains of the Eurasian Steppe. The journey might take months or years, but the sorts of plants that can grow, and the sorts of animals that can graze, are roughly the same. But this is not remotely true of an equivalent north-south journey in Africa or the Americas. If you were to walk from Peru to Canada, or from Egypt to Zimbabwe, the sorts of temperatures, day lengths, weather conditions, seasons, landscapes, soils, and diseases you would experience would change dramatically every few weeks. Plants and animals from the Peruvian Andes, like the potato or the llama, could have thrived in Canada if they had ever reached it—but the only way there was through the Colombian jungle and the shrublands of Mexico, so they never did (at least until European ships arrived). That is a major geographical point in Eurasia's favor. When it comes to food production, width wins.

Water. If you look carefully at the map of early food production, you will notice the importance of the Amazon, Nile, Yangtze, Euphrates, Indus, and Yellow rivers. We would expect that; fresh water is the most important commodity on earth. River systems provide abundantly accessible drinking water for animals and humans, which makes it possible for large numbers to gather in one place, and crucially, they make irrigation possible for growing crops. If rivers are navigable, they also make transport easier, which becomes more significant when societies develop to the point of exploring new lands, trading with other peoples, governing large territories, and taking to the seas. If, like the Fertile Crescent, you happen to be sandwiched in between a significant river system and a sea that connects you to two other continents and the open ocean, you have really landed on your feet.

Wood. When the Rapa Nui first saw the *Resolution*, they were less interested in the technical marvel of a four-hundred-ton sailing ship than they were by the sheer amount of wood it had taken to build it. Today, we largely take wood for granted. In many ways, we hardly need it and choose it more for aesthetic than functional reasons. But if you live in the Stone Age in a place where trees are either small or nonexistent, because the soils, temperature, or rainfall cannot sustain them, you face a substantial obstacle to development. Imagine living in Britain without any wood to burn as fuel or construct buildings. Imagine tilling Middle Eastern fields by hand, because there are no wooden ploughs. Clearly human beings can survive without trees—the Inuit, for example, have lived almost entirely above the tree line for a very long time—but it makes the development of farming almost impossible. That is not a problem in West Asia, as anyone who has read the Hebrew Bible will know.

Wheat. Today, cereal crops provide over half the calories that human beings eat in a day. They are effectively grasses with large edible seeds, which are either ground into flour (like wheat, maize, and barley) or cooked and eaten as grains (like sorghum and rice). Because they provide so many calories per acre of land, they form the core of the diet for a large percentage of the world's population, and have done so for about ten thousand years—which means there is a huge benefit to living in a part of the world with a native cereal crop. Rice, along with millet, is the main reason why China has always supported a large population. Maize, or corn, was the foundation of Mesoamerican civilizations like the Aztecs and the Maya. And much of the Fertile Crescent's agricultural development can be put down to the presence of three key cereals: einkorn wheat, emmer wheat, and barley. By farming these crops on a large scale, West Asians were able to produce a food surplus that freed some of their citizens to do other things. The results included developing writing, bureaucracy, trade, the wheel, and the earliest cities.

Wildlife. All animals are equal, but some animals are more equal than others.[25] If you live in southern Africa, the large mammals in your surroundings are ideal for a safari but completely unsuitable for domestication. You cannot milk a giraffe, ride a zebra into battle, make a rhino pull a plough, or breed hippos for food (and that is without mentioning carnivorous mammals like big cats and hunting dogs, which pose even more problems). In Australia, your options are fewer, but equally unpromising. Most large animals simply do not lend themselves to domestication by humans. Globally, there are only thirteen or fourteen species of herbivorous mammal that weigh over one hundred pounds and were domesticated before 1776, and only five that are so useful that they have spread all over the world.

Those animals are not distributed evenly. None are native to Australia. None are native to sub-Saharan Africa or North America. Only two, the llama and the alpaca, come from South America. The others all originated in Eurasia, including all five major farm animals (sheep, cows, goats, pigs, and horses), as well as donkeys, camels, yaks, gayals, water buffalos, and Bali cattle. That gave Stone Age Eurasians an unassailable advantage when it came to harnessing the power, skins, meat, fertilizer, and milk of the animals around them, not to mention the immunity they developed to diseases. In the race to develop farming, the Haush and the Aboriginals stood no chance.

Table 3.1   The origin of farming[26]

Area	Indigenous Cereals/ Grasses	Other Major Food Crops	Domesticated Mammals	Date of Earliest Domestication
Fertile Crescent	Einkorn wheat, emmer wheat, barley	Pea, lentil, chickpea	Sheep, goat, pig, cow, horse	8500
China	Millet, rice	Soybean, mung bean		7500
Mesoamerica	Maize	Beans, squashes	—	3500
Andes/ Amazonia	Quinoa	Beans, peanut, manioc, sweet potato, potato	Llama, alpaca	3500
West Africa/ Sahel	Sorghum, millet, rice	Cowpea, groundnut, African yam	Camel, donkey	3000
Eastern USA	Maygrass, little barley	Artichoke, squash	—	2500
New Guinea	Sugar cane	Yam, taro	—	7000?
Australia	—	—	—	—

If you put these last two factors together, you can see just how large the Eurasian head start was. But you can also see why. There is no evidence of any differences in intelligence, aptitude, or creativity between the various peoples. Rather, Eurasians had six geographical points in their favor that the indigenous Australians and the Rapa Nui did not.

The reason for making this point is not just that it gives racist theories, both in Cook's day and in ours, a punch on the nose (although there are worse reasons for saying something). It also provides a crucial part of the explanation as to why the modern world is so Western. Because of the geographical advantages they had, Eurasians developed farming earlier and more comprehensively than people elsewhere and thus also became the first to develop specialization, technology, writing, money, and so-called civilization. Their descendants spread across the world, taking their languages and farming practices with them. No matter how creative the ancestors of the Haush or the Aboriginals had been, they could never have done anything remotely like this; they were constrained by the realities of their environment. Mahine was right. *Tata meitai, fenua ino.*

Curiosity and Commerce

That, however, is only part of the puzzle. It explains why Eurasians, from 10,000 BC onward, experienced economic development faster than Native Americans, sub-Saharan Africans, New Guineans, or Aboriginal Australians. But it does not explain why some Eurasians developed faster than others. After all, as the *Resolution* sailed for the Cape of Good Hope on Cook's third and final voyage, there were at least ten major powers in Eurasia: Tokugawa Japan, Qing China, Mughal India, Ottoman Turkey, and Romanov Russia, plus the Spanish, Portuguese, Dutch, French, and British maritime empires. Each of these lands had been farming, specializing, trading, and city building for thousands of years. Several of them had been far more advanced than anywhere in Europe for long periods, including the Islamic world during the Abbasid Caliphate (750–1258) and China under the Tang (618–907) and Song (960–1279) dynasties. In 1775, Asia accounted for four-fifths of the global economy. So what was it about the Western powers in the late eighteenth century, and the most northwestern one in particular, that would give them such influence over the next two hundred and fifty years?‡

---

‡ Perhaps that is an unfair way of putting the question. If you had asked a neutral observer in 1776 to guess which of the ten would form a global empire over the next century, they would immediately have written off several of them. The Dutch empire had been getting weaker for a century after losing naval and then financial supremacy to the British. Similar things were true of the Portuguese. Tokugawa Japan had been following an isolationist policy of *sakoku* since the 1630s, which placed severe restrictions on trade and contact with foreign nations. The Mughal Empire in India, whose former glories included the Agra Fort, the Red Fort, and the Taj

Compared to many of the Eurasian empires, Britain's population was small. Their land was less suitable for growing staple crops. Their climate and even their history were unpromising. Said al-Andalusi, an eleventh-century Muslim scholar, had described England in the period of William the Conqueror as a cold and dark land populated by stupid, lazy, unscientific people who lived more like animals than humans.[27] Yet from the late eighteenth century onward, they pulled ahead of all the other Eurasian empires, including Qing China. By the early 1840s, they were sending gunships up the Yangtze River to impose a so-called treaty by force. What happened?

Much of the explanation will have to wait until chapter 9. Many historians insist that geography once again played an important role, with Western advantages including the shape of its coastlines, the Gulf Stream, its distance from the Eurasian Steppe, the depth of the Mediterranean, its lower population density, the proximity of its coal reserves to its population centers, and the distance across the ocean to the New World.[28] In a world destined to be dominated by intercontinental maritime trade, we might expect the Eurasian nations who stick out into the North Atlantic—Britain, France, Portugal, Spain, and Holland—to have been best placed to capitalize on it.

But not all differences between nations are material in nature. There are also differences in the realm of ideas—in beliefs, motivations, and hopes—and these play significant roles too, as we will see later on. And one of the most striking differences between East and West at this point is not *how* European ships sailed around the world but *why*. To see it in miniature, we can return once again to the *Resolution* as she leaves Plymouth in 1776.

James Cook had already circumnavigated the world twice. By his own admission, he had sailed farther than anyone else had done before him and fully explored the southern hemisphere. Yet less than a year after arriving home, having spent six of the previous seven years at sea, he was off for a

---

Mahal, was on the verge of total collapse after seventy years of decline. The Ottoman Empire was losing ground militarily; having lost a recent war with the Russians (1768–1774), in April 1776 they would lose Basra to the Persians. In addition, these last two powers (and especially the Mughals) faced the rising menace of a British group of mercenaries, entrepreneurs, and drug traffickers who called themselves the East India Company.

third time. The expedition was funded by the Admiralty. It required two ships to carry over a hundred and fifty people, numerous poultry, sheep, goats, pigs, and cows, and an abundance of provisions and clothing, which included "four hundred frocks and seven hundred pairs of trowsers."[29] It cost thousands of pounds and a number of lives, including those of both its captains—and all during a period when Britain was embroiled in a naval war with America, and presumably needed every able seaman they could find. What on earth were they thinking?

The question of motivation here is crucial. For obvious reasons, comparisons between Western Europe and East Asia in this period often draw attention to the superiority of Western seafaring.[§] But technological superiority does not necessarily lead to global supremacy. In the fifteenth century, a massive Chinese fleet had sailed from Nanjing under the Admiral Zheng He (1371–1435). Over the course of several voyages, Zheng reached Indonesia, Persia, Arabia, and the Horn of Africa, possibly as far south as Zanzibar. His fleet dwarfed anything that Europeans would be able to muster for centuries: two hundred and fifty vessels, with some purportedly up to 440 feet long and the total fleet carrying nearly thirty thousand men.[30] (For the sake of comparison, Christopher Columbus took three ships to America with a total company of just ninety men; at 62 feet long, his *Santa Maria* was roughly twice the size of Zheng's rudder.) As Europe was recovering from the Black Death and embroiled in the Western Schism, the Ming dynasty under the Yongle Emperor was sending fleets thousands of miles from home. Zheng could easily have sailed farther, if he had wanted to roam the oceans and discover the world.

Yet that was not the reason for the Ming treasure voyages. The Yongle Emperor had banned private trade, and Zheng had no intention of

§   It is certainly true that British navigation was world-beating at this point, thanks in no small part to John Harrison's marine chronometer, which had finally solved the riddle of how to calculate longitude at sea. Although a clock that would keep time reliably on the open ocean had been declared impossible by leading scientists, including Isaac Newton, the British Parliament had offered a prize of £20,000, or £3 million in today's terms, to anyone who could solve the problem. Harrison gave much of his life to it, and eventually succeeded. The result was not cheap—it is estimated that the early chronometers accounted for 30 percent of the total cost of a ship—but it made ocean navigation incalculably safer, and cartography far more accurate. Harrison finally died in March 1776. Three months later, the *Resolution* set sail with one of his chronometers on board: a potent symbol, like the coal she had carried a decade before, of the technological advantages Britain would take with her into the nineteenth century.

discovering new lands or shipping lanes for the sake of it. The purpose of the voyages was to protect existing trade routes, project Chinese power, and secure tribute from the peoples they visited, with a bit of pirate busting and score settling thrown in.[31] So when this was achieved, they simply came home, bringing foreign envoys and tribute with them. Nor did the voyages last. No sooner had Zheng died than Ming China stopped sending long-distance fleets like this, by order of the emperor.§

Cook's voyages, by contrast, were not mainly about tribute, protecting trade, or even the projection of power. Fundamentally, they were about discovery. The first was motivated (and funded) out of a desire to observe the transit of Venus, and there were botanists, artists, books, and scientific paraphernalia on board so that more could be learned about the natural world. The second was a three-year quest for the southern continent, with minimal trading opportunities beyond the bartering needed to keep the crew fed and watered while they continued their search.

The purpose of the third, besides taking Mai home to Polynesia, was to find the Northwest Passage. It had long been thought possible to reach the Pacific from the Atlantic via the Arctic Circle, without having to go all the way around the southern tip of either Africa or South America. It was widely believed that the sea did not freeze—because molten icebergs turned into fresh water, not salt water—so it was assumed that sea ice must come from rivers, and therefore that a route ought to exist between the ice floes, if ships could simply keep their distance from the coast. This was an exciting possibility. By the time the *Resolution* departed in 1776, the Germans were even claiming that Alaska was an island, and belief in the Northwest Passage had given rise to around fifty European attempts to find it. If it existed, it would make journey times to the East far quicker and thus cheaper, and open up the route to China in a whole new way. Cook's goal in the third voyage was to find out.

His expeditions were motivated, in other words, by a mixture of curiosity (charting new territories) and commerce (the possibility of

---

§   Some historians regard this decision, by the Zhengtong Emperor in 1435, as a key turning point in world history, especially given the great early European explorers—Columbus (1451–1506), Giovanni Caboto (ca. 1450–1500), Amerigo Vespucci (1454–1512), Vasco da Gama (1460s–1524) and Ferdinand Magellan (1480–1521)—who would be born in the next fifty years.

new trade routes). Clearly, it would be naïve to ignore their territorial implications, given the European settlement that followed within a few years, and given how regularly they discovered new islands and promptly hoisted the Union Jack. Nor can we forget the huge number of European ships in this period that were sailing the world's oceans for far less noble reasons, including plunder, piracy, warfare, and human trafficking. But nobody who has read the accounts of Cook, Banks, Forster, or anyone else on board can doubt that their basic motivation was discovery and knowledge, not wealth or territory. The first voyage was a scientific research trip. The second and third were journeys of exploration, not expropriation. Even the flag raising was very much a secondary purpose, which some evidently recognized for the farce that it was: "a flag was hoisted as I believe to signify our taking possession of this place for his Majesty, a circumstance not only contrary to the law of nations, but if seriously meant to the law of nature, as being in itself not only unjust but truly ridiculous, and perhaps fitter to excite laughter than indignation."[32] (Given that the place in question was Kerguelen Island, a piece of bare rock that the *Resolution* discovered on Christmas Day, 1776, and whose population consisted entirely of penguins, we might be inclined to agree.) When we compare the purpose of Cook's voyages with those of Zheng He, we are more struck by the differences than by the similarities. Putting cynicism aside, and with allowances made for the commercial motive, there is arguably no better way of summarizing the aims of the trips than the names of the ships: *Endeavour, Resolution, Adventure,* and *Discovery.*

The *Resolution,* and the Western nation whose flag she carried, clearly had a number of material advantages by 1776. Some of them stretched back 10,000 years to the origin of farming; some of them had emerged much more recently, through developments we will explore more fully in subsequent chapters. But she had some immaterial advantages as well, and these proved crucial in the late eighteenth century. Even in a time of war, political turbulence, and financial chaos, there was an overwhelming desire to discover, explore, chart, research, trade, and establish the existence (or not) of new islands, continents, sea lanes, and species.

To many of us, that combination of objectives might seem so natural that it is hardly worth mentioning. Surely all nations want to travel as many miles, explore as many lands, and trade with as many peoples as they can, right? Even if that was not true when Zheng set sail in the early 1400s, surely it was in the 1770s? It might seem strange, even ethnocentric, to highlight it as a source of Western advantage relative to China.

If so, then it is worth winding the clock forward seventeen years, to the summer of 1793. The American Revolutionary War has been over for a decade. All eyes are on the revolutionaries in France, who are at war with nearly everybody and have just beheaded their king. James Cook has been dead for fourteen years, after being killed in a skirmish on a Hawaiian beach on Valentine's Day, 1779. And Joseph Banks, now President of the Royal Society, has recently called for Britain to send a diplomatic mission to China for the first time. Banks's main interest is in tea growing and plant collecting, but the delegation is eventually agreed upon for other reasons: its aims include the opening of new ports to British vessels, the relaxation of trade restrictions on tea and opium, and the establishment of a permanent embassy. Led by George Macartney, the British diplomat who coined the phrase "the empire on which the sun never sets," it arrives in Beijing on August 21.

Diplomatically, the Macartney mission is a failure. It is chiefly remembered for what did not happen: Macartney did not kowtow to the Qianlong emperor, and the emperor did not grant any concessions to the British, who eventually took them by force during the First Opium War (1839–1842). But its most significant legacy, so notorious that it is still quoted by Chinese diplomats today, came in the letter written by the Qianlong emperor to George III. Amid a flurry of references to the British as barbarians, living on a remote island cut off from the world and therefore excusably ignorant, came this explanation for denying the King's request:

> Strange and costly objects do not interest me. . . . Kings of all nations have offered their costly tribute by land and sea. As your Ambassador can see for himself, we possess all things. I set no value on objects strange or ingenious, and have no use for your country's manufactures. . . . Our Celestial Empire possesses all things in prolific abundance and lacks no product within its own borders. There was therefore no need to import the manufactures of outside barbarians in exchange for our own produce.[33]

The winds of curiosity and commerce that blew the *Resolution* southward in 1776 might appear natural to us. Our entire economy is powered by strange, costly, and ingenious objects manufactured in exchange for our own produce, many of which (ironically) come from China. We do not possess all things, which is why we trade with other nations. But this did not appear natural to the Qianlong emperor in 1793. That difference would shape the next two centuries in profound ways.

Freedom and Resolution

In the same year, on the opposite side of the world, a French whaling ship called *La Liberté* had reached the end of the road.[34] After a tempestuous voyage, she arrived in Newport, Rhode Island—where the *Lord Sandwich*, formerly known as the *Endeavour*, had been scuttled fifteen years earlier—and was promptly declared unseaworthy.

Over the next few years, for reasons that are still not entirely clear, it came to be believed that *La Liberté* was in fact the same ship as the *Endeavour*. Within a few decades, pieces of the ship had become collectors' items. One of them was acquired by James Fenimore Cooper, author of *Last of the Mohicans*. Another inspired a poem by the English writer John Dix in 1852. Another was given to a yachtsman who sailed in the America's Cup in 1934. In 1971, a fragment of *La Liberté* even went to the moon aboard *Apollo 15*. Another orbited the earth with Andrew Thomas, Australia's first astronaut, in 1996.

Nobody, until very recently, had realized that these fragments were traveling under false pretenses, because nobody knew that *La Liberté* and *Endeavour* were different ships. They had fallen to the bottom of the same harbor, but when *La Liberté* arrived in Newport in 1793, the vessel that took Banks and Solander into Botany Bay had already been on the ocean floor for fifteen years. Yet in one of history's great coincidences, *La Liberté* had also circumnavigated the world in a previous life. She had also visited Tahiti and sailed around New Zealand, and to this day she lies on the ocean floor less than a mile from the *Endeavour*. So when the astronauts took a piece of her into space, believing her to be a ship who embodied the values of discovery and pioneering adventure, it turns out that they were actually right. They just had the wrong ship.

We know all this because of an English civil servant named John Barrow, who was part of the Macartney mission to Beijing in 1793. On his way to see the Qianlong emperor, he had witnessed a French whaler called *La Liberté* with his own eyes, and he knew that he had seen her somewhere before. Just months before she sailed into Newport harbor, dilapidated and exhausted, Barrow identified her as a former Whitby collier that had once been sailed by Captain James Cook.[35]

Her name was HMS *Resolution.*

4

Patriots

Becoming Democratic

*In a free country, every man thinks he has
a concern in all public matters.*

EDMUND BURKE

*It is certain in theory that the only moral foundation
of government is the consent of the people.*

JOHN ADAMS

THERE ARE ONLY SIX COUNTRIES ON EARTH that do not claim to be democratic. Four are on the Arabian peninsula: Qatar, Oman, the United Arab Emirates, and Saudi Arabia. One is Brunei, which has technically been under martial law since 1962. The other is the Vatican City.

The rest of the world's sovereign states hold some sort of elections. Over three-quarters of them have the word "republic" in their official name, including five "people's republics." Some of the most authoritarian regimes anywhere call themselves "democratic republics," including the Democratic Republic of Congo and the Democratic People's Republic of North Korea. The fact that many of these nations would lack a number of democratic hallmarks—universal suffrage, fair elections, voter security, the rule of law, a free press, an independent judiciary, and so forth—is an ironic demonstration of how widespread the democratic ideal has become. Even those states that have no intention of functioning as democracies feel the need to pretend that they do.

This is so commonplace now that we can forget what an astonishing change it represents. Today, there are around seven billion people living in countries that purport to be democratic republics.

In 1775, there were none.[1]

Any explanation of how that happened will center on the late eighteenth century, and 1776 in particular. The "age of revolution" saw democratic movements, revolutions, and/or constitutions emerge in America (1775–1789), Ireland (1778–1799), the Netherlands (1780–1787), Geneva (1782), Belgium (1789–1790), France (1789–1794), Poland (1791), Haiti (1791–1804), and Switzerland (1798–1803). They were followed in the first half of the nineteenth century by a wave of revolutions across Latin America (1808–1826) and virtually every country in mainland Europe (by 1848).[2]

But the fountainhead of this transformation was the United States. It was the first democratic domino to fall, morphing in just fifteen years from loyal subject of the Crown into rebellious colony (1775), independent country (1776), victorious nation (1781), and constitutional democracy (1789). This, alongside its sweeping rhetoric, pioneering constitution, and peaceful transfers of power, made American democracy a source of inspiration for all subsequent independence movements.

Three years after the Declaration of Independence, it was described by a man who would play a key role in the Dutch patriot revolt as "the happiest event which could have happened to the human race in general."[3] The Russian dissident Alexander Radishchev hailed George Washington as an invincible hero leading the world toward liberty: "Freedom is your leader, Washington!"[4] Soon the Venezuelan revolutionary Francisco de Miranda was an expert on the Anglo-American war, and was holding forth on "the independence of Spanish America, her immense wealth, inexhaustible resources, innumerable population, impatience under the Spanish yoke, and disposition to throw off the dominion of Spain."[5]

In France, Turgot described the American people as "the hope of the world"; the Declaration of the Rights of Man and of the Citizen (1789), the most influential civil rights text of the period, was drafted by Thomas Jefferson and the Marquis de Lafayette.[6] "Ireland has much the air of Americanizing," wrote Horace Walpole during the Irish Revolution.[7] The future president of Ecuador described the Declaration of Independence as the "true political Ten Commandments" of humanity.[8] It was even speculated that the American example could become "contagious" in South Africa.[9] American influence was everywhere. Observers witnessed a "revolution in favour of universal liberty" that "begins a new era in the history of mankind," as the Welsh pastor Richard Price put it.[10] "Next to the introduction of Christianity among mankind, the American Revolution may prove the most important step in the progressive course of human improvement."[11]

So how did it happen? And why did it produce democracy (if indeed it did)? The first question is well-trodden ground, and we will summarize the story by looking at just three moments in the turbulent year of 1776: one at the beginning, one in the middle, and one at the end. The second, which is more contested, we will come back to later.

New Year's Day

There is something rather odd about the letter dated New Year's Day 1776, written by George Washington to a commanding officer seven miles away. Those familiar with the American Revolution will spot it immediately:

> Dear Sir,   Trenton 9 Oclock P.M. Janry 1st 1776
>
> Some pieces of Intelligence renders it necessary for you to March your Troops immediately to this ~~particular~~ place—I ~~shall~~ expect your Brigade will be here by five o'clock in the Morning without fail. At any rate do not exceed 6.
>
> I am very sincerely Yr Most Obedt Sert,
>
> Gº Washington
> Bring your Baggage—at least let it follow under a guard.[12]

What is strange is not the errors, nor the ominous postscript, nor the fact that Washington is summoning a brigade at nine o'clock in the evening and expecting it to arrive by five the next morning. All of these make sense when we consider the extraordinary decision he had just made. The odd thing is that the letter was written from Trenton, New Jersey—and George Washington and his army were nowhere near Trenton on Monday January 1, 1776. They were actually four states away in Cambridge, Massachusetts, and would not reach New Jersey for another ten months.

This brief note can lay claim to being one of the most important letters in the history of America. But it was not written in 1776 at all. (We can forgive Washington for getting the date wrong, given that he had probably slept less in the previous seven days than in any week of his life.) It was written on New Year's Day, 1777, and we will return to it shortly.

As it turns out, however, the real New Year's Day 1776 was also a key moment in the Revolutionary War. To begin with, January 1 saw the official launch of the Continental Army. The joining together of the disparate colonial forces into one army for the whole continent would prove crucial to American success (although at this stage, 90 percent of the soldiers were still from New England), as Washington highlighted in a document he genuinely did write that day:

> Head Quarters, Cambridge, January 1st 1776
>
> Parole the Congress   Countersign, America
>
> This day giving commencement to the new-army, which, in every point of View is entirely Continental; the General flatters himself, that a laudable Spirit of emulation, will now take place, and pervade the whole of it; without such a Spirit, few Officers have ever arrived to any degree of Reputation, nor did any Army ever become formidable: His Excellency hopes that the Importance of the great Cause we are engaged in, will be deeply impressed upon every Man's mind.[13]

To mark the occasion, the members of this new army stood in the cold on Prospect Hill, just across the Charles River to the north of Boston, fired a thirteen-gun salute, and hoisted an American national flag for the first time.[14] The British heard the gunfire, and were half expecting the Americans to capitulate anyway. So when they saw the flag, they mistook the gesture as a sign of submission rather than defiance and prepared for the formal surrender of the Continental Army.[15] It was not forthcoming.

British confidence had been fueled by the arrival, after a long Atlantic crossing, of the speech made by King George III when he opened Parliament.[16] His Majesty had not minced his words:

> The rebellious war now levied is become more general, and is manifestly carried on for the purpose of establishing an independent empire. I need

not dwell upon the fatal effects of the success of such a plan. . . . It is now become the part of wisdom, and (in its effects) of clemency, to put a speedy end to these disorders by the most decisive exertions. For this purpose, I have increased my naval establishment, and greatly augmented my land forces. . . . When the unhappy and deluded multitude, against whom this force will be directed, shall become sensible of their error, I shall be ready to receive the misled with tenderness and mercy![17]

When the speech arrived in the American camp on January 1, 1776, it provoked outrage. It was immediately burned by the patriot soldiers, and Nathanael Greene, then a brigadier general, spoke for many when he argued that the king's rhetoric made talk of compromise impossible. "America must raise an empire of permanent duration," he argued. "Permit me then to recommend from the sincerity of my heart, ready at all times to bleed in my country's cause, a Declaration of Independence."[18]

Patriot fury would no doubt have been even greater if they had known what was happening that same afternoon, six hundred miles to the south in Norfolk, Virginia. Tensions in the harbor town had been rising for months. The colonial governor, Lord Dunmore, had declared that all slaves who fought for the British would be freed. This did not go down well with Virginia slaveowners, who lambasted him as "Devil Dunmore," an "ignoramus Negro-thief," and an "arch traitor to the rights of humanity [who] should be instantly crushd, if it takes the force of the whole colony to do it" (this last one written by the most famous Virginia slaveowner of them all, George Washington).[19] As 1776 dawned, Norfolk was under patriot control. Tory loyalists had fled the town. Four British gunships were poised menacingly along the waterfront, their broadsides pointing at the wharf.

At three o'clock on New Year's Day, after a short drumroll, over a hundred guns opened fire on the harbor, shelling it for seven hours and setting much of it ablaze. The fire was fueled by both sides: British landing craft were sent ashore to burn buildings hosting patriot snipers, while American militia began torching and looting loyalist properties. When the flames eventually subsided, the town was burned (again) by order of the Virginia Convention.[20] It was the worst damage suffered by any community in the American Revolution and a frightening foretaste of the way bombardment and fire would later be normalized in the pursuit of total war. Washington was quick to see the possible silver lining, however. "The destruction of Norfolk, and threatened devastation of other places, will have no other effect than to unite the whole country in one indissoluble band against a nation which seems to be lost to every sense of virtue, and those feelings which distinguish a civilised people from the most barbarous savages."[21]

Independence Day

The most remarkable thing about July 4, 1776, considering its totemic significance in American (and indeed world) history, is how unremarkable it was.

In popular mythology, it was a sweltering summer's day in Philadelphia. Fifty-six delegates, representing all the original thirteen colonies, voted in favor of independence from Great Britain and signed the full text of Thomas Jefferson's Declaration affirming it: "We hold these truths to be self-evident: that all men are created equal; that they are endowed by their Creator with certain unalienable rights; that among these are life, liberty and the pursuit of happiness; that to secure these rights, governments are instituted among men, deriving their just powers from the consent of the governed." The Declaration was immediately published and circulated, and proclaimed in the streets of Philadelphia by the ringing of the Liberty Bell. John Hancock, aware of the treason they had all committed, urged the signers to hang together. "We must indeed all hang together," Benjamin Franklin replied mischievously, "or most assuredly we will all hang separately."

In reality, none of that happened on July 4. It was a cool and pleasant Thursday, the steamy weather having broken on the day before. The crucial vote on the resolution took place the day before that, on Tuesday the 2nd, prompting John Adams to predict that "the second day of July 1776 will be the most memorable epoch in the history of America. . . . It ought to be solemnized with pomp and parade, with shows, games, sports, guns, bells, bonfires, and illuminations, from one end of this continent to the other." Twelve of the colonies voted for it, not all thirteen: New York abstained. The Declaration of Independence changed significantly between the 2nd and the 4th, with around a quarter of the text removed (including, notoriously, a fierce denunciation of the slave trade).* The quip about hanging separately was actually made in April by Franklin's fellow signatory Carter Braxton, and probably originated much earlier.[22] And besides John Hancock and Charles Thomson, none of the fifty-six signatories to the Declaration actually signed the original version on the 4th, despite the subsequent claims of Franklin, Adams, and Jefferson to have done so. Most of the delegates signed the engrossed copy, which did not even exist on July 4, four weeks later.

It was as close to a nonevent as such a moment could be. Some of the eventual signers were not even there, and many of those who were give a slightly underwhelming impression of it. In his voluminous papers, Adams wrote no account of the 4th at all. Neither did Franklin or Jefferson at the time; Franklin wrote to Jasper Yeates informing him of his appointment as a Commissioner of Indian Affairs,[23] and Jefferson took the opportunity to go shopping, picking himself up a thermometer and seven pairs of women's gloves.[24] Even John Hancock, whose giant signature would dominate the final form of the document, made at most passing reference to it in a letter to Washington that mostly focused on military formation.[25] Washington was a hundred miles away in New York, issuing mundane orders about pay abstracts and officer promotions.[26]

The Declaration of Independence was not printed for circulation until the Friday, did not appear in the local newspaper until the Saturday, and was not read publicly in Philadelphia until noon on the following Monday. It finally reached Washington's army in New York late in the afternoon on Tuesday, July 9, whereupon it was "received with three huzzas by the troops," some of whom went charging down Broadway in their excitement

---

* "[George III] has waged cruel war against human nature itself, violating its most sacred rights of life and liberty in the persons of a distant people who never offended him, captivating & carrying them into slavery in another hemisphere or to incur miserable death in their transportation thither. This piratical warfare, the opprobrium of infidel powers, is the warfare of the Christian King of Great Britain. Determined to keep open a market where Men should be bought & sold, he has prostituted his negative for suppressing every legislative attempt to prohibit or restrain this execrable commerce. And that this assemblage of horrors might want no fact of distinguished die, he is now exciting those very people to rise in arms among us, and to purchase that liberty of which he has deprived them, by murdering the people on whom he has obtruded them: thus paying off former crimes committed again the Liberties of one people, with crimes which he urges them to commit against the lives of another." See "A Declaration by the Representatives of the United States of America in general Congress assembled, 28 June 1776," Founders Online, National Archives, accessed December 19, 2022, https://founders .archives.gov/.

to decapitate an equestrian statue of George III and put his head on a spike, much to Washington's annoyance.[27] (The molten lead did however provide the Continental army with over 42,000 musket bullets, which produced the pleasing irony of the king's statue being fired at British soldiers "to assimilate with the brains of our infatuated adversaries, who to gain a peppercorn have lost an empire").[28] The calligraphic version familiar to most of us, and currently on display in the National Archives, was created on July 19, and eventually signed by most of the delegates on August 2.

Having said all that, the ratifying of the Declaration was not the only thing that happened on what we now call Independence Day. Another was the formation of "a Committee to prepare a device for a Seal for the United States of America."[29] We could dismiss this as irrelevant, given that it would take three committees, fourteen people, and six years to arrive at the Great Seal that appears on the back of a dollar today, and given that the original committee of Adams, Jefferson, and Franklin all came up with different designs, none of which were ever used. But the commissioning of a new seal for a new nation was a powerful statement of intent. It showed that independence was here to stay, and that it was theoretically possible to create an image that represented it graphically (as opposed to a royal face, or dynastic coat of arms). By the time it was adopted in 1782, the Great Seal had evolved to encapsulate several of the tensions that existed between the founders as to what exactly 1776 had meant: war and peace, many and one, revolutionary claims of a new world order (*novus ordo seclorum*), and gradual progress under the watchful eye of Providence (*annuit coeptis*). It is now one of the most widely printed images ever designed.

More pressing at the time, of course, was the war with Britain. It was not going well. The euphoria of driving the navy out of Boston in March, thanks to Henry Knox's munitions and the taking of Dorchester Heights, had long since dissipated. It had been replaced by fears for the security of New York, a city that was both strategically vital and virtually indefensible.

The consequences of losing New York would be devastating. Charles Lee admitted to Washington that "the consequences of the Enemy's possessing themselves of New York have appeared to me so terrible that I have scarcely been able to sleep."[30] If the British could secure the Hudson River, and simultaneously take Canada and move south into the Adirondack mountains, then they could separate New England from the other colonies and pick them off separately. Holding New York was therefore of paramount importance. "The time is now near at hand which must probably determine whether Americans are to be free men or slaves," Washington declared on July 2, just as Congress was voting for independence. "The fate of unborn millions will now depend, under God, on the courage and conduct of this army."[31]

They were doomed to failure, however. Protecting a city comprised of multiple islands separated by wide river channels would have been challenging at the best of times, given the number of places that needed to be fortified. Defending it against the world's largest navy was all but impossible. "It is so encircled with deep navigable water," Lee explained, "that whoever commands the sea must command the town."[32] As if to make this point, on Saturday, June 29, a British armada of over a hundred ships sailed past Sandy Hook and calmly dropped anchor in the Lower Bay, prompting alarm guns and panic in the city. "I could not believe my eyes," wrote one of the patriot soldiers. "In about ten minutes, the whole bay was as full of shipping as ever it could be. I do declare that I thought all London was afloat."[33]

The patriot position looked bleak. A glance at the correspondence on Independence Day alone shows just how badly things were going from an American perspective.

For one thing, the northern army had just been forced to abandon Canada. "The Retreat of the Northern Army and its present situation have spread a general alarm," wrote Jonathan Trumbull to Washington on July 4.[34] "They are now at Crown-point and Ticonderoga, in a weak state, and under necessity of an immediate reinforcement to enable them to make a stand, and prevent the enemy from passing the lake and penetrating into the country. The prevalence of the smallpox among them is every way unhappy."†

At the other end of the Hudson River, the situation on July 4 was equally perilous. The British had landed on Staten Island the previous day, completely unopposed. Here is how the Newark Committee described matters to George Washington:

---

† By one recent estimate, of the twelve thousand troops who had marched north to capture Quebec, a thousand had been killed in action, a thousand had died of smallpox, well over a thousand had been captured or deserted, and a further three thousand were sick or wounded. See Atkinson, *The British Are Coming*, 289–94.

May it please your Excellency,   Newark, 4th July 1776

As not only the levies but the main body of the militia of this and the neighbouring counties are gone to New York; and as the King's troops are in possession of Staten Island, and there being but a narrow river between them & our defenceless country; and it being thought improbable that General Howe will make any attempt on New York with his present strength, or until all his expected reinforcements arrive; and as there is great reason to apprehend that he, knowing our naked & defenceless state, will in the meantime, if his troops have no other employment, make incursions, at least, into, and ravage our country so near & exposed; we cannot behold our alarming situation without anticipating the most cruel distress.[35]

There was very little that Washington could do about it, though. He was being bombarded by requests for help, and his correspondence on Independence Day reveals a serious lack of officers ("Our men are raw & inexperienced—our officers mostly absent—want of discipline is inevitable"),[36] munitions ("the distress we are in for want of arms induces me again to urge your sending on all such as can possibly be spared with the greatest expedition"),[37] and doctors ("we are much in want of a Doctr as we have had none here since I joined the Regt").[38] Worst of all, they were woefully inexperienced, demoralized, and outnumbered:

New York,   4th July 1776

[Our present situation] is more alarming to this country than anything which has occur'd during the present contest. . . . This is a post of the greatest consequence—to be defended against 8000 disciplined Troops already arrived, a larger number hourly expected, and a mighty fleet; we cannot reckon the whole of the Land Forces at less than 18 or 20,000. . . . With an enemy of force before and a secret one behind we stand on a point of land with about 6000 old troops (if a year's service of about half can intitle them to the name) and about 1500 new. . . . Every man in the army from the General to the Private (acquainted with our true situation) is exceedingly discouraged. Had I knew the true posture of affairs no consideration would have tempted me to have taken an active part in this scene, and this sentiment is universal.[39]

History looks inevitable in hindsight. The patriotic pageantry of Independence Day, and the number of remarkable things that have happened since on its anniversary—including the Louisiana Purchase, the presentation of the Statue of Liberty, the deaths of Presidents John Adams and Thomas Jefferson fifty years to the day after the Declaration, and the death of President James Monroe five years after that—can give the impression of an iconic and triumphant moment in an inexorable march to freedom, complete with fireworks.

It was anything but. As Franklin, Adams, and Jefferson formed committees, wrote letters, and went glove shopping, the brand-new nation they had just voted for was in an incredibly vulnerable position. Its armies were retreating from Canada, disheveled and defeated, and they were on the verge of losing New York—and with it all hope.

The Twelve Days of Christmas

New Year's Day fueled the desire for freedom, and Independence Day expressed the ambition for it. But neither of them made it a reality. Aspiring nations need more than seals and ideals, flags, pamphlets, and declarations. In the end, they need allies, and they need victories. For that, Americans had to wait until Christmas.

For the most part, the Continental Army spent the second half of 1776 losing battles and retreating. The Hudson River was lost almost immediately, as British frigates breezed across the Upper Bay on July 12 and rained cannonballs on Lower Manhattan. Brooklyn fell, as it was always going to, in the last week of August. It was followed by Manhattan in mid-September, the Bronx in October, Fort Lee and Fort Washington in November, and Rhode Island in early December.

Patriotic accounts of that Autumn often emphasize the strategic brilliance of the American retreats, leaving the redcoats with tactical victories but little to show for them. There is clearly some truth to that, especially when it comes to the overnight evacuation of Brooklyn on August 29. But mostly these were calamitous defeats rather than cunning plans. The military correspondence is filled with references to cowardice, disorder, panic, and running away, with Washington himself described as dithering, caning his soldiers, throwing his hat on the ground in frustration, expostulating furiously ("are these the men with which I am to defend America?"),[40] lambasting his surgeons as "very great rascals,"[41] and bursting into tears.[42] The general knew things were not going well. "I am wearied almost to death with the retrograde motion of things," he admitted.[43] "The situation of our affairs is truly alarming."[44]

Late November and early December saw the Continental Army retreating "in a tag-rag race through the Jerseys, with General Howe and the English army at our heels."[45] The journey was cold, dispiriting, and exhausting. Supplies were low, with the patriots suffering from "the extremest want of blankets" and some soldiers marching without shoes.[46] "No nation ever saw such a set of tatterdemalions," sneered a British officer.[47] A Quaker in Burlington speculated that if things continued, the patriots might even derive an unexpected advantage: "the British troops will be scared at the sight of our men, for as they had never fought with Naked Men."[48]

Morale was low. Congress had abandoned Philadelphia for fear that it would fall, and moved south to Baltimore. General Charles Lee, who was supposed to be marching his men to join Washington on the Delaware River, was captured at a tavern where he was spending the night and taken prisoner; the British dragoon under Banastre Tarleton threatened to burn the house down if Lee did not surrender (thus providing inspiration for the infamous church-burning scene in Roland Emmerich's *The Patriot*). Meanwhile the British and Hessian troops were plundering, pillaging, and even raping as they went through New Jersey.[49] All told, it was an American crisis, fittingly immortalized by Thomas Paine: "These are the times that try men's souls. The summer soldier and the sunshine patriot will, in this crisis, shrink from the service of his country; but he that stands it now deserves the love and thanks of man and woman."[50]

Yet the patriots had two big advantages. One was that their military objective was survival rather than outright victory. The British were thousands of miles from home and had to win, either in open battle or by encircling the enemy and forcing them to surrender. The Americans were on their own turf and simply had to not lose. So if Washington could keep the Continental Army healthy, together, and alive, and away from confrontations they could not possibly win—both of which, admittedly, were easier said than done—their chances would only increase over time.

Their other advantage was the international diplomatic position. No other nations had any interest in helping Britain retain her colonies. If King

George wanted international support, he would have to rent it (which he did, in the form of Hessian auxiliaries). But there were several powers who had an interest in helping Britain lose their colonies, including the Dutch, the Spanish, and—still smarting from the loss of the Seven Years' War—the French. That is why, at the age of seventy, Benjamin Franklin had been sent across the Atlantic with two grandchildren, three trunks of clothes, thirty-five casks of indigo, and a mission "to press for the immediate and explicit declaration of France in our favour."[51] His destination: Paris.

We know how the diplomatic story ends. We know that the treaty between France and the United States, signed in February 1778, will turn the war decisively in America's favor; we know that the British will be caught in a three-way sandwich at Yorktown between the French army, the Continental army, and the French navy, and be forced to surrender their position. But the beginning of the diplomatic story is less familiar, and it began over Christmas 1776.

Franklin arrived in Paris on December 21. Within two days, he had requested an audience with the French foreign minister, the Comte de Vergennes.[52] The meeting was granted and held in secret on December 28, when Franklin formally proposed a treaty of friendship and trade. Vergennes agreed to further talks and put the Americans in touch with the Spanish ambassador for good measure; he found Franklin measured and intelligent, and subsequently expressed surprise that they had not asked for more.[53] Franklin was encouraged. The following Sunday he asked if the French could send him eight ships of the line, "twenty or thirty thousand muskets and bayonets, and a large quantity of ammunition and brass field pieces": a fitting request for the twelfth day of Christmas. Knowing that this risked drawing France into a war with Britain, he also put his cards on the table about the three-way treaty he was hoping for:

> If England should on that account declare war we conceive that by the united force of France, Spain and America, she will lose all her posses-sions in the West Indies, much the greatest part of that commerce that has render'd her so opulent, and be reduc'd to that state of weakness and humiliation, she has by her perfidy, her insolence, and her cruelty both in the East and West so justly merited. . . . North America now offers to France and Spain her amity and commerce. . . . The interest of the three

nations is the same. The opportunity of cementing them, and of securing all the advantages of that commerce, which in time will be immense, now presents itself. If neglected, it may never again return.[54]

It was a bold proposal. In the short term, Franklin was rewarded with an interest-free loan of two million livres and the promise of further help.[55] But the French were never going to give him the hardware he wanted, let alone a treaty, until the Americans looked like they could win; the risks of antagonizing the British were too great. (It is no coincidence that he was invited to resubmit his alliance proposal in December, just two days after informing Vergennes of the American victory at Saratoga. Nothing succeeds like success.)[56] To get the French assistance they needed, the Continental Army needed to start winning some battles.

Three and a half thousand miles away, with no knowledge of what was happening in Paris, George Washington was doing his best to make that happen. He was not in the most promising position to launch an attack. Holed up in a farmhouse on Christmas Eve, on the Pennsylvania side of the Delaware River, Washington had an effective army of around six thousand, just a quarter of the size it had been in September. Provisions were low, the enemy was on the New Jersey side of the river, and the freezing winter was closing in, which made crossing the river incredibly difficult: the floating chunks of ice made it dangerous to cross by boat, but the ice was not yet solid enough to cross on foot. "I can hardly believe that Washington would venture at this season of the year to pass the Delaware," concluded the British general James Grant.[57]

He was wrong. On Christmas night 1776, the Continental Army attempted three crossings of the Delaware simultaneously, hoping to attack the Hessian fort at Trenton first thing in the morning. Two of them failed, confounded by ice jams, fierce winds, heavy snow, and turbulent waters. But in one of the great military maneuvers, Washington's northern group, led by Henry Knox—who had also begun the year with a frozen river crossing—succeeded in ferrying eighteen cannons, three hundred and fifty tons of ammunition, an unknown number of horses, and two and a half thousand men (the vast majority of whom could not swim) across an eight hundred foot river covered in ice floes, in a "perfect hurricane," in the middle of the night, on a flotilla of glorified canoes.[58] Landing on the New Jersey shore in the early hours of the morning, they then marched ten miles south to Trenton, arriving at eight in the morning on the 26th and taking the Hessians completely by surprise. The result was a swift and emphatic American victory. Of the fifteen hundred Hessians defending Trenton, nine hundred were captured along with their weapons, which included six cannons, three wagons of ammunition, and thousands of muskets, bayonets, and swords.[59]

In military terms, it was an important victory. But its real significance was its impact on American and British morale. The Continental Army had been losing or running away for the best part of six months, with the redcoats in hot pursuit. At Trenton, the cat and the mouse switched places. Washington immediately sought to press home his advantage. "I am about to enter the Jerseys with a considerable force immediately," he wrote on December 28, "for the purpose of attempting a recovery of that Country from the Enemy."[60]

At nine o'clock in the evening four days later, Washington sent the (misdated) letter we read earlier, urging General Cadwalader to join him at Trenton by five in the morning. Flushed with their success, the American plan was to establish a strong defensive position at Trenton, on the south bank of the Assunpink Creek, and draw the (substantially larger) British army to attack them. It worked. At dusk on January 2, the redcoats arrived and made three attempts to force the bridge before giving up and deciding to wait until the next day. "We've got the Old Fox safe now," General Cornwallis is claimed to have said of Washington. "We'll go over and bag him in the morning."[61]

Except that in the morning, the Old Fox had disappeared. In a third consecutive move of astonishing temerity, Washington had abandoned his position and marched his troops fifteen miles through the night to attack the British garrison at Princeton. When Cornwallis and his army woke up on the tenth day of Christmas, they found the Americans gone, and "at the same time we heard a heavy cannonade in our rear, which surprised everyone. Instantly we marched back at quick step to Princeton, where we found the entire field of action from Maidenhead on to Princeton and vicinity covered with corpses."[62] They were too late. The fox had struck the chicken coop, looted the town, and vanished into thin air.

The drama of the twelve days of Christmas, and the audacity of Washington and Franklin in their very different ways, turned the tide of the war. One leading historian argues that "no single day in history was more decisive for the creation of the United States than Christmas 1776," and it has been memorialized ever since in prose, poetry, and paint.[63] But it was most poignantly evoked by the physician Benjamin Rush, in a story he told about George Washington on Christmas Eve:

> I spent a night at a farmhouse near to him and the next morning passed near an hour with him in private. He appeared much depressed, and lamented the ragged and dissolving state of his army in affecting terms. I gave him assurance of the disposition of Congress to support him, under his present difficulties and distress. While I was talking to him, I observed him to play with his pen and ink upon several small pieces of paper. One fell upon the floor near my feet. I was struck with the inscription upon it. It was "Victory or Death."[64]

We the People

We began this chapter with two questions. The first was how the American Revolution happened, and the answer is essentially a story: of 1776, British hubris, American resilience, French intervention, and what Washington called "the smiles of Providence."[65] The second question is more difficult, though. Why did the American Revolution result in democracy?

Some would reply: it didn't. Fewer than forty-four thousand people voted in the election of 1788/1789, out of a population of three million, which is roughly the same percentage of the country as are Mormons today. Virtually all women were barred from voting.[‡] So were men who did not own property. Six hundred thousand enslaved people could not vote, along with all their descendants until 1870 (in theory), and a good many of them until the 1960s (in practice). Frankly, the idea that the entire population might participate in national decision-making—male and female, slave and free—was never on the table and would have horrified most of the founders. Therefore, the argument runs, the government of late-eighteenth-century America was not a democracy at all.

Clearly, if we limit democracy to those systems of government in which every person is consulted on every decision, then the early American re-

---

‡   The exceptions were unmarried or divorced women in New Jersey.

public was not democratic. By that standard there are no democracies even now, and certainly not the United States. Outside of referendums, decisions are not made by the voters themselves, but by their elected representatives. All sorts of people are still excluded from choosing those representatives, including children, noncitizens, unregistered individuals, and various categories of people with mental disabilities or criminal convictions. Less than half the US population voted in the 2020 presidential election. So if we limit democracy to those systems that have direct decision-making and/or full enfranchisement, we effectively define it out of existence.

A more nuanced approach is to think about democracy as a system in which the government is based on consent, and in which supreme power rests with "the people," however that problematically vague term is understood. By that standard, for all its faults, the early American republic clearly qualifies. The Declaration of Independence takes it as axiomatic that "governments are instituted among men, deriving their just powers from the consent of the governed," that it is "the right of the people . . . to institute new governments," and that "all men are created equal [and] endowed by their Creator with certain inalienable rights." That trifecta of consent, popular sovereignty, and equality has a powerfully democratic logic to it, notwithstanding the massive inconsistencies of most of the founders (not least the man who wrote these words) when it came to slavery.[66] Over the coming decades, it would percolate through American society with effects that now seem irreversible. The Constitution would state its democratic foundations even more prominently: "We the people."

This is not to say that the founders all agreed that "democracy" was a good idea. Plenty of them did not. For John Adams, Alexander Hamilton, John Jay, and George Washington, among others, direct democracy was tantamount to mob rule and liable to disintegrate into anarchy if not held in check by other, more prudent influences—as the collapse of the French Revolution into self-immolating, murderous chaos surely proved. "The ancient democracies, in which the people themselves deliberated, never possessed one good feature of government," declared Hamilton at the Constitutional Convention. "Real liberty is neither found in despotism or the extremes of democracy, but in moderate governments."[67] Washington agreed. "It is one of the evils of democratical governments that the people, not always seeing and frequently misled, must often feel before they can act right," he told Lafayette. "I am not without hopes that matters will soon take a favourable turn in the federal constitution—the discerning part of the community have long since seen the necessity of giving adequate powers to Congress for national purposes; and the ignorant and designing must yield to it 'ere long."[68]

Adams was even more dismissive. "Democracy never lasts long. It soon wastes, exhausts and murders itself," he explained. "Democracy is chargeable with all the blood that has been spilled for five and twenty years."[69] What is needed instead, he argued, is a mixed government, with balance provided by competing forces. The voice of democracy is expressed by the House of Representatives, which speaks for the many. The aristocracy is represented in the Senate, which speaks for the few. And because the interests of the many and the few will always stand in tension, it is the job of the one, the President, to mediate between them, with an independent judiciary interpreting the laws that result.[70] In other words, "the people" are sovereign over one branch of the government, but not all of it.

A number of the other founders saw things very differently. For Thomas Paine, Thomas Jefferson, Benjamin Franklin, and eventually James Madison, the great threat to the republic was not so much democracy as oligarchy, or even monarchy. America had nothing to fear from "the people." The real menace was aristocracy: property qualifications for voting, the Society of the Cincinnati, Washington's monarchic pretensions, Hamilton's centralizing financial power grab, Adams's ridiculous suggestion that the President should be called "His Majesty." What was the point in escaping one form of hierarchy, only to replace it with a new one? Surely the dangers of mob rule were less than the dangers of hereditary tyranny? For Jefferson, even the bloodshed of the French Revolution was a price worth paying. "The liberty of the whole earth was depending on the issue of the contest," he wrote after the September massacres, "and was ever such a prize won with so little innocent blood? My own affections have been deeply wounded by some of the martyrs to this cause, but rather than it should have failed, I would have seen half the earth desolated. Were there but an Adam and an Eve left in every country, and left free, it would be better than as it now is."[71]

Given the strength of opinion on both sides, it is remarkable that the disagreement did not lead to the total meltdown of the young nation and its Constitution. Instead, what emerged was a creative tension that made the machinery of government far more robust than it otherwise would have been. In the end, Adams, Hamilton, and the Federalists got the institutions they wanted, with a strong central state along with the checks and balances that would prevent it from imploding into either anarchy or tyranny (as so many new republics would over the next half century). But Jefferson, Paine, and the Democratic Republicans won the battle of ideas. Everyone was created equal; the Declaration said so. Popular sovereignty rested with the people, and it covered all the branches of government and not just one of them; the Constitution said so. The forces unleashed by these statements, as well as the convictions that lay behind them, would drive a slow but relentless expansion of the franchise over the next two centuries, both within and beyond America.

This democratic conviction comes across beautifully in an exchange of letters between John Adams and his cousin Samuel in 1790. John had missed the Constitutional Convention and the crucial debates that took place there, and he still believed that although the people have "an essential share in the sovereignty" of the nation, it was as one of "a mixture of three powers forming a mutual ballance."[72] But that was not how the Constitution had been designed. It fell to Samuel to make the point:

> Is not the *whole* sovereignty, my friend, essentially in the people? Is not government designed for the welfare, and happiness of all the people? . . . They delegate the exercise of the powers of government to particular persons, who after short intervals resign their powers to the people: and they will re-elect them, or appoint others, as they think fit.[73]

It is hard to state the democratic ideal better than that.

English Whigs and French Radicals

But where did it come from?

Taking that question literally for a moment, there are two obvious answers. One is England, and the other is France.[§]

§ Naturally, there is no shortage of alternative candidates. Numerous places in Europe have been suggested as origin points for democratic ideals, including the Dutch Republic, Lutheran Germany, the Swiss Cantons, Belgian Communes, Italian city-states during the Renaissance, the Spanish Cortes, German forests after the fall of Rome, the Roman republic, and classical

For many Americans, the great prophets of democracy were English: Algernon Sidney, James Harrington, and especially the liberal philosopher John Locke (1632–1704). Needless to say, none were democrats. But Locke's ideas on freedom, equality, property, rights, and consent, adapted by Montesquieu and transposed into an American context, pulled in a decidedly democratic direction, and were of the utmost importance for the founding generation, whose letters are full of references to his writings. He was frequently cited in the newspapers and pamphlets, with correspondents praising him as "the great and judicious Mr Locke" or even "the incomparable Mr Locke."[74] The opposition to taxation without representation, which became such a flashpoint from 1765 onward, came straight out of the *Second Treatise on Government*: "If any one shall claim a power to lay and levy taxes on the people, by his own authority, and without such consent of the people, he thereby invades the fundamental law of property, and subverts the end of government."[75] John Adams copied out extended portions of Locke in his diary and wrote that he "has steered his course into the unenlightened regions of the human mind, and like Columbus has discovered a new world."[76] Jefferson identified him, along with Newton and Francis Bacon, as one of "the three greatest men that have ever lived, without any exception."[77] And the most obvious legacy of all this influence is the Declaration of Independence itself, with its talk of equality, rights, and the consent of the governed. You can tell by comparing the Declaration's "self-evident" truths with the *Second Treatise on Government*:

Athens. Some take it back even further, to ancient Israel and the critique of kingship in the Old Testament. Each of these may have played a part, but crucially, so far as eighteenth-century Americans were concerned, they were all channeled (and modified) through English or French interpreters. Others look further afield and point to democratic governance on other continents: Tlaxcala in Mesoamerica, the Huron in North America, the Mesopotamian kingdom of Mari, ancient India, and several Central African societies. But while these examples clearly show that democracy was not unique to Europe, they also show that the kind of democracies that emerged in earlier societies were not of the same form, or scale, as that which arose in the United States. See, for example, John Dunn, *Democracy: A History* (London: Penguin, 2006); Benjamin Isakhan and Stephen Stockwell, eds., *The Secret History of Democracy* (New York: Palgrave Macmillan, 2011); Roger Osborne, *Of the People, by the People: A New History of Democracy* (London: Pimlico, 2012); Daron Acemoglu and James Robinson, *The Narrow Corridor: How Nations Struggle for Liberty* (London: Penguin, 2020); Stasavage, *The Decline and Rise of Democracy*.

[Reason] teaches all mankind, who will but consult it, that being all equal and independent, no one ought to harm another in his life, health, liberty, or possessions. . . . Men being, as has been said, by nature, all free, equal, and independent, no one can be put out of this estate, and subjected to the political power of another, without his own consent. . . . The governments of the world, that were begun in peace, had their beginning laid on that foundation, and were made by the consent of the people.[78]

Another source of English influence on the democracy that emerged in America was the group of Puritans who settled there in the first place. "It is ordered and unanimously agreed upon," proclaimed the English settlers in what is now Rhode Island in March 1641, "that the government which this bodie politick doth attend unto this island, and the jurisdiction thereof, in favour of our Prince is a DEMOCRACIE, or popular government."[79] It sounds paradoxical. How can a group of Puritans submit to a monarch who rules by divine right—the same Charles I who would be decapitated eight years later—while calling themselves a democracy? But these men (and many like them) were not denying the authority of the king, or trying to set up a new state. They were merely setting up a new church, and a new town, based on the Congregationalist principles they had held for years in England. God is sovereign; churches are autonomous; church members make decisions together, subject to divine authority; the king is in charge, but three thousand miles away; so if there are decisions to be made about what to do next, we need to make those decisions ourselves.[80] By the time independence was declared, that logic had been spreading through the colonies for a hundred and fifty years.

Mix these things together, and you have many of the ingredients for American democracy. If you took a group of English Whigs with this sort of constitutional and intellectual background—philosophical clarity on equality and rights, a long history of local self-governance in the colonies, and an even longer history of parliamentary representation to approve taxation—and put them in a colony several thousand miles away with an intransigent monarch imposing unwanted new taxes, you would not be surprised if they reacted like Adams, Hancock, Washington, Jay, and Hamilton did. You even might expect them to sign a Declaration of Independence, write the Federalist Papers, or establish a new Constitution.

What you would not expect them to do, however, is to react like Paine, Jefferson, Franklin, and Thomas Young did.⁵ You could not imagine English Whigs writing *Common Sense*. You would be surprised to hear them freely criticizing hierarchy, hereditary privilege, aristocracy, and orthodox Christianity, or advocating a completely new world order in which balances of power were abolished and war disappeared. You would be amazed if they developed a state constitution with universal male suffrage and flabbergasted if they supported the Jacobins during the French Revolution. And you would not expect the language of radical equality and human rights to predominate in their speeches and pamphlets, to such an extent that revolutionaries the world over would see them as pioneers in the fight for universal democracy. Those are not the ways of English Whigs. They are the ways of French Radicals.

Two comments fifty years apart will make the point. Benjamin Rush was moving in a world of thought radically different from that of John Locke, or even John Adams, when he told a friend in July 1776 that "the republican soil is broke up, but we still have many monarchical and aristocratic weeds to pluck up from it."[81] More dramatically, on his deathbed in June 1826, Jefferson waxed lyrical that "all eyes are opened, or opening, to the rights of man. The general spread of the light of science has already laid open to every view the palpable truth, that the mass of mankind has not been born with saddles on their backs, nor a favored few booted and spurred, ready to ride them legitimately, by the grace of God."[82] There are no passages like that in Harrington, Sidney, or Locke.

There are dozens of them, however, in the writings of the radical *philosophes*. The most well-known example is also the least representative—namely, the opening line of Rousseau's *The Social Contract*: "Man is born free, and he is everywhere in chains."[83] (Virtually every radical thinker would have agreed with Rousseau that man was everywhere in chains; virtually all of them would have disagreed with him about what removing those chains might look like.) But numerous works are more typical of the republican, democratic, egalitarian instinct in the radical French Enlightenment.**

---

⁵   An irrelevant aside: an intriguing quirk of the founders' attitudes to both Britain and Christianity is the polarity between "believing Johns" like John Adams, John Jay, and John Hancock and "doubting Thomases" like Thomas Paine, Thomas Jefferson, and Thomas Young.

**   None of these ideas are unique to French writers in the period, of course. There are numerous equivalents among British, Dutch, German, Spanish, Italian, American, and even Russian

In Diderot, Helvétius, d'Holbach, Raynal, Condorcet, Volney, Mirabeau, Brissot, and others, you find many of the same ideas recurring. Monarchy is corrupt. Empire is exploitative. All men are equal. Nobody has the God-given right to rule over anybody else. Serfs should be emancipated. Universal education is imperative. Religion and aristocracy are bulwarks for privilege and obstacles to liberty. Despots who repress their people should be deposed. Most graphically, in Jean Meslier's oft-quoted phrase, "All the great men in the world and all the nobility could be hanged, and strangled with the guts of the priests."[84] And so on.

It is against that intellectual backdrop that the writings of Paine, Jefferson, and their followers make the most sense. No doubt, it is too simple to divide the Enlightenment neatly into "moderate" and "radical" streams, with the former flowing into Adams, Hamilton, Washington, the aristocratic Federalists, and the Constitution, and the latter flowing into Paine, Jefferson, Franklin, the Democratic Republicans, and the Declaration of Independence.[85] Ideas do not work like that, except in textbooks. Nevertheless, there is enough truth in this oversimplification to make it useful. Whigs wanted a stable new government; Radicals wanted a brand-new world. Radicals (like Paine) saw the American and French Revolutions as roughly equivalent in their aims. Whigs (like Edmund Burke) welcomed one and were appalled by the other.

At no point was the difference between the two clearer than in the first few months of 1776. When Paine's *Common Sense* was published in Philadelphia on January 9, it caused an immediate sensation. A politically bombastic, rhetorically brilliant, and wildly popular pamphlet, it urged Americans to separate from Britain, providing a trenchant critique of the British constitution and monarchy in particular, and proposing a new form of government in which the people are in charge and the law is king. In a paragraph of breathtaking audacity, Paine described the epoch-defining significance of the moment:

> We have every opportunity and every encouragement before us, to form the noblest, purest constitution on the face of the earth. We have it in our

---

writers, heading back to Baruch Spinoza (1632–1677) and others. But the center of gravity in the late eighteenth century was undoubtedly France.

power to begin the world over again. A situation, similar to the present, hath not happened since the days of Noah until now. The birthday of a new world is at hand, and a race of men, perhaps as numerous as all Europe contains, are to receive their portion of freedom from the event of a few months.[86]

John Adams saw things very differently. Paine, he told Abigail in March, "has a better hand at pulling down than building," with "very inadequate ideas of what is proper and necessary to be done in order to form Constitutions."[87] The very novelty of his system was the problem: where Paine felt like Noah stepping out of the ark into a brand-new world, Adams was more like Solomon asking how to govern the people wisely. Adams presented his own *Thoughts on Government* in April, with far more continuity between old and new, including a bicameral legislature and a tripartite separation of powers between judicial, executive, and legislative branches. Soon afterward, Adams explains, the two met in person:

> His business was to reprehend me for publishing my pamphlet. [He] said he was afraid it would do hurt, and that it was repugnant to the plan he had proposed in his *Common Sense*. I told him it was true it was repugnant and for that reason, I had written it and consented to the publication of it: for I was as much afraid of his work [as] he was of mine. His plan was so democratical, without any restraint or even an attempt at any equilibrium or counterpoise, that it must produce confusion and every evil work.[88]

In that exchange, colored as it is by Adams's cranky yet endearing self-importance, you have the Whig and Radical versions of the American Revolution in their purest forms. Which of them should take precedence over the other—continuity or novelty, stability or democracy, national unity or individual liberty, practicalities or idealism, prose or poetry—is something their descendants have been arguing about ever since.

The Spirit of '76

Modern democracy flourishes only in societies that share certain norms and institutions. When we consider the most obvious of those norms and institutions—universal suffrage, the rights of women, freedom of the press, freedom of religion, separation of powers, an independent judiciary, and so forth—it is striking how many of them go back to 1776.

On March 21, for example, the English radical John Wilkes became the first person to introduce a motion in the House of Commons "for a more equal representation of the people in Parliament." He lambasted the corrupt system of rotten boroughs, in which a tiny number of people in defunct rural constituencies wielded a totally disproportionate amount of power. He urged that "the rich, populous trading towns, Birmingham, Manchester, Sheffield, Leeds, and others, be permitted to send deputies to the great council of the nation" in their place. And he insisted that "the manufacturer, the cottager, the servant" should have "some share therefore in the power of making those laws which deeply interest them, and to which they are expected to pay obedience," on the grounds that "the mass of the people to be governed" are "the original fountain of power, and even of revenue, and in all events the last resource." The only person to respond was the Prime Minister, Lord North. He "supposed the honourable gentleman was not serious."[89]

Historians are still not certain whether he was. But the Welsh pastor Richard Price certainly was in February 1776, when he argued that a state was free in proportion to the number of individuals who chose their representatives.[90] So was the Commonwealth of Pennsylvania six months later, when it gave all taxpaying men the vote for the first time: "Every freemen of the full age of twenty-one years, having resided in this state for the space of one whole year next before the day of election for representatives, and paid public taxes during that time, shall enjoy the right of an elector."[91] So was Major John Cartwright in October, when he argued in his pamphlet *Take Your Choice!* that since mechanics and laborers paid taxes, "no man can be without a right to vote for a representative in the legislature." The logic of equality made universal suffrage irresistible. "All are by nature free; all are by nature equal; freedom implies choice; equality excludes degrees in freedom."[92]

Today it strikes us as strange that this logic did not extend to women, at least for Wilkes, Price, Cartwright, and the state of Pennsylvania. It would be well over a century before any nation-state gave women the vote on the same basis as men, with honors split between New Zealand, Australia, and Finland. But 1776 saw the ground shifting here as well. In July, the state of New Jersey became the first to grant the vote to women who owned property: "all inhabitants of this Colony, of full age, who are worth fifty pounds proclamation money, clear estate in the same, and have resided within the county in which they claim a vote for twelve months immediately preceding the election, shall be entitled to vote for Representatives in Council and Assembly."[93] And in March, Abigail Adams wrote a justly celebrated letter to her husband John:

> In the new Code of Laws which I suppose it will be necessary for you to make I desire you would remember the ladies, and be more generous and favourable to them than your ancestors. Do not put such unlimited power into the hands of the husbands. Remember all men would be tyrants if they could. If particular care and attention is not paid to the laidies we are determined to foment a rebellion, and will not hold ourselves bound by any laws in which we have no voice, or representation. That your sex are naturally tyrannical is a truth so thoroughly established as to admit of no dispute, but such of you as wish to be happy willingly give up the harsh title of Master for the more tender and endearing one of Friend. Why then, not put it out of the power of the vicious and the lawless to use us with cruelty and indignity with impunity. Men of sense in all ages abhor those customs which treat us only as the vassals of your sex. Regard us then as beings placed by providence under your protection and in imitation of the Supreme Being make use of that power only for our happiness.[††]

In the same letter, Abigail expresses her suspicion that "the passion for liberty cannot be equally strong in the breasts of those who have been ac-

---

†† Abigail Adams to John Adams, March 31, 1776. Three years later, Judith Sargent Murray would write in her landmark essay *On the Equality of the Sexes*: "I would calmly ask, is it reasonable, that a candidate for immortality, for the joys of heaven, an intelligent being, who is to spend an eternity in contemplating the works of Deity, should at present be so degraded, as to be allowed no other ideas, than those which are suggested by the mechanism of a pudding, or the sewing the seams of a garment? Pity that all such censurers of female improvement do not go one step further, and deny their future existence; to be consistent they surely ought. Yes, ye lordly, ye haughty sex, our souls are by nature equal to yours." Judith Sargent Murray, *Selected Writings of Judith Sargent Murray*, ed. Sharon Harris (Oxford: Oxford University Press, 1995), 7. It was published in 1790 in *Massachusetts Magazine*. A year later, Olympe de Gouges wrote her *Declaration of the Rights of Woman and the Female Citizen*, with its famous statement that "a woman has the right to mount the scaffold. She must possess equally the right to mount the speaker's platform." Olympe de Gouges, *Les Droits de la Femme* (Paris, 1791), 9. Mary Wollstonecraft's *A Vindication of the Rights of Woman* followed in 1792.

customed to deprive their fellow creatures of theirs." And there is no doubt
that the practice of race-based chattel slavery has left a permanent moral
stain on the founding generation and all their democratic pronouncements,
whether the individuals in question were advocates of slavery (as many
were), glaring hypocrites who opposed the practice in theory but refused
to emancipate all their slaves in practice (like Jefferson and Madison), or
slightly less glaring hypocrites (like Adams and Hamilton) who opposed
slavery but concluded that the liberty of black Americans was less important
than the unity—at least for now—of white ones.[94]

Yet even here, 1776 saw some steps forward. Phillis Wheatley, the first
African American to publish a work of poetry, met George Washington in
March; he thought her writings showed "great poetical talents" and even
"genius"[95] (although this did not prevent Jefferson from denying that black
people could write poetry and accusing Wheatley's work of being "below
the dignity of criticism").[96] No sooner had the Declaration of Independence
been proclaimed than the African American preacher Lemuel Haynes used
it to expose the indefensibility of slavery, in his manuscript *Liberty Further
Extended*. Abolitionists on the other side of the Atlantic were raising the
rhetorical stakes too. "If there be an object truly ridiculous in nature, it is an
American patriot, signing resolutions of independency with the one hand,
and with the other brandishing a whip over his affrighted slaves,"[97] wrote
the Lunar Society member Thomas Day, whom we will meet in chapter 7.
"It is a crime so monstrous against the human species that all those who
practise it deserve to be extirpated from the earth."[98]

The most innovative democratic text of the year was the Virginia Declaration of Rights, drafted by George Mason and adopted on June 29. It formally
established a host of things later incorporated into the Constitution: the final
authority of the people, the separation of powers, an independent judiciary,
free elections, trials by jury, and protections against unlawful searches,
self-incrimination, and cruel and unusual punishments. For the first time
in history a free press was codified in law: "That the freedom of the press
is one of the great bulwarks of liberty, and can never be restrained but by
despotic governments."[99] The final article was also emphatic: "That religion,
or the duty which we owe to our Creator, and the manner of discharging
it, can be directed only by reason and conviction, not by force or violence;
and therefore all men are equally entitled to the free exercise of religion,

according to the dictates of conscience; and that it is the mutual duty of all to practise Christian forbearance, love, and charity toward each other."[100] This commitment to religious freedom as opposed to mere toleration, at the insistence of James Madison, marked a significant break with the past, and would have profound consequences for the future of American Christianity. And all of these developments took place in 1776.

In retrospect, it is remarkable that a new nation with such seemingly contradictory commitments—to liberty and equality, popular sovereignty and separation of powers, freedom of religion and Christian virtue, a strong central government and independent states, populism and moderation, abolition and slavery, Whiggish progress and Radical upheaval, federalism and democracy—was able to last. By rights, it ought to have collapsed under the weight of its own ambition in the first few years, and it very nearly did during the acrimonious mudslinging of the 1790s. Instead, the American Revolution survived, keeping its head while all around were losing theirs (quite literally, in France's case). Whether we should put that survival down to the nature of these contradictory commitments, or a handful of exceptional individuals, or the unusual levels of wealth in eighteenth-century America, or even the smiles of Providence, continues to be debated.

A Man for A' That

George III was not the first king in history with rebellious subjects who insisted on the right to govern themselves. Nor was he the first to fight them and lose. His historic misfortune was to have rebellious subjects whose theory and practice of democracy was sufficiently radical to enthuse a nation, yet sufficiently robust to survive. Government was strong enough to prevent anarchy, and society was strong enough to prevent tyranny. America walked through the narrow corridor in between.[101]

It was the harbinger of a permanent change in the moral imagination of WEIRDER people. In the late eighteenth century, concepts like rights, consent, choice, and equality were used to discuss questions of government. But their influence quickly spread far beyond that. By the late twentieth century, they were being used to settle questions of morality in general: my right to x, your freedom to choose y, equality for z, and so forth. In many debates, they now serve as conversation stoppers, axioms with unimpeachable moral authority, unencumbered by other categories like duties, obligations, virtue, or wisdom (let alone providence).

That transformation of the imagination, rather than voting as such, is the real democratic legacy of 1776. After all, Pericles of Athens (495–429 BC) could boast of living in "a democracy, for the administration is in the hands of the many and not of the few," with "equal justice" and public office granted "not as a matter of privilege, but as the reward of merit."[102] But ancient egalitarianism, like early American democracy, had its limits. Rights did not exist independently of responsibilities. Choice was not virtuous in and of itself. And social distinctions remained. Pericles would never have put it like Robert Burns did, less than twenty years after the Declaration of Independence:

> What though on hamely fare we dine,
> Wear hoddin grey, an' a that;
> Gie fools their silks, and knaves their wine;
> A Man's a Man for a' that.
> For a' that, and a' that,
> Their tinsel show, an' a' that;
> The honest man, tho' e'er sae poor,
> Is king o' men for a' that.[103]

5

Lights

Becoming Educated

The motto of enlightenment is therefore: Sapere aude!
Have courage to use your own understanding!
IMMANUEL KANT

You can never go too far in giving people
the means to educate themselves.
JEAN-BAPTISTE LE ROND D'ALEMBERT

IT IS LUNCHTIME ON THE RUE ROYALE IN PARIS.* It is a cold, overcast Sunday in February; the chunks of ice in the Seine have only just melted. Since the winter sun is hidden by heavy cloud cover, you can already see shadows on the cobbles, cast by the lamps and candlelight shining through the town house windows. Otherwise the side street is a dull gray.

It is also very quiet, considering its location at the heart of the first arrondissement, only five minutes' walk from the Louvre. But then it is always quiet on Sunday afternoons. All of the city's one thousand cafés are closed. So are the food stalls at Les Halles. Churchgoers have been and gone, and

* Today, the Rue Royale is known as the Rue des Moulins, having had its name changed as part of Baron Haussmann's redesign of the city.

the bells have fallen silent. The merchants on the nearby Rue Saint-Honoré will be noisy tomorrow morning, but not now. There are no dignitaries on horseback visiting Louis-Philippe at the Palais-Royal, just around the corner, and no men in powdered wigs playing chess in the manicured gardens. The main noise you can hear, in fact, is the sound of chatter and laughter coming from a well-lit salon on the first floor at number ten. The date is Sunday, February 11, 1776.

The salon belongs to a wealthy German philosopher by the name of Paul-Henri Thiry, Baron d'Holbach. He and his wife have been hosting regular dinners there on Thursdays and Sundays for over twenty years. They are magnificent occasions. Dinner is served at two o'clock and lasts until eight or nine. The wine collection is grand and expensive. The menus are opulent—soup, beef, veal, fish, duck, pigeon, pheasant, lark, melon, ice cream, coffee, and liqueur—to the extent that guests complain of indigestion afterward.[1] The library contains more than three thousand volumes. But what makes the salon famous is the conversation. The guests, a dozen or so of them, talk about "art, poetry, the philosophy of love . . . the sentiment of immortality, of men, gods and kings, of space and time, of death and life."[2] Discussions are sparkling, highbrow and subversive: "the freest, most animated and most instructive conversation that ever was."[3]

Over the last two decades, the salon's guest list has read like a who's who of European intellectual life (or at least male intellectual life; many French women are important thinkers and *salonnières* in their own right, but none are invited to the d'Holbachs' on Sundays). Denis Diderot, editor of the famous *Encyclopédie*, is a regular. So, over the years, have been economists, poets, and *philosophes* like d'Alembert, Buffon, Condillac, Condorcet, von Grimm, Helvétius, Raynal, and Turgot. Rousseau was there in the early days but has since fallen out with the group and now dismisses it as a "coterie."[4] Cesare Beccaria, the influential jurist and opponent of the death penalty, has visited the salon from Italy. So have economists Ferdinando Galiani and Pietro Verri. British guests have included actor David Garrick, historian Edward Gibbon, philosopher David Hume, chemist Joseph Priestley, economist Adam Smith, *Tristram Shandy* novelist Laurence Sterne, and politicians Horace Walpole and John Wilkes. Benjamin Franklin himself has dropped in. If you want a building that encapsulates the intellectual transformation taking place in late eighteenth-century Europe, there is no better candidate than 10 Rue Royale.

Having said that, several of the greatest thinkers of their generation are definitely not at the d'Holbachs' table on Sunday, February 11, including (arguably) the four most important ones.

One is only a few hundred yards away. He has a complicated history with several members of the salon, which he himself used to attend. He spends much of 1776 wandering the streets of Paris and Montmartre in a sort of dreamworld, writing a series of beautiful and wistful reflections on nature and happiness while lamenting the fact that so many philosophers, including several members of the salon, have rejected him. His walks will be suddenly halted in October by a bizarre incident involving a Great Dane. His name is Jean-Jacques Rousseau, and we will meet him properly in chapter 8.

The most well-known *philosophe* of them all is not at the table either. He has been banned from Paris for over twenty years, and the last time he set foot here, the salon did not even exist. He is now in his eighties. As the d'Holbachs' guests take off their hats and coats and sit down for dinner, he is several days' journey away, in a chateau near Switzerland, in bed.[5] On an average day, the most he can do is sleep and write letters—although exactly two years from today, on February 11, 1778, he will make an improbable return to the city from which he has been exiled for so long and be welcomed by hundreds of adoring fans, including several members of the salon. François-Marie Arouet is the great intellectual celebrity of the period, although nobody has called him that for years. We know him as Voltaire.

Five hundred miles north of the Rue Royale, a portly, amiable Scottish philosopher is sitting at his writing desk. He has actually visited the d'Holbachs' salon himself in the past—his popularity in the city has earned him the nickname *Le Bon David*—but he is getting old now, and it is a long way from Edinburgh to Paris. He is writing to his publisher in London.[6] His main purpose is to check that his four-volume history of England has arrived safely, and to ask for a competent typesetter. But as he concludes his letter, he mentions his excitement and puzzlement about two new books by friends of his. One of them, Edward Gibbon's *The History of the Decline and Fall of the Roman Empire*, is being advertised but has not arrived, and he is eager to receive a copy. But he cannot understand why the other one, Adam Smith's *An Enquiry into the Nature and Causes of the Wealth of Nations*, has not come out yet. He is beginning to worry that Smith is deliberately waiting until after the war with America is finished, which may mean that he will die before he gets his hands on one. He concludes the letter and signs it, "I am Dear Sir Very sincerely Your most obedient humble Servant, DAVID HUME."

On the opposite side of the continent, in the Prussian city of Königsberg, a fifty-one-year-old professor rises from the table, picks up a stick, and puts on a gray coat. It is freezing outside—Königsberg will later be known as Kaliningrad in Russia—and he is something of a hypochondriac. But Immanuel Kant is also a man of routine, and his pocket watch says half past three. It is time for his daily walk.

What Is Enlightenment?

Nothing especially important happened on February 11. No books were published, laws passed, or wars started, apart from anything else because it was a Sunday. Its very ordinariness is the reason for talking about it.

No doubt, it was a memorable day for some people. Ioannis Kapodistrias, the founder of the modern Greek state, was born. In London, more comically, "in open defiance of the Sabbath day two men, partly naked, walked for a wager along the Mall in St James's Park, in the face of the numerous congregation from Charlotte Chapel. . . . The congregation were not a little obstructed in their way home by the disorderly behaviour of the rabble who attended the prize walkers."[7] On the whole, however, it was a normal, uneventful winter's day in Europe, in which people ate dinner, talked, fell asleep, wrote letters, and went for walks as they normally did. Its significance does not derive from what happened. It derives instead from three factors.

The first is that those doing the eating, talking, dozing, writing, and walking had such exceptional and pioneering minds. Ranking historical figures according to their influence is generally considered crass, something for magazine supplements rather than serious works of history. But if we were to indulge in it for a moment, we could make a good case that there was more intellectual firepower sitting down for Sunday lunch in Europe on February 11, 1776, than at any time before or since: the founding fathers of modern economics (Smith), chemistry (Antoine Lavoisier), history (Gibbon), geography (a young Alexander von Humboldt), sociology (Adam Ferguson), biology (Carl Linnaeus), comparative linguistics (William Jones), anthropology (Jean-Nicolas Démeunier), geology (James Hutton), conservatism (Edmund Burke) and educational theory (Rousseau); the founding mothers of modern physics (Laura Bassi), history (Catharine Macaulay), novel writing (Fanny Burney), and feminism (Mary Wollstonecraft); the greatest mathematician who ever lived (Leonhard Euler); the editors of history's most important encyclopedia (Diderot), anticolonial history (Raynal), and dictionary (Samuel Johnson); and the most important philosopher since Plato and Aristotle (Kant). We could all quibble with the odd name on that list. But few would deny that the collective insights of these individuals have left an indelible mark on human knowledge ever since.

The second factor is that they were all connected to each other, through an international network of letters, salons, clubs, societies, magazines, taverns, and coffee houses, stretching from Uppsala in the north to Naples in the south, and from St. Petersburg in the east to Paris in the west. We naturally imagine them meeting in coffee houses, where the combination of caffeine, newspapers and conversation provided mental as well as chemical stimulation. Plenty of them did. Others, as we have seen, met in the salons of Paris. In Britain, as you might expect, people often met in the pub.[†]

For educated elites, there were countless points of connection. Some were formal associations, like the Royal Society in London. Others were informal but regular social gatherings, like the Lunar Men of Birmingham whom we will meet in chapter 7. Others were deliberately obscure or avowedly secret, like the *Geheime Berliner Mittwochsgesellschaft* (Secret Berlin Wednesday Society), or the Masonic lodges. And the intellectual center of gravity varied

---

[†]   The Poker Club, for instance, met at Fortune's Tavern in Edinburgh on Friday afternoons; on January 26, 1776, those in attendance included David Hume, Adam Smith, Adam Ferguson, physicist William Robison, architect Robert Adam, pioneering chemist Joseph Black, and three dozen other historians, nobles, clergymen and playwrights. See Minutes of the Poker Club, January 26, 1776, in *The Book of the Old Edinburgh Club* (Edinburgh: Constable, 1910), 153–54. As the Poker Club was leaving Fortune's Tavern on Friday evenings, another group was heading into the Turk's Head Tavern on Gerrard Street, in what is now London's Chinatown, hosted by Samuel Johnson and the painter Sir Joshua Reynolds. Known simply as The Club, it also gathered Edmund Burke, playwright Oliver Goldsmith, actor David Garrick, and biographer James Boswell; others like Edward Gibbon, Adam Smith, Charles James Fox, Richard Brinsley Sheridan, and Joseph Banks (now back from the Pacific and recently installed as President of the Royal Society) were added over the next five years. For a superb recent account, see Leo Damrosch, *The Club: Johnson, Boswell, and the Friends Who Shaped an Age* (New Haven: Yale University Press, 2019).

according to where in Europe you were. In St. Petersburg, it was the court of Catherine the Great. In other Baltic cities like Riga, Königsberg, and Uppsala, it was the university. In Milan, it was the most intriguingly named society of the period, the *Accademia dei Pugni* (Academy of Fisticuffs). In some places, it was a private home. Voltaire is reckoned to have hosted around five hundred different guests at his chateau near Geneva.

The third factor, and the critical one, is that many of these luminaries thought of themselves as engaged together in a common project. Granted, at this point it did not have a name. The Germans were beginning to use the word *Aufklärung*, and the French had been talking about *les lumières* and *éclairissement* for decades, but none of these terms carried the sense of a historical movement that they do today; in English, nobody referred to this period as the Enlightenment until the twentieth century.[8] Emphases also varied dramatically. Some thinkers stressed the primacy of reason, or scientific discovery, while others focused more on experience, criticism, or common sense. There were countless divisions between theorists and practitioners, ascetics and libertines, loners and socialites, monarchists and republicans, Jews, Protestants, Catholics, deists, agnostics, and atheists.

Nevertheless, they had this in common: they believed that they were involved in a collective enterprise to free the world from the immaturity of childhood, in which authority and tradition defined the scope of knowledge, and into a more advanced, mature, and independent state, in which human beings could finally think for themselves. They believed that in their day, and thanks to their efforts, humanity was becoming educated.

Educating the World

This was the rationale behind the book that, more than any other, epitomizes the period: d'Alembert and Diderot's *Encyclopédie* (1751–1772). A hundred contributors, including Diderot, Voltaire, Montesquieu, Rousseau, and d'Holbach, filled twenty-eight volumes with seventy-two thousand articles and over three thousand illustrations; the most prolific, Louis de Jaucourt, wrote over seventeen thousand of them at a scarcely believable rate of eight articles *per day*. The *Encyclopédie* was controversial, generating splits among the authors and suppression by the papacy, and getting banned twice in France.[9] But it had a very clear purpose. Its aim, as Diderot put it, was "to gather all the knowledge scattered across the face of the earth . . .

so that our descendants, by becoming more educated, may become at the same time more virtuous, and happier."[10]

D'Alembert agreed. Explaining the project in his introduction, he provided a backstory for it—and for the entire intellectual transformation taking place in Europe at the time—that remains familiar today. After "centuries of ignorance" in which the knowledge of history and languages had been "abandoned," the world finally began to peer out of the darkness in the fifteenth and sixteenth centuries, through a combination of printing, patronage, and the collapse of the Byzantine empire. (In a fascinating phrase that brings together our ideas of Renaissance and Enlightenment, d'Alembert described this period as one in which *la lumière renaît de toutes parts*: "the light was reborn everywhere.") But it took time. "The human mind found itself, on leaving barbarism, in a sort of infancy: eager to accumulate ideas, but initially incapable of acquiring those of a higher order, because the soul's faculties had been sunk in a kind of numbness for such a long time." Finally, the day came when people stopped merely reading the classics, or copying them; "they tried to surpass them, if possible, and to think for themselves."[11] That attitude is what made the *Encyclopédie* achievable; it is also what it was trying to achieve. "You can never go too far in giving people the means to educate themselves."[12]

We find the same destination, at the end of a somewhat different journey, in Lessing's last work, entitled *The Education of the Human Race* (1780). For Lessing, humans have been educated in three distinct phases. In the first, God revealed himself to the Jews. In the second, God revealed himself to the world through Christ. In the third, we have reached maturity and become able to educate ourselves, identifying the truths of reason without need for further revelation. But the aim is the same in all three: "ever the self-same plan of the education of the race."[13]

Echoes of this can still be heard in Western education today. We used to rely on holy books and divine revelation, when we were unaware and immature, but now we have graduated: from divinity to humanity, from dogmatic theology to critical enquiry. We used to look at humanity through theological lenses; now we look at theology through human lenses (or, as we might call it, the cognitive science of religion). Ever the self-same plan of the education of the race.

Of all the attempts to define the intellectual movement taking place, the clearest was Kant's essay *An Answer to the Question: What Is*

Enlightenment? (1784). Kant saw enlightenment as leaving the state of immaturity, tutelage, and dependence that characterizes all of us—accepting what we are told by the church, the state, or society at large—and having the courage to think for ourselves. Quoting the Latin poet Horace, he provided a classic definition:

> *Enlightenment is the man's emergence from his self-incurred immaturity.* *Immaturity* is the inability to use one's own understanding without the guidance of another. This immaturity is *self-incurred* if its cause is not lack of understanding, but lack of resolution and courage to use it without the guidance of another. The motto of enlightenment is therefore: *Sapere aude!* Have courage to use your *own* understanding![14]

It is a curious slogan. It is ironic to champion the importance of thinking for yourself, free from the guidance of anyone else, by quoting the guidance of someone else. It is even more ironic to do so when proposing a belief that every single independent thinker should hold, and which others were using the same way at the same time.[‡] It is all too reminiscent of the scene in Monty Python's *Life of Brian*, when Graham Chapman tells the crowd, "You've got to think for yourselves! You are all individuals!," and the members of the crowd chant back in unison, "Yes! We are all individuals."[15]

Be that as it may, Kant's definition remains a very crisp and accurate distillation of the spirit of the age, penned by its most influential philosopher. It is also striking in its similarity to the comments of Diderot, d'Alembert, Lessing, and others. Despite being dispersed among the salons, pubs, courts, universities, and coffee houses of Europe in 1776—and despite disagreeing among themselves on all manner of important things—the *philosophes* fundamentally agreed on the essence of what was happening in their generation.[16] After centuries of darkness, tutelage, and perhaps even barbarism, people were being emancipated. The light of knowledge was banishing the darkness. Humanity was coming of age and beginning to think for itself. The world was becoming educated.

That was the story of Enlightenment. The question is: Is it true?

---

‡   *Sapere aude* was also used as a motto by the great Swedish philosopher Thomas Thorild for his journal *Den Nye Granskare* (The New Critic), which he started publishing in the same year.

Darkness to Light

It might seem odd to ask. The narrative offered by d'Alembert and others has seemed plausible for so long, and circulated so successfully within Western culture, that most of us no longer question it. Tour a medieval castle like the one near my home in southern England, and within minutes you will overhear someone talking about "the dark ages": a thousand years of stultifying grimness in which people spent all their time burning witches, eating turnips, and dying of the plague, until early modern Europeans arrived and switched on the lights. (I have noticed that people are less inclined to say this when they tour Notre Dame Cathedral or Cambridge University, for some reason.) Serious newspapers and broadcasters do it too. So do popularizers of science. John Gribbin's *Science: A History* begins in 1543 with a chapter entitled "Out of the Dark Ages." Carl Sagan's *Cosmos* depicts a "millennium gap" between the fall of Rome and "Columbus, Leonardo," which "represents a poignant lost opportunity for the human species."[17] The darkness-to-light story has seeped into the walls.

You can see why. It has all the hallmarks of a compelling historical narrative: a primeval state of happiness (the classical world), a problem (ignorance), a villain (the Roman Catholic Church), a hero (brave, independent-minded European thinkers), a conflict between the hero and the villain (especially during the Galileo controversy), and a happy ending (in which educated Westerners are comforted to find ourselves on the winning side).

It is a flexible story, too. It was originally a Protestant account, with Roman Catholics held responsible for keeping us all in the dark for so long. William Camden, who described the "midle age" as "overcast with darke clouds, or rather thicke fogges of ignorance," was an Anglican, writing in the same year that a group of Roman Catholics tried to assassinate the king by blowing up the Houses of Parliament (known in Britain as the Gunpowder Plot of 1605, and memorialized every year with bonfires and fireworks).[18] Yet by the time Edward Gibbon referred to "the darkness of the middle ages" in 1776, it had morphed into an agnostic or even anti-Christian polemic, in which the bogeyman was not Catholicism as much as religion in general.

There is also enough truth in the narrative to make it seem persuasive. The two scientific breakthroughs that did more than anything to transform our understanding of the world—Copernicus's heliocentric system (1543) and Newton's theory of gravity (1687)—did indeed take place after the Reformation had started in Europe, in Poland and England respectively. The seventeenth century did see an explosion of scientific and artistic progress, particularly in Britain and the Dutch Republic. Pope Urban VIII did not cover himself in glory through his handling of the Galileo affair (although the real story is far more complex, and interesting, than the "faith versus science" version usually told).[19] There is also an undeniable emotional resonance to the Enlightenment story. The premodern world *feels* dark to us, as in a purely literal sense it was.

But the image of light was the real masterstroke, from a public relations perspective.§ This was a period of illumination, enlightenment, *éclairissement*, *Aufklärung*, "the dawn of light."[20] In English, we have Alexander Pope's famous epitaph to thank for that:

Nature and nature's laws lay hid in night;
God said, "Let Newton be," and all was light.[21]

Scientific discoveries were bringing things to light which had previously been obscure. At the same time, it was the job of intellectuals, and of scientists in particular, not to hoard the light of knowledge but to share it with others. That is why so many experiments were done in public. Jean-Antoine Nollet, the French physicist who discovered osmosis, explained why scientific demonstrations should always be performed as transparently as possible, right down to the materials used:

Although glass is fragile, we need to introduce it when we build physics machines, preferring it to metal or other opaque materials, whenever transparency can help us see mechanical processes. As I said, our first concern should be to teach [*enseigner*] and enlighten [*éclairer*], and not to surprise or confuse.[22]

§ Arguably its most controversial legacy today is the Illuminati ("the Enlightened"), a secret society founded in Bavaria in 1776. By coincidence, the Phi Beta Kappa Society, the first and most prestigious secret honor group in the United States, was also founded in 1776.

In statements like this, enlightenment is not so much a metaphor as a methodology.

Its clearest expression came in visual form. The frontispiece to the *Encyclopédie* shows a brilliant light shining through the clouds, emanating from a veiled Lady Truth at the center (see figure 5.1). On the right, Reason is removing her veil. On the left, Imagination is hoping to adorn it. Under Imagination are four women representing the genres of poetry (pastoral, dramatic, epic, and satire), and further down, the other imaginative arts of sculpture, painting, architecture, and music. On the side of Reason, we can see Theology kneeling and holding a Bible, along with Memory, History, and Time. Beneath them are the various sciences: geometry, astronomy, and physics, and then optics, botany, chemistry, and agriculture. Finally, at the lowest level, the trades and professions gaze up expectantly from the bottom left, waiting for the light of truth to percolate the whole way down.[23] It is the entire Enlightenment narrative captured in a single image. More subtle (and indeed more beautiful) examples can be found in Joseph Wright's paintings, where scientific progress is regularly pictured taking place in the light while the rest of the room is dark.

The darkness-to-light account of history, in which eighteenth-century Europeans enlightened, emancipated, and educated the world by finally releasing people to think for themselves, was an enchanting and reassuring tale. It was narrated with verve and unblinking confidence by a remarkable number of impressive thinkers from across Europe and reinforced through paintings, slogans, engravings, poems, scientific discoveries, political propaganda (especially on behalf of "enlightened despots"), and even music.[24] It still is.

But as a historical narrative, it has come under heavy fire, especially in recent years, from both the left and the right. Its gentler critics point out that it is guilty of a certain degree of overreach, claiming credit where it is not due and flattening complex historical processes into a simplistic cartoon. Its fiercer detractors—mostly conservative then, and mostly progressive now—are less inclined to give the darkness-to-light story the benefit of the doubt. Many regard it as self-serving, bumptious, ethnocentric hogwash from start to finish.

FRONTISPICE DE L'ENCYCLOPEDIE.

Figure 5.1   Frontispiece engraving from the 1772 edition of the *Encyclopédie*, by Benoît Louis Prévost. Public domain.

Enlightenment and Its Discontents

Ironically, the poster boy for the darkness-to-light narrative did not subscribe to it himself. Isaac Newton was heralded as the man through whom a darkened world was suddenly illuminated, like the cosmos in Genesis 1.

And the hyperbole is understandable in light of Newton's *Principia Mathematica* (1687), with its groundbreaking theories of gravity, motion, and calculus. But Newton himself did not describe things that way. In February 1676, exactly a century before the Sunday lunch with which we started this chapter, he accounted for his success in a letter to his rival, Robert Hooke, with a phrase that has become proverbial: "If I have seen further it is by standing on the shoulders of giants."[25]

It is a fascinating metaphor, and not only because people are still debating it: whether it indicates modesty ("standing on the shoulders of giants") or conceit ("I have seen further"); whether Newton meant it as an intellectual or physical insult to Hooke; whether he even meant it at all.[26] But taken at face value, it is virtually the opposite of what the pope said about him. Newton, for all his extraordinary achievements, did not appear out of nowhere. He was standing on the shoulders of Galileo, Descartes, van Schooten, and Kepler. They were standing on the shoulders of Copernicus and Brahe, who were standing on the shoulders of Swineshead and Bradwardine, Grosseteste and Fibonacci, Ibn Rushd and Ibn Sina, and so on all the way back to Ptolemy, Euclid, and Aristotle. Admittedly, some discoveries are much more dramatic than others, including Newton's. But this insight on how human knowledge advances—by challenging and improving previous explanations, not by spontaneously arising in full-orbed brilliance—was in fact central to the success of Newton, Hooke, Huygens, and the scientific method in general. There would have been no "Enlightenment" without it.

And the reality is that the Middle Ages in Europe contained far more "light" and far more "giants" than most people today—steeped as we are in the Enlightenment story—could possibly imagine. Some of that becomes obvious simply by walking around a medieval city for an hour with our eyes open. The mechanical, architectural, and intellectual legacy of the period can be clearly seen in its clocks, cathedrals, and universities. Some of it is less visible, but probably of far more importance to most people at the time. We might consider, for example, medieval developments in practical fields like farming (wheeled ploughs, nailed horseshoes, rigid collars, three-field crop rotation), engineering (harnessing the power of water, wind, and coal to process grain, wood, wool, leather, and so forth), production (of clothing, cast iron, earthenware, glass), warfare (longbows, stirrups, heavy cavalry, gunpowder, cannons), and invention (eyeglasses, gears, astrolabes, magnetic compasses, chimneys, and of course clocks), as well as hospitals and navigation—not to mention a multitude of more theoretical developments in everything from art and cartography to music and astronomy. We could call them the Light Ages. Some scholars do.[27]

For a physical experience of the Light Ages, we can leave the Parisian salons of the *philosophes* and travel fifty miles to the southwest, to Chartres Cathedral. Built between 1194 and 1220, and now designated a UNESCO World Heritage Site, this astonishing piece of medieval architecture presents all sorts of challenges to the darkness-to-light story. Some of this is purely aesthetic, as evocative shards of blue and red light pour through the gorgeous stained glass into the nave. Some of it comes from the sweeping Gothic architecture, complete with flying buttresses, breathtaking vaulted ceilings, and two towers of over a hundred meters in height, all of them trumpeting the complexity and intricacy of thirteenth-century engineering.

But it is also prompted by a closer look at the famous stained glass. Underneath the south transept rose window, ten meters in diameter, are five lancets. The central one depicts Mary holding the infant Jesus, but the other four show the evangelists (Matthew, Mark, Luke, and John) literally sitting on the shoulders of giants, in this case the four major prophets (Isaiah, Jeremiah, Ezekiel, and Daniel). When compared to the glasswork in other cathedrals, it is a highly unusual image. But it highlights the fact that it was Bernard of Chartres who first used the metaphor of dwarfs sitting on giants' shoulders, over five hundred years before Newton was even born.[28] And it serves to remind us that Newton's metaphor, as much as his science, was made possible by the medieval giants upon whom he sat.

All this is without leaving Europe. If we were to consider world history as a whole and summarize the story of human education, it is far from clear that we would identify Europe in the eighteenth century as the key turning point. We might point to the emergence of language (in East Africa) or writing (in West Asia in the early Bronze Age). We might think of the development of scribal schools (in Middle Kingdom Egypt and the Old Babylonian period), religious schools (the Vedic system in ancient India), alphabets (in northeast Africa and the Levant), philosophical academies (ancient Greece), or universities (medieval Europe). We might highlight the astonishing education system that emerged in Han

China (202 BC–AD 220): a bureaucratic marvel that featured an imperial curriculum based on a Confucian syllabus, textbooks, oral and written examinations, grades, performance incentives and/or fines for teachers, and three years of formal training for over one hundred thousand civil servants—all of which was so rigorous that it continued, albeit with modifications, until the twentieth century.[29] Or we could focus on periods of exceptional intellectual flowering, like those in the Islamic world during the Abbasid Caliphate (750–1258), China under the Song dynasty (960–1227), or Renaissance Italy (1400–1550).

Against that backdrop, the tale told by d'Alembert, Lessing, Kant, and Diderot looks selective at best. Was theirs really the moment when people started thinking for themselves for the first time? Was the rest of human history really so dark? Or do the epithets we apply to early modern Europe owe more to their branding ("Renaissance," "Dutch Golden Age," "Scientific Revolution," "Enlightenment") than their importance?

Behind that lurks a more ominous concern. If the rest of history is not as dark as we thought, might it also be that the "Enlightenment" is not as light as we thought? Might the darkness-to-light propaganda disguise a more sinister motive: "a conspiracy of dead white men in periwigs to provide the intellectual foundation for Western imperialism," as the Marxist historian Eric Hobsbawm put it?[30] Hobsbawm himself did not agree with this interpretation, and neither do I. But it is hard to deny that the darkness-to-light narrative reflects a combination of ethnocentrism and chronological snobbery, however defensible (or not) that was at the time. And nowhere was it less defensible than over the issue of race.

Heart of Darkness

It would have taken David Hume around ten minutes to walk from his house to the Poker Club in 1776. A short walk south across the bridge to the High Street, then left for about a hundred yards, and Fortune's Tavern is on your left. Retracing his footsteps today takes a similar amount of time, although the bridge now crosses Waverley Station rather than the canal, and Fortune's Tavern is long gone. If you're looking for a memorial to Hume, you can simply turn right, rather than left, when you reach the High Street. Walk for a hundred yards toward Edinburgh Castle, and you will encounter a prominent statue of Hume, dressed and reclining like a

Greek philosopher. He has a blank tablet in his hand to represent his skepticism, and an unusually shiny big toe, a touch of which—ironically, given Hume's disdain for superstition of all kinds—is meant to bring good luck.

If you had visited the statue in the summer of 2020, during the protests following the death of George Floyd, you would have noticed something else. Hanging around Hume's neck was a piece of cardboard. Written on it in permanent marker was his most infamous quotation: "I am apt to suspect the negroes to be naturally inferior to the whites." Soon afterward, the University of Edinburgh formally removed his name from one of its principal buildings, changing it from David Hume Tower to 40 George Square. In a statement, the university explained that Hume's "comments on matters of race, though not uncommon at the time, rightly cause distress today."[31] They certainly do, and in a way that raises questions about how "enlightened" the major Enlighteners actually were. If anything, Hume's comments are even more indefensible when you read them in context:

> I am apt to suspect the negroes to be naturally inferior to the whites. There scarcely ever was a civilized nation of that complexion, nor even any individual eminent either in action or speculation. No ingenious manufactures amongst them, no arts, no sciences. On the other hand, the most rude and barbarous of the whites, such as the ancient Germans, the present Tartars, have still something eminent about them, in their valour, form of government, or some other particular. Such a uniform and constant difference could not happen, in so many countries and ages, if nature had not made an original distinction between these breeds of men. Not to mention our colonies, there are Negroe slaves dispersed all over Europe, of whom none ever discovered any symptoms of ingenuity; though low people, without education, will start up amongst us, and distinguish themselves in every profession. In Jamaica, indeed, they talk of one negroe as a man of parts and learning; but it is likely he is admired for slender accomplishments, like a parrot, who speaks a few words plainly.[32]

The Jamaican man Hume is talking about here is Francis Williams: a scholar who was admitted to Lincoln's Inn, wrote Latin poetry, founded a free school for black children, taught mathematics and literacy, and is thought to have been the first black student at Cambridge University.[33]

Needless to say, he was no "parrot." And Williams was just one of many eminent Africans in Europe at the time, several of whom were known to Hume.⁵ So we cannot wave away Hume's racist comments as if they result from sheer ignorance or defend him on the grounds that everyone at the time agreed. Many did not.

We could say the same of Voltaire, whose Parisian statue was also defaced (and eventually removed) in the summer of 2020. Voltaire's antisemitism is well known, appearing frequently in his writings; the Jews are regularly used as a stick with which to beat the Bible, and hence the church. Less known, but no less egregious, are his comments on Africans. "The Negro race is a different species of human to ours," he declared in 1756. "You could say that if their intelligence is not of a different species to ours, it is certainly inferior."[34] Thirteen years later, the *Letters from Amabed* included this notorious passage:

> No art is known amongst these people. It is a big question among them whether they are descended from monkeys or whether the monkeys come from them. Our wise men have said that man is the image of God. Here is a pleasant image of the eternal Being: a flat, black nose, with little or no intelligence! A time will surely come when these animals will know well how to cultivate the land, beautify their houses and gardens, and know the paths of the stars. Everything takes time.[35]

Immanuel Kant's views, clearly influenced by Hume, are equally appalling:

⁵ We will meet Olaudah Equiano in chapter 11. Abram Petrovich Gannibal (1696–1781) was born in what is now Cameroon and taken to the court of Peter the Great in Russia, where he trained as an engineer and married, eventually becoming the great-grandfather of the poet Alexander Pushkin. Anton Wilhelm Amo (1703–1759), a philosopher who taught at the universities of Halle and Jena in Germany, came from modern-day Ghana. Angelo Soliman (1721–1796), originally called Mmadi Make, was enslaved as a child in Nigeria and wound up in Vienna, where he became tutor to the future Prince of Lichtenstein, an influential freemason, a friend of Joseph II, and an acquaintance of Mozart and Salieri; he was almost certainly the inspiration for Bassa Selim's character in Mozart's *The Abduction from the Seraglio*. Closer to home, Hume shared a number of mutual acquaintances with both Samuel Johnson's valet Francis Barber (1742–1801) and the writer and composer Ignatius Sancho (1729–1780), who despite being born on a slave ship became the first black person to vote in a British election (as well as the subject of one of the century's most famous paintings, Allan Ramsay's *Portrait of an African*). See Michael Bundock, *The Fortunes of Francis Barber: The True Story of the Jamaican Slave Who Became Samuel Johnson's Heir* (New Haven, CT: Yale University Press, 2015); Jerry White, *London in the Eighteenth Century: A Great and Monstrous Thing* (London: Bodley Head, 2012), 125–37.

The Negroes of Africa have by nature no feeling that rises above the trifling . . . not a single one was ever found who presented anything great in art or science or any other praiseworthy quality, even though among the whites some continually rise aloft from the lowest rabble, and through superior gifts earn respect in the world. So fundamental is the difference between these two races of man, and it appears to be as great in regard to mental capacities as in colour. . . . The blacks are very vain but in the Negro's way, and so talkative that they must be driven apart from each other with thrashings.[36]

Two paragraphs later, Kant dismisses the opinion of a carpenter because "this fellow was quite black from head to foot, a clear proof that what he said was stupid."[37]

These are not marginal figures. Quite the opposite: Hume, Voltaire, and Kant are the giants of the Scottish, French, and German Enlightenments, respectively, read and respected by virtually all the key figures in the period. Nor are they unique in their views. Opinions like this flourished in Enlightenment soil, generated by three things the *philosophes* were passionate about: categorizing human beings, the superiority of European culture, and anti-Christian polemic, especially with regard to the Genesis story. Despite repeated attempts to minimize the significance of these passages, whether by contextualizing them or by highlighting the work of other writers, there is no escaping the reality that many of the leading *philosophes* defended profoundly racist ideas.[38] So whatever the merits of renaming their buildings and removing their statues, it will always seem to many as if there is something fundamentally rotten at the heart of the "Enlightenment."[39]

That is the case for the prosecution, so to speak. The *philosophes* got an awful lot wrong. They exaggerated their own importance, had some large and inexcusable blind spots (including, but not limited to, the subject of race), left a very ambiguous legacy for subsequent generations, and regarded themselves as the high point of world history. Perhaps we all do.

The case for the defense is that in spite of all these things, they gradually but permanently transformed the way human beings think.[40] We might think it patronizing that they described that change as illuminating the darkness, educating humanity, or daring to think for themselves for the first time. It certainly was. But the change was real, dramatic, and lasting nonetheless. Everybody reading this book—and, in all likelihood, everybody within a hundred miles of us—conceives of the world in ways that go back to the "dead white men in periwigs."

That transformation is evident in all kinds of fields. But we can sample it by considering a handful of things that happened in 1776 in five subject areas (biology, geology, history, physics, and philosophy), in five different countries (Sweden, Britain, France, Italy, and Prussia). In each case, the most obvious changes do not relate to *what* people think—although that changed significantly too—but *how*.

Thinking about Species

The year 1776 was when the great Carl Linnaeus retired from his post at the University of Uppsala in Sweden. He had been a professor there for thirty-five years, during which time he had achieved an international reputation as a botanist, ecologist, physician, and zoologist. But his health was failing. A second stroke had left him able to admire his own writings, but without realizing that he had written them. Two years later he died. He left behind his wife and five children, a collection of 40,000 specimens, and a binomial classification system (*tyrannosaurus rex, homo sapiens*, and so on) that has been used throughout the world ever since.

Linnaeus could never be accused of modesty. "No one has more completely changed a whole science and initiated a new epoch," he announced in one of his five autobiographies. "No one has become more of a household name throughout the world."[41] He pictured himself as the second Adam, naming and ordering the natural world, and designated seventeen of his students as "apostles" who would travel the world collecting specimens. (In chapter 3, we met Daniel Solander, who was one of the luckier ones; seven of them never made it back alive.) As grandiose as this seems now, the Linnaean system was undoubtedly a substantial breakthrough in our understanding of the natural world. Instead of classifying creatures by physical similarities or modes of movement, Linnaeus saw all organic life as arranged hierarchically (kingdom, class, order, genus, species, variety), and proposed a far simpler way of naming things, replacing long and ornate descriptions with just two words, a genus (*homo*) and a trivial name (*sapiens*). To this day, his body remains the official type specimen for *homo sapiens*, because the only specimen he is known to have examined was himself.

He also developed the sexual system for identifying plants, according to the number and placement of their stamens (male) and pistils (female). This was probably more significant at the time. Linnaeus certainly thought so. It was also highly controversial. In the popular imagination, plants were female, not androgynous. And it caused a certain level of embarrassment to refer to stamens and stigmas as "genitals" or to calyxes as "nuptial beds," not to mention the use of more explicit terms like *labia minora, labia majora,* and *clitoria.* When William Withering wrote *The Botanical Arrangement of All the Vegetables Naturally Growing in Great Britain,* also in 1776, he removed all the sexual references so as not to offend women, even renaming stamens as "chives" and pistils as "pointals."[42] The Prussian botanist Johann Siegesbeck referred to the sexual system as "loathsome harlotry," mocking the idea that twenty males could share one female.[43] Linnaeus retaliated by naming an ugly, foul-smelling weed after him, which we still call *siegesbeckia orientalis.***

In the long run, however, the most momentous aspect of the Linnaean system was the decision to include human beings alongside all other species. In many ways, this was not new. Everybody knew that humans were animals as opposed to plants and mammals as opposed to reptiles; and anyone who had seen a chimpanzee would notice the resemblance. But by placing us in his taxonomy of all life, and designating us as "primates" alongside monkeys, apes, lemurs, and bats, Linnaeus had made a significant move: humans can and should be classified and analyzed like any other animal. He was not the only one to make this point. The Comte de Buffon, whom we met briefly in d'Holbach's salon, noted the family likenesses and even dared to ask whether they meant that humans and apes had a common ancestor like the horse and the donkey.[44] But it was Linnaeus's system that ensured we would be seen as primates, and members of the *homo* genus, from now on. (He originally went for *homo diurnis,* "man of the day," but later settled on *homo sapiens* or "wise man.") The repercussions of this development would gradually become clear over the next few decades.

**   The screenwriter Richard Curtis did something similar after losing a girlfriend to a rival. Most of his scripts, including *Four Weddings and a Funeral, Notting Hill, Blackadder,* and *Love Actually,* contain a buffoonish or idiotic character called Bernard, named after the Conservative MP Bernard Jenkin.

There is an interesting English footnote to this Swedish story. William Withering's book on botany, applying the Linnaean system to British flora, was very successful despite its apparent prudery. It was republished numerous times for another hundred years and gained him a reputation on the continent as the English Linnaeus. It did however have an absurdly long title, which ran to well over a hundred words. An older physician, who shared Withering's interests in botany and zoology, advised him to make it "easily remember'd," and made a number of suggestions, including "The Scientific Herbal," "English Botany" and "Linnaean Herbal."[45] But Withering was having none of it and stuck with his gargantuan front page. The two physicians later fell out, when the older man took credit for one of Withering's discoveries, observed while they were treating a patient together in 1776. They hardly spoke to each other again.

But it was the older man whose family name we remember today. He speculated that perhaps life had developed underwater, that "all warm-blooded animals have arisen from one living filament," and that this first living thing had gradually developed "the faculty of continuing to improve by its own inherent activity, and of delivering down those improvements by generation to its posterity, world without end!"[46] He had no idea how this might work. Nobody did for another fifty years, when his more famous grandson wrote a bestselling book explaining it. But he was so enthused by the possibility that he adopted the motto *e conchis omnia*, adding it to his family coat of arms and having it painted on his carriage. His name was Erasmus Darwin, and his grandson's name was Charles. *E conchis omnia* means "everything from shells."

Thinking about Rocks

Erasmus Darwin was one of the first to order a copy of John Whitehurst's book *An Inquiry into the Original State and Formation of the Earth* when it was announced in 1776.[47] Whitehurst had been researching it for fifteen years, and minerals and fossils were a source of fascination to most natural philosophers at the time. The growth of mining had made geology more important, for obvious reasons. It was also becoming a more controversial subject as its implications became clearer, especially those relating to the origins and antiquity of the earth.

It was increasingly obvious, for instance, that the layers of rock near the earth's surface were a good deal younger, more sedimentary and more likely to contain fossils than the layers farther down, which were more crystalline. This raised some important questions about the age of the earth. Was it really just a few thousand years old, as many argued from the book of Genesis? Should it perhaps be measured in the tens of thousands, or even millions? Why did some strata contain fossils and not others? How long had species been dying on earth? Could a global deluge account for all of this? If not, what could?

Whitehurst had struggled for years to integrate his empirical investigations with his interpretation of Scripture, particularly when it came to the global flood. There were numerous reasons to think that rocks were both older, and more likely to have been formed by fire than water, than a literal reading of Genesis would imply. He handled the problem by structuring his book in two parts: an inquiry, in which he attempts to fit the geological evidence into the timeline provided by the book of Genesis, and an appendix, which meticulously analyzes the rock strata in Derbyshire. The differences between the two sections are glaring. The appendix reads like a detailed scientific study, while the inquiry looks more like an exercise in theological-geological harmonization. And some of the evidence he provides in the appendix, particularly relating to marine fossils, seems decidedly at odds with the account he gives in the inquiry. To some at the time, it appeared as if his scientific evidence was in conflict with his theological narrative. The potter Josiah Wedgwood was a friend of Whitehurst's, and he agreed: "I own myself astonished beyond measure at the laboured and repeated efforts to bring in and justify the Mosaic accounts beyond all rhime or reason."[48]

This was a relatively new phenomenon. Most scientific research did not collide with biblical interpretation at all. The seventeenth century was full of scientific and mathematical breakthroughs by a wide range of Christian thinkers—Boyle, Descartes, Fermat, Halley, Hooke, Huygens, Kepler, Leibniz, Newton, and Pascal, to name just ten—but these discoveries simply illuminated the way that God had designed the world, and presented few if any challenges to the religious convictions of the scientists who made them. (This was true even when those religious convictions were less than orthodox; Newton's heretical Christology had nothing to do with his mathematics.) The obvious exception would seem to be Galileo's *Dialogue concerning the Two Chief World Systems* (1633), which was banned by the Roman Catholic Church. But Galileo's book was almost the opposite of Whitehurst's. Galileo was compelled by the Church to present a view that conflicted with his scientific research, despite being certain he was right.[††] Whitehurst was compelled by his conscience to present scientific research that conflicted with his theological beliefs, because he thought he might be wrong. We might admire him for presenting evidence that did not suit his case, or pity him for not reviewing his interpretation of Genesis, but either way his attempt was a brave one. It was not the last time that piety and professionalism would come into conflict.

Thinking about the Past

One of the most intriguing characters of the eighteenth century had one of its most evocative names. Abraham Hyacinthe Anquetil-Duperron was the French equivalent of Indiana Jones: an adventurer and linguist whose search for ancient oriental manuscripts involved fighting a duel, visiting ancient ceremonies in disguise, carrying a sword and a pistol, fleeing through a jungle, and negotiating with foreign powers in the middle of a war. Over the course of seven years, much of it travelling on foot, he tracked down one hundred and eighty manuscripts written in dozens of Indian languages, scattered across a vast country that he had never previously visited and learning languages as he went. The end product was a three-volume translation of the Zend-Avesta, the main sacred text of Zoroastrianism. He would later become the first person to render the Hindu Upanishads into a European language.[49]

His work received mixed reviews. Edmund Burke declared it "impossible not to be impressed by the number of discoveries contained in this book. . . . No one can be more respected than this true virtuoso."[50] Voltaire and Diderot were less enthusiastic; they were frustrated that the book did

---

[††] Galileo was asked to present both cases, the Copernican and the Ptolemaic, and admit that nobody knew which was right. He did—but the fact that he made a much more convincing case for the heliocentric system than the geocentric one, and put the latter in the mouth of a character called Simplicio ("Simpleton"), caused personal offence to Pope Urban VIII, a former friend and patron of his. He spent the rest of his life under house arrest.

not give them further ammunition against Christianity. One anonymous pamphlet claimed it was fraudulent drivel.[51]

Amid all the controversy swirling around the book, its most startling insight went largely unnoticed. It was an observation not about Persian religion, but world history in general. Anquetil-Duperron was the first to highlight what we now call the "Axial Age": the ethical transition that took place all across Eurasia in the sixth century BC, under the influence of great thinkers like Confucius, Lao Tzu, Buddha, Zoroaster, the Hebrew prophets, and the early Greek philosophers.[52] Although these individuals were totally independent of one another, and in most cases had not heard of each other, they all appeared at roughly the same time and brought changes in social and religious thought that still shape us now. Anquetil-Duperron called it a "natural kind of revolution, which produced geniuses who would set the tone for the whole world."[53]

This was a significant contribution to world history. It represented a global, or at least Eurasian, perspective without shoehorning in contemporary Enlightenment concerns. It was not a positive narrative of steady development toward commercial European society (like those of Turgot or Robertson), but nor did it center Europeans negatively by building the story around how they conquered and pillaged everybody else (like those of Raynal and Diderot).[54] It was an attempt at comparative and universal history, with both the distinctives and commonalities between different civilizations noted and appreciated. And it was remarkably sympathetic history for its time, partly because Anquetil-Duperron had actually visited the places he was writing about.

If you were trying to create the exact opposite of Anquetil-Duperron, you would probably make Edward Gibbon. It is hard to think of a historian less likely to walk around India on foot collecting manuscripts. He did not have the constitution for it, for a start, and in his later years he became extremely obese.[‡‡] Gibbon was a sedentary scholar, whose sources were not gathered by hand but assembled into a vast library of six thousand volumes. As far as we know, despite being the Member of Parliament for Liskeard, he never even visited Cornwall.

---

‡‡ Gibbon's parents were so convinced he would die as a child that they christened his younger brother Edward as well, presumably as a replacement.

Nevertheless, in an age full of great historians—Hume, Catharine Macaulay, Raynal, Robertson, Friedrich Schiller, August Ludwig Schlözer—Gibbon's *Decline and Fall* was the undoubted historical masterpiece. "My book was on every table," Gibbon boasted, "and almost on every toilette."[55] After reading an advance copy a few days before its official release, Horace Walpole wrote a gushing letter to him on Valentine's Day 1776. "You have, unexpectedly, given the world a classic history," he concluded. "The fame it must acquire will tend every day to acquit this panegyric of flattery."[56] So it has proved.

Much of this fame stems from Gibbon's argument about Rome's decline, and in particular his controversial assessment of Christianity's role in it, which we will return to in chapter 6. It also owes much to his style, which combines mellifluous prose, impish irony, and punchy aphorisms: "The various modes of worship which prevailed in the Roman world were all considered by the people as equally true; by the philosopher as equally false; and by the magistrate as equally useful."[57]

But what impresses most, and demonstrates best why he can be called the founding father of modern historians, is the historical method. The extent of his research is extraordinary. His analysis moves effortlessly between the macrocosm of nations and religions, and the microcosm of human psychology. The book contains eight thousand footnotes, so that subsequent scholars can interrogate his claims; this is common practice now, but it was not at the time. (There are no footnotes in Voltaire, for instance.) He avoids making what happened sound inevitable, occasionally suggesting some intriguing counterfactuals.[58] Admittedly, he is antisemitic by modern standards, and he does not hold back in his criticism of Christianity. But he is aware of his own biases and makes abundant use of Christian sources, drawing conclusions that are surprisingly evenhanded when compared to many of the *philosophes*. When he does not know what happened, he admits it and gives his best guess. And in all this, the flow of the narrative never gets lost.

"Two paths can lead us to the knowledge of man," wrote Anquetil-Duperron at the start of his first volume. "Metaphysics takes the first path, breaking man down and analysing his faculties, power and relationships. . . . History proceeds differently. It shows us man in action, which is to say as he is: the only proper way to give us exact knowledge."[59] For all their differences, he and Gibbon were united in their conviction that history can show us who we really are, and that the knowledge of humanity comes to us bottom-up (through the study of sources and artifacts) rather than top-down (through philosophical or theological reasoning). True or not, it is a conviction that shapes us still.[§§]

Thinking about Women

One aspect of the Enlightenment that continually baffles modern readers is its paradoxical view of women. On the one hand, women could be celebrated thinkers, authors, scholars, and even empresses. The *philosophes* met in salons hosted by women, and many agreed that the rules of Maria Theresa in Austria (r. 1740–1780) and Catherine the Great in Russia (r. 1762–1796) were more enlightened and effective than those of many men. Yet on the other hand, the clubs, universities, writings, and marriages of the Enlighteners—let alone their views of politics—assumed a much more limited role for women, based on their perceived weakness, emotion, and lack of aptitude for abstract thought.[60] Two things happened in 1776, one in Holland and one in Italy, that encapsulate the paradox.

One was the publication of a new book by the French philosopher Gabriel Bonnot de Mably.[61] It was mostly about law, not the place of women in society, and its republican arguments were destined to play an important role in the French Revolution. But the suitability (or not) of women for education, and of education for women, was a live subject of debate at the time, and Mably weighed in. Adam Smith, also writing in 1776, argued that the lack of schools for women was a good thing, because it kept them away from irrelevance: "There are no public schools for the education of women, and there is accordingly nothing useless, absurd, or fantastical in the common course of their education."[62] Mably disagreed. "The Republic is not only made up of men," he explained, "and I warn you that you will have achieved nothing if you neglect the education of women."[63] It sounds like something Mary Wollstonecraft might say a few years later. But then Mably gives his reasons:

§§ An interesting recent example: In their popular podcast, *The Rest Is History*, Dominic Sandbrook and Tom Holland consider the historical Jesus (episode 288, "Jesus Christ: The History," December 21, 2022). Sandbrook asks whether, given Occam's razor, the simplest explanation for all the historical evidence they have surveyed is simply that Jesus was the Son of God. Holland says no, on the grounds that historians cannot invoke supernatural causes to explain historical events—and to support his case, he immediately quotes Edward Gibbon.

They want to dominate like us, but in small ways: cunning, trickery, tears, sulking, pity, and all the inexhaustible resources of coquetry. . . . I defy you to point out any state where women have had power without destroying morals, laws and government. So raise young women in modesty and love of work. Form their morals early on, in such a way that they will have no ambition besides the glory of being excellent mothers in their families.[64]

Eight hundred miles to the south, the world's oldest university was honoring a woman whose career suggested otherwise. Laura Bassi was an exceptional physicist. By the age of twenty-one, she had publicly defended theses on Newtonian optics and the properties of water, become the second woman in history to earn a PhD and the first to enter the Bologna Academy of Sciences, and been appointed professor of universal philosophy at the University of Bologna. As a woman, she was not formally allowed to teach at the university, and it was difficult to publish her own work. But over the next forty years, she conducted experiments, corresponded with scientists, wrote papers, gave lectures, and taught students—much of it from home, while also giving birth to eight children and raising five. Her research ranged from electricity to hydraulics, and she was instrumental in spreading Newton's ideas in the Italian peninsula.

Bassi became something of a celebrity.[65] Her initial appointment was met with public celebrations in Bologna and a presentation of poetry in her honor, and as her reputation grew, she was held up as an example of what women could achieve on both sides of the Atlantic. The astronomer Jérôme de Lalande argued that her example should be followed in France.[66] John Morgan, who founded the University of Pennsylvania's medical school, visited the laboratory in her home in 1764, and hailed her as a "celebrated Doctress and Professor of Natural Philosophy" who "discoursed very learnedly on Electricity and several other Philosophical subjects."[67] Voltaire compared her to Newton.[68] It was probably this international reputation that made her among the highest paid faculty members in the university in the early 1760s, with a salary of twelve hundred lire.[69]

Her career culminated in the prestigious award of the Chair of Experimental Physics in 1776. It was an honorific rather than a practical appointment, in recognition of a lifetime's research. She held it for only two years before she died. But after a lifetime of arguing that she should be able to teach alongside men, to no avail, she had become the first female physics professor in history. Her husband, himself an anatomy lecturer at Bologna University, became her assistant. We can guess what Mably would have made of that.

Today, Laura Bassi has a crater on Venus named after her. Even that honor reflects our relative disregard for female scientists: a thirty-kilometer hole that nobody has heard of in a planet a hundred million miles away. It is in stark contrast to the way we remember one of the young male scientists who corresponded with her in the 1770s, whose name (or initial) is almost certainly a few feet away from where you are sitting right now. As a twenty-six-year-old physicist, he was keen for an expert opinion of his work on electricity, and enthusiastically sent Bassi a copy, admitting it was merely *mia giovanil produzione*, or "my youthful effort." (Everything sounds better in Italian.) Like her, he would be appointed as a professor of experimental physics at a major Italian university. He would also experience a landmark year in 1776, performing experiments on "flammable air," and eventually discovering methane. But electricity was always Alessandro Volta's first love. A few years later, he invented the chemical battery.

Thinking about Knowledge

Immanuel Kant is the very model of a modern major philosopher. He stares out of his portraits, contemplative and intense. His giant forehead, "built for thought," gestures toward the range and depth of subjects in which he is an expert: mechanics, cosmology, ethics, theology, metaphysics, geography, aesthetics, even weather.[70] He writes books that everybody admires and nobody understands. When we hear that he is obsessed with duty and highly disciplined, with a servant who wakes him at five each morning with the phrase "It is time," we are not surprised. We find his numerous eccentricities—eating one meal a day, never leaving East Prussia, disliking all music that is not military, changing into a nightgown after his morning lectures, refusing to have conversations outside to avoid breathing through his mouth—strangely reassuring. He publishes continuously for twenty years, then goes completely silent for a decade, then explodes into life again and revolutionizes Western thought. This is what all philosophers should be like, we think: brilliant, quirky, mysterious, incomprehensible, and German.

The year 1776 came at the midpoint of this "silent decade" of Kant's career, in which he published nothing except advertisements for his classes. It is also when he first wrote an outline for what would become the foundational text of modern philosophy. In a lengthy note, he lays out an overview of a future work in four sections: "Dialectic of Sensibility," "Dialectic of the Understanding," "Transcendental Doctrine of Appearance," and "Transcendental Doctrine of Experience."[71] Though it would evolve a great deal in the following five years, this is clearly recognizable as a summary of the *Critique of Pure Reason* (1781), a complex, original, and breathtaking book that would turn philosophy on its head. Madame de Staël, writing thirty years after it was published, declared that "virtually everything which has been done since, in literature as well as philosophy, comes from the impulse given by this work."[72] Kant himself described it as a Copernican revolution in philosophy, inverting the relationship between the observer and the observed in such a way that we could never go back. As arrogant as that sounds, he was right.

The *Critique of Pure Reason* is extremely difficult to understand, let alone summarize.[73] But in simple terms, it is Kant's attempt to resolve one of the Enlightenment's major problems, which is the question of what we can know and how we can know it. We all know how the world *appears* to be, based on our observation of it. But how can we know the world as it really *is*? And if that turns out to be impossible, then what hope is there for the objective truths we value: in science, theology, metaphysics, or anywhere?

Prior to Kant, two main answers were available, running in parallel tracks. One track, running from Descartes and Spinoza to Leibniz and Wolff, was what we now call *rationalism*. Our minds have intuitive knowledge of necessary truths, and we can achieve an objective, "God's-eye view" of the world through the use of our reason. The other track, which went from Bacon and Locke to Berkeley and Hume, was what we now call *empiricism*. This was the opposite position. Everything we know comes from experience, and the ideas that are generated by our sensory impressions, so objective knowledge is ultimately impossible: we cannot separate the known (the world) from the knower (the self).

Kant rejected both tracks. He thought Hume was wrong because there are certain truths that are neither true by definition nor established by experience (like "every event has a cause"). And he thought Leibniz was wrong because reason alone, without experience, would lead only to illusion, fallacy, and self-contradiction (as he argues with his famous "antinomies"). Knowledge is possible, Kant insisted, only when you combine reason *and* experience. If you have sensory impressions without rational concepts, you have no ability to think. But if you have rational concepts without sensory impressions, you have nothing to think *about*. "Without sensibility no object would be given to us," he wrote, "and without understanding none would be thought. Thoughts without content are empty, intuitions without concepts are blind."[74] (Picture the mind as an ice cube mold: cubes only form where there is both a structured set of categories, like reason (the mold), and an external object for them to act upon, like experience (the water). These "categories", for Kant, are basic concepts without which we cannot make sense of the world.) When understanding and sensibility come together, however, it is possible to have objective knowledge of an independent world that "transcends" the perspective of the knower—even if this world is still "ideal" (the world as it is perceived) rather than real (the world as it is). He called this *transcendental idealism*.

The *Critique of Pure Reason* was the start of a new phase for Kant, and for Western thought in general. Kant wrote two further "critiques," on moral philosophy and aesthetics, as well as several other works on politics, morality, and religion. His moral philosophy is probably better known today, and it is certainly easier to understand. But it was his Copernican revolution in metaphysics, and his idealism in particular, that transformed European philosophy, prompting a wide variety of responses in the work of Fichte, Schelling, Hegel, Schopenhauer, Marx, and many since. No philosopher since Plato and Aristotle had forced such a fundamental rethink of what human beings can know, and how we can know it.

The Enlightenment Legacy

The shadow of the Enlighteners is longer than we realize.

Jane Austen does not feel like an "Enlightenment" figure, any more than we do. She was only two weeks old at the start of 1776, and she wrote her novels a generation later. Her characters seem light-years away from the Poker Club, the Turk's Head Tavern, and the d'Holbachs' salon on Rue Royale. To the extent that she engages with that world at all, it is through ironic critique of its manners and pretensions rather than fawning adulation of its ideas. There seems to be a chasm between Austen and the work of Linnaeus, Whitehurst, Anquetil-Duperron, Gibbon, Bassi, and Kant that was taking place during the first twelve months of her life.

But the gap is much smaller than it appears. She is unmistakably a child of the Enlightenment. The connection between botany and romance that so intrigued Linnaeus, and concerned Withering, emerges clearly in *Emma*, *Mansfield Park* and especially *Northanger Abbey*: "a taste for flowers is always desirable in your sex. . . . I am pleased that you have learnt to love a hyacinth. The mere habit of learning to love is the thing."[75] In *Persuasion*, Austen describes the rocks and cliffs at Lyme Regis on the Jurassic Coast, which were already known as a geologically important area, rich with fossils and visible rock strata (the first ichthyosaur skull had been found there just six years earlier). At the age of fifteen, she wrote *The History of England*, mimicking historians like Goldsmith, Hume, Macaulay, and Gibbon and satirizing the pretense of historical objectivity. The women in her books reflect both halves of the paradox we saw earlier: for every Elinor, Emma, or Elizabeth Bennet, celebrated for having "more quickness of observation and less pliancy of temper than her sister," there is a corresponding Lucy Steele, Jane Fairfax or Mary Bennet, mocked for having "neither genius nor taste." And in Elinor and Marianne Dashwood, we have a memorable pair of heroines to represent the parallel tracks that Kant was trying to bring together in the *Critique of Pure Reason*. Philosophers called them rationalism and empiricism, or understanding and sensation, or reason and experience. Austen called them *Sense and Sensibility*.

Over two centuries later, the Western world stands in a similar position. We feel a long way removed from the *philosophes*, both in form and substance. Like Austen, we find their self-importance and stylized manners a little ridiculous. But we are profoundly influenced by them nonetheless. Like it or not, the Enlighteners have educated us all.

It seems obvious to us, for example, that we should classify species along biological lines and analyze the earth scientifically, even if some of our interpretative assumptions are challenged in the process. We instinctively use critical methods to reconstruct the past. We are committed to the education of all people of both sexes. We think of knowledge as a dialogue between the knower and the known, and take it for granted that information should be classified and shared in dictionaries or encyclopedias. When it is, we expect them to look pretty much like Johnson's Dictionary (1755), Diderot's *Ency-clopédie* (1751–1772), or the *Encyclopaedia Britannica* (1768–1771), and not remotely like the *Siku Quanshu* (1772–1783), which was being compiled in Qing China at the same time. We expect truth claims to be established by persuasion, not imposed by fiat. If we are honest with ourselves, we will admit that our society has absorbed many of the Enlighteners' more odious traits as well: their self-exalting narrative of world history, their dismissive view of "backward" and "outdated" cultures, their intellectual condescension, and racial superiority.

Ideally, we would keep their strengths and weaknesses separate, appropriating the former and rejecting the latter. Every *philosophe* would become either a pioneering genius who embodies our contemporary standards perfectly or a villainous caricature who must be thrown under the bus. But history is more complex than that. Heroes and villains are often the same people; good ideas and bad ideas come tangled together, growing like wheat and tares in the same soil. So it is hardly surprising that the Enlighteners have bequeathed to us a mixed legacy. The Western world has been illuminated by their powerful blend of sense and sensibility, and their laudable commitment to persuasion—but we have also been darkened by their pride, and prejudice.

6

Skeptics

Becoming Ex-Christian

Écrasez l'infâme!

VOLTAIRE

We hold these truths to be ~~sacred and undeniable~~ self-evident.

THE DECLARATION OF INDEPENDENCE

ON JULY 7, 1776, THE BIOGRAPHER James Boswell went to visit David Hume as he lay dying and discovered to his horror that Hume did not believe in the afterlife.

Boswell's surprise is itself surprising. The two men had known each other for years, and Hume's religious skepticism was no secret. His argument against miracles, "that no testimony is sufficient to establish a miracle, unless the testimony be of such a kind that its falsehood would be more miraculous than the fact," was famous across Europe (and is still influential today).[1] In his *Dialogues concerning Natural Religion*, which he had just completed, Hume would offer a powerful critique of several arguments for the existence of God, particularly the argument from design, and give a crisp statement of the problem of evil for belief.

Furthermore, Hume's unbelief was well-known by the population at large, not just by readers of philosophical essays. He liked to tell of how he once got stuck in a bog in Edinburgh and a group of fishwives refused to help him out until he had recited the Lord's Prayer because they recognized him as "the wicked unbeliever David Hume."[2] Boswell himself had jestingly referred to him as "the Great Infidel."[3]

Nevertheless, Boswell was clearly unsettled by the cheerful unbelief of someone so close to death:

> I had a strong curiosity to be satisfied if he persisted in disbelieving a future state even when he had death before his eyes. I was persuaded from what he now said, and from his manner saying it, that he did persist. . . . I asked him if the thought of annihilation never gave him any uneasiness. He said not the least. . . . I however felt a degree of horror, mixed with a sort of wild, strange, hurrying recollection of my excellent mother's pious instructions, of Doctor Johnson's noble lessons, and of my religious sentiments and affections during the course of my life. I was like a man in sudden danger eagerly seeking his defensive arms; and I could not but be assailed by momentary doubts while I had actually before me a man of such strong abilities and extensive inquiry dying in the persuasion of being annihilated. But I maintained my faith.[4]

For modern readers, the enigma in this story is not Hume. We are used to thoroughgoing religious skepticism. There is nothing remotely odd to us about meeting someone who denies miracles, rejects organized religion, and does not believe in heaven or hell.

For us, the puzzle is Boswell. He hardly fits the stereotype of a committed Christian. He was frequently drunk, garishly arrogant, addicted to gambling, and infected with gonorrhea on seventeen occasions. His diaries and letters are full of his sexual exploits with married women, Rousseau's mistress, various actresses, and dozens of prostitutes, many of which came after his marriage to his cousin and several of which are described in lurid and self-congratulatory detail. Yet not only does he identify as a lifelong Christian ("my religious sentiments and affections during the course of my life"), and proudly so ("I could not but be assailed by momentary doubts . . . but I maintained my faith"), but he is genuinely disturbed by the fact that Hume does not. His moral and intellectual framework is so thoroughly Christianized, despite his dissipation and debauchery, that he cannot conceive of a godless world. Nor does he want to.

This is what I have in mind when I talk about the modern West being ex-Christian. It is not that everybody today thinks like Hume. The vast majority of people do not, with polls regularly showing the stubborn persistence of belief in God(s), spirits, miracles, heaven, prayer, or all five, even in our most secular countries and cities. Rather, it is that nobody today thinks like Boswell. Christianity is definitely still an option, but it is just that: an option. The religious and secular menu has plenty of alternatives—and many of them will feel easier to believe and/or practice for much of the time.

Hume finally died on August 25. According to his doctor, he was "in such a happy composure of mind that nothing could have made it better."[5] Adam Smith was quick to write a glowing tribute to his old friend, describing him as "approaching as nearly to the idea of a perfectly wise and virtuous man as perhaps the nature of human frailty will permit."[6] Referring to an unbeliever as a paragon of virtue was always going to be controversial, and so it proved; Smith later claimed his brief eulogy brought him "ten times more abuse than the very violent attack I had made upon the whole commercial system of Great Britain."[7] Boswell was especially unimpressed. He saw Smith's remarks as "daring effrontery" and told Samuel Johnson how much he hated the "poisonous productions with which this age is infested" in a passage that sounds more like Mary Whitehouse or Phyllis Schlafly than a man who had slept with over sixty prostitutes. "You might knock Hume's and Smith's heads together," he added, "and make vain and ostentatious infidelity exceedingly ridiculous. Would it not be worth your while to crush such noxious weeds in the moral garden?"[8] Sadly, Johnson never replied.

Self-Evident

Two weeks before Boswell's visit to Hume, Thomas Jefferson wrote to Benjamin Franklin asking him to edit the Declaration of Independence in time for a meeting the following morning. "The inclosed paper has been read and with some small alterations approved of by the committee," Jefferson explained. "Will Doctr. Franklyn be so good as to peruse it and suggest such alterations as his more enlarged view of the subject will dictate?"[9]

Franklin was at home recovering from gout and made very few changes. But one of them would have epochal significance. Jefferson had originally written that "we hold these truths to be sacred and undeniable."

Franklin crossed out the last three words and replaced them with one: "self-evident."[10]

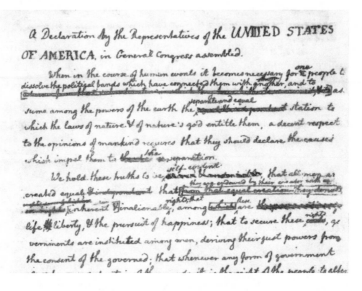

Figure 6.1   Declaration of Independence rough draft with Benjamin Franklin's edits. Public domain. {{PD–US}}

It was a portentous edit. Jefferson's version, despite his theological skepticism, presented the equality of men and the rights they held as grounded in *religion*: they are "undeniable" because they are "sacred" truths that originate with the Creator. By contrast, Franklin's version grounded them in *reason*. They are "self-evident" truths, which are not dependent on any particular religious tradition but can easily be grasped as logically necessary by anyone who thinks about them for long enough.[11]

To which the obvious response is: no, they are not. There are plenty of cultures in which it is not remotely self-evident to people that all men are created equal and endowed by their Creator with certain inalienable rights, let alone that these rights include life, liberty, the pursuit of happiness, and the prerogative to abolish any government that does not preserve them. Most human beings in 1776 did not believe that at all, which is partly why the Declaration was required in the first place.* (This accounts for the

---

* The philosopher Jeremy Bentham was one of many to pen a robust response, in his *An Answer to the Declaration of the American Congress* (London: Cadell, 1776).

otherwise inexplicable phrase *"we hold* these truths to be self-evident," as opposed to saying simply "these truths *are* self-evident.") Some of the founders had not quite believed it themselves just fifteen years earlier. Billions of people today still don't.

The fundamental equality of human beings, and their endowment with inalienable rights by their Creator, are essentially theological beliefs. They are neither innately obvious axioms nor universally accepted empirical truths nor rational deductions from things that are. There is no logical syllogism that begins with undeniable premises and concludes with "all people are equal" or "humans have God-given rights." The Russian philosopher Vladimir Solovyov expressed the non sequitur at the heart of Western civilization with a deliciously sarcastic aphorism: "Man descended from apes, therefore we must love one another."[12]

Many of us find this unsettling. We are inclined to see equality and human rights as universal norms, obvious to everyone who can think for themselves. But in reality they are culturally conditioned beliefs that depend on fundamentally Christian assumptions about the world. Friedrich Nietzsche made this point with angry brilliance: the obsession with alleviating the suffering of the weak and marginalized, within an ethical framework that valorizes humility, fairness, charity, equality, and freedom (as opposed to nobility, pride, courage, and power), is the result of the "slave morality" introduced by Christianity, with its crucified Savior and its claims about weak things being chosen to shame the strong.[13] Coming from a very different angle, Yuval Noah Harari shows how human rights, likewise, have no foundation if they are not rooted in Christian anthropology. "There are no such things as rights in biology," he explains. Expressed in biological terms, the Declaration of Independence would read very differently: "We hold these truths to be self-evident, that all men evolved differently, that they are born with certain mutable characteristics, and that among these are life and the pursuit of pleasure."[14]

Jefferson was right the first time.[15] Equality and human rights are "sacred" truths, not "self-evident" ones. They are irreducibly theological, grounded in specifically Judeo-Christian beliefs about God and his creation of humans in his image, and there is no particular reason why societies with different theological foundations should not reach very different conclusions. Many have.

We can see this even if we limit ourselves to the language used in the paragraph Franklin was editing. As we saw in chapter 4, the Declaration's famous preamble depends heavily on Algernon Sidney and especially John Locke, who argued that there was "nothing more evident" than the equality of human beings and that "being all equal and independent, no one ought to harm another in his life, health, liberty, or possessions."[16] In saying this, Locke was not innovating. He made it very explicit that he was also borrowing, in his case from a passage in the *Laws of Ecclesiastical Polity* by the Reformed theologian Richard Hooker (1554–1600): "This equality of men by nature, the judicious Hooker looks upon as so evident in itself, and beyond all question, that he makes it the foundation of that obligation to mutual love amongst men, on which he builds the duties they owe one another, and from whence he derives the great maxims of justice and charity."[17] And Hooker was not being original either. He was standing in a rich tradition of Christian reflection on theology and government stretching back to the church fathers and beyond; in the passage cited by Locke, Hooker was quoting directly from the Code of Justinian and Christ's words in Matthew's Gospel.[18] So yes, the equality of all humans seemed staringly obvious (at least in theory) to Franklin and Jefferson. But that was because their culture was saturated with Christian assumptions—so much so that the concepts and phrases they used were taken from Locke, who had got them from Hooker, who had got them from Scripture.[19]

Franklin's brief, scribbled correction is a marvelous metaphor for the ex-Christian West. His replacement of the words "sacred and undeniable" with "self-evident" echoes what was happening across European society as a whole in 1776, at least among elites. It was an attempt to retain Christianity's moral conclusions while scrubbing out its theological foundations: keeping the fruits while severing the roots, if you will. And it resulted in the insistence that Judeo-Christian convictions on anthropology and ethics were now to be regarded as universal norms on which all reasonable people would agree.

The last two centuries have provided plenty of other metaphors for post-Christianity. Consider the common academic practice of replacing BC and AD with BCE and CE, as if the Common Era was grounded in "self-evident" truth rather than "sacred" belief. Or take the 9/11 wars, in which

Western nations were so convinced of the universality and "self-evidence" of their values that they cheerfully deposed foreign governments, on the assumption that equality, democracy, and human rights would flourish naturally in their place. We could look at Communist Russia, a murderous state committed to doctrinaire atheism, yet motivated by a desire to inaugurate a new world of peace and justice, according to the teaching of its founding Jewish prophet in which the first shall be last and the last shall be first. ("The measure of how Christian we as a society remain," suggests Tom Holland, "is that mass murder precipitated by racism tends to be seen as vastly more abhorrent than mass murder precipitated by an ambition to usher in a classless paradise.")[20] Even the Beatles, announcing themselves to be bigger than Jesus while singing songs about the ultimacy of love and peace that could only have been written, let alone sold millions of copies, within a thoroughly Christianized culture, embody the irony.[21]

But for sheer directness, and indeed chutzpah, Ben Franklin's deletion takes pride of place. His edit is a lasting witness to the fact that the modern West is not so much *ex*-Christian, in the sense of having renounced Christ and all his works, as it is abidingly and distinctively ex-*Christian*. Contingent religious beliefs now sound like self-evident secular truths. The year of our Lord has been universalized, the rights of humanity have been standardized, the redistribution of wealth has been normalized, and all you need is love.

Christianity, in that sense, became a victim of its own success. It baked its moral norms so deeply into Western culture that people eventually forgot where they came from. There are plenty of examples in this book. The Enlightenment adapted the thoroughly Christian imagery of conversion from darkness to light through a moment of rebirth, and the emancipation of the whole world from slavery into a future of hope and justice (chapter 5). The rise of science was powered by the belief in an all-powerful Creator whose world follows predictable laws (chapters 5 and 7). Industrialization and enrichment both depended on the centrality of written texts, literacy, and diligence to godly living, alongside the eschatological belief that history is progressing rather than stagnating or declining (chapters 7 and 9). No matter how self-evident it seemed to Franklin, modern democracy would never have developed in the way it did without the cocktail of equality, rights, and freedom it inherited from medieval theologians, church fathers, and biblical texts from Genesis to Galatians (chapter 4). Even the Romantic movement would have been inconceivable without the Christian virtues of compassion and charity, the self-understanding of Paul and Augustine, and the "inward turn" of first Protestantism and then German Pietism (chapter 8).

And here is the great irony. In many ways, the transition to a WEIRDER world—Enlightenment, industrialization, enrichment, democracy, pluralism, Romanticism, and so forth—has made practicing Christianity harder. Increases in wealth, power, sexual permissiveness, independence, and individualism have generally been associated with smaller families, lower church attendance, and weaker religious observance, for a variety of (very contested) reasons. Yet the WEIRDER transition is itself a product of Christian influence. It would never have happened without it.

Christendom, in effect, was hoisted by its own petard.[†] And at the same time, the *philosophes* were making war on the institutional church using rhetorical weapons they had stolen from the church's own arsenal: light, hope, rights, *liberté, égalité, fraternité*. It was a powerful one-two punch. Simultaneously, Christianity was being edited out of elite discourse because its values were "self-evident," and condemned for not living up to them.

And nowhere was this one-two punch more devastating than in France.

Écrasez l'Infâme!

In December 1776, as Franklin was heading through western France toward Paris, the eighty-two-year-old Voltaire wrote a touching letter to another *philosophe*. "I am inconsolable to be dying without having met you," he lamented. "I would happily come back to spend my last quarter of an hour having the pleasure of hearing your voice."[22]

It is remarkable that the two men had never met. Voltaire and Denis Diderot were the two brightest stars of the French Enlightenment, and they had been corresponding since 1749, when Voltaire invited Diderot to din-

---

[†] Another striking example of this phenomenon is demography. As we saw in chapter 2, Joseph Henrich has shown how the Western church's "marriage and family programme" was instrumental in the formation of modernity, not least because it generated smaller families. But in the long run, as demographers have often pointed out, smaller families are associated with declining religious commitment (although the direction of causality here is more contested). Put starkly: Christianity grows, which eventually makes families shrink, which makes Christianity shrink. See Philip Jenkins, *Fertility and Faith: The Demographic Revolution and the Transformation of World Religions* (Waco, TX: Baylor University Press, 2020).

ner (and Diderot turned him down).[23] Since then, they had led the charge for reason and the spread of knowledge, collaborated on the *Encyclopédie*, and fought together for years against the censorship of philosophical ideas, often at significant personal cost.

They were also well-known for their sustained and scathing attacks on Christianity. Voltaire had been lampooning the bigotry and irrationality of the church for years, for which Diderot had affectionately addressed him as a "sublime, honest and dear Antichrist."[24] Since 1759, he had made the furious slogan *Écrasez l'infâme!* ("Crush the abomination!") a personal catchphrase, to the point of signing letters with it. Diderot had moved beyond him into full-blown atheism, which he preached "with visionary fervour" verging on "fanaticism" at every opportunity; he saw Christianity as "the most absurd and atrocious of dogmas, the most incomprehensible, metaphysical, twisted and therefore subject to divisions."[25] After thirty years of correspondence and cobelligerency, these two great scourges of the church finally met in 1778, in Paris—whereupon they somewhat anticlimactically spent much of the time arguing about Shakespeare. (Diderot, reflecting on the encounter, described the ageing Voltaire as an enchanted castle, falling to pieces, but with an old sorcerer still wandering its corridors.)[26] Within a few weeks, Voltaire was dead.

Yet despite their mutual respect, and shared hatred for Christianity, the two men were on very different pages when it came to the existence of God. Diderot saw it as part of his mission in life to subvert the divine, while disguising his true objective. "I would sacrifice my life, perhaps, if I could annihilate forever the notion of God," he wrote privately (although he also admitted to being drawn to it from time to time).[27] Having left Christianity behind as a young man, Diderot spent a brief period as a deist before coming to embrace a more robust form of atheism, eventually championing the wholesale materialism of his friend Baron d'Holbach. In his *Interview between a Philosopher and the Marshal of* ***, published in July 1776, Diderot made clear that the abolition of all religious belief could only be a good thing for humanity:

CRUDELI: Tell me: if a misanthrope had set about bringing misfortune upon the human race, what invention could be better than belief in an

incomprehensible being on whom people would never be able to agree, and
upon whom they would place more importance than their own lives? . . .

MARSHAL: But you have to have something that frightens people away
from wicked deeds that escape the severity of the law—and if you
destroy religion, what will you put in its place?

CRUDELI: Supposing I had nothing to put in its place, that would always
be one less terrible prejudice.[28]

Voltaire could not have disagreed more. He despised Christianity and
the Catholic Church in particular, mercilessly satirizing her apologetics in
Candide (1759), pillorying her homicidal God in his *Sermon of the Fifty*
(1762), and savaging her bigotry in his *Treatise on Tolerance* (1763). But
unlike Diderot, he thought that belief in God was crucial for public morality. His strongest statement of the case came in verse, and culminated in
his most famous one-liner:

Criticise the servant, but respect the master.
God mustn't suffer for the stupidity of the priest, . . .
This sublime system is needed for humanity.
It is the sacred tie that binds society,
The primary foundation of holy equity,
The restraint of the villain, the hope of the just.
If the skies, stripped of his noble imprint,
Could ever cease to witness to it,
If God did not exist, we would have to invent him.[29]

There is a fascinating ambivalence to Voltaire's writings on Christianity. On the one hand, he is uncompromising in his condemnation and/or
ridicule of the institutional Church and its Scriptures, miracles, sacraments,
divisions, persecutions, superstitions and wealth. On the other hand he is
deeply troubled by the idea of atheism, and his idea of what should replace
it is remarkably Christian in its shape. He effectively envisages a new universal monotheistic religion in which all the nations worship the God of
tolerance, hope and justice, and sees himself in the tradition of Luther and
Calvin (both of whom he mentions in this very poem), banishing superstitious nonsense and purifying the Church from foolishness. Even more

explicitly, after pouring scorn on Old Testament religion in his *Sermon of the Fifty* (1762)—itself an intriguing title—he makes a very revealing pitch for an alternative:

> Haven't our fathers [the Protestant Reformers] already taken away from the people transubstantiation, the worship of creatures and dead bones, auricular confession, indulgences, exorcisms, fake miracles and ridiculous statues? Haven't the people got used to missing out on these superstitious foods? You have to have the courage to take a few more steps. The people are not as stupid as you think; they will have no problem embracing a wise and simple monotheistic cult.[30]

This is Western ex-Christianity in miniature: hyper-Protestantism, thinly disguised. The Reformation was a start, but it was incomplete. Now it needs "the courage to take a few more steps," which means getting rid of biblical authority, miracles, doctrinal disputes, and the power of the church while retaining a God of love and justice and keeping the moral scaffolding of Christendom intact.

The strange twist is that when this eventually happened, Voltaire himself would become a victim of it. One day the iconoclastic, statue-toppling, hyper-Protestant preachers of peace, tolerance, and justice would come for him too (and David Hume, as we saw in chapter 5), on the grounds of his racism and antisemitism. His image would be covered in red paint in the summer of 2020, and subsequently removed by the city authorities, ostensibly for cleaning. *Écrasez l'infâme*, indeed.

Diderot scoffed at Voltaire's moderation. He had no time for God and no time for despotism, and regarded Voltaire's deist, monarchist, and gradualist approach to Enlightenment as part of the problem, not part of the solution. For Diderot, a much more thorough overhaul of the *ancien régime* was needed. Kings, empires, priests, gods, and miracles all belonged on the same bonfire of arbitrary powers. It was a conviction he shared with d'Holbach, whose *Système de la Nature* made the fullest philosophical case for atheism in the eighteenth century (and arguably ever). The world is nothing but matter—there is no soul, no spirit, no final cause, no free will, no god, and no afterlife—and the sooner people accept that and learn to see the world as it truly is, the happier they will all be.

This was not a minor disagreement. In fact, for Princeton historian Jonathan Israel and his followers, Diderot's more robust approach represents the true, unsullied, radical Enlightenment, in contrast to the more squeamish, decaffeinated, emollient version favored by Voltaire. According to this view, the "moderate" group (which also included Locke, Montesquieu, d'Alembert, Hume, and Kant) never quite broke free from the ideological shackles of Christendom, with their continued belief in God and acceptance of hereditary privilege, monarchy, and empire. But the "radicals" (like Diderot, d'Holbach, Condorcet, Helvétius, and Brissot) saw the project all the way through. Having rejected belief in God, and therefore any divine basis for law or politics, they sought emancipation for everybody, including serfs, slaves, women, and subjected nations. Their ideological fountainhead was not Christianity, which they wholeheartedly rejected, but the Dutch philosopher, monist, and panentheist Baruch de Spinoza. And it is they, Israel claims, who should really receive the credit for American Independence (though not the Constitution), and the French Revolution (though not the Terror).[31] Christianity had nothing to do with it.

What should we make of this? Was there a "radical Enlightenment" that left Christendom behind completely, running in parallel to the "moderate Enlightenment" in which Christianity's ghost continued to haunt the halls? Well, we might have questions, as we saw in chapter 4, about the neat way in which the two groups are divided and the way they map onto American politics, not just in the eighteenth century but also the twenty-first. We might also be suspicious at how nicely one of the two groups lines up with contemporary Western academia on virtually everything (empire, slavery, feminism, tolerance, republicanism, theism, race, democracy, education, and sex, to name just ten), and wonder whether the tale is really quite that simple.[32] We might even be struck by the thoroughly Christian shape of Israel's story, in which a radical thirtysomething Jewish prophet (Spinoza) confronts the scribes and elders of his day, gets chased out of the synagogue, challenges everybody's view of God, dies at a tragically young age, and leaves behind a group of disciples who meditate on his teachings, confront the imperial powers, emancipate the poor, elevate the status of women, and preach the gospel of light throughout the world.

But all of these responses are beside the point. The key thing to notice is that even if Jonathan Israel was right in every detail, the "radical" Enlightenment was still every bit as Christian in its shape, controlling narrative and moral substance as the "moderate" one. Yes, Voltaire believed in God and thought others should too, and Diderot did not. But Diderot's story of a world seeing the light and being born again, into a future of liberty, equality, and brotherhood where there are neither Jew nor Greek, male nor female, slave nor free was Christian all the way down. So were his ethical convictions on self-sacrifice, love, compassion, freedom for the captives, and the corrupting power of wealth. So was the French Revolution itself. *Liberté, égalité, fraternité!* Blessed are the poor! Woe to the rich! Whoever exalts himself will be humbled!

No matter how strenuously Diderot (and Voltaire) opposed Christian teachings, and no matter how flagrantly the French Church failed to live up to them, the reality is that most of these convictions could have come from only one place.‡ They did not come from Greek philosophers or Roman poets. They had nothing in common with the views of the barbarian tribes—the Franks, Angles, Saxons, Norsemen, and so forth—who had lived in Europe before the coming of Christianity. (The difference in the two moral universes is essentially that between *Lord of the Rings* and *Game of Thrones*.) They clearly had not reached Paris from the Qing, Mughal, or Ottoman empires. Worse: they were unknown by, and largely incomprehensible to, the numerous peoples that Europeans had "discovered" in the last three centuries, which showed that they were not innately obvious either. They had come, rather, from the very religion that Diderot and Voltaire were so zealously attempting to debunk.[33] Leaving Christianity behind was more troublesome than it sounded.

As it happens, though, there was one French atheist in 1776 who did jettison Judeo-Christian anthropology and morality altogether. But he may

---

‡   This point is often made by contemporary philosophers, as well as intellectual historians like Larry Siedentop, Tom Holland, and Charles Taylor. We could quote Jacques Derrida ("Today the cornerstone of international law is the sacred. . . . In that sense, the concept of crime against humanity is a Christian concept and I think there would be no such thing in the law today without the Christian heritage, the Abrahamic heritage, the biblical heritage"), Jürgen Habermas (see chapter 11), Luc Ferry ("Christianity was to introduce the notion that humanity was fundamentally identical, that men were equal in dignity—an unprecedented idea at the time, and one to which our world owes its entire democratic inheritance"), as well as Nietzsche, Horkheimer, and many others. See Jacques Derrida, "On Forgiveness: A Roundtable Discussion with Jacques Derrida," in *Questioning God*, ed. John D. Caputo, Mark Dooley, and Michael J. Scanlon (Bloomington: Indiana University Press, 2001), 70; Luc Ferry, *A Brief History of Thought: A Philosophical Guide to Living*, trans. Theo Cuffe (New York: Harper Perennial, 2011), 72–73.

not have been the best advert for it. He quickly became not just the most notorious figure in eighteenth-century France but one of the most reviled people in human history, and a byword ever since for moral degradation and wanton cruelty.

Sadist Atheism

Ten days before the Bastille was stormed by a Parisian mob, effectively starting the French Revolution, one of the prison's inmates was removed from his cell and transferred elsewhere. He was completely naked at the time. He had been shouting at the urban crowds through an improvised megaphone, alleging that prisoners were being killed, and urging people to free him. The authorities decided he was a liability in such a febrile context, and moved him to a lunatic asylum a few miles away.

When the Bastille fell on July 14, 1789, he was in despair. "I have shed tears of blood," he said. He was convinced that the revolutionaries had destroyed a document he had started work on four years earlier, having painstakingly glued together smuggled pieces of paper into a scroll nearly forty feet long and then hidden the manuscript in the wall of his cell. But in fact, in a remarkable stroke of luck, the scroll had been found and rescued just two days before the revolution started. It would later become one of the most expensive manuscripts in history, with a price tag roughly equivalent to the Declaration of Independence or *The Canterbury Tales*.[34]

It was also one of the most diabolical texts in history. Even today, it is almost unreadable for its lurid descriptions of orgies, sexual abuse, torture, and murder. It was entitled *120 Days of Sodom*, which may give an idea of its contents; the plot and the author's macabre boast that it was "the most impure tale that has ever been written since the world began" serve as graphic illustrations of why its author was imprisoned in the first place. All told, he would be incarcerated in prisons or asylums for about thirty of his seventy-four years, not to mention several periods of exile, for crimes including sexual abuse, poisoning, sodomy, orgies, and blasphemy. His name was Donatien Alphonse François, Marquis de Sade.

Few people have lived lives of such unapologetic depravity. Sexually voracious, famously cruel, financially incontinent, and grotesquely fat, Sade was embroiled in numerous major scandals: flogging a poor widow and pouring hot wax into her wounds (1768), lacing sweets with aphrodisiacs that poisoned the young women who ate them, for which he was burned in effigy and sentenced to death (1772), trapping several young people in his fortified chateau for weeks of orgies (1774–1775), hiring young women as domestic servants so that he could have sex with them, for which he was very nearly shot by a protective father (1776–1777), and beginning a sexual relationship with a fourteen-year-old girl at the age of seventy (1810).[35]

At the time, however, his writings were even more inflammatory than his lifestyle. They constituted a full frontal assault on Christian morality, from someone who did not so much disbelieve in God as despise him. In one of his earliest works, *A Dialogue between a Priest and a Dying Man*, his disdain for God is already clear:

> You have confused but not enlightened my mind, and I owe you not gratitude but hatred. . . . God, if he exists as you are mad enough to believe, cannot possibly have set out to convince us by using means as ludicrous as those employed by your Jesus. . . . He was a seditious influence, an agitator, a bearer of false witness, a scoundrel, a lecher, a showman who performed crude tricks, a wicked and dangerous man. He knew exactly how to set about hoodwinking the public and was therefore eminently punishable in the type of kingdom and state of which Jerusalem was then a part.[36]

But it is in his novels that we really encounter the implications of abandoning Christianity altogether. Sade had no time for the idea that we should hold onto Christian morality despite rejecting Christian theology. Instead, he thought we should admit that there is no natural basis whatsoever for loving other people, forgiving them, or showing compassion. "The doctrine of loving one's neighbor is a fantasy that we owe to Christianity and not to Nature," he explained.[37] Virtue, likewise, is "just a way of behaving that varies according to climate and consequently has nothing real about it."[38]

In fact, if we could rid ourselves of the teaching and example of "that wily little sneak Jesus,"[39] we would realize that "nature has given the weak to be slaves"[40] and see the world as it really is: "wolves eating lambs, lambs devoured by wolves, the strong killing the weak, the weak falling victim to the strong."[41] The ancient Persians, Greeks, and Romans were happy to sanction torture, sexual exploitation, infanticide, and/or watching other people being killed for fun—and if it were not for Christianity, so would we. The natural world is not run by love, but by power. Nietzsche would make a similar point a century later.

This contrast was savagely dramatized through a pair of novels so shocking that even Sade would not put his name to them. (Not that the attempt at anonymity did Sade any good: he was arrested by order of Napoleon himself and spent the last thirteen years of his life incarcerated, first in prison and then in an asylum.) *Justine: The Misfortunes of Virtue* is the tale of a sweet, virtuous, loving girl who believes that people are essentially good and experiences an obscene sequence of abuse, rape, and brutality. *Juliette: Vice Amply Rewarded* is the story of her sister, who is the exact opposite: a wanton, amoral, nymphomaniac murderer who winds up successful and happy. The point could not be clearer. In a world with no God, subject simply to the dark whims of fate and the malevolent forces of nature, the strong triumph and the weak suffer. "Nature has elaborated no statutes, instituted no code; her single law is writ deep in every man's heart: it is to satisfy himself, deny his passions nothing, and this regardless of the cost to others."[42]

Sade's odious behavior, and the pornographic depravity of his writings, can obscure the serious point that is being made here. Voltaire is wrong; Diderot, d'Holbach, Condorcet, and company are wrong. If God does not exist, then you do not have to invent him. You have to submit to the brutal sovereignty of Nature instead. At the same time, if the *infâme* is crushed and the world comes to recognize that there is no God and Christianity is consigned to the dustbin of history and the way of the cross is replaced by the way of Sodom, then you cannot continue to function as if Christian moral values—love, pity, humility, compassion, forgiveness, let alone sexual fidelity—are still normative. They are not, and nor should they be. Christian ethics are nothing more than the fruits of Christian theology, and if the roots are cut down they will quickly wither, to be replaced (in Sade's vision) by a world of filth, incest, cruelty, and death.

We recoil from this vision with horror, and rightly so. But for Sade, it was a price worth paying to get rid of the God he hated so much. Believing in God, he declared, "is the sole wrong for which I cannot forgive mankind."[43]

The Ex-Christian Scale

Based on the individuals we have considered so far, we could construct a sort of scale of ex-Christianity in 1776, moving from "softer" to "harder" varieties. At the lower, softer end you have (1) professing Christians like James Boswell, coming to terms with the fact that Christian beliefs are now optional rather than assumed, even as he holds them himself. Next to him you have (2) irenic deists like Ben Franklin, arguing that certain values should henceforth be regarded as universal and self-evident rather than specifically Christian, although without any particular hostility toward Christianity itself. In the middle you have (3) polemic deists like Voltaire, raging against the Church while insisting that belief in God remains important for society. Then you have (4) combative atheists like Diderot and d'Holbach, adamantly rejecting theism and seeking to extirpate it but continuing to celebrate values and even narratives that derive from Christendom. And at the hard end you have (5) God haters like Sade, for whom Christianity's entire moral framework should be upended and eliminated along with its theology.

If we wanted to make the scale more granular, we could add other ex-Christian thinkers from the period. Immanuel Kant's "religion within the bounds of mere reason" is at the softer end between (1) and (2), along with Rousseau's "civil religion."[44] Hume is skeptical without being hostile, which puts him with Franklin at (2); this is also where we could put many of Franklin's fellow Freemasons. Jefferson and Paine oscillate between (2) benevolent skepticism and (3) a more polemical response to Christian theism, depending on their ages and political circumstances.[45] Franz Anton Mesmer, the founder of animal magnetism (or "mesmerism," the precursor of hypnosis), sits somewhere between (3) and (4), although more as the leader of a scientific cult than as a serious thinker. The Cult of Reason, the atheistic religion founded at the height of the French Revolution (in which numerous churches, including Notre Dame, were desecrated and became "Temples of Reason"), is at the harder end of the spectrum between (4) and (5)—though undoubtedly sillier than both. And so forth.§

§ Clearly a scale like this cannot cover everybody. It has no place for Gotthold Ephraim Lessing, for example, one of the most intriguing and controversial religious thinkers of the period. Lessing's tone and posture toward Christianity was remarkably gentle, as befits a man who wrote so much about religious tolerance, which on its own would put him between (1) and

Positions (2) to (5) are still with us in some form.[46] The nineteenth and twentieth centuries saw an explosion of political atheism, quasiscientific cults and New Age movements, from Chinese Communism in the east to Californian Scientology in the west, that bear a striking resemblance to the religious ideas circulating in Paris between the American and French Revolutions. The progressive secular humanism that prevails in Western universities and media outlets is essentially that of Hume, Voltaire, and Jefferson (though with rather less tolerance for dissent these days). Equally, the New Atheism that emerged in the first decade of the twenty-first century would not have sounded remotely "new" to the members of d'Holbach's salon. Even the hatred of God we find in Sade, with the attempt to overthrow Christian morality and replace it with an ethic based on Nature, finds a disturbing echo in the twentieth century's most diabolical figure: Adolf Hitler. The ex-Christianity of the late eighteenth century has cast a long shadow.

The Origins of Ex-Christianity

The question that will occupy us for the rest of this chapter is simply: Where did this ex-Christianity come from?

The popular explanation goes something like this. In the Middle Ages, everyone believed in God, miracles, relics, saints, sacraments, angels, demons, and witches. The world was in the center of the cosmos and was created a few thousand years ago along with all its life forms. Spiritual power was universally recognized, and could be harnessed by a combination of piety, perseverance, and prayer. The Bible was true. Everybody went to either heaven, hell, or (most likely) purgatory when they died; the Catholic Church had the authority to say which, and for how long, and used this power to hold people in thrall, suppressing dissent through a combination of excommunications, burnings, and inquisitions. The alignment of the stars was a better predictor of what would happen next than the detailed study of natural processes. Physical phenomena were interpreted theologically: eclipses mean God is warning us, good harvests mean God is favoring us,

---

(2). At the same time, his theology was basically pantheist ("Ἐν καὶ Πᾶν, or "One and All") and had plenty in common with Spinoza; he insisted that contingent historical truths, like those affirmed in Christianity, could never ground necessary religious ones ("Lessing's Ditch"); and he was responsible for publishing Hermann Samuel Reimarus's argument that Jesus was not divine, the apostles were frauds, and Christianity was false. If we were assessing content alone, we would put him at (4).

plagues mean God is angry with us, and so on. They were simple people, and nobody knew any better. No other explanation was available.

Then two things happened at the same time. One was science. Gradually, the assumptions of medieval Europeans were challenged by encounters with reality. The earth moved from the center of the cosmos to the periphery; gravity, orbits, and vacuums provided better explanations for celestial and terrestrial phenomena than theological or mystical accounts; rocks, and the life forms they contained, suggested that the world was much older than originally thought, and that some species used to exist that had since died out. All of these discoveries raised uncomfortable questions about the authority of both the Bible and the Church—questions that only became more acute with Charles Darwin's theory of evolution by natural selection—and meant there was less and less work for God to do. The "God of the gaps" got smaller every time a new mystery was explained, until eventually he disappeared altogether.

The other was war. The Protestant Reformation split Europe down the middle: Protestants killed Catholics, Catholics killed Protestants, and both Protestants and Catholics killed Anabaptists. The unity of Christendom was shattered. Wars of religion became commonplace, culminating in the terrible destruction of the Thirty Years' War (1618–1648), in which a third of the German population died. The moral authority of the church, which had been unquestioned for so long, started to look untenable in the light of all this division and violence—and it was not enhanced by reports of the brutality of Christian invaders toward indigenous peoples in Africa, the Americas, and the East Indies. Over time, enlightened Europeans came to see the need for tolerance at home and benevolence abroad, which would ultimately lead to the abolition of slavery, empire, state religion, absolute monarchy, patriarchy, sexual restrictions, and God him/her/itself.

"Religion loses ground as philosophy advances," wrote Diderot.[47] And so it was that over five centuries, we went from a united Christendom, last seen in the early 1520s—a now unimaginable world in which the church was authoritative, everyone in Europe assumed the Nicene Creed was true, Martin Luther was swearing at the devil, Hernán Cortés was advancing the gospel by destroying Tenochtitlán, William Tyndale's life was in danger for translating the Bible into English, and Huldrych Zwingli was sparking a Reformation by eating a sausage—to the thoroughly post-Christian, pluralist landscape of the 2020s. In the exact middle of that five-hundred-year process sit the *philosophes* of the 1770s, pens at the ready, clustering in their salons to denounce the ignorant and intolerant church for its backward, irrational bigotry. It feels like an extraordinary change, but it is really not that complicated. As knowledge and tolerance grew, God shrank. Sectarian violence made Christianity undesirable; scientific progress made it unnecessary. May it rest in peace.

The only problem with this story is that it is almost entirely wrong. As Charles Taylor has shown in great detail, human beings do not change our social and cosmic imaginaries by "subtracting" old illusions, limitations, and misconceptions from them (like God, supernaturalism, or whatever). Rather, we construe the world in *new* ways, based not just on new ideas but also on new practices, symbols, rituals, self-understandings, and constructions of space and time.[48]

But the details are thoroughly inaccurate as well.[49] Early skeptics of Christian belief did not frame their objections in anything like this form, as we shall see. Medieval Europe witnessed far more doubt, dissent, and protest than this caricature implies. The scientific and mechanical breakthroughs of the sixteenth and seventeenth centuries did not challenge belief in God at all; they were virtually all made by Christians (many of whom also believed in alchemy and/or astrology, but that is another story), and caused no discernible damage to the religious convictions of the individuals in question, let alone to those of society as a whole. Priests and missionaries had been objecting to European conquest, slavery, and genocide for over two centuries before the *philosophes* got involved.[§] The "wars of religion" resulted far more from political and dynastic disputes than theological concerns (as evidenced by the fact that Protestant Denmark fought Protestant Sweden, Catholic Bourbons fought Catholic Habsburgs, Protestant Saxony supported Catholic Bohemia, Catholic France supported Protestant Germany, and so forth). And many of the most dehumanizing verdicts on indigenous peoples came from Enlightenment thinkers who were explicitly rejecting ecclesial authority and biblical anthropology, as we saw in chapter 5. Frankly, the religion-versus-science and bigotry-versus-tolerance narratives tell us far

---

§   The works of the Spanish theologian Francisco de Vitoria (1483–1546) and the Dominican friar Bartolomé de las Casas (1484–1566) were written over two hundred years before the *Encyclopédie* or Raynal's *Histoire des Deux-Indes*, for example.

more about the cultural battles of twentieth-century America than they do about the rise of ex-Christianity between the Reformation and the First World War.

The real story is somewhat different. As we have seen, the ex-Christianity of the modern West emerges in the social, economic, and institutional context that we have been considering for the last few chapters: the beginnings of globalization, Enlightenment, industrialization, enrichment, and representative government. Without that context, it is unthinkable that modern secularism would have come about in the way that it did. But although these transformations all catalyze the emergence of post-Christian society, they do not cause it by themselves. The primary progenitors of ex-Christianity—the two theological parents who came together unexpectedly, generated it unintentionally, and have been squabbling ever since over who gets custody—were *paganism* and *Protestantism*.

Paganism

When the intellectual historian Peter Gay published his analysis of the Enlightenment, he entitled the prizewinning first volume *The Rise of Modern Paganism*. This is not because he thought Hume, Kant, and Voltaire were offering sacrifices, indulging in Bacchanalian revelry and dancing round the maypole. It is because he regarded the *philosophes* as fundamentally unified by their shared appreciation of pagan antiquity and their use of classical learning to shake off Christian assumptions about the world. "The Enlightenment was a volatile mixture of classicism, impiety and science," he explained. "The philosophes, in a phrase, were modern pagans."[50]

It is hard to deny. The Enlighteners were constantly enthusing about the brilliance of ancient pagans, often in direct contrast to Christianity. The Greeks were variously credited with inventing philosophy (by Diderot), inquiry (by Gibbon), mathematics (by Kant), science (by Hume), and evidence-based research (by Yvon).[51] Voltaire thought they were the fountainhead of beautiful architecture, sculpture, painting, music, poetry, eloquence, and history.[52]

If anything, the Romans were quoted even more, partly owing to familiarity with Latin. Seneca was revered for his philosophy and wisdom; Cicero for his rhetoric and *humanitas*; Horace for his wit; Livy, Virgil, and Ovid for their lyrical beauty and sheer entertainment value. Lucretius was especially celebrated for his polemical poem *On the Nature of Things*, a sustained assault on religion in which supernatural explanations of the world are dismissed, on both moral and intellectual grounds, in favor of a skeptical, materialist, and protoevolutionist account of reality:

> Nothing from nothing ever yet was born.
> Fear holds dominion over mortality
> Only because, seeing in land and sky
> So much the cause whereof no wise they know,
> Men think Divinities are working there.
> Meantime, when once we know from nothing still
> Nothing can be create, we shall divine
> More clearly what we seek: those elements
> From which alone all things created are,
> And how accomplished by no tool of Gods.[53]

The reigns of Augustus (37 BC–AD 14) and the Antonines (138–192), which modern people might consider periods of imperial brutality, slavery, and warmongering, were seen as golden ages. Edward Gibbon famously remarked that "if a man were called to fix the period in the history of the world during which the condition of the human race was most happy and prosperous, he would, without hesitation, name that which elapsed from the death of Domitian to the accession of Commodus."[54] (Presumably slaves, Jews, women, and barbarians might hesitate, at least momentarily.) Taken together, the critical inquiry, high art, material prosperity, and literary style of the ancient pagan elites were incredibly attractive to European philosophers—even if their gods were not.

Pagan tolerance was attractive too. Gibbon himself would argue this at great length, but David Hume made the point concisely in his *Natural History of Religion*: "The tolerating spirit of both ancient and modern idolaters is very obvious to anyone with the least knowledge of the writings of historians or travellers."[55] Unlike monotheism, Hume declared, paganism is "sociable."[56] The Greeks and the Romans accepted the local deities of the people they conquered, and often included them in their pantheon. Meanwhile their stories and legends were such a contradictory tangle that pagan religion could never be dogmatically pinned down, which made religious persecution unnecessary and even absurd. Judaism, Christianity, and Islam, with their singular deities and inspired scriptures, are radically different: "The intolerance of almost all religions that have maintained the unity of God is as remarkable as the contrary principle of polytheists." The Jews, he explained, are "implacably narrow." Islam operates on "still more bloody principles." The Catholics launched the Inquisition. Zoroastrians "shut the doors of heaven against all but the Magians." Admittedly the English and Dutch Protestants have been more tolerant, but "this has come from the steady resolution of the civil magistrate in opposition to the continued efforts of priests and bigots." With that exception aside, theism is incalculably more intolerant than paganism.[57]

Clearly we could raise all sorts of questions about Hume's narrative here (let alone Gibbon's). Many scholars have.[58] For our purposes here, though, his essay serves as a good illustration of the connection between the paganism of the ancients and the post-Christianity of the Enlighteners. It also shows why Peter Gay called Hume "the complete modern pagan."[59]

But there is a deeper sense in which the shift to post-Christianity is tied to paganism. As the Jewish philosopher Abraham Heschel points out, all humans experience a sense of awe and wonder at the sublime, or the "holy," which leads us to adoration and even worship. In response, we can either locate the sacred *within* the world, or in something (or Someone) *beyond* the world.[60]

For ancient pagans, the sacred was located within the cosmos: "To the Greek mind the universe is the sum and substance of all there is; even the gods are a part of, rather than the cause of the universe."[61] Zeus, Apollo, Aphrodite, and the other Olympian deities do not transcend the world. Rather, they are somehow included within it, albeit as its most powerful agents. In "the biblical mind," by contrast, the sacred is identified with a transcendent, eternal, all-powerful God, who created all things. And that essential choice—between paganism and theism, or what Peter Jones calls "oneism" and "twoism"—has always been there.[62] Indeed, Heschel argues, it still is: "The Western man must choose between the worship of God and the worship of nature."[63]

The French philosopher Chantal Delsol makes a similar point in her recent book *Le Fin de la Chrétienté*.[64] For millennia, she explains, there have been two sorts of religious systems. There are the immanent varieties of polytheism, paganism, and "cosmotheism," which seem natural to us, and there are transcendent monotheisms, which depend on revelation and require constant effort to maintain. Without that maintenance, we become cosmotheists by default, and that is what is happening in the post-Christian West:

> Our Western contemporaries no longer believe in a beyond or in a transcendence. The meaning of life must therefore be found in this life itself, and not above it, where there is nothing. The sacred is found here: in the landscapes, in the life of the earth, and in humans themselves. . . . For the monotheist, this world is only a temporary lodging. For the cosmotheist, it is a home.[65]

Framed that way, much of the Enlightenment was indisputably pagan. From the genial deism of Franklin to the dark misotheism of Sade, ultimacy was located within the material world. True happiness was to be found in this life, not the next (a point that is central to Ritchie Robertson's magisterial *The Enlightenment*).[66] The proper object of study was nature rather than Scripture, and humanity rather than divinity.

This analogy between ancient paganism and modern atheism was noticed by some of the Enlighteners themselves. But they turned it on its head. Rather than saying (like Gay, Heschel, or Delsol) that modern skeptics were effectively pagans, they suggested that the ancient pagans were effectively atheists. Here is Hume again:

> To anyone who thinks soundly about this matter, it will appear that the "gods" of all polytheists do not deserve pious worship or veneration any more than did the elves or fairies of our ancestors. *These pretended religionists are really a kind of superstitious atheists, and acknowledge no being answering to our idea of a deity.* No first principle of mind or thought; no supreme government and administration; no divine planning or intention in the structure of the world. . . . If we open any classic author we'll meet with these gross representations of the deities; and Longinus was right to say that *such ideas of the divine nature, if taken literally, contain a true atheism.*[67]

Whatever we make of this argument, it is clear that ancient pagans and Enlightenment ex-Christians agreed on this much: the sacral was located within the cosmos rather than beyond it. The holy, the numinous and the sublime were essentially immanent rather than transcendent. And right across the ex-Christian spectrum, this had a significant impact on the way people thought about nature, art, sex, life, liberty, and the pursuit of happiness.

On its own, this does not really explain much. After all, paganism was hardly new in 1776. European elites had been reading, studying, painting, and quoting the stories and poems of pagan antiquity since the Renaissance. At a popular level, you could argue that paganism had never really disappeared.[68] Yet late medieval and early modern Europe was as Christian as it had ever been, and virtually all of the great Renaissance writers, artists, and patrons were good Catholics. Clearly, reading and enjoying pagan writings did not stop people from practicing Christianity. So what changed?

The answer is that paganism was combined with a much newer and more revolutionary force, and the reaction between the two—which was catalyzed by the social, economic, and political changes we have sketched in the last few chapters—was explosive. This newer movement challenged the authority of the church and the unity of Christendom at a far more fundamental level than paganism ever could, not least because it challenged the church from within. It was of course Protestantism.

Protestantism

There are a number of ways of making that case, and some are more compelling than others. Depending on who you ask, the Protestant Reformation is variously charged with bringing disaster, division, disenchantment, and doubt.

Disaster

A popular Roman Catholic version of the story puts the blame for the evils of modernity squarely on the shoulders of the Reformers themselves, and Luther in particular. By opposing the papacy as he did, grounded in nothing more than his own personal conviction about what Scripture teaches, Luther put the autonomous self rather than the authoritative and unified Church at the center of reality. He was not only an anti-intellectual who pitted reason against faith, and did not really understand the theological traditions he was rejecting, but also an egocentric subjectivist, an emotivist, even "the first great Romantic," whose passionate commitment to the spirit of the individual, in defiance of authority and convention, quickly caught on among his followers.[69]

The results were devastating. Salvation was defined in terms of subjective personal experiences (like individual faith or encounters with the Holy Spirit) rather than objective corporate practices (like the seven sacraments). Sectarianism became endemic. Worse still, without the canons and councils of the Catholic Church to guide them, no two Protestants could agree on what Scripture actually meant, which quickly brought disagreement, which brought conflict and then war. Thus medieval Christendom was shattered into a thousand pieces, each filled with people who thought their personal view of reality mattered more than Church doctrine, and it was all the Reformers' fault. Western Christianity never recovered.[**]

Division

Brad Gregory's *The Unintended Reformation* offers a more nuanced version of this story.[70] The crucial turning point in his account is the moment, somewhere around 1520, when the ethical critique of late medieval Catholicism became a doctrinal one as well. People had been saying for centuries that the Church's *leaders* were corrupt, superstitious, and greedy. Many of them were. But the early Protestants, starting with Luther himself, began to insist that the Church's *teachings* were wrong and that her authority to define Christian doctrine was therefore compromised.

As soon as that move was made, Gregory argues, the writing was on the wall. It was all but certain that some people would start defining what they thought Scripture meant for themselves, and refusing to belong to a

---

[**] This caricature, which continues to circulate through the influence of Jacques Maritain (and to a lesser extent G. K. Chesterton), prompts a mixture of bemusement and exasperation from Protestant historians. The subjectivist portrait of Luther is absurdly anachronistic. The harmonious unity of late medieval Catholicism is wildly overstated in light of both the numerous reform movements swirling around Europe, and the papal schism of the late fourteenth and early fifteenth centuries. Neither theological factionalism nor violence against one's opponents began in 1517. The Reformed confessions and catechisms can be searched in vain for any evidence of emotivist, antiauthoritarian individualism. Most importantly, the Reformation, like several other reform movements, was sparked not by a desire to put the autonomous self at the center of things, let alone by an early form of Romanticism, but by a problem that already existed in the late medieval Church: the widespread abuses taking place under the auspices of papal authority, and the failure of the Church to address them.

Church that taught otherwise. Inevitably, this would destabilize the unity of Christendom. Luther, Eck, Erasmus, Zwingli, and Müntzer could not all be right. Gradually, "churches" would replace "the Church," which would lead inexorably to calls for religious toleration and then religious pluralism and ultimately the privatization of religion. It would also contribute to the rising prestige of experimental science: in a world where people disagreed about Scripture, tradition, and religious experience, science produced the same results whether you were Protestant or Catholic, and this made it a prime candidate to replace the Church as the umpire of modern thought. And it would have huge implications for the roles of the state, the market, and the university, which were set to become the only institutions whose authority was effectively uncontested. Gregory's subtitle sums it up nicely: *How a Religious Revolution Secularized Society.* Protestantism brought division, which over time would bring theological, ecclesial, moral, and intellectual pluralism. That is modern secularism in a nutshell.

Disenchantment

The most comprehensive genealogy of secularism in this century so far is Charles Taylor's seminal book *A Secular Age.* It goes something like this: The medieval world was enchanted.[71] The cosmos was filled with spirits, angels, and demons. Magic and miracles were widespread, even if there was occasional debate about which was which (or witch). Curses were effective, and frightening. The living could interact with dead saints. Objects had powers too: shrines, bones, remedies, relics, blessed candles, indulgences, and obviously the bread and wine. The individual was "porous," or vulnerable to all these cosmic forces and the powers they exerted. There was no "buffer" separating the person from the things that might get to them, as there is in modern understandings of the self.

Medieval Christianity was also two-tiered. Some people lived a higher, religious form of life, renouncing worldly passions and pursuing spirituality wholeheartedly as priests, monks, nuns, or friars. Everybody else lived ordinary lives, in which they recognized that the demands of perfection were largely unattainable but continued religious practices like fasts, feasts, attending Mass, and popular devotion to Mary and the saints. Generally, this two-tiered approach was accepted by Church authorities and the population at large. But beginning in the eleventh century, the High Middle Ages saw a growing desire in various quarters for reform: the desire to convert ordinary people to a higher, more observant form of Christianity, in which Christocentric spirituality, confession of sin, and personal devotion were for everybody, not just a hyperpious elite.

In this enchanted and two-tiered world, the Protestant Reformation came as a disruptive double whammy. On the one hand, it contributed to disenchantment by insisting on the authority of Scripture alone, re-interpreting the Mass, and challenging the practices and superstitions of popular piety: relics, indulgences, shrines, magic, pilgrimages, the cult of saints, and so forth.[72] Interior convictions and experiences, like personal faith and the work of the Holy Spirit, were more important than external symbols, objects, and cosmic forces. On the other hand, it insisted that no vocation was any "higher" or more spiritual than any other: "There were not to be any more ordinary Christians and super-Christians. The renunciative vocations were abolished. All Christians alike were to be totally dedicated."[73] A shoemaker could be just as godly as a monk. And that focus on the holiness of ordinary activities—eating, drinking, work, sex, and all to the glory of God—gradually made possible what Taylor calls the "anthropocentric shift," which he describes as "a revision downward of God's purposes for us, inscribing these within an immanent order which allows for a certain kind of human flourishing, consonant with the order of mutual benefit."[74] This combination of disenchantment and anthropocentrism is crucial for the development of modern secularism, and both of them were turbo-charged by the Protestant Reformation.[75]

Doubt

One further angle on the relationship between Protestantism and ex-Christianity is found in Alec Ryrie's recent book *Unbelievers*, which provides what Ryrie calls "an emotional history of doubt." His central contention is that unbelief existed in practice, even in the apparently devout Christendom of the High Middle Ages, long before it existed in theory. (The book begins in 1239, when Pope Gregory IX accused the Holy Roman Emperor of being an unbeliever.) Across medieval Europe, some people felt angry toward God. Some clashed with or hated his appointed representatives on earth. Some blasphemed. Some mocked the Church's doctrines, miraculous claims, priestly corruption, or political ineptitude. Many simply lived as if Christianity made little difference.

So Protestantism did not create religious doubt. What it did do, however, was to weaponize it. Skepticism—of papal authority, of Church councils, of the power of relics or shrines, of doctrines like transubstantiation—became a crucial tool in the Reformers' battle against Roman Catholicism. Sermons and pamphlets were scornfully skeptical of Catholic theology and practice. Before long, Catholics were returning the favor, highlighting the areas where Protestants were most vulnerable. As Christians openly ridiculed and expressed incredulity toward the beliefs of other Christians, unquestioning belief became harder to sustain (ironically, just as "faith alone" was becoming more important), and these doubts were only increased by the regular discoveries of peoples and nations who knew nothing of Christianity, and did not seem minded to accept it. It turned out that the power of skepticism, once unleashed, did not easily go back in the box. "Once you have thrown into the balance of doubt and uncertainty any articles of their religion," wrote Montaigne in 1580, "they soon cast all the rest of their beliefs into similar uncertainty."[76]

Thus doubt became a fact of life, even for those who continued to believe. "The Reformation, by choosing scepticism as its key religious weapon, in effect required believers to transition to a different kind of post-sceptical faith, a journey many of them struggled to complete," Ryrie concludes. "As their anxieties dissolved one certainty after another, they were left with nothing except their commitment to their moral vision, which increasingly seem[ed] . . . to be detachable from the Christian tradition itself." And when the Church who proclaimed that moral tradition in theory was found not to live up to it in practice, it was fiercely critiqued by its own standards. "The moral force of the unbelief of anger and the moral urgency of the unbelief of anxiety mixed into a gathering flow of insistent, ethically driven doubts that began carving Christendom's old-established landscape into something new."[77]

Protestant Pagans

Ex-Christianity in the modern West is the unwitting product of both of these forces working together. Paganism, which has always seen the sacred as immanent and ultimacy as located within this world of space and time, reacted with the divisions and doubts brought by Protestantism, and produced a new entity. The result is as fascinating as it is confusing, combining disenchantment with re-enchantment, and spiritual ambiguity with moral certainty. We could call it Protestant paganism.[††]

You can see it around you in every city center, university campus, or coffee shop noticeboard. In its twenty-first-century form, it combines a very broad menu of spiritual practices and experiences with a very narrow range of dogmatic commitments. The spiritual options are hugely diverse. They have little in common beyond a preference for intuitions over institutions, "spirituality" over "religion," and the therapeutic over the theological; otherwise virtually anything goes, from mindfulness to wicca to Kabbalah to traditional faith.[78] By contrast, the doctrinal convictions are clearly defined, defended with Puritanical zeal, and sometimes even expressed in creedal form: In this house, we believe that science is real, women's rights are human rights, black lives matter, no human is illegal, love is love and kindness is everything. If you step outside the confessional boundaries—which are deeply Christian in their shape, as we saw earlier in this chapter—you will be called to repentance, ideally in front of the whole community, and either excommunicated or urged to spend more time in the catechism until you have an experience of awakening.[‡‡] If you are dead, you may have your image defaced or desecrated. This sounds like a baffling combination. Religious pluralism and moralistic fervor do not

---

†† Needless to say, nobody self-identifies as a Protestant pagan. Most of us prefer the term "secular" instead. But as Tom Holland demonstrates in his remarkable book *Dominion*, this term is far less neutral and far more Christian than it first appears. "Secularism was not a neutral concept. The very word came trailing incense clouds of meaning that were irrevocably and venerably Christian. That there existed twin dimensions, the secular and the religious, was an assumption that reached back centuries beyond the Reformation: to Gregory VII, and to Columbanus, and to Augustine. The concept of secularism—for all that it was promoted by the editor who invented the word as an antidote to religion—testified not to Christianity's decline, but to its seemingly infinite capacity for evolution" (411). By contrast, the idea that it is possible to separate "religion" from the remit of the state makes very little sense within an Islamic or Hindu context: secularism "depended on the care with which it covered its tracks. If it were to be embraced by Jews, or Muslims, or Hindus as a neutral holder of the ring between them and people of other faiths, then it could not afford to be seen as what it was: a concept that had little meaning outside of a Christian context.... To sign up to its premises was unavoidably to become just that bit more Christian" (505).

‡‡ In October 2021, a viral video showed a group of protesters outside the Netflix headquarters in California, objecting to remarks made by the comedian Dave Chappelle; one woman was waving a tambourine and shouting, "Repent, motherf*****!"

usually go together. But it makes perfect sense in light of its origins. The post-Christian West is full of Protestant pagans.

Admittedly, this particular iteration of Protestant paganism is a recent phenomenon. It clearly reflects the specific social, political, and economic anxieties (and technological possibilities) of the West in the early twenty-first century. But its basic features—a this-worldly sense of ultimacy, happiness, and meaning, combined with reformist zeal, moral certainty, commitment to progress, and an inescapably Christian ethical framework—go back much further. As we have seen, we find them coming together in different ways in Voltaire, Diderot, Franklin, Jefferson, and several other writings from 1776.

Gibbon's *Decline and Fall* is an obvious example. It is nothing if not a tribute to pagan antiquity, even a lament for its disintegration at the hands of the church. Pagan learning is hailed as groundbreaking and profound. Ancient polytheism is celebrated as harmonious, tolerant, elegant, and beautiful, and characterized by a mild spirit; pagan empire, at least in the second century, is valorized as the product of wisdom and virtue by emperors who rejoiced in liberty and saw themselves as accountable for the law. Yet the shape of Gibbon's narrative is decidedly Protestant. History has three phases: ancient, middle, and modern. The villain of the piece is the Catholic Church: superstitious, dogmatic, controlling, arcane, and intolerant. Her reign was an age of ignorance and gloom, even if "the darkness of the middle ages exhibits some scenes not unworthy of our notice."[79] Only now that her spell has been broken is humanity marching upward again toward the light.

Or take Hume's *Dialogues concerning Natural Religion*. One of the greatest critiques of theism ever written, the *Dialogues* take the quintessentially pagan form of a three-way discussion, modelled specifically on Cicero's *De Natura Deorum*, right down to its famously cryptic final paragraph. Classical quotations are sprinkled throughout. The strongest argument against God's existence is lifted straight from Epicurus: "Is he willing to prevent evil, but not able? Then he is impotent. Is he able, but not willing? Then he is malevolent. Is he both able and willing? Whence then is evil?"[80] Again and again, Hume insists that present happiness and benevolence matter far more than religious commitments to a world beyond:

> Consider, I beg you, how much we care about present things, and how little concern we express for objects so remote and uncertain [as the

rewards or punishments promised in the afterlife]. . . . It is certain, from experience, that the smallest grain of natural honesty and benevolence has more effect on men's conduct than the most pompous views suggested by theological theories and systems. . . . The steady attention alone to so important an interest as that of eternal salvation is apt to extinguish the benevolent affections, and beget a narrow, contracted selfishness. And when such a temper is encouraged, it easily eludes all the general precepts of charity and benevolence.[81]

All of this is classic Hume, and as pagan as we might expect. Yet there also is a Protestant feel to the argument, and not only because of the reference to "the superstition of the Popes, who preserved a little jargon of Latin in order to support the appearance of an ancient and universal church."[82] Consider this contrast, for example:

Formerly it was a most popular theological topic to maintain that human life was vanity and misery, and to exaggerate all the ills and pains which are incident to men. But of late years, divines, we find, begin to retract this position. . . . When religion stood entirely upon temper and education, it was thought proper to encourage melancholy; as indeed, mankind never have recourse to superior powers so readily as in that disposition. But as men have now learned to form principles, and to draw consequences, it is necessary to change the batteries, and to make use of such arguments as will endure at least some scrutiny and examination.[83]

A similar fusion of paganism and Protestantism is detectable in the famous opening pages of Jeremy Bentham's *Fragment on Government*, also written in 1776. "The age we live in is a busy age, in which knowledge is rapidly advancing towards perfection," it begins. "Correspondent to discovery and improvement in the natural world is reformation in the moral."[84] At the heart of this moral reformation is one fundamental axiom: "it is the greatest happiness of the greatest number that is the measure of right and wrong."[85] The tone here may be Protestant—reform and moral clarity suffused with a millenarian confidence in the direction of travel—but the content is pagan. Transcendent morality is redundant. The only ethical framework you need is a calculation of the immanent, present, this-worldly happiness of the largest possible group of people.

If we were feeling cheeky, we might speculate that the most influential statement of Protestant paganism to be published in 1776 was the Declaration of Independence. It is a remarkable hybrid of Puritan and classical thought, signed by a mixture of Presbyterians, Anglicans, Unitarians, and deists. And it certainly gave rise to a nation where, over the next two generations, fervent evangelicalism (in the form of the Second Great Awakening) would grow alongside a passion for material prosperity, immanent contentment, and the "pursuit of happiness." It was a combination that intrigued Alexis de Tocqueville. "In the United States," he remarked, "Christian sects vary infinitely and are constantly modified, but Christianity itself is an established and irresistible fact that no one undertakes either to attack or defend. The Americans, having accepted the principal dogmas of the Christian religion without examination, are obliged to receive in the same manner a great number of moral truths that flow from them and depend on them."[86] Yet at the same time, no generation had ever been so enamored with immanent contentment and worldly welfare:

> It is a strange thing to see with what sort of feverish ardour Americans pursue well-being and how they show themselves constantly tormented by a vague fear of not having chosen the shortest route that can lead to it. The inhabitant of the United States attaches himself to the goods of this world as if he were assured of not dying, and he rushes so precipitately to grasp those that pass within his reach that one would say he fears at each instant he will cease to live before he has enjoyed them. He grasps them all but without clutching them, and he soon allows them to escape from his hands so as to run after new enjoyments. . . . Death finally comes, and it stops him before he has grown weary of this useless pursuit of a complete felicity that always flees from him.[87]

It is hard to describe modern paganism better than that.

The Christian Inheritance

The modern West is post-Christian in the same sort of way that it is postindustrial. Neither Christianity nor industrialization have been truly left behind, for all that our use of "post-" language implies they have. Their cultural footprints remain enormous, even when the churches and factories have been turned into flats. What has happened, rather, is that society has been so irrevocably shaped by their influence that we can think of their legacy as secure and begin to contemplate moving "beyond" them into a wide variety of new possibilities, according to the demands of the market. So we make postindustrial choices—going vegan, converting our power plants into urban gardens, replacing gas boilers with wood-burning stoves, and so forth—precisely because we live in the age of the machine, and we do not fear running out of calories, power, or heat. Likewise, our post-Christian spiritual menu is as broad as it is because we live in the age of the cross, and we have no fear that accepting pagan spirituality will end in the ethics of the Colosseum, Westeros, or the Marquis de Sade.

In that sense, the ex-Christian world is living off its inheritance. The disturbing question is: What if the legacy runs out? Is there a finite amount of leftover Christian capital available, and if so, what happens when we have spent it? One pessimistic take, available in all good bookshops, is that without the substructure of Christianity to support it, the West will increasingly lose its moral consensus, intellectual coherence, and economic advantage, and collapse into a weird chimera of nihilism, tribalism, and decadence. A more optimistic person might draw on T. S. Eliot's observation that "a society has not ceased to be Christian until it has become positively something else" and contend that, as yet, there is no sign of anything close to a religious, moral, and imaginative system that could replace Christianity.[88] They might welcome the church's retreat to the margins as a much-needed step in a cruciform direction, pregnant with new opportunities, or even hail it as the victory of Christianity over Christendom.[89]

But there is another scenario for an ex-Christian world that has spent all its inheritance. In this story, having squandered his legacy and run into trouble, even to the point of hiring himself out to other masters to make ends meet, the estranged son finally remembers that his father is still alive and his family home is still there. He comes to his senses, swallows his pride, and begins the long walk home—whereupon he lifts his eyes to the horizon and sees his father, jubilant and tearful, sprinting down the road toward him.

Machines

Becoming Industrialized

To behold the secrets of Chymistry, and the mechanick powers, so employ'd and exerted, is very delightful. I consider the Machines you have at work as so many useful subjects to Great Britain.

ELIZABETH MONTAGU

I sell here, Sir, what all the world desires to have—POWER.

MATTHEW BOULTON

BENEATH THE NORTHWEST VIEWING PLATFORM on the *premier étage* of the Eiffel Tower, engraved in golden letters two feet high, is the word LAVOISIER.

Western Paris is an advert for industrialization, and the Eiffel Tower is its icon. Conjured out of nothing but wrought iron, engineering, and thrusting ambition, it was the high point of an industrial overhaul that lasted half a century, carpeting Paris with new roads, sewers, public buildings, and railway stations, and transforming it from the city of *Les Misérables* to that of the Belle Époque. So when it was completed in 1889, as an "invocation of science," Gustave Eiffel decided to engrave the names of seventy-two French scientists, mathematicians, engineers, and industrialists on the frieze beneath the first floor, as a tribute to those who had made his tower, and the industrialization of France, possible. The earliest, greatest, and most colorful of the seventy-two men—and the only one to be separated from his head on two separate occasions—was the father of modern chemistry, Antoine Lavoisier.

Lavoisier was the great pioneer of the chemical revolution. His first work, an investigation of what we now call carbon dioxide, was translated into English in 1776. He subsequently isolated and named both oxygen and hydrogen, demonstrated that sulfur was an element and that water was not, predicted the existence of silicon, transformed the way people think about the chemistry of combustion (including the proposal that respiration and combustion were essentially the same thing), and confirmed the law of the conservation of mass. His binomial system for naming chemicals, based on the Linnaean system in biology, is why we call it "copper sulphate" instead of "vitriol of Venus" to this day.

His personal life was equally eventful. He married Marie-Anne Paulze, later a significant chemist in her own right, when she was just fourteen, to help her escape the suit of a lecherous fifty-year-old count whom she regarded as a "fool" and an "ogre."[1] As chairman of the commission on weights and measures, he was responsible for the adoption of the metric system. When he was honored with a giant Parisian statue in 1900, the sculptor gave him someone else's head by mistake, confusing him with the Marquis de Condorcet. (In a curious coincidence, the Americans did the exact opposite, even though the two men do not look very similar: the bust of Condorcet in Philadelphia is actually Lavoisier.)[2] And this was the second time Lavoisier had lost his head. At the height of the Terror he was accused of defrauding the state, and sent to the guillotine on May 8, 1794.

"It only took them a moment to cut off this head," a fellow scientist lamented the following day, "and a hundred years might not be enough to reproduce an equivalent."[3] The charges against him were clearly politically motivated—tax farming, stealing from the Treasury, diluting the quality of tobacco, corresponding with foreign scientists—and they were eventually retracted after his death. The judge himself was executed a few weeks later.

But one of those charges, as innocuous as it sounds today, was essentially accurate. Lavoisier had been writing letters to the Lunar Men.

Hell on Earth

For every Paris—advertising the benefits of industrialization with its railways, boulevards, iron, and glass—there was a Manchester.

It is hard to overstate how shocked people were by the filth, clatter, gloom, and stench of Manchester's dark, satanic mills. "The town is abominably filthy," remarked a visitor in 1808. "The Steam Engine is pestiferous, the Dyehouses noisesome and offensive, and the water of the river as black as ink."[4] Alexis de Tocqueville, the greatest travel writer of his generation, was horrified by the "noise of furnaces, the whistle of steam," but more so by the state of the people: "humanity attains its most complete development and its most brutish; here civilisation works its miracles, and civilised man is turned back almost into a savage."[5] The philosopher Hippolyte Taine agreed, describing the city as "a large bazaar for the sale of low-priced goods, a workhouse to accommodate four hundred thousand persons, a prison for convicts condemned to penal servitude."[6] So did the American Henry Colman, who saw "wretched, defrauded, oppressed, crushed human nature lying in bleeding fragments all over the face of society."[7]

For many who encountered Manchester in the industrial age, the vileness could be expressed only through metaphor. For General Charles Napier, it was "the chimney of the world" in which soot had mixed with rain and formed a paste: "The only view is a long chimney. What a place! The entrance to hell realised."[8] The Swedish novelist Fredrika Bremer called it "that Queen of spiders, surrounded by a mass of ugly houses and factories, veiled in a thick cloud of rain, not unlike a spider's web. It produced a dark, oppressive impression on me."[9] Friedrich Engels was blunter: it was "hell upon earth."[10] Engels had been sent to Manchester to cure him of his radical beliefs, but seeing industrial capitalism first hand had precisely the opposite effect. Three years later, he wrote *The Communist Manifesto* with Karl Marx.

Despite the horrific conditions of industrial cities, a great many people still moved there. Manchester grew from a market town of around ten thousand people in 1715 to a massive city of four hundred thousand by 1860, and twice that fifty years later. The explanation for this was infamously summarized by a middle class man who heard Engels lamenting the condition of the city: "And yet there is a great deal of money made here. Good morning, sir."[11] Manchester prospered because it became Cottonopolis, the beating heart of the Industrial Revolution with all the wealth and jobs that it generated. And this happened as a result of two things that were built in 1776.

One was Richard Arkwright's massive second cotton mill at Cromford in Derbyshire. Seven stories high and one hundred and thirty feet long, and with every part of the process mechanized for the first time, it was built with a row of terraced houses for his workers. Six years later Arkwright would open his first mill in Manchester, and within a century there would be a hundred mills in the city, accounting for a staggering 30 percent of the world's cotton production. The other was the Bridgewater canal, which connected Manchester by water to Liverpool, and hence the oceans of the world. That combination of mechanized production and easy access to raw cotton and international markets, in a region that already had an abundance of skilled spinners and weavers, secured her position as a global manufacturing center. It also created living conditions of unspeakable squalor for many of her inhabitants.

"From this filthy sewer pure gold flows," wrote Tocqueville.[12] He was talking about Manchester, but he could have been talking about industrialization in general. All of us are beneficiaries of the gold: the Eiffel Tower, the cotton we are wearing right now, and the dramatic changes in power, transport, communications, and productivity that have so enhanced human welfare in the last two hundred and fifty years. But we also know about the sewers from which it flowed. We all know who picked the cotton, who swept the chimneys, who lost their lands, lives, or livelihoods—and who was beating or even shooting them at the time. Industrialization, like Enlightenment, was riddled with ambiguities. We will return to that in chapter 9.

In the meantime, there is a striking parable of industrialization in another transport link that opened between Liverpool and Manchester, on September 15, 1830.[13] It was the official launch of the world's first passenger railway. Large crowds watched as Robert Stephenson's new steam engine *Northumbria* left Liverpool, pulling a train with passengers including the Duke of Wellington, hero of Waterloo and now prime minister, and the local member of Parliament William Huskisson. Following the *Northumbria* on a parallel track was Stephenson's more famous engine, *Rocket*. When *Northumbria* stopped to take on water, many of the guests got out to stretch their legs. Huskisson, hoping to be reconciled to the prime minister after a political disagreement, approached Wellington's carriage to shake his hand, but before he was able to climb aboard, *Rocket* appeared in the distance on the adjacent track.

Rocket was a prototype and did not have brakes. The driver immediately changed into reverse, but it took a vital ten seconds to engage. Several people shouted to Huskisson to move out of the way. Although there was plenty of time to reach safety, Huskisson hesitated between the tracks and then tried to avoid *Rocket* by clambering into the duke's carriage. There were no fixed steps, so he tried to haul himself up by the carriage door. At the last minute, the door swung open, with Huskisson still holding it, straight in front of the oncoming *Rocket*. His leg was horribly mangled, and despite a valiant effort to get him medical care in time—the *Northumbrian* traveled toward Manchester at thirty-six miles per hour for fifteen miles, breaking the world speed record in the process—he died of blood loss that evening. The story made headlines everywhere. Industrialization brought unprecedented power, but it also brought death.

In the pocket of Huskisson's jacket when he died was a tribute to the man who had made steam travel possible (and thus, ironically, Huskisson's own death). The man in question—who was also, as it happens, one of the "Lunar Men" to whom Lavoisier had been writing—was a Scottish inventor named James Watt.

The Light of the Moon

Watt's steam engine, like Arkwright's mill and the Bridgewater canal, was launched commercially in 1776. Taken together, those three breakthroughs make 1776 a pretty good starting point for the Industrial Revolution.[14] It was also the year that Watt, his business partner, and a number of other key figures in the history of industrialization began meeting regularly for dinner on the Monday nearest the full moon, calling themselves the Lunar Society.[15]

At the center of the Lunar Circle was the friendship between Birmingham manufacturer Matthew Boulton and the physician Erasmus Darwin, from nearby Lichfield. The union of these two men, and these two towns, encapsulates the marriage of theoretical science and practical industry that would characterize the Lunar Men, and indeed the British Industrial Revolution as a whole. Samuel Johnson, who was from Lichfield himself, mischievously described the relationship between the two towns in 1776: "Sir, we are a city of philosophers; we work with our heads, and make the boobies of Birmingham work for us with their hands."* But the Lunar Society would bring the philosophers and boobies together. The "heads" of leading scientists, in combination with the "hands" of leading manufacturers, would have powerful consequences, as ideas, instruments, investments, and inventions flowed between them.[†]

In practice, most of the Lunar Men transcended that divide. John Whitehurst, whom we met in chapter 5, made clocks and wrote books on geology. Samuel Galton was a gunsmith who made groundbreaking discoveries on optics, light, and color. Darwin wrote *Zoonomia*, but he also wrote to Boulton with detailed sketches of his "Scheme for a fiery Chariot" (today we would call it a car). James Keir was a chemist and geologist who managed a glassworks, ran Boulton and Watt's factory for a few years, and then made his fortune manufacturing soap. Watt, best known as an inventor, was an early pioneer in the chemical properties of water.

Nevertheless, the genius of the group lay in the combination of theoretical and practical skills, with the research of one member triggering an innovation by another, which could then fuel the research of another, and so on. To take one example of many: Joseph Priestley's work on gases shaped Josiah Wedgwood's process for making ceramics, which enabled him to help Keir understand the gravity of glass and thereby make clearer lenses, which he then sold to Boulton for use in his factory, which was producing Watt's engines. Geology, chemistry, and industry were interconnected. Manufacturing was impossible without minerals, gases, and heat; chemistry and geology were impossible without tools, precision instruments, and increasingly power.

---

* A "booby" was a dope or stupid person. See James Boswell, *The Life of Samuel Johnson* (1791; repr., London: Penguin, 2008), 512.

† At different times, the Lunar Circle also included the writer Thomas Day, the inventor Richard Lovell Edgeworth, the physician William Small (who died in 1775), the botanist Jonathan Stokes and the clergyman Robert Augustus Johnson, who do not really feature in our story—although the "profoundly scientific and eminently absent" Stokes did on one occasion accidentally release a large yellow and black snake into the room, having picked it up for dissection on the assumption that it had frozen to death, and then forgotten about it as it gradually thawed in his pocket. See Mary Anne Schimmelpenninck, *Life of Mary Anne Schimmelpenninck: Author of "Select Memoirs of Port Royal" and Other Works*, 4th ed., 2 vols., Christina C. Hankin (London: Longman, 1860), 31.

The synergy between these Lunar interests was captured nicely in a letter from Darwin to Boulton, after visiting caves in Derbyshire with John Whitehurst:

> I have been into the Bowels of old Mother Earth, and seen Wonders and learnt much curious knowledge in the Regions of Darkness. . . . And am going to make innumerable Experiments on aquaeous, suphureous, metallic and saline Vapours. Food for Fire-Engines![16]

The possibilities of chemistry in particular were very exciting. Of the 118 elements in a periodic table today, fewer than 15 had been known in 1700.[‡] The middle of the century saw 4 new metals identified (platinum, cobalt, nickel, and magnesium), alongside significant improvements in the production of iron and steel.[§] But things really took off in the 1770s, and the Lunar Men were at the heart of it. Watt was studying "latent heat" as part of his work on steam. Small and Boulton were working on new metals, including manganese, which was first isolated in 1774 and would soon become indispensable in steelmaking. James Keir was researching alkalis, which were needed in the manufacture of soap, textiles, glass, and pottery. In a busy 1776, he published a seminal article on crystallization in glass, as well as translating Pierre-Joseph Macquer's *Dictionary of Chemistry*, to which he added his own work as an appendix the following year.[17]

Most significantly, Joseph Priestley was making a series of extraordinary discoveries about air, which he wrote up in his *Experiments and Observations on Different Kinds of Air* (1774–1777). If you put a mouse in a jar with "pure air," or what we call oxygen, it can survive for twice as long as it does with "common air."[18] If you put a sprig of mint in a jar with "putrid air," caused by the decay of a dead mouse, the mint grows better than it does normally. If you put the mouse and the mint in the same jar, they both survive indefinitely, which suggests a symbiotic relationship between animal and plant respiration (a fact that prompted Benjamin Franklin to remark, as presciently as ever, "I hope this will give some check to the

---

‡ Antinomy, arsenic, bismuth, carbon, copper, gold, iron, lead, mercury, phosphorus, silver, sulfur, tin, zinc.

§ Magnesium was not isolated until 1808, but its discovery is often dated to the work of Joseph Black in 1755.

rage to destroying trees that grow near houses").[19] If you take the air that results from fermentation and "impregnate" water with it, you can create fizzy drinks, which combine a pleasant acidic taste with apparent medicinal benefits.[20] This was one of Priestley's favorite discoveries, and a source of great personal pride; he spent ten pages refuting the charge that it possessed a "strange urinous flavour."[21] Soda water quickly caught the attention of a Swiss-German watchmaker named Johann Jacob Schweppe, who began mass producing it. (Boulton and Darwin were particular fans.) It even went around the world on HMS *Resolution*.

Experiments on "airs," or what we now call gases, were taking place all over Europe in the 1770s. We have already seen that Alessandro Volta discovered methane in Italy. Chlorine was identified by Carl Wilhelm Scheele in Sweden.[§] Priestley discovered sulfur dioxide in England, where Henry Cavendish had just produced "inflammable air." Scheele was the first to produce "fire air" in 1771, and a year later Daniel Rutherford isolated "noxious air" in Scotland, which is where Joseph Black had previously studied "fixed air." Eventually Lavoisier, in France, described how these last four gases (and combustion itself) actually worked, and it was his approach to naming and classifying them that was ultimately adopted. We now know them as hydrogen, oxygen, nitrogen, and carbon dioxide.

This presents us with a puzzle, however. Scientific discoveries were proliferating across Europe in the late eighteenth century. New metals and gases were identified in Austria, Britain, France, Germany, Italy, Spain, and Sweden in the decades either side of 1776, to say nothing of the developments in Holland, Russia, Switzerland, and elsewhere. Yet it was only in Britain that they became, in Darwin's phrase, "food for fire-engines." Clearly industrialization was not an inevitable result of scientific progress: the Lunar Men made engines and factories while the French made hot air balloons, the Austrians made music, and the Dutch did not make much of anything for the next few decades.[22] So why did the Industrial Revolution start in Britain? And why now?

It is a vast question, one of the most important in economic history. But in simplistic terms we can distinguish between "deep" and "shallow" causes.

---

§   Scheele did not realize chlorine was an element in its own right, believing it to be an oxide.

The deep causes—the factors that, over multiple centuries and indeed millennia, caused the breakthrough to happen in early modern Western Europe as opposed to elsewhere in history or elsewhere in the world—will have to wait until chapter 9.[23] The shallow causes are slightly easier to define, because they relate to what triggered industrialization in eighteenth-century England in particular: the reasons why, as Robert Allen puts it, "there was only one route to the twentieth century, and it traversed northern Britain."[24] If we narrow our focus to that question, then we can answer it in terms of three interlocking stories, all of which collide in 1776, and all of which feature members of the Lunar Society in a starring role. They are the stories of power, of manufacturing, and of invention.

The Making of Power

Until 1700, only three sources of useful power were available to human beings. Anyone hoping to move something—to lift an object, pull a plough, grind wheat into flour, crush ore, pump water, transport goods, or operate machinery—had to power it using the wind or a river or muscles. The wind was good for certain things, but its inconsistency of availability, speed, and direction made it hard to harness for most human activity. Rivers were much steadier, but you could not take them with you, so mills, pumps, looms, and the like had to be built in very specific places. The only other option was to use muscles. Either you got an animal to work for you, in which case you had to provide it with food, land, and rest; or you paid (or forced) a person to work for you; or you did the work yourself.

The seventeenth century saw a lot of attention given to the possibility of a fourth source of power: nothing.

For two thousand years, educated opinion in Europe had mostly agreed with Aristotle that vacuums, or voids, did not and could not exist. "Nature abhors a vacuum," as Rabelais quotably put it.[25] But this consensus began to crumble in the 1640s and 1650s, as the possibility and power of vacuums became apparent. Evangelista Torricelli demonstrated that a sealed tube filled with mercury would create a vacuum at the top as it emptied (thus inventing the barometer, almost by accident). Otto von Guericke built the first vacuum pump, with a design that was subsequently improved by Robert Boyle and Robert Hooke. Before long it had demonstrated the power of vacuums in the most dramatic fashion, as people gathered in Magdeburg, in central Germany, to watch a team of horses try to pull apart two empty copper hemispheres. In front of a large crowd, including the Holy Roman Emperor, they failed—and in doing so, showed just how powerful nothing could be.

In and of itself, this was more spectacular than useful. But it coincided with increasing interest in the possibilities of steam, and whether it might one day be capable of pumping water out of mines, running mills, or even propelling vehicles.** It was fairly obvious that water expanded when it boiled—steam fills roughly eighteen hundred times more space than the equivalent amount of water—and that steam could therefore produce enough "push" to raise a piston in a cylinder. But the real power came from the realization that the reverse was also true. When the steam condensed back into water, it became eighteen hundred times smaller, creating a vacuum within the cylinder that would "pull" the piston back down again with terrific force.[26] Steam could be used to make vacuums, which could be used to make power.

That basic insight belonged to a French Huguenot, Denis Papin. So it might seem strange that the idea was taken forward in Britain rather than France. But the reign of Louis XIV was a torrid time for French Protestants, and Papin spent his most productive years in Italy, Germany, and particularly England. It was in London that he invented the pressure cooker (giving it the rather macabre name of "bone digester") and in London that he worked alongside both Hooke and Boyle in the Royal Society. And it was in London that, in 1699, the Royal Society saw the first demonstration of a working steam-powered pump: Thomas Savery's "New Invention for Raiseing of Water and Occassioning Motion to all sorts of Mill Work by the Impellent Force of Fire."[27] It was dangerous, prohibitively inefficient, incapable of pulling anything other than water, and incapable of pulling it more than ten meters upward. But in a country with cold winters, diminishing supplies of wood, and plentiful supplies of cheap coal (if only it could be mined efficiently), it was a start.

Two hundred miles to the southwest, a Baptist preacher and ironmonger named Thomas Newcomen was working on his own project, which would

***

** Patent no. 50 (1631) was awarded to the Scottish clockmaker David Ramsay "to Raise Water from Lowe Pitts by Fire," "to Make any Sort of Mills to goe on Standing Waters by Continual Moc'on without the Helpe of Windes, Waite or Horse," and "to make Boates, Shippes and Barges to goe against stronge Winde and Tyde." Sadly there is no evidence that he ever succeeded.

eventually become the first steam engine. The key challenge, Newcomen realized, was not the "push" but the "pull." It was easy enough to heat water into steam, raise a piston in a cylinder, and lift a wooden beam. But it was far more difficult to cool the steam back into water, thus creating the vacuum needed to bring the beam back down—let alone to do this quickly enough, and securely enough, to make the engine run continuously. After ten years of fiddling, Newcomen finally stumbled across the solution quite by accident, as a tiny hole caused cold water to rush into the cylinder, condensing the steam immediately and causing a blast of "tremendous power" that broke the chain, crushed the bottom of the cylinder, and "convinced the very senses of the onlookers that they had discovered an incomparably powerful force which had hitherto been entirely unknown in nature."[28] It was a genuine breakthrough, and the first steam engine was built near Birmingham in 1712. By 1776, there were six hundred of them, draining mines across Britain, Europe and even America. When Newcomen died, his only obituary remembered him as the "sole inventor of that surprising machine for raising water by fire."[29]

Steam power was now possible. But outside of draining coal mines it was thoroughly impractical, and would remain so for another sixty years. Newcomen's engine was so inefficient, and used so much coal relative to the amount of water it drained, that to use it anywhere other than a coal mine would have been a complete waste of money. Various tweaks were made to the design, but they could not overcome the fundamental problem: the vast majority of the heat in the system was wasted. Water had to be boiled into steam and then condensed back into water in the same cylinder, which was spectacularly inefficient in terms of heat, coal, and cost. Consequently, until James Watt, there was no way that steam could be used to power mills or machinery, let alone Darwin's "fire engines." A radical new idea was needed.

Watt's solution came to him gradually, and then suddenly.[30] He worked on steam throughout the 1760s, researching latent heat while becoming increasingly frustrated with a Newcomen engine he had been asked to fix. But the key innovation—cooling the steam in a separate, cold condenser— came to him in a flash of inspiration in 1765:

It was in the Green of Glasgow. . . . I was thinking upon the engine at the time and had gone as far as the Herd's house when the idea came into my

mind, that as steam was an elastic body it would rush into a vacuum, and if
a communication was made between the cylinder and an exhausted vessel,
it would rush into it, and might be there condensed without cooling the
cylinder. I then saw that I must get quit of the condensed steam and injection
water, if I used a jet as in Newcomon's engine. . . . I had not walked further
than the Golf-house when the whole thing was arranged in my mind.[31]

Like most great innovations, it seems very obvious afterward. The way to
avoid the continuous cycle of heating and cooling, with all its inefficiency,
was to make the engine both hot and cold at the same time, but with the
hot and cold parts kept separate, connected through valves and a pipe.
But its implications were seismic. If it could be made to work, it would cut
the amount of fuel needed by up to 75 percent, dramatically increase the
cost-effectiveness of steam power, and make it useful in a variety of other
settings, not just in coal mines.

Watt was convinced that it could. "I have now made an Engine that shall
not waste a particle of Steam," he proclaimed in 1765, before he had even
built it. "It shall all be boiling hot—ay, and hot water injected, if I please."[32]
Ten years later, he had designed the engine, made a prototype, patented it,
and gone into business with Boulton to build it. The first one started running at Bloomfield colliery on March 8, 1776. It drained the pit of nearly
sixty feet of water in under an hour.

The new engine caught on quickly. A second opened at an ironworks in
Shropshire in April, then another at a London distillery in the summer, then
another at a colliery in Warwickshire. The first engines for the Cornish tin
and copper mines—a vast potential market, which would see forty engines
installed in the first ten years—were ordered in November. Boulton could
see the window of opportunity opening. "I hope and flater myself that we
are at the eve of a fortune," he told Watt. "People are daily coming to see
the engines."[33] Orders were coming in from Bristol, London, Scotland, and
Wales, and Boulton was keen that their advantage not be lost to inventors
with better engines, "serpents like Moses' that devour all others."[34] Soon he
was urging Watt to develop a rotary engine that could turn wheels, which
would enable it to be used in manufacturing cotton; Watt delivered with
his famous sun-and-planet system in 1784. "I think Fire Mills will in the
end rival Water Mills," Boulton predicted.[35]

Not all of the visitors in 1776 were potential customers. Some were simply nosy. James Boswell toured the factory out of sheer curiosity, and was astonished by "the vastness and the contrivance of some of the machinery," the seven hundred people who worked for Boulton as an "iron chieftain" and "father to his tribe," and Boulton's zeitgeist-embodying remark: "I sell here, Sir, what all the world desires to have—POWER."[36]

Other visitors had more nefarious motives. A group of Cornish mine captains arrived that summer, ostensibly to consider buying an engine, but when they left, Watt noticed that a crucial drawing of the engine design had mysteriously vanished along with them. Boulton responded with a furious letter, insisting that he was running a factory rather than "a school to teach fire-engine making." The drawing promptly turned up again. It had been taken by one of the mine captains, a certain Richard Trevithick, "under a misapprehension," they explained.[37]

This incident provides another peculiar link between Watt, *Rocket*, and the world's first railway accident. Trevithick's son, also named Richard, was only five years old when his father tried to snaffle Watt's design in 1776. But he would soon grow into a giant of the steam industry himself. By the age of twenty-five, the younger Trevithick had built a model of a new kind of engine powered by high-pressure steam, rather than atmospheric pressure. It was smaller, simpler, and more portable than Watt's atmospheric engine, and this was vital if moveable "fire-engines" were ever going to be possible.

Trevithick did not stop there. At thirty, he was the first to build a working locomotive, announcing the arrival of steam travel in breathtaking fashion by riding his *Puffing Devil* up Camborne Hill, without warning and to widespread astonishment, on Christmas Eve 1801.[38] (The locomotive did not survive until the New Year, after its drivers went off to the pub for the evening, leaving it unattended in a shed with the engine still on. It quickly boiled dry and then burst into flames, and "nothing that was combustible remained either of the Engine or the house").[39] At thirty-five, he started work on a tunnel under the River Thames, which was never completed. At forty he was declared bankrupt. At forty-five he left for South America to make his fortune in mining, but quickly got swept up in the fight for independence under Simón Bolívar, in the course of which he designed a new gun for the army, fled from the Spanish in Peru, crossed the jungle on foot, narrowly escaped being eaten by an alligator, and finally wound up in

Cartagena, Colombia, where he managed to persuade a young Englishman to lend him £50 for his ticket home. In an extraordinary coincidence, after spending more than a decade five thousand miles from home, Richard Trevithick had bumped into one of only two people on earth who knew more about steam locomotives than he did.

The young Englishman's name was Robert Stephenson. Two years later, he designed and built *Rocket*.

The Power of Making

Industrial man cannot live by steam alone. Engines were harbingers of the future, but they would have been rather pointless, and indeed impossible to make, if they had not developed in symbiosis with British manufacturing. Engines needed parts; factories needed power. Neither could bring about industrialization on their own, but in combination, they would prove transformative.

The transformation in British manufacturing was multifaceted, and so is the explanation for it.[††] But we can summarize it as the product of metals, mechanization, management, marketing, and money.

Metals

Britain is undoubtedly lucky in her allocation of coal. There is plenty of it, mostly at or near the earth's surface, and the location of her coalfields means that even in the eighteenth century, coal could be transported to

---

[††] Unsurprisingly, the Lunar Men were at the heart of it. Matthew Boulton worked in "toy-making," an industry that employed twenty thousand people in Birmingham alone, manufacturing small metal goods like buckles, corkscrews, inkstands, snuffboxes, toothpicks, tweezers, watch chains, and the like. So did Samuel Galton, although his company focused on manufacturing guns. James Keir ran a glassworks, then a chemical works, then a soap factory. Josiah Wedgwood industrialized European pottery. Joseph Priestley's brother-in-law, John "Iron Mad" Wilkinson, was the ironmaster whose precision iron cylinders were essential to making the Boulton and Watt engine work. (Wilkinson was so obsessed with iron that he made his own coffin out of it and kept it in his office. After he died, it was discovered to be too small for his corpse, and then too large for the grave; he was buried four times in total, most recently in 1928.) The greatest industrialist of them all, cotton manufacturer Richard Arkwright, not only visited the Lunar Society but managed to get their two most prominent members, James Watt and Erasmus Darwin, to testify for him in court. Again, alongside the "philosophers" in the group who used their heads to research and make discoveries, there were plenty of "boobies" who used their hands to manufacture and make money—quite literally in Boulton's case, after he set up the Soho Mint in 1788.

major population centers (most notably London) with relative ease. But her subterranean good fortune does not end there. Her geological history has also given her an impressive diversity of metals—copper, lead, tin, zinc, and iron in particular—which are often found near each other. Moreover, many deposits of iron ore happen to be found near rich seams of coal, which is one major reason why Britain was able to produce iron and steel so abundantly, and so early.

The other is the diligence, know-how and persistence of four pioneering individuals. In 1709, at Coalbrookdale in Shropshire, Abraham Darby had made the first breakthrough of the industrial age, producing cast iron using coke (which is baked coal) as opposed to charcoal. Forty years later, Benjamin Huntsman worked out how to use clay crucibles for the production of high-quality steel in Sheffield; this was a significant advance because steel, though far stronger and less brittle than iron, was also fiendishly difficult to forge. John "Iron Mad" Wilkinson's boring machine was probably the first machine tool, and critical to the manufacture of precision instruments and components. And high-quality iron became much cheaper thanks to Henry Cort's puddling and rolling technique, which enabled people to use coke to make wrought iron (the type used to make nails, pipes, nuts, and bolts), and was described in 1786 as "more advantageous to Great Britain than the possession of the thirteen colonies of America."[40]

The effect of all these innovations was to dramatically increase British production of iron and steel, at precisely the point in history when it was most needed to make tools, engines, and machinery. The chronological alignment is remarkable. In the year that steelmaker Benjamin Huntsman died, Abraham Darby III was commissioned to build the world's first iron bridge, Henry Cort started running his first iron forge, and blowers were installed at John Wilkinson's ironworks in Broseley, powered by Boulton and Watt's brand-new steam engine. That year, of course, was 1776.

Mechanization

The most obvious feature of early British industrialization, at least from the perspective of today, is the use of machines. Water mills, wheels, turning machines, lathes, and eventually engines proliferated. Though mechanization would later be seen as dehumanizing and grotesque, as we have already seen in Manchester, it initially prompted a mixture of admiration and wonder. When Italian author Carlo Castone visited Boulton's factory, he described the use of machinery as "the most interesting and well-done part of English industry," in which "wheels, vices, pincers, pedals, lathes, sewing awls, scissors and hammers, dropping from a height" meant that "women, men and children do a huge amount of work" with "little effort."[41] Elizabeth Montagu, founder of the Blue Stockings Society, found it "exquisite": "To behold the secrets of Chymistry, and the mechanick powers, so employ'd and exerted, is very delightful. I consider the Machines you have at work as so many useful subjects to Great Britain."[42] The idea, as James Keir put it, was "to convert such trades as were usually carried on by individuals into great manufactures by the help of machinery, which might enable the articles to be made with greater precision and cheaper than those commonly sold."[43]

Nowhere was the impact of mechanization greater than in the manufacture of cotton. There were five major new inventions in the cotton industry between 1765 and 1785 (the spinning jenny, the water frame, Samuel Crompton's mule, Arkwright's carding machine, and Edmund Cartwright's power loom), which dramatically increased the amount of cotton that could be carded, spun, and weaved at once, thus increasing production, lowering costs, and driving demand all at the same time. But machines were doing more of the heavy lifting across the board: cutting patterns for Wedgwood's pots, boring cylinders for Galton's guns, polishing Boulton's buttons, and powering Wilkinson's ironworks and Trevithick's mines. Mechanization was spreading, transforming every industry it touched. Erasmus Darwin could not contain his enthusiasm (although we might wish he had):

> Press'd by the ponderous air the Piston falls
> Resistless, sliding through its iron walls;
> Quick moves the balanced beam, of giant-birth,
> Wields his large limbs, and nodding shakes the earth.[44]

Management

Separating complex processes into simpler ones, whereby ten people are assigned one task each rather than one person doing ten, is such a basic feature of our world that we can forget how astonishing it was to many at the time. Jabez Fisher, visiting Boulton's factory from Philadelphia in 1776, described "a theatre of business, all conducted like one piece of mechanism, men, women and children full of employment according to their strength and docility. The very air buzzes with the variety of noises. All seems like one vast machine. . . . Tis wonderful, astonishing, amazing."[45] The German aphorist Georg Christoph Lichtenberg was similarly impressed: "Each workman has only a very limited range, so that he does not need constantly to change his position and tools, and by this means an incredible amount of time is saved. Thus, for example, each button, fashioned in box-wood, ivory, or anything else, passes through at least ten hands."[46]

By breaking production down into small pieces, managers could maximize productivity, minimize the skills required of each worker, and defend against industrial espionage, all at once. The division of labor changed everything. It was, as Adam Smith declared in the opening sentence of *The Wealth of Nations* (also written in 1776), responsible for "the greatest improvement in the productive powers of labour, and the greater part of the skill, dexterity, and judgment with which it is anywhere directed or applied."[47] Equally, however, Smith realized that it risked turning "minds" into mere "hands." This separation of intellectual and manual labor would later be severely criticized by Karl Marx, with sweeping consequences.

Factories presented all sorts of new management challenges, and their owners had to work out how to solve them. Some were financial. Wedgwood was one of the first to examine his production costs in detail, negotiate with his workers over the cost of each piece of pottery, increase production in order to minimize the cost of overheads per unit—"making the greatest quantity possible in a given time," as he put it—and recognize that lowering prices of his wares could actually *increase* profits, because more of "the middling People" could afford to buy them.[48]

Other challenges related to the practicalities of managing a large workforce. Wedgwood's factory had a system for checking in and out, set mealtimes, high standards of cleanliness and language, and a process to prevent people from starting their shifts late. Wedgwood, Boulton, and Arkwright all imposed fines for bad behavior (skiving, drunkenness, theft, vandalism); in Jedidiah Strutt's factory, offenses included "riding on each other's backs," "throwing tea on Josh Bridworth," "calling thro' window to some soldiers," "putting Josh Hayne's dog into a bucket of hot water" and "throwing water on Ann Gregory very frequently."[49] But there were carrots as well as sticks. Wedgwood employed a midwife and three apothecaries. Boulton distributed gifts for good work, and arranged for an insurance scheme in the case of sickness, injury, or death. Both men, like Arkwright, built homes for their workers. The management of people, as well as financial accounts, would become increasingly important for industrialists in the years ahead.

Marketing

In some ways, Josiah Wedgwood was an unlikely potter.[50] The youngest of thirteen children, he saw the family pottery pass to his older brother Thomas, to whom he was later apprenticed. He was physically unable to kick the treadle to turn the potter's wheel, thanks to a childhood bout of smallpox that left him with permanent pain in his right knee (which was later sawn off). But he had a flair for what we now call marketing. He practically invented it: loss leaders, celebrity endorsements, traveling salesmen, advertisements, catalogues, buy one get one free, direct mail, public relations campaigns, free delivery, and money-back guarantees all go back to Josiah Wedgwood. He was arguably the first manufacturer to think seriously about why ordinary people bought things, where they heard about them, and how they could be persuaded to buy more.

He was quick to see the power of what we would now call influencer endorsements. Making tea sets for the royal family was laborious and relatively unprofitable, so many potters declined the orders. But Wedgwood realized that it was extremely effective at getting *other* people to buy them, so he accepted royal commissions, both at home and abroad: "if a royal or noble introduction be as necessary to the sale of an article of luxury as real elegance and beauty, then the manufacturer, if he consults his own interest, will bestow as much pains, and expence too, if necessary, in gaining the favour of these advantages as he would in bestowing the latter."[51] He reacted to fashions quickly, responding to the fad for hand bleaching by pointing out that his black basalt teaware would create a tasteful contrast.[52] Knowing that his wealthier customers "will not mix with the rest of the World any farther than their amusements or conveniencys make it necessary," he established exclusive showrooms for them.[53] Famously, he mass-produced abolitionist medallions, featuring a kneeling slave in chains made from black basalt against a background of white jasper, surrounded by the words "Am I Not a Man and a Brother?" And most farsightedly, he recognized that the future of his trade lay with selling large numbers of reasonably priced products to the "Middling Class of People," rather than small numbers of expensive items to the rich. This was counterintuitive in many industries, and nowhere more so than in the manufacturing of tea sets and tableware. But Wedgwood had seen the future. "The middling People would probably buy quantitys of them at a reduced price," he explained.[54]

Needless to say, none of these four things would have brought about a transformation in British manufacturing if it was not for the availability of the fifth one: money. But that is a subject that needs more space than we can give it here. We will return to it in chapter 9.

The Mother of Invention

It is something of a cliché to say that the Industrial Revolution's greatest invention was invention itself.[55] But like most clichés, it is essentially true. Even if we limit ourselves to the innovations in mining, metallurgy, engine design, and manufacturing we have mentioned so far, it is striking how many significant breakthroughs occurred in the 1770s—and not only relative to the 1470s or 570s, which we might have expected, but also relative to the 1970s or even 2010s, which we might not.[56]

There were countless others. Watt also developed a copying machine, the screw micrometer, the rangefinder telemeter, and the flexible water main. Priestley invented the eraser, Edgeworth the optical telegraph, Darwin the canal lift and horizontal windmill. The year 1776 also saw the world's first submarine: David Bushnell's *Turtle*, used by the Continental Army against the British in New York harbor. (It failed; Washington told Jefferson that "one accident or another was always intervening," although he still considered it "an effort of genius.")[57] A few months earlier, in 1775, Alexander Cumming had invented the one item from this period that you almost certainly have in your home: the S-trap toilet, which prevents foul smells from entering the bathroom through the waste pipe. It was improved in 1778 by Joseph Bramah, who then went on to invent the unpickable lock and the hydraulic press.

In Spring 1774, Benjamin Jesty discovered something that would make an even greater contribution to human well being than either flush toilets or steam engines, when he deliberately infected his wife and sons with cowpox. The Turkish practice of inoculation, or deliberately infecting people with smallpox, had been introduced to Britain decades earlier. But Jesty took it to the next level by infecting humans with pus from a cow's udders using a darning needle.[58] He was widely ridiculed for making his family ill on purpose, with some claiming cowpox would give them horns. They quickly recovered, however, and by the end of the century the practice of vaccination (from the Latin *vacca* for "cow") would be vindicated by Edward Jenner as both safer than inoculation, and less likely to lead to transmission. Smallpox was finally eradicated in 1980.

Here is what's curious about each of these innovations: they were all made by English-speaking people. This is odd, because science was advancing across Europe in the seventeenth and eighteenth centuries, not just in Britain. We have already seen how new physical laws, mathematical formulae, biological species, and chemical elements were being identified all over the continent. Another good example of scientific internationalism in the period is electricity; to this day, we measure electrical components using Volts, Watts, Amps, and Ohms, reflecting the contributions of Italian, Scottish, French, and German scientists respectively.[‡‡] Yet when we strip out experiments with purely theoretical or curiosity value and focus instead on practical inventions that changed the way individuals, businesses, and entire nations operated—pumps, engines, tools, locks, machines, factories, toilets, vaccines, trains—the list becomes disproportionately Anglophone, with nearly all of them created in England, Wales, Scotland, or America. Which invites the question: Why?

There are a variety of explanations. One is geography. Britain was fast running out of wood, so she had to find an alternative source of fuel, and coal (which was plentiful and accessible) was the ideal candidate—which soon prompted experiments and inventions to mine it more efficiently, which then had knock-on effects in the production of iron and steam. Another is the role of the state: the combination of the Glorious Revolution of 1688,

---

‡‡ The first electrostatic generator was made by a German; the Leyden jar by a Dutchman; lightning rods by a Czech, an American, and perhaps a Russian; the electroscope by a Frenchman; and the battery by an Italian. Additionally, electromagnetism was discovered by a Dane, conduction by an Englishman, bioelectricity by an Italian, and the one-fluid theory of electricity by an American. The largest scale experiment of the period, in which hundreds of monks and soldiers formed a line a mile long and were given an electric shock simultaneously, was conducted by a Frenchman. And much of this was written up and added to by an Englishman (and Lunar Society member), the ubiquitous Joseph Priestley. See Priestley, *The History and Present State of Electricity* (London: Dodsley, Johnson and Cadell, 1767).

economic protectionism, and more or less continual warmongering by the British state in the eighteenth century provided favorable conditions for the growth of various industries, including cotton, textiles, munitions, and metalwork. A third is relatively high wages, which incentivized the development of labor-saving machinery. A fourth is the improvement of the British travel network in the second half of the century, which witnessed a dramatic expansion in the number of turnpike roads as well as the start of a canal boom that would make the transport of goods far cheaper, thanks in no small part to the efforts of Lunar Men like Darwin, Wedgwood, Small, and Boulton.

But material factors like minerals, wages, wars, and roads do not tell the whole story. We can see that from the counterexample of France in particular, whose natural resources, militarization, transport networks, and wages were roughly equivalent to Britain's, if not greater.[59] Ideas played a role too. They always do.

Take religion, for instance. The inventors we have met so far were virtually all Protestant.[60] Most of them were Nonconformists as well, even though Dissenters made up less than 10 percent of the British population.[61] Naturally, there is plenty of debate as to why this might be true. Is it the intellectual freedom that comes from being outside the mainstream of acceptable thought? Is it the Protestant work ethic, in which hard work is proof that you are part of the elect? Is it the high view of diligence, education, and useful knowledge found among the Puritans? Is it the lack of church meddling in scientific matters (in contrast to the colleges in France, where the Jesuits insisted on Cartesianism being taught rather than Newtonian mechanics)? Is it the greater levels of literacy, generated by the Protestant emphasis on reading the Bible? Is it a classic example of the creative minority principle, in which people who are excluded from traditional power structures have to find other ways to rise up in the world? It may have been any of these, a combination, or something else entirely—and it is very difficult to prove which—but whatever explanation(s) we choose, the correlation between religion and invention in this period is too strong to be overlooked.

Or take the idea behind the success, and indeed the very existence, of the Lunar Society. Most cultures in history have had clear blue water between intellectuals and craftsmen, thinkers and doers, Lichfield philosophers and Birmingham boobies. You can either pursue knowledge or power, theoretical truth or practical utility, but not both (and the thinkers usually look down on the doers). But in early modern England, that paradigm began to change. In a series of works, Francis Bacon called for the *savants* to join forces with the *fabricants*, the knowers with the makers, in order to seek understanding that was practically useful. Contemplating truth is all well and good, he wrote in 1592, but surely our aim should be "the happy match between the mind of man and the nature of things," in order "to produce worthy effects, and to endow the life of man with infinite commodities?"[62]

Bacon's ideas soon took root. In 1663, Robert Boyle confessed his relative lack of interest in "pleasing Speculations to entertain [man's] Understanding without at all increasing his Power." He then applied the principle to himself: "I shall not dare to think myself a true naturalist till my skill can make my garden yield better herbs and flowers, or my orchard better fruit, or my field better corn, or my dairy better cheese, than theirs that are strangers to physiology."[63] Thomas Sprat went further, arguing that philosophy "will attain perfection when either mechanic laborers shall have philosophical heads, or the philosophers shall have mechanical hands."[64] This did not happen overnight, of course, nor exclusively in Britain. But it was in Britain, more than anywhere else, that Bacon's vision for the purpose of science—"to endow human life with new discoveries and resources"—became a reality.[65] Ideas have consequences.

Another example is the idea that inventions are a form of property. Today, we take intellectual property for granted. It seems right to us that people who come up with new ideas should have the opportunity to profit from them for a period of time, without other people copying their ideas and peddling their own imitations. Indeed, by providing a financial incentive for "the first and true inventor" of a new product, patents are foundational to our pursuit of innovation. But that idea is by no means a universal one. It evolved in seventeenth- and eighteenth-century Britain, emerging from the work of men like Bacon, Edward Coke, and John Locke, and finding legal expression in the Statute on Monopolies (1623–1624), the Copyright Act (1710), and the Engraving Copyright Act (1734–1735). These laws were not without problems and eventually became the subject of significant controversies involving Watt, Boulton, Trevithick, Arkwright, Darwin, and many others. But without them, and without the underlying assumption that ideas were something you could own, it is highly unlikely that Matthew

Boulton would have put up the money for James Watt's steam engine, or that Watt would have bothered persevering with it. "Of all things in life," Watt remarked just three months after receiving his patent, "there is nothing more foolish than inventing."[66]

Necessity is not the mother of invention. It provides a powerful incentive to think of better ways of doing things, and this is undoubtedly important. But historically speaking, inventions typically come from the privileged rather than those in desperate need, because innovation flourishes where there are not only incentives but also expertise, resources, time to experiment, and freedom to fail.[67] For a variety of geographical, economic, political, religious, intellectual, and legal reasons, those conditions were more fully met in Britain and America than in most of Europe in the late eighteenth century, and this generated a virtuous circle in which steam power, manufacturing, and invention developed symbiotically, with each drawing life from the other two. The Lunar Men and their friends seized the moment, and shot for the moon.

The Modern Prometheus

Maybe Prometheus was the first industrialist. He stole the secrets of fire from the gods in order to share them with humanity, and they brought huge power, enabling great progress in the arts and sciences. But they also brought unintended consequences of suffering and conflict.

There is something unmistakably Promethean, for example, about Benjamin Franklin snatching fire from the heavens with a key and a kite. Matthew Boulton's quest for power, with which we started this chapter, is similarly audacious. The same spirit characterizes Erasmus Darwin and John Whitehurst as they rummage underground for wonders that might fuel fire engines, and indeed Richard Trevithick's boast that while others had put the boiler in the fire, he had put the fire in the boiler. There is something Promethean, too, about the ambiguous aftermath: Eiffel's tower and Tocqueville's sewer, the power and danger of Stephenson's *Rocket*, the military consequences of industrial technology. You can see why the poets of the first industrial generation, including Goethe, Byron, and Shelley, found the myth such a source of creative inspiration.[68]

The most famous example was the extraordinary novel *The Modern Prometheus*, written by Mary Shelley—wife of Percy, daughter of Mary

Wollstonecraft and the anarchist William Godwin—when she was just eighteen. Generally recognized as the first piece of science fiction, it is a tale of scientific progress gone awry. Several of the inventors we have met in this chapter appear in the novel: there are allusions early on to Franklin's work on lightning and Luigi Galvani's on bioelectricity (from which we get our word *galvanize*), alongside various developments in chemistry and steam, and Erasmus Darwin appears in the book's first sentence. Besides being a novel, it is a parable of the dangers of industrial knowledge.

An eager young student goes to university in Ingolstadt. He learns for the first time about chemistry and particularly electricity, and marvels at the wondrous possibilities of modern science: "these philosophers, whose hands seem only made to dabble in dirt, and their eyes to pore over the microscope or the crucible, have indeed performed miracles. They penetrate into the recesses of nature. . . . They have acquired new and almost unlimited powers."[69] So he resolves to use these powers for good, either by abolishing disease, or by overcoming death. But his experiment backfires terribly. He creates something that is far beyond his control—like fire, and indeed industrialization—unleashing alienation; horror; the destruction of children, families, and communities; and death.

Eventually, he comes to understand what responsibilities creators have toward their creatures. But it is too late to save him. The reader is left pondering whether the benefits of technology outweigh the dangers of creating a monster that we cannot control, and which might at any moment wreak havoc upon our communities, our children, and our very planet. (The same question haunts one of the great TV series of recent times, Craig Mazin's *Chernobyl*.) Today we know Mary Shelley's novel by its other title: *Frankenstein*.

In a sense, industrialization was indeed a monster. It unleashed all sorts of consequences that would have horrified the Lunar Men, from Dickensian London and nineteenth-century Chicago to machine guns, nuclear weapons, and climate change.[70] Communities and family structures that had been stable for thousands of years were swept away in a matter of decades, with profound consequences for the practice of Christianity. Landscapes were destroyed. Millions of human beings were reduced to machines. Weaponry became immeasurably more deadly and sophisticated, with devastating consequences; as Captain Blood puts it in Hilaire Belloc's poem, "Whatever happens, we have got / the Maxim gun, and they have not."[71] Today, for every mile of railway track in the world, there are a hundred AK-47s.

Yet for all that, industrialization (like fire) is a Promethean triumph as well as a Frankensteinian monster. Which of the two metaphors predominates—whether running water compensates for Hiroshima, or antibiotics for the Somme, or the growth in wealth for the overweening pride that accompanies it—probably depends on where you are sitting.[72]

8

Lovers

Becoming Romantic

I return into myself, and find a world.
JOHANN WOLFGANG VON GOETHE

Not that he blushed to show compassion;
It chanced that year to be the fashion.
HANNAH MORE

ANYONE WRITING ABOUT 1776 and the origins of Romanticism has two
fairly obvious problems.

One is that it is doubtful whether Romanticism existed in 1776. The word
certainly did not. While some scholars date the start of the movement as
early as 1770, others say it began a generation later, with the Revolution in
France (1789), the development of the word *romantisch* in Germany (from
1793), or the publication of Wordsworth and Coleridge's *Lyrical Ballads* in
England (1798).[1]

Virtually all of the iconic figures of early Romanticism were children in
1776. Beethoven, whose Eroica symphony heralded the dawn of Romantic
music, was just six. So were William Wordsworth and Friedrich Hölderlin,
widely seen as the first Romantic poets along with Samuel Taylor Coleridge,

Friedrich Schlegel, and Novalis, who were all four. Friedrich Schleiermacher was eight. Napoleon was seven. Walter Scott was five. The great pioneers of Romantic art were younger still: Caspar David Friedrich, J. M. W. Turner and John Constable were all infants.* So were Jane Austen and Friedrich Schelling. Robert Burns, Jean Paul, Friedrich Schiller, and William Blake were a few years older, but all of them were still teenagers when America declared independence. Of the great nineteenth-century Romantics who are now household names—whether writers (Byron, Keats, the Shelleys, the Brontës, Pushkin, Hugo, Dumas), painters (Géricault, Delacroix), or composers (Schubert, Schumann, Rossini, Berlioz, Chopin, Mendelssohn, Liszt)—none had been born yet.

The second problem is that nobody can agree on exactly what Romanticism is. Pinning it down is like nailing jelly to a wall; there have been literally thousands of definitions suggested, and many are either so narrow that they exclude important figures or so broad as to be virtually meaningless. The etymology of the word is convoluted. We move from Rome to the vernacular Roman language to popular Romance languages more generally to popular writings more generally ("romances") to the *roman* or novel to the identification of poetry that is *romantische* ("romantic") as opposed to *klassische* ("classical") and only then to a movement called "Romanticism," by which time the first generation of Romantics had already died. And none of this quite explains why we also use the word "romantic" to describe the mystery of love—although it is a delightful coincidence that *Amor* is *Roma* spelled backward.

The term is nebulous by design. Friedrich Schlegel, credited with coining it in something like its modern sense, wrote to his brother in 1793: "I cannot send you my explanation of the word 'romantic' because it would be 125 sheets long."[2] When Isaiah Berlin delivered the Mellon Lectures on Romanticism—which he viewed as "the greatest single shift in the consciousness of the West that has occurred,"[3] and "a gigantic and radical transformation, after which nothing was ever the same"[4]—he began by saying that although people might expect him to define the term or at least explain what he meant by it, "I do not propose to walk into that particular trap."[5] He then

---

* There are, of course, exceptions, including the Swiss painter Henry Fuseli (1741–1825) and the Spanish artist Francisco Goya (1746–1828), sometimes described as the last of the Old Masters.

demonstrated what a hopeless tangle it was by quoting a wide range of thoroughly irreconcilable definitions, drawn from many of the movement's key thinkers, before offering an (admittedly brilliant) eight-hundred-word summary of his own.[6]

If describing Romanticism takes Isaiah Berlin eight hundred words, it is clearly foolhardy to try and outline it in just eight. Nevertheless, for the sake of clarifying how I will be using the term in this chapter, here it goes:

1. *Inwardness.* All that is most important in life, from personal feelings to artistic creativity, comes from inside a person rather than outside. Introspection is good, and authenticity matters more than compliance with expectations. In Hegel's oft-cited definition, Romanticism is about "absolute inwardness."[7]

2. *Infinity.* There is a longing for the indescribable and inexplicable over the delineated and defined, whether in nature, art, architecture, or (especially) music. "Art is for us none other than the mystic ladder from earth to heaven," wrote Liszt, "from the finite to the infinite, from mankind to God."[8]

3. *Imagination.* Only by allowing one's ideas to run free, unconstrained by schools, rules, or reason, is genuine creativity possible. This is why death, sex, dreams, and nightmares are such important sources of inspiration; it is why Blake desired "to cast off Bacon, Locke, and Newton from Albion's covering, to take off his filthy garments and clothe him with imagination."[9]

4. *Individuality.* What counts is the specific rather than the universal. "I am made unlike anyone I have ever met," declared Rousseau on the opening page of his *Confessions.* "I will even venture to say that I am like no one in the whole world. I may be no better, but at least I am different."[10]

5. *Inspiration.* Great artists began to be viewed as geniuses: inspired and inspiring figures who broke rules, transformed art, lived differently, and became iconic. The obvious example is the cult-like admiration of Beethoven, for his behavior and image as much as his music; it was of a completely different order to the admiration of the equally gifted Mozart just a generation before.[11]

6. *Intensity.* There is an emphasis on deep, vivid, and visceral emotional experiences, whether paroxysms of rapturous joy, furious rage, or suicidal melancholy. In Wordsworth's famous preface to the *Lyrical Ballads*, it was made explicit: "All good poetry is the spontaneous overflow of powerful feelings."[12]

7. *Innocence.* Many leading Romantics were fascinated by childhood, by rustic idylls, and by "noble savages," all three of which pointed to the purity of a former time, an Eden uncorrupted by society, war, or industrialization. Rousseau, Wordsworth, and Blake are classic examples, especially the latter's *Songs of Innocence and Experience* (1789).

8. *Ineffability.* Some Enlighteners talked as if everything in the world could be categorized, analyzed, and understood by the use of reason. The Romantics protested against this, often fiercely. Some realities, they insisted—passion, art, poetry, sex, feeling, music, the soul, God—were beyond words and could not be dissected like physical laws. (The idea of defining Romanticism in eight alliterated bullet points, for instance, would no doubt have made many of them physically nauseous.)

Some of these seem quite alien to us today. The focus on innocence, deep emotions, wild and remote landscapes, Gothic architecture, and indescribable experiences strikes us as very nineteenth century, evoking images of foppish, ruffle-haired, misty-eyed young white men staring wistfully into the middle distance.

Others, by contrast, seem thoroughly natural to us, to the extent that we do not even notice them. Inwardness and individuality, in particular, are so central to our understanding of identity and the self that we cannot fathom how people in previous centuries could possibly have thought about personhood differently. We find it thoroughly unintelligible that the English Puritan John Owen (1616–1683), to take just one example, could lose his wife and all eleven of his children, yet say nothing about it or his personal response to it in any of his works; we just assume that a person's inner journey of pain, love, and transformation is pretty much the most interesting thing about them, and the main reason other people would listen to what they had to say.[13] Owen, for whom the meaning of Scripture and the work of Christ were far more important than his own personal anguish, would have found our obsession with authenticity, identity, and self-discovery equally incomprehensible.

These eight words hopefully serve as an answer, however simplistic, to the question of what Romanticism is. But our other question still stands. In what sense can we talk about the origins of Romanticism in 1776, given that the artistic movement had not started, the word did not exist, and its pioneering poets, painters, and composers had not reached adulthood?

The short answer is that while Romanticism flowered in the early 1800s, its roots—temperamentally, artistically, sexually, and philosophically—lie in the 1770s. The longer answer involves visiting four European cities in 1776, where these roots were particularly prominent: Paris, London, Weimar, and the city that to this day is often hailed as the most romantic place in the world.

Venice: Sexuality and Self-Discovery

It is early summer in 1776, and a fifty-one-year-old Venetian is sitting outside Caffè Quadri on the Piazza San Marco. It is the best time of day for people watching. The light is golden, the mist on the canals has cleared, the air is warm but not yet hot, and there is already plenty of bustle at the heart of Europe's most densely populated city. The gondoliers are noisily touting for business. Tourists are peering up at the basilica to his left. The markets are open, and the imperious bell tower, which sits halfway between him and the Palazzo Ducale in the far corner, is supervising it all carefully. He is at home here. Often he takes his coffee at Florian's on the other side of the square, but Quadri's opened last year and he rather likes it.

He does not look like a spy. Well dressed, thick set, and wearing a short chestnut-colored wig, he is unusually dark for a local, and at six foot one, unusually tall. If you engage him in conversation, he is affable, attentive, even charming. If you ask him where he is from, he points to the west and says he grew up half a mile away on the Calle della Commedia. If you ask him what he does for a living, he says quite truthfully that he is working on a modern translation of Homer's *Iliad* and that his second volume is out this year. He does not reveal that he has also just accepted a salary of fifteen ducats per month to work as an informer for the Venetian Inquisition, under the alias Antonio Pratolini.

It is an unexpected development, to put it mildly. Until two years ago, he was not allowed in the city at all. Jailed by the Inquisition at the age of thirty, for "a question of religion," he pulled off one of history's most dramatic prison breaks in 1756—involving a renegade priest, a plate of butter-soaked macaroni, an iron spike hidden inside a Bible, and a hole in the ceiling covered up by a painting—from the building behind the bell tower on the far side of the square.[†] He was exiled for eighteen years. Now he is back, being paid by the people who imprisoned him and sipping coffee in plain view of the building from which he escaped. Insouciance does not begin to describe it.

By any standard, "Antonio Pratolini" has led an extraordinary life. He has traveled over forty thousand miles across Europe, from Madrid to St. Petersburg and London to Constantinople, punctuated by "sword fights at midnight and complots at the palace, bugs in the bed and bedlam in the tavern, masked balls, balls-ups and shinnying up drainpipes, flummery, mummery and summary executions," as Clive James vividly put it.[14] Under various names, he has gained audiences with Frederick the Great, George III, Madame de Pompadour, Catherine the Great, Pope Benedict XIV, and Pope Clement XIII, to say nothing of artists and intellectuals like Mozart, Voltaire, Goethe, and Rousseau.

He has been expelled from seminary, attacked, banished, arrested, imprisoned, robbed, and shot. Radiating self-confidence, he has convinced numerous patrons to sponsor him (making him respectable), the French government to set up a state lottery (making him rich), and the Marquise d'Urfé that he could turn her into a man (making him notorious). His career has been as varied as his itinerary: clergyman, diplomat, army officer, theater promoter, professional gambler, charlatan, librarian, spy. And he has had sexual encounters with several men and over one hundred and twenty women and girls—including fifteen members of royalty, two nuns, his niece, and (appallingly) his own daughter—many of which he will describe in prurient detail in his autobiography.[15] His real name is Giacomo Casanova.

---

†   This breakout is presumably the inspiration for Stephen King's short story *Rita Hayworth and the Shawshank Redemption* and Frank Darabont's subsequent film. Indeed, the parallels go further still: after escaping, he deliberately left behind a Bible verse in his cell for his captors to find ("I shall not die, but live, and declare the works of the Lord"). See Giacomo Casanova, *The Memoirs of Jacques Casanova de Seingalt*, vol. 2, *To Paris and Prison*, trans. Arthur Machen (New York: Putnam, 1894), 28.

Today Casanova's name is proverbial, and his legacy is dominated by his reputation as a philanderer. This he undoubtedly was. Even in our hypersexualized age, his narrative has the capacity to shock with its descriptions of incest, orgies, affairs with women he assumed were castrated men, and what we would now call pedophilia (around one in five of his sexual relationships took place with girls between the ages of eleven and fifteen). But however distasteful we may find it, Casanova's sex life was not as exceptional as it might appear by the standards of his day. When we consider some of his rich, itinerant, urban male contemporaries—people like James Boswell, John Wilkes, and the Marquis de Sade, let alone Lord Byron, who claimed to have had two hundred liaisons during just three years in Venice himself—it is not the number of people Casanova slept with, or their ages, that stands out.[16]

Even his fabled gallivanting is not unique. The eighteenth century was the age of the Grand Tour, and occasionally the Grand Sex Tour, as young upper-class men explored, researched, and sometimes slept their way around Europe, and Italy in particular. It was also the age of the itinerant mountebank.[17] Casanova's contemporaries included the Italian mystic, magician, and mischief-maker Alessandro Cagliostro (1743–1795), implicated in the Diamond Necklace Affair that so damaged Marie Antoinette; the French impostor George Psalmanazar (1679–1763), who claimed to be from Taiwan, convinced people that his skin was pale because everyone there lived underground, and published a bestselling book about it, including an entirely fictional language and alphabet; and the enigmatic Comte de Saint Germain (1712?–1784), who claimed he was many centuries old and had witnessed the crucifixion himself, along with his valet.[18] Even the distances Casanova travelled, though undeniably impressive, pale in comparison to the circumnavigations of James Cook (1728–1779), or the staggering mileage accumulated by the Methodist preacher John Wesley (1703–1791). Neither Casanova's adventuring nor his womanizing are sufficient to explain our fascination with him centuries later, or his significance as a Romantic figure *avant la lettre*.

What makes him so important, rather, is the *way* he wrote about both himself and his sexual exploits—and in particular, the way he made the latter central to understanding the former. Today we take this as read. It seems obvious to us that a person's sexuality is integral to one's sense of identity and something without which you cannot really understand who one is. But almost nobody at the time believed either of those things. No one had ever written, far less read, an autobiography in which sexual encounters were the central point of interest. No one had made sexuality the focal point of a description of oneself.

Very few people wrote books about themselves in the first place. Interest in the personal narrative of an individual for its own sake, of the sort we see everywhere in bookshops today, was only just beginning.[‡] To the extent that autobiographies existed, they were typically written for theological edification, historical interest, or perhaps geographical fascination rather than to explore the inner life of a person as a subject in its own right. (The difference becomes obvious when you compare Boswell's *Life of Samuel Johnson*, which is groundbreaking in its level of intimacy, verisimilitude, and personal detail, with the travelogue of James Cook that we considered in chapter 3, which is rich with information but sparse on what we would call personality.) As such, the flurry of autobiographies that appeared in the final third of the eighteenth century—including Casanova's, Gibbon's, Franklin's, and Rousseau's *Confessions*—were the advance guard of a genre that would soon become wildly popular. Inwardness was becoming interesting.

But Casanova did not just write about himself. And he did not just write about sex and seduction; this would hardly have been noteworthy in the age of *Don Giovanni* and *Les Liaisons Dangereuses*. What was unique was that he wrote about sex and seduction *as a means of explaining and defining himself*, in a breezy, unashamed, and candid fashion, with unprecedented levels of self-disclosure and honesty. He talked frankly about his sexual disappointments and diseases, his fears, frustrations, and failures. He laughed at himself—again, something very few of his contemporaries were able or willing to do in print—and acknowledged the dissonance between who he was and who he seemed. He did not see his affairs as mere conquests, or notches on the proverbial bedpost, but as deeply personal romantic entanglements that revealed the essence of who he was. "He was a libertine

---

[‡] Most autobiographies before the eighteenth century were theological or devotional in nature, from Augustine's *Confessions* and Abelard's *Historia Calamitum* to St. Teresa of Avila's *Life* and *The Book of Margery Kempe*. There are occasional exceptions to this general rule, however; see, for example, the extraordinary *Vita* of Benvenuto Cellini, a Florentine goldsmith and sculptor in the mid-sixteenth century.

on the cusp of being a romantic," writes Ian Kelly in his recent biography.[19] "What shocked, amused, inspired and aroused [his contemporaries] was the unique manner in which he suggested that an understanding of his sexual journey was vital to understanding him."[20]

In that sense, the Venetian sipping coffee on the Piazza San Marco was not just a romantic but a Romantic figure: a daring and adventurous womanizer, for sure, but also a pioneer in the realms of introspection, intimacy, and inwardness. For better or worse, he was a man whose elucidation of sexuality and self-discovery, and the relationship between the two, was decades ahead of its time.

Weimar: Storm and Stress

Five hundred miles to the north, a group of passionate young writers were clustering together in the central German town of Weimar, and it was beginning to cause problems for their most famous member.

It was partly a problem of his own making. Most of them were in town because he was. He had recently become an international celebrity with his breakthrough novel, *The Sorrows of Young Werther* (1774), and the quirky outfits that the group enjoyed wearing—yellow vests, blue coats with brass buttons, yellow breeches, brown boots, knobbly walking sticks, and gray felt hats with yellow trim—were copied from the book's main character. Several of them had followed him to Weimar because they were hoping for his support. In the previous few months, he had joined with a gang of them in a display of raucous behavior that had scandalized the small town: dressing inappropriately, climbing trees at night, cracking whips in the marketplace, swearing, drinking, firing pistols in the palace, and swimming naked in the river.[21] As long as he was a private citizen this was tolerated, if frowned upon. But when he was appointed Privy Councillor on June 11, 1776, his exuberant antics became unacceptable and some of his friends became an embarrassment. He began to distance himself from the group. By November, he had used his influence to get one of them banned from the duchy altogether.

Today, Johann Wolfgang von Goethe is widely recognized as the greatest German writer who ever lived. He would later regard his wild, intense, early stage as a youthful phase that he (like the rest of the group) left behind as he matured. But his most celebrated work, *Faust*, was already drafted by the time he reached Weimar, a product of this passionate and short-lived movement that is often identified as the dawn of Romanticism in literature. It has come to be known as *Sturm und Drang* ("Storm and Stress").[22]

Like most literary movements, the *Sturm und Drang* defies precise description. Peaking in the mid-1770s, and born in reaction to the formulaic torpor of French literature at the time, it was dramatic, original, and self-consciously German, with a preference for the theater, where words combined with gestures and immediacy was everything. It emphasized extremes: of feeling, language, genius, spontaneity, and violence. Fierce, authentic, raw emotions that led people to take action were celebrated. So were nature, friendship, and self-expression.

It divided the crowd. Goethe described the movement as a "creative whirl" in which "a throng of young geniuses burst forth with all the boldness and arrogance peculiar to their years," prompted by "a group of unbuttoned youths recklessly following their individual innate characters without any theoretical guidance."[23] Some contemporaries were more dismissive. Kaspar Riesbeck was contemptuous of "this ridiculous fashion of wanting to stand out through neglect of the common good and of the aesthetic rules, through affected wildness, fantastic situations, repulsive grimaces and wretched deformities."[24] Georg Christoph Lichtenberg found it irritating. "It is as if our tongues were confused: when we want to have a thought, they give us a word, when we ask for a word, a dash, and where we expected a dash stands an obscenity."[25]

The group was personified in many ways by Friedrich Klinger, whose play *Sturm und Drang* coined the name.[26] Klinger was not just a flamboyant, well-spoken, and sociable young man who traveled to Weimar and enjoyed dressing up in Werther costumes. He was also a talented and productive dramatist, who weaved allusions to Petrarch, Shakespeare, and Rousseau into his emotionally fraught and intense plays. In 1776 alone, he published four: *The Twin Brothers*, which won a national competition for its simple tale of jealousy and fratricide; *The Modern Arria*, featuring young lovers in Renaissance Italy; *Simsone Grisaldo*, in which a medieval knight rides through Spain and drinks lion's blood; and *Sturm und Drang* itself, set in the American Revolutionary War. The outlandish settings, rhapsodic language, and extreme characters were the whole point. When he read *Sturm und Drang* aloud, even Goethe jumped up and told him it was rubbish, and nobody would put up with it. Klinger was delighted to provoke such a reaction. "The most profoundly tragic feeling always alternates with horse-laughs," he explained.[27]

Not all of the young writers were so breezy. Jakob Lenz was a complex man: fervent, morally serious, naïve, frequently infatuated with unattainable women, and perennially in Goethe's shadow, despite being a gifted writer in his own right. The only word Goethe could think of to describe him was the English word "whimsical," and the relationship between the two men—the rich, handsome, confident genius and his talented, adoring but awkward outrider—is reminiscent of that between Tom Ripley and Dickie Greenleaf in Patricia Highsmith's *The Talented Mr. Ripley*. 1776 was the turning point for Lenz. Anxious that he would be exposed as the author of his new play *The Soldiers*, which was based on real (and potentially compromising) events, Lenz moved to join Goethe in Weimar, where he was initially accepted into his boisterous social circle. But when Goethe was appointed to the Privy Council in June, Lenz was increasingly marginalized, sometimes misreading his social standing in ways that embarrassed his friend, and eventually doing something that Goethe cryptically refers to in his diary as "Lenz's asinine behaviour."[28] Whatever it was, it proved to be the last straw. At Goethe's urging, he was forced to leave Weimar in early December.[§]

The most significant writer who came to town in 1776 was not a playwright at all. Thanks to Goethe's influence, the philosopher-theologian Johann Gottfried Herder was appointed as General Superintendent in Weimar, where he would spend the rest of his life. Herder had already played a vital role in the emergence of the *Sturm und Drang* by befriending Goethe in 1770 and introducing him to the mysterious, brilliant philosophy of Johann Georg Hamann, whom we will meet in chapter 10. It is not possible to do justice here to Herder's writings on literature, history, religion and especially language, nor to his originality (he coined the word "empathy," for example), nor to the influence he had on the *Sturm und Drang* and indeed

---

§   Tragically, on leaving Weimar, Lenz increasingly struggled with his mental health: he attempted suicide, was chained to a bed for ten days, and on one occasion was dunked in iced water by Klinger as a way of curing his obsessions. Eventually he moved to Moscow, where he died in 1792.

Romanticism in general. But this early passage shows how indebted the young men in Weimar were to their new court pastor:

> [The poet] is supposed to give voice to *feelings*. . . . Now, miserable poet! You are asked to portray your feelings on paper, to pour them out through a conduit of black liquid, to write so that others may *feel*, and you are asked to forgo the *real expression* of feeling. You must not wet your paper with tears dissolving the ink, you must put down your whole living soul in dead letters and parley instead of giving expression. . . . You must present synthetically the *natural expression* of feeling.[29]

Among the various likeminded young writers we could mention, the other one who stands out—and the only one whose poetry every reader of this chapter will have heard in the original German, whether they realize it or not—is Friedrich Schiller. Admittedly he was younger than the rest of the group and came a little later to the party. His first play was only finished in 1781, and he did not settle in Weimar until 1787. Nevertheless, his early work represents the high point of *Sturm und Drang* drama. *The Robbers* was a milestone in German theatre, with its criminal hero, sibling rivalry, and melodramatic protest against convention, and it broke box office records across the country.[30] It is a mark of Schiller's genius that it was only four years later, at the age of twenty-five, that he wrote *An die Freude* ("Ode to Joy"), which would be immortalized in the fourth movement of Beethoven's Ninth Symphony and provide the soundtrack to Romanticism ever since. And this was not the only time Schiller's writing would inspire Romantic composers. Verdi wrote operas based on four of his plays. Rossini's last and most famous opera was drawn from Schiller's *William Tell*.

Most of the *Sturm und Drang* playwrights have been forgotten outside of Germany. Few people today read or perform Klinger, Lenz, Merck, or Leisewitz. In fact, for modern English speakers, the most familiar contribution of the *Sturm und Drang* is not a play but a painting: Henry Fuseli's terrifying *The Nightmare* (1781), with its proto-Romantic nocturnal setting, haunting supernaturalism, and interest in the subconscious. Besides that, and the works of Goethe and Schiller we have already mentioned, the creative output of the group has largely faded from popular memory.

Figure 8.1   *The Nightmare*, by John Henry Fuseli. Public domain.

But Romanticism in art might never have existed without it. The urgent intensity, the ungovernable emotions resulting in action, the longing for spontaneity and authenticity, the wild gestures and defiance of convention, the cult of genius: much of what makes Romantic creativity so arresting was pioneered by a group of young Germans in the 1770s. So was the direct challenge to the Enlightenment. The *Stürmer und Dränger* were the first group of artists to stand together against the totalizing Reason™ of the *philosophes*, with their insistence on classifying, dividing, and proving everything. "Now we have got the freedom of believing in public nothing but what can be rationally demonstrated," lamented Johann Heinrich Merck. "They have deprived religion of all its sensuous elements, that is, of all its relish. They have carved it up into parts and reduced it to a skeleton without colour and light . . . and now it's put in a jar and nobody wants to taste it."[31]

They also articulated many of the core convictions of Romanticism for the first time, convictions which continue to shape artists, poets, musicians and scriptwriters to this day. In 1773, Goethe asserted that art was only genuine "if its influence arises from deep, harmonious, independent feeling, from feeling peculiar to itself."[32] The following year he encapsulated the inwardness that would become so characteristic of Romantic art: "I return into myself, and find a world!"[33] Herder, in a statement that could almost have appeared in *Frozen* or *Toy Story*, told his fiancée in 1773 that "all our actions should be self-determined, in accordance with our innermost character—we must be true to ourselves."[34] And Schiller's aesthetic philosophy would become crucial to the movement, particularly his understanding of the nature of beauty and the importance of *Spiel* ("play"): "It is only through beauty that man makes his way to freedom. . . . Man only plays when he is in the fullest sense of the word a human being, and he is only fully a human being when he plays."[35]

We probably take it for granted that great art comes from the inside out, and is a product of great imagination, emotion, and authenticity. We revel in genius and assume that those who possess it will behave in audacious, untamable ways. We expect artists to push boundaries and do things that have never been done before: inserting a choral movement into a symphony, inventing new terms, painting abstract shapes, writing a four-thousand-word sentence to close a modernist novel. The way we think about the role of the artist and the essence of art has far more in common with van Gogh than van Eyck, even if we think *The Arnolfini Portrait* is a much better painting than *The Starry Night*. And much of that goes back to the boisterous young Germans swimming naked in the river in 1776, and their circle of playwright friends.[36] The road from Amsterdam to Arles—and Los Angeles, for that matter—runs through Weimar.

London: Sex and Celebrity

Two sexual revolutions have shaped the West, one at the start of Christendom and one at the end.

Both of them took centuries. Most moral revolutions do. The ancient one began with the dawn of Christianity in the first century—the heart of it is captured in Paul's letters to the Corinthians, for example—but it did not become widespread until the fourth century, and was not dominant until the fifth or sixth.[37] The modern one, likewise, took several hundred years. It is often assumed to have started in the 1960s, with the marked change in public opinion toward extramarital sex, contraception, pornography, abortion, and homosexuality, the legal aftershock of which is still being experienced today. Some would date it slightly earlier, to Freud,

D. H. Lawrence, Margaret Mead, and the Roaring Twenties, when the term "sexual revolution" was first used.[38] But in effect, these twentieth-century movements represented the entrance into the popular mainstream of ideas and practices that a minority, beginning with elite men in Britain, had been pursuing since the eighteenth century. That, as Faramerz Dabhoiwala has shown, was when the modern sexual revolution really started.[39]

It is hard to exaggerate the scale of the change that took place during the course of a single lifetime—say, that of Voltaire (1694–1778).[40] England in the early 1690s was a strict place when it came to public sexual morality. Sex outside of marriage was illegal: around a hundred prosecutions for adultery or fornication were brought every year in London alone. Prostitutes were regularly flogged. The king wrote to every parish in the country urging them to prosecute sexual immorality more vigorously. Reformers were drafting a bill that would send fornicators to prison, put brothel keepers in the pillory, and execute adulterers.

By the late 1770s, all this was a distant memory. Prostitutes were still harassed, but arresting them was rare, unpopular, expensive, and ultimately ineffective. The rapid growth of London had made sexual discipline more difficult to enforce, and the rapid growth of the navy had led to a dramatic rise in the demand for, and hence supply of, streetwalkers, brothels, sex clubs, and bagnios (as a quick look at Boswell's diaries or Hogarth's paintings will show). The illegitimacy rate had tripled.[41] A French novel circulating in the city had introduced a new term, *le pornographe*, into the lexicon. Moralists were increasingly seen as worse than the disease they were trying to cure, and the hypocrisy of sexual policing, whereby rich people got away with behavior that poor people did not, rankled. Proving sexual immorality in court had become a legal minefield; nobody had been prosecuted for adultery in thirty years. Jeremy Bentham was even formulating arguments for the legalization of sodomy.[42]

There were a variety of reasons for this transformation. Several stem from changes we are considering elsewhere in this book: the Enlightenment (chapter 5), the decline of religious authority (chapter 6), urbanization (chapter 7), the expansion of the military (chapter 9), and encounters with cultures whose sexual mores were very different (chapter 3). We could also point to developments in contraception, specifically the "cundum." But one factor we have not considered yet—and there are further parallels here with the changes of the 1960s—is the impact of celebrity. Eighteenth-century London saw the dawn of a new mass media culture, with the rise of literacy, newspapers, periodicals, broadside ballads, novels, cheap printed portraits, and public opinion. Without this media revolution, the sexual revolution would almost certainly not have happened.[43] And at the heart of this explosion of popular culture were two things with which popular media have been obsessed ever since: celebrity and sex. Take just three examples from London in 1776.

On January 7, a French spy known in London as the Chevalier d'Éon wrote a thirty-eight-page letter to the Caron de Beaumarchais, accusing him of profiting from the knowledge that he was secretly a woman.[44] The tale is every bit as strange as it sounds. Rumors had been circulating in London for years that d'Éon—a forty-seven-year-old former diplomat and soldier who regularly dressed in a dragoon's uniform and who was known to be an excellent swordsman—was in fact female and was presenting as male to receive an inheritance. The public was captivated by the story. A betting pool on d'Éon's sex was launched on the London Stock Exchange, and it soon became difficult for him to leave the house without armed guards because so many people wanted to see him naked. On November 11, 1775, the *Morning Post* announced the latest odds and claimed that the truth would be out within a fortnight: "betts now run 7 to 4 a woman against a man, and a nobleman well known on the turf has pledged himself to bring the matter to a clear decision before the expiration of fourteen days."[45]

D'Éon suspected Beaumarchais of using his personal knowledge of the situation to make money out of it—a kind of insider trading based on sexual identity, if you will—and wrote to him to complain. Beaumarchais responded with an ultimatum, urging him to "cool down, reconsider and repent" within eight days or risk losing all contact; d'Éon renewed his accusations; and so it continued.[46] The controversy rumbled on through 1776, intensifying over the summer as scurrilous newspaper articles were published and duels were threatened, accompanied by intense public speculation about d'Éon's true identity. It would not subside until eighteen months later, when d'Éon finally returned to France and began living as a woman. He was known as Mademoiselle d'Éon for the next thirty years, until his death at the age of eighty-one—whereupon a postmortem examination proved definitively that he was in fact a man, although with certain female characteristics.[47]

The only public scandal that drew more attention from Londoners in 1776 was the trial of the Duchess of Kingston for bigamy.[48] Elizabeth Chudleigh had been secretly married in 1744 to the Earl of Bristol's grandson. The marriage was a disaster, and rather than get divorced, she had insisted that they simply deny that it had ever happened. She very nearly succeeded in covering it up. Twenty-five years later, legally deemed a spinster, she had married the Duke of Kingston and become Elizabeth Pierrepoint, Duchess of Kingston. Unfortunately for her, a combination of gossip, legal challenge, and documentary evidence eventually exposed the fact that her first marriage had indeed happened: she was both the Duchess of Kingston and, on the basis of her first husband, the Countess of Bristol. She was charged with bigamy in 1775.

The trial began on April 15, 1776. It was a sensation. "No chaos ever equalled my head at present, and I will venture to pronounce the heads of half ye people in this great town," wrote eighteen-year-old Anna Porter to a friend. "This day the Duchess of Kingston is tried for bigamy—the whole town has talked of nothing else for this week past."[49] Four thousand people crammed into Westminster Hall to watch it. It was "a sight which, for beauty and magnificence, exceeded anything which those who were never present at a coronation, or a trial by peers, can have the least notion of," declared Hannah More. "There was a great deal of ceremony, a great deal of splendour, and a great deal of nonsense."[50] The trial, full of gasps and dramatic disclosures, concluded on April 22 with the Duchess-Countess found guilty of bigamy, having successfully distracted the capital from the war in America for a full week. She promptly absconded to Calais with her fortune and reinvented herself yet again; she would soon appear at the court of Catherine the Great in St. Petersburg, sailing up the Neva in a spectacular new yacht, audaciously named the *Duchess of Kingston*.

For one more example, we can eavesdrop on the meetings that took place in the Spring of 1776 between Mai, the young Polynesian who traveled back to London with James Cook, and the Christian reformer and abolitionist Granville Sharp. Mai had met numerous wealthy Londoners during his stay, most of whom saw him as an exotic curiosity. But Sharp wanted to talk to him about Christianity. In a series of meetings in February and March, he sought to explain the Scriptures to the young Ra'iatean, and when they reached the subject of the Ten Commandments, Sharp found that adultery was an unfamiliar concept to him. His explanation prompted a fascinating response from Mai:

> This new state of the case produced a deep consideration and silence, for some time, on the part of Mr Omai. But he soon afterwards gave me ample proof that he thoroughly comprehended. . . . He took one pen and laid it on the table, saying, "There lies Lord Sandwich" (a noble with whom he was well acquainted, and in whose family he had spent some time); and then he took another pen and laid it close by the side of the former pen, saying, "and there lies Miss Ray" (who was an accomplished young woman in many respects, but unhappily for herself, she lived in a state of adultery with that nobleman); and he then took a third pen, and placing it on the table at a considerable distance from the other two pens . . . in a pensive posture, he said, "and there lie Lady Sandwich, and cry!"[51]

Lord Sandwich's affair with the opera singer Martha Ray was the worst-kept secret in London. She was twenty-five years younger than him, but they openly cohabited for years and had five children together as Lady Sandwich's health deteriorated.[§] Everybody knew about it: witness the fact that Mai, who had been in town for only a few months, could use it as a definition of adultery to a man he had met just twice. It was also a source of widespread ridicule. When Sandwich met the actor Samuel Foote, and said he was unsure whether Foote would die from syphilis or by hanging, Foote famously responded, "That will depend on one of two contingencies—whether I embrace your lordship's mistress, or your lordship's principles."[52] Yet despite the publicity of the affair, there was no suggestion that Sandwich should try to conceal the relationship, or keep a low profile, let alone resign from his position as First Lord of the Admiralty. Quite the opposite: he stayed in post for another six years, oversaw the navy during the war with America, and ended up giving his name to a transport vessel, a dozen islands, and a billion commuter lunches. In that sense, when it came to elite males, British society was arguably more tolerant of sexual infidelity in the mid-1770s than the early 1960s.[53]

---

§   The affair came to a tragic conclusion when James Hackman, a Church of England priest who became besotted with Martha Ray, murdered her in 1779 in the foyer of the Royal Opera House.

Celebrity sex scandals do not change a society overnight. Sexual habits change slowly, over many years and indeed generations, for a variety of theological, philosophical, legal, economic, and technological reasons. Most people in eighteenth-century London did not want to have sex lives like the Chevalier, the Duchess-Countess, or Lord Sandwich. "There have been always two different schemes or systems of morality current at the same time," remarked Adam Smith in March, "of which the one may be called the strict or austere; the other the liberal, or, if you will, the loose system. The former is generally admired and revered by the common people: the latter is commonly more esteemed and adopted by what are called people of fashion." When famous people behave in unchaste or immoral ways, they are "generally treated with a good deal of indulgence, and are easily either excused or pardoned altogether. In the austere system, on the contrary, those excesses are regarded with the utmost abhorrence and detestation."[54] It could be a comment about Hollywood and Middle America today.

Yet at the same time, by provoking intrigue and prurient gossip, the sex lives of celebrities do play an important role in naming and then normalizing sexual practices that would otherwise be unspeakable in public and unthinkable in private. They raise questions. They challenge taboos. They move the Overton window. They provide fuel for erotic images in pop culture, from Thomas Rowlandson to Hugh Hefner. And in societies where ordinary people know what celebrities are getting up to (and away with), they can destabilize sexual norms, with deviance gradually spreading from a tiny handful of aristocrats and libertines, to poets and artists, to elites more generally, to the educated bourgeoisie and then to society as a whole—even if that process involves several reversals and takes two hundred years.

So it feels fitting that on the other side of the street from the Duchess of Kingston's trial in 1776, learning his trade in Westminster Abbey, was an eighteen-year-old artist named William Blake. He would become Britain's greatest Romantic genius, and his poems and paintings would articulate as passionately as anybody the sexual revolution taking place in London:

> I went to the Garden of Love,
> And saw what I never had seen:
> A Chapel was built in the midst,
> Where I used to play on the green.

And the gates of this Chapel were shut,
And "Thou shalt not" writ over the door;
So I turned to the Garden of Love,
That so many sweet flowers bore.

And I saw it was filled with graves,
And tomb-stones where flowers should be:
And priests in black gowns were walking their rounds,
And binding with briars my joys and desires.[55]

Paris: Solitude, Sincerity, and Selfhood

The life of Jean-Jacques Rousseau was filled with events that ranged from the eccentric to the downright bizarre, but two of the strangest took place exactly eight months apart in 1776.

On Saturday, February 24, he entered Notre-Dame de Paris with a view to sneaking his book manuscript onto the high altar. It was marked: "A deposit committed to providence." His hope, it seems, was that God would lead the manuscript to the king of France, who would then be able to circulate the book to "a better generation" than the *philosophes* who had rejected him (as we saw in chapter 5). Rousseau had been planning the quixotic attempt for some time, having visited the cathedral on several occasions before concluding that Saturday afternoons would be the quietest time to make his move. But to his dismay, the area was closed and locked. He left crestfallen. Changing his distribution strategy, he gave the manuscript to a friend, entrusted copies of the first three sections to an English aristocrat of his acquaintance, and took to handing out pamphlets in the street. The *Dialogues* were published in 1780.[56]

Then on October 24, while working on his next (and final) book, he was walking down a narrow Parisian street when he was mowed down by a massive dog galloping at full speed: "one of those Great Danes which rich people in their vanity make run down the streets ahead of their carriages, to the misfortune of pedestrians."[57] He was seriously injured. Initially knocked unconscious, and left bleeding on the roadside by the owner of the carriage (who did not slow down), Rousseau's face was badly swollen; given the deterioration in his health from that point on, it is likely that he also suffered neurological damage, probably experiencing epileptic seizures brought on by the collision.[58] Less than two years later he was dead, his last book still unfinished. It was called *The Reveries of the Solitary Walker*.

It was a remarkable end to an extraordinary literary career. Few individuals have matched the diversity and originality of Rousseau's written output: the greatest autobiography since Augustine (*Confessions*), the most important work on education since Plato (*Emile*), a wide-ranging and provocative *Dictionary of Music*, the most influential piece of political thought of his generation (*The Social Contract*), and the eighteenth century's bestselling novel (*Julie*). But readers today might find the *Reveries* to be the most beautiful work he ever wrote. In ten essays, based on a series of walks he took around Paris from 1776 until his death in 1778, Rousseau blends observations on plant life and scenery with daydreams and remembrances, as he meditates wistfully on nature, isolation, pleasure, and tranquility.

The *Reveries* show many of the hallmarks of Romanticism we identified earlier. Inwardness, imagination, individuality, inspiration, innocence, and intensity are all here in abundance. So are other emphases that would influence Romantic writers and artists in subsequent generations: pity, solitude, enthusiasm for botany, nostalgia, and an attachment to wild and remote places. You cannot read, say, Wordsworth after reading the *Reveries* and fail to see the connection, from "I wandered lonely as a cloud" to "society has parted man from man."[59] "No other eighteenth century writer so inspired the Romantic movement," writes Robert Wokler, "through the intensity of his feelings, the rapture of his dreams, and the spontaneity of his imagination."[60]

Above all, Rousseau's *Reveries* are about himself. "Behold me, then, as if alone upon the earth, having neither brother, relative, friend, or society, but my own thoughts," he begins.** "What am I? This remains to be sought."[61] We could be forgiven for thinking that a man who had already written the *Confessions* and the *Dialogues* had said all there was to say about himself.

** Rousseau had a gift for writing opening lines. "Man is born free, and he is everywhere in chains." *The Social Contract*, trans. Henry Tozer (New York: Scribner, 1895), 100. "Everything is good as it leaves the hands of the Author of things; everything degenerates in the hands of man." *Emile*, trans. Allan Bloom (New York: Basic Books, 1979), 37. "I have resolved on an enterprise which has no precedent and which, once complete, will have no imitator. My purpose is to display to my kind a portrait in every way true to nature, and the man I shall portray will be myself." *The Confessions of Jean-Jacques Rousseau*, trans. J. M. Cohen (London: Penguin, 1953), 17. And so on.

But for Rousseau, there was plenty more where that came from. Because society had rejected him, or so he believed, he was better off alone, peering into his own soul and disclosing what he found there. The world outside had let him down, so he would look within instead.

Indeed, there may be no better statement of the "inward turn" that would characterize Romanticism, and eventually Western society in general, than this paragraph from the opening walk of the *Reveries*, written in late 1776:

> I will endeavour, henceforward, to banish from my mind all painful ideas, which unavailingly distress me. Alone for the rest of my life, I must only look for consolation, hope, or peace, *in my own breast*; and neither ought or will henceforward think of anything but *myself*. It is in this state, that I return to the continuation of that severe and just examination which I formerly called my Confessions; I consecrate my latter days to *the study of myself*; and to the preparation of that account, which I must shortly render up of my actions. I resign my thoughts entirely to *the pleasure of conversing with my own soul*. . . . I shall forget my misfortunes, disgraces and persecutors, on recollecting and contemplating *the integrity of my own heart*.[62]

This project of self-discovery went hand-in-glove with Rousseau's commitment to what he called *véracité* ("truthfulness") and *sincérité de coeur* ("sincerity of heart"). We might call it authenticity. Rousseau had long considered himself a truth teller in a world of vanity and pandering. He saw society as a corrupting influence and regarded the *philosophes* as mired in social expectations and obligations—honor, gratitude, comparison, duty, and so forth—whereas he alone was free to live authentically: "one follows one's heart and everything is done."[63] Inevitably, insisting on such radical freedom from social norms led to problems in most of his friendships, including high-profile fallouts with Diderot and Hume, which gradually pushed him into isolation. But Rousseau was unrepentant. Solitude, sincerity, and self-reflection were a package deal. He was proud to have gone further in expressing his true self than anyone ever had:

> I carried veracity and freedom as far, or I dare believe further, in [the *Confessions*] than ever man did; for feeling that the good outweighed the

evil, I was proud to divulge all; accordingly nothing was concealed. I have
never said less than the truth, I have sometimes said more, not in regard
to facts, but the feelings they produced. . . . . If we should be just to our
neighbour, we certainly should be so to ourselves; it is an homage which
every honest man should pay to his own dignity.[64]

For twenty-first century Western people, the kind of sincerity and inwardness Rousseau is talking about in these passages is almost second nature
(even if the peculiar manner in which Rousseau expressed it is not). Of
course we need to look deep within ourselves and find out who we really
are. Of course we owe it to ourselves to be true to the authentic self we find
there, in the face of social pressures and expectations to conform, since we
are essentially benevolent and authenticity is an unalloyed good. That is
the narrative of numerous movies, countless educational programs, and
the entire sexual revolution; you can almost hear *The Greatest Showman*
playing in the background. But it was virtually unheard of before Jean-
Jacques Rousseau.[65]

As such, Rousseau represents a watershed in the development of our concept of the self. As numerous sociologists have pointed out, the WEIRDER
understanding of selfhood is highly distinctive. Robert Bellah calls it
"expressive individualism": the idea that at the heart of each person is a
unique emotional core that needs to find expression for our individuality
to be realized.[66] Philip Rieff talks about the "triumph of the therapeutic"
in Western culture, in which the fulfilment of the inner self is paramount:
"an infinity of created needs can now be satisfied," and if that fails, the
psychological-industrial complex can pick up the pieces.[67] Charles Taylor
describes it as the "age of authenticity," which he defines as "the understanding of life which emerges with the Romantic expressivism of the late
eighteenth century, that each of us has his/her own way of realising our
humanity, and that it is important to find and live out one's own."[68] Plenty
of WEIRDER people will read such descriptions and wonder how else
selfhood and identity could possibly be construed. To which Bellah, Rieff,
and Taylor would presumably respond: exactly.

Needless to say, Rousseau did not bring about this transformation on
his own. His ideas did not appear out of nowhere but reflected the age
of sentiment and sensibility in which he lived; they were refracted and

expanded through the Romantic movement, especially its poets; they were later mixed with the ideas of Marx, Nietzsche, Darwin, and Freud to make a cocktail that WEIRDER people, especially in the second half of the twentieth century, would find intoxicating; and their aura of plausibility was substantially enhanced by industrialization, which made it increasingly conceivable that the external world could be adapted to suit the demands of the inner self.[69] Nor could Rousseau have foreseen the directions in which his account of authenticity, selfhood, and identity would be taken. If a man had told Rousseau that he felt his authentic inner self was female even though his body was male, Rousseau would likely have been just as incredulous as the next person.

Nevertheless, the fact that people do say things like that—and the fact that disagreeing with them is viewed as hate speech or even violence in some quarters, since it strikes at the heart of who they are—owes a good deal to the view of the self, and the need to be true to it, that Rousseau was articulating in the *Reveries* in 1776. The inner self, unlike the outer world, is fundamentally good: "If I had remained free, obscure and alone, placed in the situation Nature designed me for, I would have done nothing but what was right, for my heart bears not the seeds of any mischievous passion."[70] Only by following it wherever it leads can a person find contentment. "I learned by my own experience that the source of true happiness is in ourselves."[71]

The Goldfinch

One of the finest expressions of Romanticism today is Donna Tartt's prize-winning novel *The Goldfinch*. Published in 2013 to critical acclaim and commercial success, it is a classic *Bildungsroman* in which a teenage boy, grief-stricken by the death of his mother, follows his emotions into a series of increasingly unwise decisions, complex relationships, and the criminal underworld. At the same time, it is the tale of a piece of art: a small Dutch painting of a chained goldfinch, the theft and concealment of which drive much of the plot.

The book is full of quintessentially Romantic themes: childhood innocence, pity, the sublime, unrequited love, introspection, solitude, intense emotions, drug addiction, and self-discovery. The characters remind you of the people in Dickens or Victor Hugo. The descriptions of paintings and antiques, in which one work of art examines another, sound like Keats on the *Grecian Urn* or Shelley on Leonardo's Medusa. And the novel also raises some profoundly Romantic questions. Do aesthetics trump ethics? Does our attachment to beauty necessarily ennoble us, or might it lead us into moral squalor? Is our enjoyment of art essentially about self-discovery, and if so, is that a problem? Will reaching for perfection, or trying to hold onto it, make us miserable?

The richest questions come in the novel's final few pages. These are the ones that most clearly show the influence of the things people were saying and doing in Venice, Weimar, London, and Paris in 1776: the inwardness, the solitude and self-discovery, the art and emotion, the storm and stress. "I watch the clouds reflected on sliding panes and marvel how even my sadness can make me happy," explains Theo, our protagonist. "I've been thinking a lot about what Hobie said: about those images that strike the heart and set it blooming like a flower, images that open up some much, much larger beauty that you can spend your whole life looking for and never find. And it's been good for me, my time alone on the road. A year is how long it's taken me to quietly wander round on my own."[72] You could be reading Rousseau or Wordsworth.

Yet in the midst of this introspective monologue comes the most direct challenge to WEIRDER morality that I have seen in contemporary literature:

From William Blake to Lady Gaga, from Rousseau to Rumi to *Tosca* to Mister Rogers, it's a curiously uniform message, accepted from high to low: when in doubt, what to do? How do we know what's right for us? Every shrink, every career counsellor, every Disney princess knows the answer: "Be yourself." "Follow your heart."

Only here's what I really, really want someone to explain to me. *What if one happens to be possessed of a heart that can't be trusted?* What if the heart, for its own unfathomable reasons, leads one wilfully and in a cloud of unspeakable radiance away from health, domesticity, civic responsibility and strong social connections and all the blandly-held common virtues and instead straight towards a beautiful flare of ruin, self-immolation, disaster? Is Kitsey right? If your deepest self is singing and coaxing you straight toward the bonfire, is it better to turn away?[73]

9

Profits

Becoming Rich

*He intends only his own gain, and he is in this, as in
many other cases, led by an invisible hand to promote
an end which was no part of his intention.*
ADAM SMITH

*He that is of the opinion that money will do everything
may well be suspected of doing everything for money.*
BENJAMIN FRANKLIN

A THOUSAND YEARS FROM NOW, the most significant legacy of the late
eighteenth century will not be Cook's voyages to the South Seas, or the
Industrial Revolution (which will presumably no longer be called that),
or the European Enlightenment (which will definitely no longer be called
that). It will not be Kant's *Critiques* or Mozart's *Requiem*. Nor will it be the
French Revolution, the most tangible heritage of which will be the metric
system, or even the Declaration of Independence, whose date, location, and
text will be just as fuzzy in the minds of most people on earth as those of
the Magna Carta are today. From the standpoint of the early fourth millennium, the most significant impact of the late eighteenth century on world

history will surely be the transformation in health, wealth, and prosperity that it launched. Economic historians call it "the great escape," "the great divergence," "the great enrichment," or "the European miracle."[1] The rest of us know it as normal life.

It is anything but normal. For the previous thousand years, the living standards of the average human had hardly changed. History had consisted of small, incremental improvements in productivity and wealth, which were quickly swallowed up by a rise in population. A new crop, tool, or technique was introduced; productivity went up, causing a brief increase in standards of living; people took advantage by having more children, or by nurturing more of them through to adulthood; so average living standards went back down again.

It seems unfathomable to us, who take economic growth for granted, but gross domestic product per person when Shakespeare wrote his plays, estimated at roughly $550 per year, was barely higher than it was in the age of King David. Global productivity had increased tenfold between 1000 BC and AD 1600, but so had the population—so living standards had hardly changed in two and a half thousand years. (Some economists argue that living standards for the bulk of humanity were actually *lower* in early modern Europe than they were in the Stone Age, but we will leave that for now.)[2] This economic loop, known as the "Malthusian trap," was first described by the British economist Thomas Malthus in 1798—ironically, as it turned out, just as people were beginning to escape it for the first time.

The late eighteenth century saw the start of something completely new. Living standards began to increase dramatically, first in northwestern Europe and then across the world, as productivity outstripped population growth by an order of magnitude. Today, human beings consume around *seventy times* more goods and services than we did two centuries ago—an increase not of 70 percent but of 7,000 percent—while world population has only increased by a factor of seven. That means that the average person today, in very rough terms, has a standard of living around ten times higher than in 1776. If the Pilgrim Fathers lived on $2 a day in today's terms, and the average person in the eighteenth century lived on $3 a day, the average person now lives on more like $30. In richer countries, it is closer to $100.[3]

The result of this economic explosion is not only that you are much richer than you would have been in the eighteenth century, or at any time before that. You are also much taller, healthier, safer, and more comfortable; you are far less likely to lose a child, lose a limb, or die in great pain; and you are far more likely to be able to read, go to school, go to university, travel the world, and live to see your grandchildren. This represents the greatest transformation in human economic and physical well-being since the origin of farming, if not ever.

We could amass literally hundreds of charts and tables to show this transformation visually. Some scholars have.[4] But for now, consider just three graphs that make the point especially clearly. The first shows income per person, which bounces along under the Malthusian ceiling for thousands of years before suddenly turning a corner in the 1770s and shooting upward:

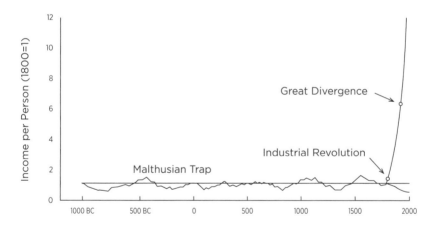

Figure 9.1   Income per person over time. (Adapted from Clark, *Farewell to Alms*, 2.)

The second shows the dramatic change in global life expectancy. Although the flat line is obviously an estimate, there is a general consensus that global life expectancy at birth was between twenty-five and thirty until the nineteenth century; it is now more than seventy. The result is a graph that looks even more like a hockey stick than the previous one:

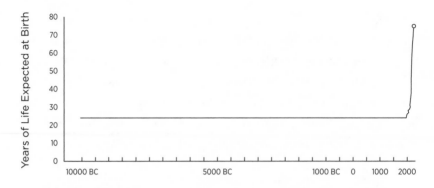

Figure 9.2   Life expectancy over time. (Adapted from Cato Institute, Our
World in Data, cited in Jeff Desjardins, "Animation: The World's Rapid Rise in
Life Expectancy, in Just 13 Seconds," Visual Capitalist [website], May 11, 2020,
https://www.visualcapitalist.com/.)

The third graph needs a bit more explanation. It portrays what Ian Morris
calls a "social development index," which is a way of quantifying a community's ability to get things done by mastering its physical and intellectual
environment.[5] It is made up of four metrics that reflect a society's level
of sophistication. The first is energy capture: the number of kilocalories
consumed as food or fuel every day (ranging from 4,000 kcal per person
in the Stone Age to 228,000 kcal per person in modern America). The
second is organizational capacity, derived from the size of the largest city
at the time. The third is information technology, which is a combination of
literacy levels and the speed and reach of communication technologies. The
fourth, lamentably but realistically, is the capacity to make war. These four
metrics, Morris argues, give us a reasonable proxy for the sophistication of
a society, and enable us to compare social development across time (from
14,000 BC onward) and space (contrasting Eastern and Western Eurasia).

The result, unsurprisingly, is yet another hockey stick that skyrockets
from the 1770s onward. The precise year in which the West overtakes the
East, according to Morris's model, is 1773.

No matter what we measure—income, life expectancy, energy capture,
social organization, information technology, military capacity, social development, or various other things—we keep seeing the same picture. Roughly
three quarters of the way through the eighteenth century, prosperity punched
through the Malthusian ceiling, and has not stopped rising since.

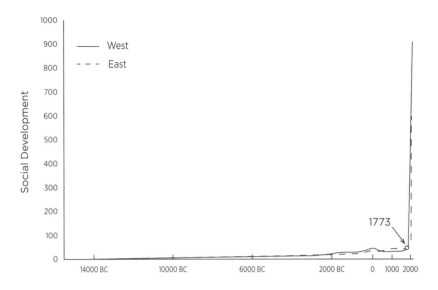

Figure 9.3   Social development in the East and the West over time. (Adapted from Morris, *Why the West Rules*, 161.)

We could obviously issue all sorts of caveats about that. Growth has not been evenly distributed. Some people and nations have got even poorer, widening global inequalities to egregious levels. Unbridled economic expansion presents all sorts of challenges in our relationship with the natural world. Being richer is not the same as being happier, let alone more virtuous. Rising wealth does not do much for the poorest people if it is accompanied by rising violence. And so forth.

Still, the fact remains that somewhere around the 1770s, people started to escape from the Malthusian trap for the first time in humanity's long history. Beginning in northwestern Europe, economic growth began outpacing population growth, and people found themselves getting richer than their parents. The obvious question is: Why?

A tempting response is simply to say: the Industrial Revolution happened. But this is inadequate for at least three reasons. First, there had been periods of major technological breakthrough before—in Song China, for example—but they had never become self-sustaining feedback loops of innovation and economic growth. Second, industrial technology has now been disseminated throughout the world, but its economic impacts have varied dramatically from place to place: some groups are fifty times richer than they were in the eighteenth century, and others are just as poor (and in some cases poorer). So whether or not industrial technology is a necessary condition for dramatic enrichment, it is clearly not a sufficient one. Third, we still need to explain why the breakthrough happened in eighteenth-century Europe in the first place—not just the decades-long "shallow" causes that triggered it in Britain as opposed to France or the Netherlands, which we considered in chapter 7, but the centuries-long "deep" causes that meant it happened in northwestern Europe as opposed to India, Japan, Persia, China, or nowhere at all. That will be our task in this chapter.

We are in distinguished company. That question—effectively, what makes some nations richer than others—has been asked by many of our greatest thinkers over the last two and a half centuries. As it happens, one of the first attempts to answer it, and the most influential by some distance, was published on March 9, 1776.

The Wealth of Nations

In 1726, a three-year-old boy from Kirkcaldy in Scotland was temporarily abducted by a group of vagrant tinkers. Fortunately, he was taken only a few miles. The boy was crying so hard that he was noticed by a passing gentle-man, who later found the boy's mother and explained that he had seen her son howling in the arms of a gypsy woman. A search party was assembled, and they soon found the woman in some nearby woods—whereupon she immediately dropped the boy and disappeared into the forest. Before long, the young Adam Smith was back in the arms of his mother. It is just as well, remarked his biographer John Rae. "He would have made, I fear, a poor gipsy."[6]

Questions remain as to whether Smith was really abducted. Perhaps he simply wandered off and got lost, as three-year olds sometimes do. It would be very much in character for someone whose absentmindedness would become proverbial in later life: signing an official document by copying the signature of the person before him, falling into a tanning pit while holding forth on the division of labor, putting bread and butter into boiling water and complaining about the quality of the resulting tea, and the like.[7] So the explanation for his disappearance may never be known. What we do know is that exactly fifty years later, this forgetful, eccentric philosopher, described by Samuel Johnson as "a most disagreeable fellow" who was "as dull a dog as he had ever met with," published the most influential of all the books that appeared in 1776, practically inventing modern economics in the process.[8] It was called *An Inquiry into the Nature and Causes of the Wealth of Nations.*

The full title is significant. Most people today, if they know the book at all, think of it as a book about the "causes" of wealth: free trade, abolishing monopolies, the "invisible hand" of the market, the division of labor, and the importance of self-interest in generating economic growth. But Smith was also trying to explain its "nature": what national wealth actually *was.* And the answer is not as simple as it looks. How exactly do you define the wealth of a country?

The dominant view in France was what Smith called the "agricultural system": national wealth consists in what is produced by the land, or as Frederick the Great put it, "the only true form of wealth is that produced by the soil."[9] The main alternative was the "mercantile system": national wealth is a matter of how much gold and silver you have, so the way to maximize national wealth is to maintain a positive balance of trade (by selling more than you buy), and to establish profitable colonies.[10] Smith rejected both.[11] The nature of wealth is far different, as he explained in a landmark paragraph:

> But *the annual revenue of every society is always precisely equal to the exchangeable value of the whole annual produce of its industry*, or rather is precisely the same thing with that exchangeable value. As every individual, therefore, endeavours as much as he can both to employ his capital in the support of domestic industry, and so to direct that industry that its produce may be of the greatest value; every individual necessarily labours to render the annual revenue of the society as great as he can. He generally, indeed, neither intends to promote the public interest, nor knows how much he is promoting it. By preferring the support of domestic to that of foreign industry, he intends only his own security; and by directing that industry in such a manner as its produce may be of the greatest value, *he intends only his own gain, and he is in this, as in many other cases, led by an invisible hand to promote an end which was no part of his intention.*[12]

National wealth, in other words, is not ultimately based on land, or money, but the productivity of labor. Wealth is "equal to the exchangeable value of the whole annual produce of its industry": what today we would call its "gross domestic product." And if that is the case, then the best ways to maximize it—the "causes" of the wealth of nations, if you like—have nothing to do with trade surpluses, bullion hoarding, or extractive colonialism. Wealth grows as both capital and labor are freed to be as productive as possible, in competition with others, motivated by their own self-interest, and with prices set by the market. "Every man, as long as he does not violate the laws of justice, is left perfectly free to pursue his own interest his own way, and to bring both his industry and capital into competition with those of any other man, or order of men."[13] The only criterion for success is how well the interests of the consumer have been served by the product: "Consumption is the sole end and purpose of all production; and the interest of the producer ought to be attended to only so far as it may be necessary for promoting that of the consumer."[14] The customer, you might say, is always right.

All of this is illuminating, convincing, and ahead of its time in various ways. But it does not really answer our question about the causes of the wealth of different nations. It does not explain why the people of northwestern Europe were about to get a lot richer (a phenomenon that Smith did not anticipate), nor indeed how rapid economic growth through innovation was even possible. After all, when northwestern Europeans found their wealth beginning to increase in the late eighteenth century, in contrast to the economies of China, India, Japan, Persia, and the Ottoman empire, it was not because Europeans were practicing open competition and free trade. The whole point of Smith's argument, especially in book 4 of *The Wealth of Nations*, is that they weren't. The reasons for the great enrichment, then, must lie elsewhere.

Scholars have proposed dozens of different explanations for it. At the risk of oversimplifying a very complex discussion, we can roughly allocate these explanations into four groups.[15] Some are essentially *institutional* (legal and constitutional framework, parliamentary government, patent law, taxation, property rights, religious toleration, trade policy). Some are *socioeconomic* and can be traced back to the combined effects of the Black Death (population size, wage levels, urbanization, downward mobility, cheap capital), and particularly the discovery of the New World (colonialism, resource extraction, slavery, luxury imports, global trade pressures, warmongering, the rise of consumerism). Some are *ideological and cultural* (Christianity, Protestantism, literacy, religious dissent, industriousness, scientific culture, empirical tradition, curiosity). And some are *geographical* (navigable rivers, shallow coal deposits, wood shortages, indented coastlines, abundance of minerals, soil quality, distance from the Eurasian steppe, proximity to the New World). Many interpreters opt for a combination of these.

All four of these broad approaches to explaining the "great enrichment"—institutions, socioeconomics, culture, and geography—have some truth to them, even if some are more foundational than others (as we shall see). And all four of them go back, in principle if not in detail, to people who were working and writing in 1776, before anyone knew the great enrichment had even started.

Explanation 1: Institutions

Adam Smith believed that some nations were richer than others because they had better institutions. China, for example, has always been "one of the most fertile, best cultivated, most industrious, and most populous countries in the world." But in economic terms, he says, it has been "stationary" since the visit of Marco Polo five hundred years ago. This is not because the Chinese people are lazy or ignorant. It is because China has "acquired that full complement of riches which *the nature of its laws and institutions* permits it to acquire."[16]

If property is not secure, Smith argues, and if the rich can plunder the poor, and if "the law does not enforce the performance of contracts," then people will keep their wealth safely hidden away rather than investing it for future growth, because they are worried they will lose it. "This is said to be a common practice in Turkey, in Indostan, and, I believe, in most other governments of Asia."[17] In Britain, by contrast, the legal and political environment encourages investment and trade. "The English legislature has been peculiarly attentive to the interests of commerce and manufactures. . . . Commerce and manufacturing have accordingly been continually advancing during all this period."[18] Good institutions encourage the wealth of nations to grow; bad institutions stunt it. And nothing illustrates that more clearly than Britain's own colonies. America is protected by "the genius of the British constitution," and is therefore rich. Bengal is not, which exposes her to the ruthless predations of the East India Company. She is therefore poor.[19]

 ⟋   We will come back to British India in a moment. A more popular case study today, which features in two recent bestsellers on this subject and appears to support Smith's case for the power of institutions, is the contrast between Spanish-speaking and English-speaking America.

Daron Acemoglu and James Robinson begin their book *Why Nations Fail* in the city of Nogales, on the border between the US and Mexico.[20] It is cut in half by a fence. Half of the city is in Arizona, where household income is around $30,000 a year. The other half is in Sonora, where it is a third of that. Genetically, geographically, culturally, and even linguistically, the two halves of the city are virtually identical. The crucial difference, they argue, lies in the economic and political institutions that exist on both sides of the border, which provide very different incentives for the individuals and businesses based there. For historical reasons stretching back to the Pilgrim Fathers and the *conquistadores*, Arizona has more incentives and fewer barriers to innovate, start a business, invest money, follow the law, get a good education and adopt new technologies than Sonora. So the levels of prosperity on either side of the fence are widely different. Inequality exists because of institutions.

Niall Ferguson makes a similar point in *Civilization*. The European conquest of the Americas represents one of the great natural experiments in history: impose British rule on North America, and Spanish and Portuguese rule in South America, and see which one does better economically.[21] The results are obvious. And this is not because the land in the north is more fertile or bountiful than the south. Quite the opposite, in fact: the early British colonies in the north faced continual risk of starvation, while the Spanish to the south were planting tropical gardens and mining mountains of silver. The key difference, Ferguson argues, was institutional. The north had enumerated property rights, representative government, religious pluralism, and the rule of law. The south had none of these things; each of them had been opposed by Simón Bolívar, *El Libertador* himself.[22] North and South America have been on different political and economic trajectories ever since. And we could say similar things about North and South Korea, East and West Germany, Botswana and Zimbabwe, and others.

In the same way, the argument runs, it is institutions—particularly those that resulted from the Glorious Revolution in England (1688), and later the revolutions in America and France—that explain the rapid growth in prosperity of those countries. That was essentially Adam Smith's view, and plenty of economic historians agree with him.[23] Institutions created incentives, which generated investments and then innovations, which facilitated industrialization, which brought enrichment.

Clearly this institutional explanation of the wealth of nations is at least partially right. Few would deny that bad institutions can limit growth through poor incentives, extractive practices, and corruption. But as a historical explanation for the great enrichment, or the divergence between the West and the Rest that was getting underway in 1776, it is limited in a couple of ways.

One is that it does not explain enough. Institutions do not spring up out of nowhere; they are the products of long-term social, cultural, theological, legal, and economic developments. What needs explaining is *why* the institutions that emerged in northwestern Europe were so different from those in the Ottoman, Zand, Mughal, or Qing empires (if indeed they were).[24] This involves asking deeper historical questions about causality.

It is also inadequate at a historical level. Adam Smith's view that China had been "stationary" for five hundred years is obviously incorrect, however widely held it was in Europe at the time. So is the view we encountered in chapter 5, that Eastern empires were stagnant under Oriental despotism. But the contemporary version, in which the West pulls ahead of the East as a result of its superior institutions following the Glorious Revolution, is overstated as well. In the decades after 1688, Britain was so riddled with bribery, sinecures, scandals, rigged elections, sale of offices, and abuses of power that when William Cobbett called it "Old Corruption," the label stuck. In fact, the Glorious Revolution may even have made corruption worse, by giving absolute power to an unrepresentative Parliament. And much of the institutional and legal framework needed to incentivize economic growth had been present since the thirteenth century. As Gregory Clark mischievously points out, if the International Monetary Fund and the World Bank had carried out a series of assessments on Britain over the last millennium, her economic incentives (security of property and person, low tax rates and public debt, free markets for goods, labor, capital, and land) would have ranked higher in the medieval period than they would today.[25]

China, by contrast, compared favorably with Europe in the eighteenth century on a whole host of institutional metrics. It had relatively secure property rights, few if any monopolies, high personal mobility, even commodity prices, low and uniform tax rates, good transport connections, low tariffs, relatively efficient markets, and widely enforced commercial contracts.[26] Admittedly, China faced corruption problems of her own, and of course it was not democratic. But then again, neither was Britain—and it is far from clear that democracy causes prosperity anyway.

Bad institutions inhibit growth. There is little doubt about that. But there is a great deal of doubt about whether good institutions are enough to generate it, and whether European institutions in general (and Britain's in particular) were as "good" as all that in the first place. So for many interpreters, Adam Smith's explanation is inadequately self-critical at best, inaccurately self-serving at worst.

Maybe the great enrichment was more a result of Western vice than Western virtue. Maybe it did not stem from WEIRD institutions but from nothing more than old-fashioned GREED: Guns, Resource Extraction, Enslavement, and Death.

Explanation 2: GREED

Dozens of Indian words have entered the English language. Most of them, as you might expect, were adopted because they identified things British people had not encountered outside of India: foods (*curry, chutney, tiffin, kedgeree*), geographical features (*atoll, jungle, teak*), or religious terms (*mantra, guru, karma, avatar, nirvana*).

The largest group of words relates to clothing and fabrics: *bandana, calico, cashmere, chintz, cummerbund, dungarees, jodhpurs, khaki, pashmina, pyjamas, sari, shawl*. That tells us a lot about how strong the Indian textile industry was in the seventeenth and eighteenth centuries, just as the word *mogul* gives us a sense of how wealthy the Mughal emperors became as a result.[27] But despite that strength, and that wealth, and despite the centrality of textiles to the Industrial Revolution, the great enrichment did not begin in India. And one of the reasons for that is hinted at by another Hindustani word that entered the English language: *loot*.

It is a story that can be told very briefly or at great length. The short version is that Europeans stumbled across the New World, subjugated it quickly through a combination of disease and weaponry, and then plundered it for gold and silver, which enabled them to strengthen their military capacity; forcibly take control of the trade in lucrative Asian products like spices, textiles, and tea; establish slave plantations in the Americas to grow sugar, indigo, and tobacco; and eventually connect the whole world through a commercial web in which they were the spider.

The long version has been told many times, but its definitive first draft was compiled by the abbé Raynal in his *Histoire des Deux Indes*, which was first translated into English (and, as it happens, banned by the Spanish Inquisition) in 1776.[28] Over the course of about a million words, it narrated the history of European colonization in unflinching detail, beginning in the East Indies with the Portuguese (book 1), Dutch (book 2), English (book 3), French (book 4), and other European powers (book 5), before moving to the conquest of the Americas under the Spanish (books 6–8) and Portuguese (book 9), then the slave trade and the colonization of the Caribbean (books 10–14), and finally the British and French settlements in North America (books 15–18). It does not pull its punches. The greed of the Europeans and the horrors visited upon the native peoples are vividly described, from the massacres of men, women, and children in Mexico and Peru to the barbarities of the slave trade and the devastations of the Bengal famine. You can get a sense of it from the conclusion:

> We have travelled, and continue to travel, to all climates and from one pole to the other, in search of continents to invade, islands to ravage, peoples to plunder, to subdue, to massacre. . . . This insatiable thirst for gold gave birth to the most insane and atrocious of trades: that of slaves. We are talking about crimes against nature. . . . I am speaking to the cruellest of Europeans, and I say to him: there are regions that will furnish you with rich metals, nice clothes, and delicious meals. But read this history, and consider the price of the discovery you have been promised.[29]

Notice that the *Histoire* presents this as a European problem rather than something limited to a particular nation. Quite so. The savagery of the Spanish under Cortés and Pizarro had been well documented since Bartolomé de las Casas published *A Short Account of the Destruction of the Indies* in 1552. The Portuguese began the Atlantic slave trade, and were responsible for nearly half of it, shipping around six million people to work their sugar plantations in Brazil. The Dutch were guilty of brutality verging on ethnic cleansing in the Spice Islands, killing or removing the Bandanese and replacing them with slaves and settlers to grow nutmeg, and forcibly establishing monopolies on pepper, cinnamon, cloves, and even elephants; Jan Pieterszoon Coen infamously told the directors of the United East India Company that "we cannot make war without trade, or trade without war."[30] Britain developed the diabolical triangular trade in the Atlantic, subsequently adopted by the Danish and others, whereby guns and manufactures went from England to West Africa, slaves went from West Africa to the Americas, and cash crops went from the Americas back to England. (Britain could also lay claim to the worst man in the world, in the form of slaver and Jamaican landowner Thomas Thistlewood.)* And in Saint Domingue, France had the most lucrative Caribbean slave colony of all, governed under arguably the cruelest regime in the Americas.†

Despite the universality of European GREED, much of the anger was focused on Britain in the 1770s. Particular ire was reserved for the East India Company, whose ruthlessness and greed during the Bengal famine of 1770 had made a bad situation immeasurably worse. Approximately 1.2 million Bengalis had starved to death, while Company executives expropriated up to £100 million in today's terms; a report to the Company directors in 1771 made the chilling remark that "notwithstanding

---

* Thistlewood's tortures are almost unprintable in their gruesomeness, but a measure of the man is provided by the fact that he meticulously recorded them all in his diary, as well as detailing 3,852 occurrences of sexual intercourse with (which effectively meant "rape of") 138 Jamaican women. In a grim irony, Thistlewood was also the person who introduced cricket in the West Indies, in June 1778. See Trevor Burnard, *Mastery, Tyranny, and Desire: Thomas Thistlewood and His Slaves in the Anglo-Jamaican World* (Chapel Hill: University of North Carolina Press, 2004).

† In an interesting twist, Raynal's *Histoire* was partly responsible for Saint Domingue eventually casting off French rule. Toussaint Louverture read the *Histoire* enthusiastically after his manumission in 1776, and the book inspired him to lead what remains the only successful slave revolt in history. And he achieved this despite the best efforts of another avid reader of Raynal, who was busy trying to reintroduce slavery and take over the known world. His name was Napoleon Bonaparte.

the great severity of the late famine, and the great reduction of people thereby, some increase [in revenue] has been made."[31] The horrific news soon spread. "In order to earn a few million rupees for the Company," thundered the *Histoire*, "it coldly devoted millions of people to death, and the cruelest death at that."[32]

It is undeniable that expropriation made India, and many other subjugated nations, poorer. The more complicated question is whether or not it actually made Europe richer. It clearly made a number of individuals extremely wealthy, from Cortés and Coen to Colston and Clive. But did European GREED—Guns, Resource Extraction, Enslavement, and Death—really generate more wealth overall for the European nations in question?

Many of its critics at the time, including Smith, Raynal, and Diderot, argued that it did not. The military resources it required were a huge drain on the national budget, and the fruits of colonial economics were mixed at best, as the implosion of the Spanish, Portuguese, and Dutch empires showed. The British were doing better, but this was in spite of GREED rather than because of it: monopolies and slavery are economically counterproductive in the end because they do not incentivize trade, innovation, or increases in productivity. Therefore, the argument runs, colonial expropriation did not really make European nations wealthier—let alone by a factor of seventy.

Looked at another way, however, the connection between GREED and enrichment is harder to avoid. Imagine you are having breakfast in your pajamas. You have a cup of tea or coffee; you have a bowl of cereal, or perhaps toast with jam; you serve it on porcelain crockery; perhaps you smoke afterward. Your experience is entirely made up of items—tea, coffee, sugar, china, tobacco—that changed in the course of the eighteenth century from exotic foreign luxuries, to aspirational consumables, to everyday necessities.[33] You are unintentionally embodying the great enrichment. And you are doing this while wearing the original global consumer commodity, the first to be produced industrially, and the one without which the industrial world might not even exist: cotton.

Luxury goods are an important part of this story. European demand for them served to encourage both trade abroad and diligence at home, as families worked longer hours to afford them (the so-called industrious revolution).[34] And wages in early modern Europe were already higher than in other parts of the world, for reasons stretching back to the Black Death.[‡] With high wages, hard work, and global trade in consumable commodities, you have the major building blocks of a consumer culture. Each of them was fueled by GREED, and all of them are reflected in what you had for breakfast this morning.

But the game changer was cotton. As we saw in chapter 7, cotton was integral to the development of factories, the transformation of productivity, the prosperity of Manchester and Liverpool in the late eighteenth and nineteenth centuries, and the industrialization of Britain. By 1830, the industry employed one in six British workers and was responsible for over a fifth of the British economy, with productivity having risen by an astounding 37,000 percent in just three decades.[35] Naturally, this explosive growth proved a blessing to some. Cotton accounted for over half of all US exports between the presidencies of James Madison and Abraham Lincoln, to meet skyrocketing demand from the mills of Lancashire.[36] But it was a curse to others. In the Bengali district of Dhaka, to take one example, eighty thousand spinners and twenty-five thousand weavers had been employed in 1776—but prices collapsed in the face of British competition, forcing many to migrate or even starve.[37] A century of Indian deindustrialization followed.

This may sound like nothing more than the invisible hand of Adam Smith's market, rewarding labor-saving machinery with lower costs, higher volumes, and larger sales, and driving weaker competitors out of business. But there was nothing invisible about it. Plenty of technological innovation was taking place in the cotton industry, as we have seen. Yet it would have been impossible and/or irrelevant without the fruits of GREED: industrial espionage in India, protectionist legislation in Europe, expropriated American land, and forced African labor. To that extent, the "lords of the loom" depended on the "lords of the lash." Cotton production needed colonial plantations and coerced peoples, and no amount of jennies, mules, and gins would have been any use without them.

[‡] If a third of the population dies, as happened in Europe in the late 1340s, the people who survive can become much more valuable. This drives up wages, empowers the peasantry, destabilizes feudalism, and incentivizes agricultural improvements. For the question of why the Black Death did not have the same effect in Eastern Europe, see Acemoglu and Robinson, *Why Nations Fail*, 96–101.

So did European GREED cause "the great escape"? Yes and no. Yes, in that industrialization, globalization, enrichment, and divergence would not have happened in the way that they did without it (if indeed they had happened at all). Much as we might want to, we cannot disentangle the story of modern economic growth from the guns, resource extraction, enslavement, and death that made much of it possible. But also no, in that even if these things were necessary for the great enrichment—and there is plenty of debate about that—they were clearly not sufficient for it. Early modern Europeans were not, alas, the first people in history to subdue other nations with superior weaponry, expropriate their resources, enslave or kill their peoples, and leverage these things for economic gain. They weren't even the only people doing this in the eighteenth and nineteenth centuries. So if we are looking to explain the great enrichment, as opposed to merely describing it, we need to go deeper. We need to enter the realm of ideas, beliefs, and culture.

Explanation 3: Culture

It seems to me that of all the characters in the eighteenth century, the one who would feel the most at home in today's world is the man on the one hundred dollar bill. It might be his pragmatism, his sense of humor, his cosmopolitanism, or something else entirely, but there is something strikingly modern about Benjamin Franklin.

Granted, his abilities were somewhat freakish. Printer, self-help author, philosopher, entrepreneur, inventor, scientist, diplomat: you could count on one hand the number of people in history whose career has taken so many turns with such impressive impact. We still use his inventions (lightning rods, bifocal glasses); we still treasure his financial advice ("money makes money, and the money that money makes, makes money"); we still laugh at his witticisms ("nothing can be certain but death and taxes"); we still quote his one-liners on politics ("a republic, if you can keep it"), gossip ("three may keep a secret if two of them are dead"), perseverance ("no gains without pains"), hospitality ("fish and guests stink after three days"), and diligence ("early to bed, early to rise, makes a man healthy, wealthy, and wise"). But as a person, when set alongside his contemporaries, Franklin seems incongruously normal. His lifestyle and outlook—diligent, frugal, prosperous, can-do, upwardly mobile, democratic, optimistic, Protestant-lite—are those of bourgeois middle America today. Some of his letters would almost work as emails. It is as if he was accidentally allocated to the wrong century.

I mention this because for many interpreters, the cultural traits that make Ben Franklin seem so familiar to us—curiosity, innovation, experimentation, self-improvement, a commitment to discovering and disseminating useful knowledge—provide the best explanation of the great divergence. Modern economic historians talk about the "culture of growth" that developed in early modern Europe and North America, or the "bourgeois values" that took root.[38] They point to the number of individuals who (like Franklin) were coming up with new ideas, fiddling with things to make them work better, starting new companies, testing products on the open market, researching new areas, sharing their findings, criticizing and learning from one other, and trying to work out how to solve problems and make money. In this account, enrichment was not primarily the result of institutions, or of GREED. It was a matter of ideas, of habits, of *culture*.

At the time, Franklin's contemporaries had no concept of the great enrichment, but many of them were aware of the increasing divergence between East and West. And they saw the explanation for it in essentially cultural terms. Here is how Diderot described it in the *Encyclopédie*:

> In a word, [the Chinese] do not have the genius of invention and discovery that shines today in Europe. . . . In general the spirit of the East is quieter, lazier, more withdrawn into their essential needs, more limited to what is already common knowledge, and less eager for novelties than the spirit of the West. In China in particular, this makes customs more constant, government more consistent and laws more lasting; but the sciences and the arts require more restless activity, a curiosity that never stops searching, a sort of inability to be satisfied. We are more suited to that, so it is not surprising that although the Chinese are the most ancient society, we are ahead of them so far.[39]

Plenty of this is indefensible, Orientalist bunk. Particularly absurd is the claim that the Chinese were lazier than Europeans, which was not true then and likely never has been.[40] On the other hand, as we saw in chapter 3, there are good reasons to think that early modern Europeans were indeed "eager for novelties" and filled with a "curiosity that never stops searching" to an extent that their counterparts in China were not. To sharpen the point: Benjamin Franklin could not have been Chinese. Although Qing education was widely admired for its rigor and intensity, its content was dominated by antiquity rather than novelty. The Confucian Four Books and Five Classics were at the heart of the curriculum, along with certain select commentaries. Wise government, and knowledge in general, were deemed more likely to come from ancient learning than experimental progress.[§] Similar things were true in the Islamic world.[41]

Europeans were the anomaly here. Historically speaking, virtually all cultures put a higher value on tried and tested ancestral wisdom than on newfangled, unproven contemporary innovation. That is easy to forget in in the contemporary West, where we are so shaped by the notion of progress and the expectation that we will know more tomorrow than we do today. But from an eighteenth-century perspective, what needs explaining is not why Chinese education centered on two-thousand-year-old Confucian texts, or Islamic learning on the Koran, or why traditional societies prized certainty over possibility. These represent the norm in almost all times and places, including medieval Europe. What needs explaining is why early modern Westerners started doing the opposite. Why did their cafes, museums, and stately homes fill with "curiosities"? Why did the pursuit of novelty, discovery, and possibility begin to win out over antiquity, familiarity, and fidelity?

Three factors were particularly significant. The first was Christianity, whose influence on the psychology, sociology, eschatology, and theology of Western Europeans over the course of a millennium or more can scarcely be exaggerated. Psychologically, as we saw from Joseph Henrich's work in chapter 2, we can thank the Roman Catholic Church and its theology of marriage for the "highly individualistic, self-obsessed, control-oriented, nonconformist and analytical" way our brains work.[42] Sociologically, the

---

§ Consider, for example, the competition between Jesuit and Confucian astronomers over the traditional Chinese calendar. In a series of experiments between 1644 and 1668, the Jesuit missionaries were shown beyond doubt to be more accurate at predicting solar eclipses than local experts—but opposition to Christianity, and the insistence that Western methods were ultimately Chinese in origin, prompted the Kangxi emperor to marginalize the Jesuits' science along with their religion. Good riddance, argued the Confucian astronomer Yang Guangxian: "It is better to have no good astronomy than to have Westerners in China." See Jonathan Spence, *Emperor of China: Self-Portrait of K'ang-Hsi* (1957; repr., New York: Knopf, 1974), 72–75; George Wong, "China's Opposition to Western Science during Late Ming and Early Ching," *Isis* 54, no. 1 (1963), 34–35.

Western Church also created the European bourgeoisie—the urbanized middle class of "burghers" or "townsfolk" with their charters, guilds, and universities—as an unintentional by-product of the papal revolution in the eleventh and twelfth centuries.[43] Eschatologically, the hope of the coming kingdom generated an expectation that the future would be better than the present, and that progress was therefore possible (in contrast to religious systems in which history is a series of cycles, or even a steady decline from a Golden Age in the distant past).[44] And theologically, the conviction that the world was created and sustained by a single rational intelligence, rather than being subject to the whims of different deities or the manipulation of divination, fostered what A. N. Whitehead called

> the inexpungable belief that every detailed occurrence can be correlated with its antecedents in a perfectly definite manner, exemplifying general principles. Without this belief the incredible labours of scientists would be without hope. It is this instinctive conviction, vividly poised before the imagination, which is the motive power of research: that there is a secret, a secret which can be unveiled. How has this conviction been so vividly implanted in the European mind? When we compare this tone of thought in Europe with the attitude of other civilisations when left to themselves, there seems but one source of its origin. It must come from the medieval insistence on the rationality of God.[45]

The implications for Western culture are obvious. If you put control-oriented, analytic people in an individualistic, urban environment, give them a sense that the world will one day be better than it is now, and suffuse them with a deep conviction that there is an intelligence behind all things whose secrets are just waiting to be unveiled, then you would expect such a society to value novelty and discovery—even if most of them remain religiously devout farmers. Give them a few centuries, and you might even expect them to produce Ben Franklin.

The second factor is what Yuval Noah Harari calls "the discovery of ignorance."[46] Human beings do not tend to explore or experiment when we think we know everything worth knowing. We are inclined to preserve our knowledge, teach it to our children, and record it for posterity. But when we are confronted by the extent of our ignorance—when we encounter entirely new things that we know nothing about and that appear to be surprising and/or important—we are driven to investigate. We become more interested by what we don't know than by what we do know. Curiosity begins to trump familiarity.

This is exactly what happened in early modern Europe. Consider the lifetime of Henry VIII of England. When Henry was born in 1491, educated Europeans were confident that there was no major landmass besides Afro-Eurasia, that the quickest route to India would be across the Atlantic Ocean if only they could carry enough supplies to make it, that the sun revolved around the earth and the planets did as well, and that Christendom would forever remain united under the leadership of the pope. A divided church, a heliocentric cosmos, and America were as unimaginable as each other.

But by the time Henry died in 1547, the fathomless depths of Western ignorance had been revealed. An entirely new continent had been discovered. Cape Horn and the Cape of Good Hope had been rounded, and the world circumnavigated. Christendom (including England, and even Henry's own family) was fracturing along confessional lines in response to Martin Luther's Reformation, and it was far from clear that all the king's horses and all the king's men would be able to put it back together again. It was even being argued that the earth and other planets went around the sun, with all the questions that raised for cosmology and theology. The snowball of European ignorance was picking up momentum. The more people knew, the more they realized they didn't know, and the more motivated they became to find out.[¶]

¶ The reception of Aristotle in this period illustrates the point. While Confucius continued to be studied intensively in the East, Aristotle—the closest thing to a European equivalent of the great Chinese sage—was increasingly becoming the subject of criticism, debunking and even ridicule in the West. As early as 1536, Petrus Ramus defended his Master's thesis in Paris with a lecture entitled "Everything That Aristotle Ever Said Is Made Up." A few decades later, Giordano Bruno called Aristotle "the stupidest of all philosophers." The natural philosopher John Wilkins, Oliver Cromwell's brother-in-law, argued that "Aristotle's works are not necessarily true, and hee himselfe hath by sufficient Arguments proved himselfe to be liable unto errour," and quoted Francis Bacon in a revealing explanation: "In such Learning as may be increased by fresh experiments and new discoveries, 'tis we are the Fathers, and of more Authority than former Ages, because wee have the advantage of more time than they had, and Truth (wee say) is the Daughter of Time." Galileo, whose experimental work dealt the death blow to ancient cosmology, lumped Aristotle in with "plague, urinals and debt" as among the most miserable things in all of life. Needless to say, for a leading Chinese intellectual to speak about Confucius in anything like this way would have been unthinkable. See Giordano Bruno, *Opere Italiane*,

And this interacted in vital ways with the third and most obvious factor: books. It is no great surprise that a culture in which lots of people can read fluently and write freely is a culture in which useful knowledge spreads quickly. What may be a bit more surprising is that Europe's advantage here was not just the result of printing, nor of a more literate population in general. China, after all, had been printing books for centuries before the Gutenberg press was invented in 1443 and had widespread schooling and higher literacy rates than Europe until around 1700.[47] What was distinctive to Europe was the combination of moveable type printing (which made books much cheaper), Protestantism (which encouraged families and individuals to read the Bible and other Christian texts for themselves), eyeglasses (which enabled people to read past middle age), and a relatively free press, especially in the vernacular in areas where the Reformation was flourishing. None of these things were as true in China, and the result was a significant divergence between East and West in the quantity of printed books. A detailed recent study estimates that over a billion books were printed in Europe in the eighteenth century, covering forty times as many titles as were published in China during the same period.[48]

Literacy increases the flow of ideas, enabling new concepts and discoveries to spread. It also facilitates commerce. Correspondence, advertising, double entry bookkeeping, written contracts, and joint stock companies become possible. Middle class occupations soon follow: accountants, actuaries, bankers, insurers, judges, lawyers, notaries, and secretaries. People start pooling their risk through mutual organizations like insurance markets and building societies, the first examples of which launched in 1774 (in London) and 1775 (in Birmingham), respectively. Numeracy often rises as well, and ordinary people get better at counting, estimating, measuring, and budgeting.[49] In Shakespeare's plays (1585–1615), for example, mathematics is a source of confusion and comedy, money a distraction to be avoided, and finance the preserve of sinister Jews. Yet somehow by 1776, even a traditionalist, arch-Tory, Anglican moralist like Samuel Johnson is calculating and measuring everything, holding forth on economics and profits, and saying things like "no man but a blockhead ever wrote, except for money."[50] Social norms have changed.

---

ed. Giovanni Aquilecchia, 2 vols. (Turin: Unione Tipografico-Editrice Torinese, 2002), 1:182; John Wilkins, *A Discourse concerning a New World and Another Planet in 2 Bookes* (London: Norton, 1640), 2:7; Holland, *Dominion*, 337.

Culture is very difficult to define. It runs the risk of being a bit of a blunderbuss: by explaining everything, it explains nothing. Yet when we specify what we mean—a commitment to novelty, curiosity, possibility, and discovery, fostered by the combination of Christianity, the discovery of ignorance, and the rise of literacy—it has significant explanatory power in accounting for the great enrichment.

What it does not explain, however, is perhaps the strangest feature of Western growth—namely, the intensity of competition and productive fragmentation that existed in early modern Europe (and which in many ways endures to this day). To make sense of that, we need geography.

Explanation 4: Fragmentation

David Hume's explanation for the rise of the West was somewhat different to those of Smith, Raynal, and Diderot. He essentially agreed with these writers in condemning Western GREED and arguing that institutions and culture had played important roles. But Europe's key advantage, he argued, was more fundamental. The continent was divided into small, competitive, independent states.

"Where a number of neighboring states have a great intercourse of arts and commerce," Hume explained, "their mutual jealousy keeps them from receiving too lightly the law from each other, in matters of taste and of reasoning, and makes them examine every work of art with the greatest care and accuracy." So the French study Newton and notice Descartes's weaknesses. The English observe the decency and morality of French theatre and realizes the "scandalous licentiousness" of their own. Competition sparks progress, and thus "the divisions into small states are favourable to learning." In large empires, on the other hand, this does not happen. United by language, law and culture, it is too easy for the state (like China) to suppress dissent, and for authoritative teachers (like Confucius) to be above criticism.[51]

Why, then, is Europe fragmented into small independent states? Hume continues,

If we consider the face of the globe, Europe, of all the four parts of the world, is the most broken by seas, rivers, and mountains; and Greece of all countries of Europe. Hence these regions were naturally divided into several distinct governments. And hence the sciences arose in Greece; and Europe has been hitherto the most constant habitation of them.[52]

Six years later, the same point was made by the gloriously named Charles-Louis de Secondat, Baron de La Brède et de Montesquieu:

> In Asia one has always seen great empires; in Europe they were never able to continue to exist. This is because the Asia we know has larger plains; it is cut into larger parts by seas; and, as it is more to the south, its springs dry up more easily, its mountains are less covered with snow, and its smaller rivers form slighter barriers.[53]

You do not have to know much about Eurasian geography (or history) to have some fairly serious objections to this analysis. Are the Indus, Mekong, Yangtze, and Yellow Rivers really so small? Didn't the Roman empire last five hundred years? Are the Himalayas or the Tibetan plateau any less snowy than the Alps? Do equatorial river systems dry up as much as all that?

Nevertheless, there are two important ideas here. One is that the political fragmentation of Western Europe has created high levels of competition between different states, at least since the fall of Rome, and this competition has contributed to Western advances in learning and commerce (and military technology). The other is that this political fragmentation is itself largely a result of geography, in that large land empires are much harder to sustain in Western Europe than they are in Asia. In a nutshell: natural barriers generate division, which generates competition, which (eventually) generates growth.

And this, according to Stanford professor Walter Scheidel, is pretty much exactly what happened. In a wide-ranging and brilliant book, Scheidel argues that the great enrichment was made possible by a single condition: polycentrism, or the "competitive fragmentation of power." In contrast to much of Eurasia, where large traditional empires have held sway for most of the last few thousand years, Europe has been divided since the fall of the Western Roman Empire in 476. No imperial power has been able to maintain control over more than a fifth of the population. Consequently, fragmentation has been a permanent feature of the European political landscape: city against city and nation against nation, but also church against state, kings against barons, knights against merchants, and Catholics against Protestants.

You can see why competition, diversity and innovation would flourish in a context like this. The continent is covered in natural experiments. When an advance or new discovery is made—in learning, commerce, politics, navigation, or technology—it is quickly copied and/or improved upon in neighboring nations, who do not want to fall behind. So if the Dutch gain a financial advantage through public debt, joint stock companies, and South Asian trade, then the English can simply snaffle their ideas. If Portugal discover a new maritime route, other nations will quickly exploit it. If England establishes a lucrative sugar colony in the Caribbean or pelt trade in the American Midwest, France will be there like a shot. The benefits of competition are especially obvious in warfare, where the "tournament" of continuous battles between rival states fuels frequent innovation and in the long run gives Europe a significant military advantage.[54] Failures, likewise, are noted and learned from.

Rivalries ensure that creative types have plenty of options. If a heavy-handed ruler takes exception to a particular idea, the writer in question can simply move abroad and write there—as many leading thinkers did, including Bayle, Calvin, Descartes, Galileo, Hobbes, Locke, Raynal, and Voltaire. If an Italian explorer's madcap scheme to sail across the Atlantic to India is rejected by the Portuguese, then he can pitch it to the Spanish instead. Even the conflict between skeptical Enlighteners and traditional Christianity was ideologically fertile. And this environment of nonstop competition was integral to the rise of modern commerce, war, science, industry, and statecraft in Europe. None of it could have emerged under a hegemonic empire that could "flip the switch off" and summarily decide to change the syllabus, cancel overseas voyages, destroy observatories, or ban printing.[55] In the end, Scheidel argues, this competitive fragmentation is the cause that stands behind all the other explanations that have been put forward for the great enrichment, including institutions, GREED, and culture.[56] He offers it as a fundamental axiom: "without polycentrism, no modernity."[57]

But why is Europe so fragmented? Why has it not fallen subject to a dominant imperial power since Rome? The answer is similar in outline, if not in detail, to that provided by Hume and Montesquieu: it is mostly a matter of maps, not chaps. Numerous geographical features have combined to make Europe harder to unite than equivalent areas of territory in China, India, Central Asia, the Middle East, and North Africa.

Start with the point made by both Hume and Montesquieu, that Europe is more divided by seas than Asia. This is undoubtedly true. A tenth of Western Europe is made up of islands, and nearly half of it sits on peninsulas; in China, India, the Middle East, and North Africa, the total insular and peninsular land mass is less than 4 percent of the total.[58] The major islands of Japan and the Indonesian archipelago are several times farther from the mainland than any major European island besides Iceland. There is over four times as much coastline in Western Europe as there is in either China or India. All other things being equal, this ought to make it significantly harder to build a continuous land empire across a large area. History would suggest that it has.

Or take mountains and rivers. The key point is not how small the rivers or how snowy the mountains, as Montesquieu thought. Rather, it is the extent to which the continent is (in Hume's words) "broken by seas, rivers and mountains": in effect, how far you can travel on relatively flat land before encountering a mountain range or impassable river that serves as a natural break between states. The Alps, Pyrenees, and Carpathians, together with the coasts, marshlands, and rivers like the Rhine and the Danube, divide Europe west of the steppe into a number of distinct regions—Iberia, Ireland, Britain, France, the Low Countries, the Italian peninsula, the Alpine region, Scandinavia, Austro-Hungary, Transylvania, and Greece—that have proved monstrously difficult to unite (as the Habsburgs, Napoleon, and Hitler can testify).[59] In "core China," by contrast, you can travel from the Pacific to the Tibetan plateau without encountering peaks of anything like that size, and much of the land is served by the tributaries and flood plains of the Yangtze and Yellow rivers, making it one of the most naturally fertile areas in the world. Similar things are true of India between the Indus and the Ganges. If all you had was a good relief map and a sprinkling of common sense, you would expect it to be easier to establish large land empires in Asia than in Europe.**

** One geographical feature that Hume and Montesquieu did not mention is the Eurasian steppe. This five-thousand-mile area of grassy shrubland, stretching from Hungary to Manchuria, seems to have played a significant role in the development (or not) of large states: the vast majority

Geography was not the only major factor driving the fragmentation of power in Europe. The other, once again, was Western Christianity. The separation of church and state, whereby kings and queens have a different (and in some ways lesser) kind of power than popes and bishops, is a uniquely Christian idea. The notion that a religious leader might excommunicate the Emperor, as Pope Gregory VII did in 1076—let alone the idea that the emperor might do penance for his sins by kneeling and waiting barefoot in the snow for three days, as Henry IV did in response—would be completely unthinkable in a Chinese, Indian, or Islamic context. Within Christendom, however, it made sense. The disaggregation of sacred and secular power generated polycentrism within states, just as surely as geography generated it between them. Indeed, in many parts of Europe, over the course of a millennium or more, the church often had more power, wealth, and stability than the state.

At the same time, Christianity provided a set of shared norms, values, and language that prevented Western states from becoming isolated from one another. This, too, was essential to "productive fragmentation." Medieval Europe was not just divided; it was divided into principalities that had enough in common to keep talking, writing, visiting, intermarrying, squabbling, trading, and debating with each other. And that was particularly significant for intellectual development. The Republic of Letters, a "market for ideas" in which European thinkers shared knowledge, methods, and experimental results on what we would now call an open-source basis, was integral to the expansion of Western learning in the seventeenth and eighteenth centuries, and like any academic environment it was driven

---

of land empires in history to cover more than a million square kilometers have emerged in close proximity to it. Zones that are "exposed" to the steppe—like China, continental India, and southwest Asia—typically develop larger states and empires than zones that are "protected" from it, like Western Europe, Southeast Asia, Japan and Korea. Why? Because the steppe is home to pastoral nomads (like the Mongols) who graze sheep, ride horses, keep moving, and gain access to other goods either by trading with or raiding them from local farming communities. And since small states are mostly unable to defend themselves against lightning strikes by skillful archers mounted on horseback, this provides a powerful motivation for peoples near the steppe to collaborate, unify, and welcome the increase of state power. Western Europe, on the other hand, never experienced this pressure; even the Mongols only reached Poland. See Peter Turchin, "A Theory for Formation of Large Empires," *Journal of Global History* 4 (2009): 191–217; cf. Scheidel, *Escape from Rome*, 270–306; Victor Lieberman, *Strange Parallels: Southeast Asia in Global Context, c. 80–1830*, 2 vols. (Cambridge: Cambridge University Press, 2003–2010), 2:92–117.

by competition, jealousy, and the struggle for patronage and honor.[60] But it would not have emerged without Christianity. Christendom provided a transnational sense of commonality: scholars communicated in Latin, appealed to the same sources and cultural heritage, researched at the same universities, and treated one another as colleagues in a joint endeavor as well as rivals. Indeed, the very concept of a *Respublica Literaria* grew out of the *Respublica Christiana* in Augustine's *City of God*.

That blend of cultural unity and political fragmentation was a unique and ultimately potent combination, sparking competition, commerce, curiosity, and growth. Connected by Roman Catholicism, Latin, canon law, and a shared intellectual tradition yet separated by geographical, linguistic, historic, and political boundaries, Europe was somehow divided enough to compete yet united enough to cohere. Some would say it still is.

Virtue and Vice

The great enrichment is a case study in moral ambiguity, especially for Christians. On one hand it is the product of institutions (explanation 1) and culture (explanation 3) that owe a great deal to Christian influence, and it has dramatically increased living standards and life expectancy for billions of people, as well as enabling a massive expansion in global mission. On the other hand, its origins lie in the fragmentation, competition, and warfare of what used to be Christendom (explanation 4) and the exploitative GREED of professing Christians (explanation 2), and its results also include the amplification of most of the seven deadly sins, the emergence of white supremacy, the widespread veneration of Mammon, and the swatting aside of traditional moral and social structures by the invisible hand of the market. Understandably, therefore, it has met with ambivalent responses from the church. Some have seen the increase in prosperity as a providential gift from God to humanity, or a sign of divine favor. Others have seen it as a curse that only looks like a blessing, like Pandora's Box or Turkish Delight, or even proof of divine judgment. Perhaps it is both.

One of the most powerful statements of this ambivalence, whereby evil motives produce good results (and vice versa), came many decades before the great enrichment even started. The words of the Dutch satirist Bernard Mandeville, written twenty years before Adam Smith was born, were to prove prophetic:

    Luxury
Employ'd a Million of the Poor,
And odious pride a million more.
Envy itself, and vanity
Were ministers of industry . . .
Thus vice nursed ingenuity
Which, joined with time and industry,
Had carried life's conveniencies,
Its real pleasures, comforts, ease,
To such a height, the very poor
Lived better than the rich before.[61]

PART 3

RESPONSES

Christians

Grace, Freedom, and Truth

My memory is nearly gone, but I remember two things:
that I am a great sinner and that Christ is a great Saviour.

JOHN NEWTON

Liberty is a jewel which was handed down
to man from the cabinet of heaven.

LEMUEL HAYNES

"CHRISTIANITY WAS SOMETIMES AT WAR with modernity," writes Harvard professor David Hempton in his history of the eighteenth-century church, "and sometimes was its midwife."[1] We have seen that dynamic throughout this book. The church is frequently concerned by the social, intellectual, and economic changes taking place in the West, and is often directly threatened by them. But she is also indirectly responsible for bringing many of them about. As the sociologist of religion Peter Berger memorably put it, "historically speaking, Christianity has been its own gravedigger."[2]

Having said that, we should not imagine Christians in this period as a passive, embattled minority, watching helplessly as global forces beyond their control slowly squeeze their convictions to the margins of public life. Quite the opposite, in fact. "The eighteenth century," Hempton continues, "was as much a century of religious enthusiasm, renewal and revivalism, albeit influenced by the Enlightenment, as it was a century of cold rationalism and proto-secularisation."[3]

It certainly was. Indeed, the changes within Western Christianity in this period—great awakenings and evangelical revivals, Moravians and Methodists, the decline of Tridentine Catholicism, the suppression of the Jesuits, the religious Enlightenment, the rise of abolitionism, hymn writing, the modern missions movement, and many others—are so numerous and varied that it would take a whole book just to summarize them.[4]

That is clearly beyond the scope of this chapter. So instead, we will focus on just three crucial developments taking place among Christians in the 1770s: the celebration of *grace*, the pursuit of *freedom*, and an articulation of Christian *truth* that offered a metacritique of the Enlightenment and pointed the way to a postsecular future. In part, I have chosen these three because they reflect such different aspects of the Christian life: our *pathos* (how we feel), our *ethos* (how we act), and our *logos* (how we think). But I am also convinced that each of them has the potential to help Christians thrive in the WEIRDER world of the twenty-first century, as much as (if not more than) the eighteenth. We will come back to that in the final chapter.

Amazing Grace

To mark the start of 1776, the English hymnwriter Augustus Toplady made a few notes for the year ahead. "Our highest acknowledgements are due to him, whose mercy endureth forever," he began. "He alone is worthy to receive the love of our hearts."[5] The beginning of the year was a chance to give thanks for the goodness of God, remember the sinfulness of man, and rejoice in "the free grace of the Father, the redeeming merit of Jesus, and the sanctifying omnipotence of the Holy Ghost." But it was also a moment to ponder the certainty of death, especially in light of the war with America, and the providential grace of God that would carry believers through it:

> Many a lofty head will be laid low before the expiration of 1776. The sad ravages of civil war will, too probably, people the regions of the grave with additional thousands, over and above the myriads who never fail to swell the ordinary bills of mortality. But providence, unerring providence, governs all events (Daniel 4:35). And grace, unchangeable grace, is faithful to its purpose (Romans 8:28). May we live by faith on both.[6]

Toplady practiced what he preached. When a general fast for the war with America was announced later that year, to pray for "the pardon of sins, averting judgments, imploring victory, and perpetuating peace to the British Empire," many pastors gave sermons on exactly that. Toplady took a different approach. After explaining why pastors should generally avoid meddling in politics, and making some comments about the English constitution and religious liberty, he spent the rest of his message talking about the transforming power of grace:

> When the citadel of the human heart is taken by grace, the enemy's colours are displaced; satan's usurped authority is superseded; the standard of the cross is erected on the walls; and the spiritual rebel takes the vow of willing allegiance to Christ, his rightful sovereign.[7]

> From the moment of conversion, grace introduces a total change. The renewed sinner abhors himself, as in dust and ashes, for all that he has done, and can never sufficiently adore, admire, and revere that infinite goodness which, instead of turning him into hell, has turned him to God, and made him a living monument, not of deserved vengeance, but of unmerited mercy.[8]

> And may such of us, as are awakened by grace, to the experimental knowledge, love, and imitation of Christ, be led, farther and deeper, into acquaintance with God, and communion with his blessed Spirit: gaining, day by day, brighter evidences of our election to eternal life, and more substantial marks of our interest in the covenant of grace.[9]

Grace was a controversial subject in the 1770s, which is partly why Toplady was talking about it so much. He and his fellow Calvinists believed that God's grace was "insuperable": it was so powerful that it would overcome human resistance, with the result that everyone to whom it was given would inevitably be saved. John Wesley and his followers disagreed. They taught that grace was "prevenient": it was given to everybody, not just the elect, and it could be either received or rejected. The age-old debate had been given a new lease of life in Britain by the Methodist revival, whose two key leaders—Wesley and the Calvinist preacher George Whitefield—had passionately disagreed on the matter.

The controversy about grace became acrimonious in the extreme. Toplady referred to Wesley as "the most rancorous hater of the gospel-system that ever appeared in this island," an "enraged porcupine" who has "dipt his quills in the ink of forgery on occasion, as Indians tinge the points of their arrows in poison."[10] Wesley did not mince his words either. "Mr Augustus Toplady I know well," he wrote, "but I do not fight with chimney sweepers. He is too dirty a writer for me to meddle with. I should only foul my fingers. I read his title page, and troubled myself no farther."[11]

Neither Wesley nor Toplady come out well from their exchanges. Toplady emerges as a bad-tempered and bumptious controversialist, and Wesley as a proud man who almost certainly did forge Toplady's work for his own purposes and never apologized. But as it turned out, the divine grace they were arguing about was powerful enough to make up for it. Two and a half centuries later, the most lasting result of the dispute—and probably the most frequently quoted poem published in 1776—was Toplady's hymn "Rock of Ages," a meditation on grace so powerful that Wesleyans have been singing it ever since:

> Rock of Ages, cleft for me,
> Let me hide myself in thee!
> Let the water and the blood
> From thy riven side which flowed
> Be for sin the double cure,
> Cleanse me from its guilt and power.
>
> Not the labours of my hands
> Can fulfil thy law's demands;
> Could my zeal no respite know,
> Could my tears forever flow,
> All for sin could not atone:
> Thou must save, and thou alone!
>
> Nothing in my hands I bring;
> Simply to thy cross I cling.

Naked, come to thee for dress,
Helpless, look to thee for grace.
Foul, I to the fountain fly:
Wash me, Saviour, or I die!

Whilst I draw this fleeting breath,
When my eye-strings break in death,
When I sour through tracts unknown,
See thee on thy judgment throne,
Rock of Ages, cleft for me,
Let my hide myself in thee![12]

In any ordinary decade, Toplady's 1776 collection would have represented the high-water mark of English hymnody.[13] But the 1770s were not an ordinary decade. In 1779, Wesley launched *A Collection of Hymns for the Use of the People Called Methodists*, which he regarded as the best hymn-book yet published in English: "In these hymns there is no doggerel, no botches, nothing put in to patch up the rhyme, no feeble expletives. Here there is nothing turgid or bombast on the one hand, or low and creeping on the other."[14] It contained over a thousand hymns, mostly written by his brother Charles and plenty still in use today, including "And Can It Be," "Love Divine All Loves Excelling," "O for a Thousand Tongues," and "Hark! The Herald Angels Sing."

In Bedfordshire, the Anglican vicar John Berridge was writing *Sion's Songs* during a long illness. Just down the road from him, John Newton and William Cowper were writing the *Olney Hymns* (1773–1779), a collection destined for even greater fame than Berridge's or the Wesleys'. Many of their lyrics ("How Sweet the Name of Jesus Sounds," "Glorious Things of Thee Are Spoken," "With Christ in My Vessel I Smile at the Storm") are sung today by people who have never heard of Newton or Cowper. Some of them have passed into everyday speech:

God moves in a mysterious way
His wonders to perform.
He plants his footsteps in the sea,
And rides upon the storm.[15]

And their most famous hymn has become one of the world's most familiar songs in any genre, recorded in nearly thirteen thousand versions and
performed around ten million times every year:

Amazing grace! (How sweet the sound!)
That saved a wretch like me!
I once was lost, but now am found,
Was blind, but now I see.

'Twas grace that taught my heart to fear,
And grace my fears relieved;
How precious did that grace appear
The hour I first believed!

Through many dangers, toils and snares
I have already come;
'Tis grace has brought me safe thus far,
And grace will lead me home.[16]

It was not obvious at the time that "Amazing Grace" would become so
well-known. It barely registered in Britain. Initially, it was not even called
that; Newton's original title was the rather less pithy "Faith's Review and
Expectation." The explosive popularity of the hymn came later, in nineteenth
century America, as a result of a new tune, a new name, a new verse, and
the Second Great Awakening. And it was elevated to iconic status by its
association with the fight against slavery. Newton's personal transformation from slaver to abolitionist, and the hymn's message of grace even to
a "wretch" like him, made it an ideal candidate for this, as did Harriet
Beecher Stowe's decision to include it in *Uncle Tom's Cabin*, complete with
a new verse ("When we've been there ten thousand years") that had been
shared among African American communities for fifty years.[17] Later, the
hymn would become an anthem of the struggle for civil rights and racial
justice more generally, from Mahalia Jackson and Fannie Lou Hamer to
Nelson Mandela and Barack Obama. It would also give its name to numerous books, two major movies, and (inexplicably) a Superman villain in the
DC Comics universe.

But it was by no means the only hymn Newton wrote about grace. Some would argue it was not even the best one. In 348 Olney hymns, "grace" is mentioned 270 times, which astonishingly is more than the words "God," "Jesus," "Christ," or "Spirit." When you read the collection, you are struck on every page by Newton's passion for the doctrines of grace, which he described in the preface as "essential to my peace; I could not live comfortably a day, or an hour, without them."[18] Newton was genuinely amazed by the free gift of God in Christ, unmerited and unmeritable, and wrote about it with the air of someone who is still trying to come to terms with it:

> Who can faint while such a river
> Ever flows, their thirst to assuage?
> Grace, which like the Lord, the giver,
> Ever flows from age to age.[19]

> Sovereign grace has power alone
> To subdue a heart of stone,
> And the moment grace is felt,
> Then the hardest heart will melt.[20]

> My grace would soon exhausted be,
> But his is boundless as the sea.
> Then let me boast with holy Paul
> That I am nothing. Christ is all.[21]

Newton's letters display the same relentless emphasis. "By nature we are separated from the divine life, as branches broken off, withered and fruitless," he wrote in a typical example.[22] "But grace, through faith, unites us to Christ the living Vine. . . . How inviolable is the security, how inestimable the privilege, how inexpressible the happiness, of a believer! How greatly is he indebted to grace! He was once afar off, but he is brought near to God by the blood of Christ: he was once a child of wrath, but is now an heir of everlasting life."[23] So too do his last recorded words: "My memory is nearly gone, but I remember two things: that I am a great sinner and that Christ is a great Saviour."[24]

His sermons, likewise, reach their highest points when waxing lyrical about the grace of God:

The great God is pleased to manifest himself in Christ, as the God of grace. This grace is manifold, pardoning, converting, restoring, persevering grace, bestowed upon the miserable and worthless. Grace finds the sinner in a hopeless, helpless state, sitting in darkness, and in the shadow of death. Grace pardons the guilt, cleanses the pollution, and subdues the power of sin. Grace sustains the bruised reed, binds up the broken heart, and cherishes the smoking flax into a flame. Grace restores the soul when wandering, revives it when fainting, heals it when wounded, upholds it when ready to fall, teaches it to fight, goes before it in the battle, and at last makes it more than conqueror over all opposition, and then bestows a crown of everlasting life.[25]

And grace was Newton's theme in perhaps the most famous sermon outline in the history of the church:

I am not what I *ought to be*. Ah! how imperfect and deficient. Not what I *might be*, considering my privileges and opportunities. Not what I *wish to be*. God, who knows my heart, knows I wish to be like him. I am not what I *hope to be*; ere long to drop this clay tabernacle, to be like him and see him as he is. Not what I *once was*, a child of sin and slave of the devil. Though not all these, not what I *ought to be*, not what I *might be*, not what I *wish or hope to be*, and not what I *once was*, I think I can truly say with the apostle, "By the grace of God I am *what I am*" (1 Cor 15:10).[26]

Newton's obsession with grace, no doubt, flowed in part from what a paradigmatically bad man he had previously been. Like Paul and Augustine before him, Newton's agonizing awareness of how wicked and undeserving he was—a greedy, foul-mouthed, blaspheming, cowardly, drunken, violent slaver and (probably) rapist—corresponded to his open-mouthed amazement that God would rescue him, of all people.[27] If he could be saved, then anybody could. "If the Lord were to leave me one hour, I should fall into gross evil," he explained. "I am like a child who dares not go across Cheapside unless someone holds his hand."[28]

His preoccupation with grace was driven by other personal factors too. A heartfelt desire to reassure his friend and cowriter William Cowper, who wrestled so desperately with his own salvation, was probably one.[*] Newton's Calvinism, at a time when Wesleyanism was in the ascendancy, was another.[29] His passion for John Bunyan's *The Pilgrim's Progress*, which he says he had virtually memorized (and for which he wrote a preface in 1776), was another.[30]

Yet at the same time, Newton's focus on grace is representative of a broader shift in the way British Protestants were articulating their theology and experience of salvation. Grace—the unmerited, transforming favor of God—had obviously been foundational to Christian theology since the very beginning. But eighteenth-century Britain saw a change in the way people talked about it, through a combination of Puritan theology, Pietist experience, poetic expression, and personal narrative. The past was summarized more graphically, and indeed more personally, than had been typical before ("a wretch like me," "O Lord how vile am I," "foul, I to the fountain fly," "when we were more loathsome than the beggar on the dunghill").[31] The moment of transformation was described more suddenly ("my chains fell off, my heart was free," "I once was lost but now am found," "I woke, the dungeon flamed with light"), and indeed a singular conversion experience was often seen as essential, even for those raised in Christian families.[32] Grace began to be personified as an agent of change as much as a divine attribute ("Twas grace that taught my heart to fear, and grace my fears relieved.") And the difference between law-based and grace-based obedience was celebrated with stanzas that are still widely quoted today:

Run, John, and work, the law commands,
Yet finds me neither feet nor hands.
But sweeter news the gospel brings:
It bids me fly, and lends me wings.[33]

[*] The first use of "Amazing Grace" was on the morning of New Year's Day, 1773. Cowper, who had struggled with depression for years, wrote "God Moves in a Mysterious Way" that same afternoon, but by the middle of the night he was wracked with hallucinations and nightmares and attempted suicide, believing God had told him to sacrifice himself. Though he recovered, and later wrote many other hymns, he never attended church again.

To see the law by Christ fulfilled
And hear his pardoning voice
Changes a slave into a child
And duty into choice.[34]

Admittedly, people like Toplady, Newton, Berridge, and the Wesleys—preachers, pastors, and hymnwriters during a time of spiritual revival—are precisely the sorts of people we would expect to champion grace and stress the importance of experiencing it personally. But it was by no means unique to them. Indeed, one of the most remarkable testimonies of grace from the period came from someone whose life experience was the exact opposite of Newton's: a former slave from Benin, whose eloquence on the subject matched that of the former slaver from Bedfordshire.

Olaudah Equiano was born in around 1745 in what is now southeastern Nigeria.[35] Kidnapped along with his sister at the age of eleven, he was sold to English slave traders and transported to Barbados before being taken to Virginia and sold to a Lieutenant in the Royal Navy. In some ways, his decade of enslavement was typical, and his account of its unspeakable horrors made a huge contribution to the abolitionist cause when it was published in 1789. But in other ways, Equiano's experience was quite unprecedented. He served in the Seven Years' War, converted to Christianity, was sent to Britain to learn English, traded on his own behalf, and was eventually able to purchase his freedom, upon which he spent the next ten years continuing to travel, from Turkey to the Arctic Circle to the Caribbean. In 1776, appalled by the behavior of his colleagues, he returned to England, where he quickly became a pioneering abolitionist, campaigner, celebrated author, and eventually husband and father.

It is no surprise that his autobiography, *The Interesting Narrative of the Life of Olaudah Equiano*, lays bare the vileness of Atlantic slavery and the grievous hypocrisy of the so-called Christians who perpetuated it. The book's most harrowing paragraph begins with an account of two Africans, chained to one another, jumping into the sea to escape the gruesome conditions of the ship, followed by the merciless flogging of another who attempted to follow them; it concludes with a gut-wrenching passage on the practice of separating families:

O, ye nominal Christians! Might not an African ask you, learned you this from your God? . . . Why are parents to lose their children, brothers their sisters, or husbands their wives? Surely this is a new refinement in cruelty, which, while it has no advantage to atone for it, thus aggravates distress, and adds fresh horrors even to the wretchedness of slavery.[36]

What is astonishing is that, having suffered such inhumanity at the hands of people who professed to be Christians, Equiano not only converts to Christianity (as so many enslaved people did), but writes about his own sin and God's grace like this:

Again, I was convinced that the Lord was better to me than I deserved, and I was better off in the world than many. . . . I was sensible of the invisible hand of God, which guided and protected me, when in truth I knew it not; still the Lord pursued me although I slighted and disregarded it; this mercy melted me down. When I considered my poor, wretched state, I wept, seeing what a great debtor I was to sovereign free grace. . . . Oh! the amazing things of that hour can never be told—it was joy in the Holy Ghost! I felt an astonishing change. . . . By free grace I was persuaded that I had a part and lot in the first resurrection, and was enlightened with the "light of the living."[37]

For many of us, it is hard to fathom how a person could undergo such cruelties and still talk like this, let alone worship alongside English Christians, singing their hymns and reading their books. But Equiano genuinely seems to have been more aware of his own sin than theirs, and convinced that far from owing him anything, God in Christ had actually given him far *more* than he deserved. His comments after attending his first "soul-feast" in 1774 are a wonderful distillation of the evangelical theology of grace:

I could not but admire the goodness of God, in directing the blind, blasphemous sinner in the path that he knew not of, even among the just; and instead of judgment he has shown mercy, and will hear and answer the prayers and supplications of every returning prodigal:

O! to grace how great a debtor
Daily I'm constrained to be.[38]

We should not overstate how widespread this sort of piety was at the time. Even in Britain, evangelicals represented a small proportion of the Christian population in the 1770s, and from the perspective of global Christianity as a whole, they were a drop in the ocean. But several factors meant that they were destined to play a much larger role in the next two centuries. One was the spread of the British empire, the English language and British cultural norms. Another was the rise of America, where the First Great Awakening had already ensured that much popular Christianity was increasingly conversionist, Biblicist, and revivalist, and the next century would see it become more so, not least because of the growth of African American Christianity. More important still was the growth of the missions movement, which often exported British evangelical theology and practice—whether in its Baptist, Methodist, Presbyterian, or evangelical Anglican forms—to parts of the world where the Christian population was small or nonexistent, from India and Korea to Polynesia, sub-Saharan Africa, and inland China. And the way evangelicals engaged socially and politically, which was most obvious in (but not limited to) the abolition of the slave trade, gave them disproportionate influence in the two nations that would most shape the nineteenth and twentieth centuries.

The legacy of this influence has been both varied and complicated. Most legacies are. But one of them is that you can find up to a billion people today, gathering every Sunday in virtually every city on earth, whose views of divine mercy and human sinfulness, and whose stories of their own personal conversion and transformation, bear a striking resemblance to those of Toplady, Wesley, Newton, and Equiano. "I am not what I ought to be," they will tell you in hundreds of different languages, "and I am not what I'm going to be. But I am not what I was. And by the grace of God, I am what I am."

Free Indeed

It is a warm August day in 1776, in what is now Accra in Ghana, and an African American missionary has just been offered a free voyage home. It puts her in an unusual position. Most of the people on board the *Ada*, a Danish slave ship armed with twelve cannons and manned by a crew of twenty-five, are destined for the sugar plantations in the Danish West Indies, or what today we call the US Virgin Islands.[39] But for all that she might resemble them physically, Rebecca Protten is a free woman. The decision to sail or not is entirely hers.

Unusually she has lived out the transatlantic slave trade in reverse: from slavery in the Caribbean as a child, to freedom on the African Gold Coast in her fifties.[40] Born in Antigua, Rebecca was liberated at the age of twelve when her owner died, and then she spent a decade preaching the gospel to African slaves on the island of St. Thomas, before leaving for Germany and joining the Moravian community in Herrnhut. Eventually she moved to be with her husband in West Africa, where she has spent the last few years teaching local children. She has recently been widowed for the second time. As she considers whether to take up the owners of the *Ada* on their offer, she has to weigh up the benefits of returning home with the health risks of the voyage and the prospect of continued ministry to the local children. She decides to stay.

In a world where gospel preachers, foreign missionaries, and ordained ministers are almost entirely European men, Rebecca Protten stands out as exceptional. As a teenage evangelist who could speak multiple languages, she was indispensable to the Moravian mission among the slave population in the 1730s. "She has done the work of the Saviour by teaching the Negro women and speaking about that which the Holy Spirit himself has shown her," wrote the German missionary who mentored her. "I have found nothing in her other than a love of God and his servants."[41] Since then, she has broken numerous boundaries in forty years of Christian ministry. Together with her fellow Moravians, she was evangelizing in the open air several years before Wesley and Whitefield started doing the same. When Rebecca and a fellow West Indian were appointed as deaconesses, licensing them to preach to women and serve Communion on their own, they may well have been the first women of African descent to be ordained in the history of Protestantism.[42] And she is surely unique in having prophesied the means of her own escape from jail, after being given, along with her husband Matthäus, a life sentence.[43]

This last incident, which marked a turning point in her life, is emblematic of the complicated relationship between conversion, freedom from slavery, and religious liberty within eighteenth-century Christianity. It would be nice to think that the conversion of enslaved people would be greeted with joy by all professing Christians, and that the sight of hundreds of black believers gathering for worship on a Moravian plantation would be celebrated by the Dutch Reformed Church. Sadly the opposite was true. The local planters were so troubled by the mission, and by the mixed-race married couple at the heart of it, that Matthäus and Rebecca were charged with multiple offences, fined, and jailed. Moravian teaching was "contrary to the commands of God and the King"; Rebecca had been "seduced by the heretical religion of these people, which is in conflict with what she was previously, namely Reformed"; and worse, since their marriage was conducted in the Moravian church, it was effectively illegal, and "their unchristian and scandalous living on this small island causes great disturbances."[44] Since they could not pay their hefty fines, and refused to back down on conscience grounds, Matthäus would spend the rest of his life in prison, and Rebecca would return to slavery. They were delivered from this terrible fate only by the dramatic appearance of Count Zinzendorf, the leader of the Moravian Church himself, to intercede on their behalf—impressively, just as Rebecca had predicted two days before.[†]

We find it almost unimaginable that a woman in her early twenties could be imprisoned and threatened with re-enslavement by her fellow Christians, essentially for being too evangelistically effective in the wrong denomination. But for most of Rebecca Protten's life, Christians generally regarded spiritual redemption, personal freedom, and religious liberty as three quite different things. Even Count Zinzendorf, whose intervention saved Rebecca and her husband (and who introduced 24/7 prayer to the slaves on the island on the same visit), defended the practice of slavery, teaching their three-hundred-strong congregation that "God has punished the first Negroes with slavery. The blessed state of your souls does not make your bodies accordingly free."[45] Freedom in Christ, for most eighteenth-century

---

[†]   It was described this way at a Moravian Synod in 1739: "The Brethren in St Thomas had languished for three months. Two days before Zinzendorf's arrival, Freundlich said to Rebecca, 'I would dearly love to leave this prison.' Rebecca said, 'If we are to leave, the Saviour will send us a key, perhaps Count Zinzendorf.' In two days came Zinzendorf, and two days later they were given permission to leave the prison." Her own account of it was characteristically modest: "I have spent fifteen weeks in prison and I have enjoyed sweetness in prison. We were brought seven times before the court, and if I was brought before the justices it was sublime to me that the dear Saviour used me, poor worm, to testify. The 30th January we came out of prison through his miracles" (Rebecca Freundlich to Anna Nitschmann, February 16, 1739). See Sensbach, *Rebecca's Revival*, 128–29.

Christians, did not necessarily mean freedom from enslavement, let alone freedom to choose how and with whom to worship.

Yet as Rebecca considered her options on the Gold Coast in the summer of 1776, this was beginning to change. She could not possibly know it, but several developments were taking place elsewhere in the world at exactly the same time—the American Revolution, the anticolonial turn of the radical Enlightenment, the rising evangelical abolitionist movement, and the work of her fellow black Christians, among others—which would have huge significance for the way freedom was understood and experienced in the future.

A good example of how these four developments came together in 1776 is the pamphlet *Liberty Further Extended, or Free Thoughts on the Illegality of Slave-Keeping*. It was written by the African American preacher Lemuel Haynes, just as Rebecca was deciding whether or not to board the *Ada*:

> Liberty is equally as precious to a black man, as it is to a white one, and bondage equally as intolerable to the one as it is to the other, seeing it effects the laws of nature equally as much in the one as it does in the other. But, as I observed before, those privileges that are granted to us by the Divine Being, no one has the least right to take them from us without our consent; and there is not the least precept or practise in the sacred Scriptures that constitutes a black man a slave, any more than a white one.[46]

Haynes was a true pioneer. The most influential black abolitionist works, like Ottobah Cugoano's *Thoughts and Sentiments on the Evil and Wicked Traffic of the Slavery and Commerce of the Human Species* (1787) and Equiano's *Interesting Narrative* (1789), did not start to be published for another decade.[47] But their essential arguments are all here in miniature. There is a political appeal, using the democratic language of rights and consent ("no one has the least right to take them from us without our consent"); there is a rational appeal to nature ("seeing it effects the laws of nature equally as much in the one as it does in the other"); there is a theological appeal, based on the providence of God ("granted to us by the Divine Being") and the authority of the Bible ("not the least precept or practise in the sacred Scriptures"); and there is an emotional appeal to empathize with enslaved people ("liberty is equally as precious to a black man as it is to a white one"). Those four lines of argument, which roughly correspond to the developments we traced in chapters 4, 5, 6, and 8 of this book, would recur again and again in abolitionist literature. And Haynes's groundbreaking ministry was just beginning. In 1785, he would become the first black American to be ordained as a pastor.

The same arguments were being made by white American pastors as well, and not just by Quakers (who are usually remembered for their contribution), but by northern evangelical Calvinists (who are not). The year 1776 saw the Congregationalist pastor Samuel Hopkins, a leading disciple of Jonathan Edwards, publish *A Dialogue concerning the Slavery of the Africans, Shewing It to Be the Duty and Interest of the American States to Emancipate All Their African Slaves*, in which he argued that the war was God's judgment on America for practicing slavery.[48] Later in the year, he went further in a furious sermon on Isaiah 1:15:

> This whole country have their hands full of blood this day, while the blood of millions who have perished by means of the accursed slave trade long practised by these states is crying to heaven for vengeance on them. . . . Since nothing can be more contrary to the gospel than the slavery this country practises towards fellow-creatures, it being built upon the ruins of that law of our Saviour, do as ye would be done by, which is the basis of all morality among men.[49]

A much more comprehensive denouncement of slavery had just been published in Britain, by none other than John Wesley. His *Thoughts on Slavery* (1774) represented a blistering attack on the institution by one of the nation's most influential Christians, full of detailed arguments, legal and economic reflections, gruesome descriptions of the realities of slavery, and appeals to Christian conscience: "Is there a God? You know there is. Is he a just God? Then there must be a state of retribution. . . . O think betimes, before you drop into eternity! Think now: He shall have judgment without mercy that showed no mercy."[50] His conclusion was a theological and rhetorical masterpiece, and shows how evangelical Christians were beginning to think about the obligation to bring freedom to their brothers and sisters:

If, therefore, you have any regard to justice, (to say nothing of mercy, nor the revealed law of God), render unto all their due. Give liberty to whom liberty is due, that is, to every child of man, to every partaker of human nature. Let none serve you but by his own act and deed, by his own voluntary choice. Away with all whips, all chains, all compulsion! Be gentle toward all men; and see that you invariably do unto every one as you would he should do unto you.

O thou God of love, . . . Arise, and help these that have no helper, whose blood is spilt upon the ground like water! Are not these also the work of thine own hands, the purchase of thy Son's blood? Stir them up to cry unto thee in the land of their captivity; and let their complaint come up before thee; let it enter into thy ears! Make even those that lead them away captive to pity them, and turn their captivity as the rivers in the south. O burst thou all their chains in sunder; more especially the chains of their sins! Thou Saviour of all, make them free, that they may be free indeed![51]

Although Wesley's intervention was not especially original, much of it having been lifted from the Philadelphia Quaker Anthony Benezet, his national prominence and fiery prose had a galvanizing effect on British abolitionism.[52]

The man who did more than anybody to pull the antislavery movement together in Britain was the biblical scholar and campaigner Granville Sharp. In a career spanning fifty years, Sharp was involved in virtually every significant development in British abolitionism: defending slaves who had been abused by their masters (1765), publishing the first tract in England opposing slavery (1769), bringing the case that clarified that slavery was unsupported by English common law (1772), prosecuting the perpetrators of the *Zong* slave ship massacre, at the urging of Olaudah Equiano (1781), and cofounding the Society for Effecting the Abolition of the Slave Trade (1787). His work rate was prodigious. Besides his activism, he wrote prolifically; established the British and Foreign Bible Society; corresponded on tactics and ideas with American abolitionists like Benezet, Hopkins, and Benjamin Rush; defined a rule of Greek grammar that is still taught in seminaries today; and cofounded Sierra Leone. In 1776 alone, he published four different antislavery tracts, lambasting those who call themselves Christians and treat other humans as their property:

Let slaveholders be mindful of the approaching consummation of all earthly things, when perhaps they will see thousands of those men, who were formerly esteemed mere chattels and private property, coming in the clouds with their heavenly Master, to judge tyrants and oppressors and to call them to account for their want of brotherly love! . . . The slaveholder deceives himself if he thinks he can really be a Christian and yet hold such property. . . . If we carefully examine the Scriptures we shall find that slavery and oppression were ever abominable in the sight of God.[53]

It is therefore a happy coincidence that the summer of 1776 also witnessed the opening of Holy Trinity Church Clapham, whose members and their associates—Sharp, William Wilberforce, Henry Thornton, Hannah More, Zachary Macaulay, Henry Venn, and the rest of the "Clapham Sect"—would be so influential in passing the Slave Trade Act (1807) and the Slavery Abolition Act (1833).[‡]

On the other side of the Atlantic, the journey toward abolition would be slower. But the journey toward religious freedom would be much faster, with things moving at a breathtaking pace through the summer of 1776. On May 17, the Presbyterian pastor John Witherspoon preached a crucial message in which he argued that civil and religious liberty were inseparable, and that it was a Christian duty to promote virtue without descending into acrimonious squabbles over the "circumstantials of religion" or the "peculiar distinctions" of different sects. "Perhaps there are few surer marks of the reality of religion," he explained, "than when a man feels himself more joined in spirit to a true holy person of a different denomination, than to an irregular liver of his own."[54] (This, to put it mildly, was not Rebecca Protten's experience.) Days later, George Mason submitted his draft of the Virginia Declaration of Rights, with its formal insistence that "all men should enjoy the fullest toleration in the exercise of religion." This did not go far enough for Witherspoon's former student James Madison, who proposed two amendments over the following fortnight. One, arguing that "no man or class of men ought on account of religion to be invested with peculiar emoluments or privileges, nor subjected to any penalties or disabilities,"

---

‡   It is sobering, however, to consider that it took exactly two hundred years for slavery to become illegal in every nation on earth, after Mauritania finally legislated against it in 2007.

was rejected; Virginia's political leaders were not yet ready to disestablish the church.[55] But the other, with its crucial upgrade from religious toleration to religious freedom, was formally adopted on June 12: "That religion, or the duty which we owe to our Creator, and the manner of discharging it, can be directed only by reason and conviction, not by force or violence; and therefore, *that all men are equally entitled to enjoy the free exercise of religion*, according to the dictates of conscience."[56]

This was a historic pronouncement. Madison was not merely arguing that the state should tolerate all religions and allow people to worship as they chose. People had argued that before. He was saying—and Virginia was saying, and soon the United States would be saying—that the state ("force and violence") had no authority over religious belief and practice at all, because "the duty which we owe to our Creator, and the manner of discharging it, can be directed only by reason and conscience." Religious liberty was a natural right, not a gift of the government. This was made even more explicit a few weeks later by the constitutional convention in Pennsylvania, under the presidency of Benjamin Franklin:

That all men have a natural and unalienable right to worship Almighty God according to the dictates of their own consciences and understanding. And that no man ought or of right can be compelled to attend any religious worship, or erect or support any place of worship, or maintain any ministry, contrary to, or against, his own free will and consent. Nor can any man, who acknowledges the being of a God, be justly deprived or abridged of any civil right as a citizen, on account of his religious sentiments or peculiar mode of religious worship. And that no authority can or ought to be vested in, or assumed by any power whatever, that shall in any case interfere with, or in any manner control, the right of conscience in the free exercise of religious worship.[57]

The American commitment to freedom of religion was the fruit of an unlikely union. On one side were evangelical dissenters, motivated by a zeal for preaching the true gospel without being harassed by (or having to pay for) the established church. On the other side were Enlightenment skeptics who, though slightly embarrassed by that evangelical zeal, nevertheless agreed that the state should not serve as an arbiter of religion.[58]

These fiery preachers and aloof rationalists made strangely effective bed-fellows. The skeptics receive most of the credit today. After all, they wrote the articles and laws in question, and their names are still carried on our buildings, books, and banknotes. But the pressure and public support for religious freedom, and the disestablishment of the state churches in particular, came mostly from the dissenters. Thomas Jefferson admitted as much, in a fascinating account of the struggle for religious freedom in Virginia:

> The established clergy, secure for life in their glebes and salaries . . . devoted Sunday only to the edification of their flock, by service, and a sermon at their parish church. Their other pastoral functions were little attended to. Against this inactivity the zeal and industry of sectarian preachers had an open and undisputed field; and by the time of the revolution, a majority of the inhabitants had become dissenters from the established church, but still obliged to pay contributions to support the pastors of the minority. This unrighteous compulsion to maintain teachers of what they deemed religious errors was grievously felt during the regal government, and without a hope of relief. But the first republican legislature which met in '76 was crowded with petitions to abolish this spiritual tyranny. These brought on the severest contests in which I have ever been engaged.[59]

Evangelical Christians, not Enlightenment rationalists, were behind this "crowd" of petitions in October 1776. The Hanover Presbyterians argued that establishing Christianity was no different in principle from establishing Islam or Catholicism, and that it also inhibited the progress of "arts, sciences and manufactories."[60] The Baptists submitted a petition for "equal liberty" with ten thousand signatures on it, representing roughly 2 percent of the total population of Virginia. And there were plenty of others. The bill that all these dissenters wanted would not be passed for another ten years, owing to the "severest contests" that Jefferson refers to in this passage. But when it was, on January 16, 1786, the Statute for Religious Freedom was worth the wait.

Rebecca Protten never lived to see it, hear the wording of the First Amendment, or witness the abolition of the slave trade. She died in 1780, before any of them had been passed, and long before they would have guaranteed religious or physical liberty for her Caribbean brothers and sisters. Yet the developments taking place within the church in 1776 were destined to have long, lasting, liberating consequences for millions of people in the West, as both freedom of religion and freedom from slavery became first thinkable, then achievable, and finally inevitable. "Liberty is a jewel which was handed down to man from the cabinet of heaven," was how Lemuel Haynes put it that summer. "And as it proceeds from the Supreme Legislator of the universe, so it is he which hath a sole right to take it away."[61]

A Postsecular Vision of Truth

If you had never heard of Johann Georg Hamann (1730–1788), and you encountered this picture of him in 1776 (see figure 10.1), you would never guess that he was one of the most brilliant thinkers of his generation.[62] You might even mistake him for a pirate. Somehow he does not look like a theorist of language, a pioneering critic of the Enlightenment, or even a Christian. His mouth looks like he is suppressing a smile; his left eyebrow is arched upward, mischievously; his flamboyant headscarf is hardly standard issue for German philosophers, and would look thoroughly ridiculous on, say, his friend Immanuel Kant. The overall impression of the portrait is one of impishness mixed with defiance— which, as it turns out, is a good summary of both the man and his message.

Figure 10.1   *Johann Georg Hamann.* Public domain.

Most people today have never heard of Hamann. His writings are fragmentary, baffling, and often untranslated, and they are peppered with allusions, riddles, jokes, epigrams, parodies, parables, and pranks, often in multiple languages (he knew German, Latin, Greek, Hebrew, English, French, Italian, Arabic, Spanish, Portuguese, Latvian, and Chaldaic).[63] The results can be anywhere between idiosyncratic and impenetrable. Reading him is like reading *Ulysses* in German.

His contemporaries, however, were convinced of his genius. Goethe praised the "unique mind" of this "modern wizard" who "made me laugh on nearly every page," and hailed him as "the brightest mind of his day."[64] Schlegel called him an "immensely wise and profound thinker" who would have saved philosophers from years of confusion if only they had listened to him.[65] For Jean Paul, Hamann was "a deep heaven full of telescopic stars"; Lavater said he would be happy to "collect the golden crumbs from his table";[66] Herder, in a similar vein, was prepared to be "a Turkish camel-driver gathering up sacred apples before his ambling holy beast, which bears the Koran."[67] Hegel devoted an entire monograph to his work and thought he possessed a "penetrating genius."[68] Kierkegaard would later call him "the greatest humourist in Christendom" and rank him along with Socrates as one of "the most brilliant minds of all time."[69] Yet for all these laudatory epithets from his fellow philosophers—to which we could add others by Kant, Jacobi, Schelling, and more—the nickname that stuck was coined by a politician, Friedrich von Moser. He called Hamann the *Magus im Norden*: the Wizard of the North.[70]

At the heart of this wizard's work is a theological vision of truth that stems from his conversion experience.[71] In the spring of 1758, after a turbulent period in London in which he alternated between desperation ("I went about depressed, staggering to and fro, without a soul with whom to share my burden") and dissipation ("I ate for free, I drank for free, I made love for free, I raced around for free; I fruitlessly alternated between gluttony and reflection, between reading and knavery, between industriousness and complete inactivity"), Hamann reached the end of himself.[72] Lonely, in debt and with his health deteriorating, he was inspired to pick up a Bible. He was in Deuteronomy 5, of all places, when he was suddenly struck by the story of Cain and Abel. It changed his life:

> I fell into deep reflection, thought about Abel, of whom God said: the earth *opened its mouth* to receive the *blood* of your *brother*. . . . I felt at once my

heart swelling, it poured itself out in tears, and I could no longer—I could no longer hide from God that I was the murderer of my brother, that I was the murderer of his only begotten Son. The Spirit of God continued, in spite of my great weakness, in spite of the long resistance that I had previously mounted against his witness and his stirrings, to reveal to me more and more the mystery of divine love and the benefit of faith in our merciful and only Saviour.[73]

The results were immediate. Hamann immersed himself in the Bible and wrote a commentary on it that ran to several hundred pages, as well as an account of his conversion and several other essays, in just three months.[74] He was utterly amazed by Scripture's capacity to disclose the truth about God, reveal mysteries, and serve as an allegory of his own life. It was, he marveled,

> the only bread and manna of our souls, which a Christian can no more do without than the earthly man can do without his daily necessities and sustenance—indeed, I confess that this Word of God accomplishes just as great wonders in the soul of a devout Christian, whether he be simple or learned, as those described in it.[75]

He was equally awestruck by the condescension of God in Christ, the "twofold drama of majesty and abasement, of Divinity and the profoundest level of human misery," in which God's grace was revealed and creation transformed forever:

> It is finished—this password, which the man of God called out on Golgotha, deafened all of nature, created a new heaven and a new earth, transfigured God, transfigured man, and revealed to all the world, angels and men, that God is just and that all should be justified who would come to believe in him.[76]

Hamann's conversion completely changed how he saw the world. Like Blaise Pascal, to whom he is sometimes compared, he became a thoroughly Christian philosopher, as opposed to a philosopher who merely happened to be a Christian. From that point on he would offer a provocative critique of the Enlightenment, rooted in specifically Christian truth claims. Let me highlight just four.

First, since God took on *flesh* in the incarnation of Christ, the rationalist tendency toward asceticism and gnosticism must be resisted. Far too many Enlighteners, he felt, were obsessed by abstraction: the pursuit of pure thought, of reason unencumbered by senses, passions, or bodies. Hamann dismissed this as gnostic nonsense. "Nature works through the senses and the passions," he thundered. "But those who maim these instruments, how can they feel? Are crippled sinews fit for movement? Your lying, murderous philosophy has cleared nature out of the way."[77] His passion on this point would influence the *Sturm und Drang* and the emergence of Romanticism, as we saw in chapter 8. It would also shape his response to Kant's *Critique of Pure Reason*, which he facetiously entitled *Metacritique of the Purism of Reason*; he saw Kant's system as motivated by "a Gnostic hatred of matter" and "an old, cold prejudice for mathematics before and behind it."[78] Fortunately for their friendship, Hamann never published it.

Second, because the message of the cross is *foolishness*, we must also resist the temptation to self-exaltation and pride that plagues all people, and philosophers in particular. God has humbled himself in Christ. Intellectuals have always struggled with that: "The pagan, the philosopher, recognises the omnipotence, majesty, holiness and goodness of God; but of the *humility* of his love for man he knows nothing."[79] The cross of Jesus is folly to the wise; the inspiration of Scripture is offensive to the philosophers of this age.[80] So in order to be truly wise, the Enlighteners need to realize how darkened they still are, and how little they actually know. But despite their professions of doubt, they remain remarkably confident in their own reason: "However much the ancient and modern sceptics wrap themselves in the lion's skin of Socratic ignorance, they nevertheless betray themselves by their *voice* and their *ears*. If they know nothing, why does the world need a learned demonstration of it? Their hypocrisy is ludicrous and shameless."[81] The *philosophes* claim to be skeptics, but when it comes to their own beliefs they are nowhere near skeptical enough. Only by genuinely humbling themselves, admitting their ignorance, and doubting their doubts can they gain self-knowledge—a task in which Hamann, as you might expect, is very eager to help.§

§ Interestingly, this conviction accounts for Hamann's notoriously cryptic and allusive style. God, for Hamann, has hidden himself in Scripture using signs, parables, and other seemingly foolish forms, like David disguising himself as a madman before Achish (1 Sam. 21). In the

Third, just as the message of the gospel is received by *faith*, so we need faith if we are to know anything at all. Reason on its own, divorced from faith, gets us nowhere. Hamann uses David Hume to devastating effect here: Hume argued that our knowledge of the external world is grounded in belief, not reason, and Hamann insists that he was absolutely right. Hume needed faith, not mere reason, to know that the sun would rise tomorrow, to realize that he would die, to eat an egg or drink a glass of water, to know that the world was there at all.[82] None of those things followed logically from undeniable premises. In the same way, "our own existence and the existence of all things outside us must be believed and can be made out in no other way."[83] Fundamentally, we know things—ourselves, other people, the external world, philosophy, God—in exactly the same way as we are saved: by faith. And as it happens, faith also makes life immeasurably more meaningful than reason alone. "What a Nothing, smoke, what a pestilent nothing are [our days] in our eyes when reason counts them! What an All, what a treasure, what an eternity, when they are counted by faith!"[84]

Fourth, and most originally, Hamann uses *Christology* to resolve the most sticky Enlightenment dilemma: how to reconcile idealism and realism, form and matter, subjective and objective, reason and experience. We summarized this apparent problem, and Kant's answer to it, in chapter 5. But Hamann finds Kant's answer ridiculously complicated, and indeed unnecessary, because it is caused by the needless philosophical habit of separating things—sensibility and understanding, form and matter, concept and intuition, and so forth—that God has joined together. The clearest evidence for that is the existence of language. Every time we speak to each other, we participate in a process that is *both* rational *and* empirical, involving abstract concepts on the one hand and sensations on the other. Separating them is fruitless. And ultimately, the reason why sensibility and understanding come together in words is because they come together in the Word: the Lord Jesus Christ, in whom Value becomes fact, Reason is experienced by the senses, the Ideal becomes real, and the Word is made

---

same way, Hamann himself "puts on faces and masks; he too hides behind the appearance of a madman, painting the doors of his writings with bizarre signs, allusions and ciphers—not out of mere eccentricity, but as an appropriate, calculated posture before a proudly rational audience . . . a faithful enacting of divine folly in an age that proudly considered itself the age of 'Enlightenment.'" See Betz, *After Enlightenment*, 50.

flesh. Human and divine natures are perfectly united in the person of Christ, such that the properties of each can be attributed to the other, and we provide a picture of these profound theological mysteries every time we have a conversation. "Popular language," Hamann concludes, "gives us the finest parable of the hypostatic union of the sensible and intelligible natures, the joint communication of the idiom and their powers."[85]

We might find it jarring to see Christian theological concepts like these used so freely in philosophical debate. It was rare then, and it is even rarer now. But Hamann has no time for the idea that "pure reason" should be kept separate from the contingencies of history, faith, tradition, culture, and language.[86] And he thinks this for an extremely good theological reason: Jesus Christ, the Truth himself, was fully immersed in all of them. Free-floating rationality, abstracted and liberated from the shackles of its specific cultural, religious, and linguistic contexts, is a chimera. It is not good for reason to be alone.

For a perfect illustration as to why, consider Hamann's whimsical and hilarious essay defending the letter *h*.[87] In a fit of enlightened fervor that verges on self-parody, the rationalist theologian Christian Tobias Damm had recently argued that the *h* should be removed from German words when it appeared unpronounced at the end. (Americans pulled the same trick with the letter *u* in English words like *colour*, albeit with rather more success.) The silent terminal *h*, Damm claimed, was "a pointless, groundless custom that appears barbaric in the eyes of all foreigners"—and since people who are not rational about spelling will not be rational about important things like "universal, sound, and practical human reason," it should henceforth be abolished.[88] Hamann demurred. If reason requires getting rid of the terminal *h*, he responded, why stop there? Why not remove double conso-nants, like those that the author has hypocritically retained in his own last name? Why not get rid of all silent letters? Why not publish a new edition of Damm's work, but with all the unpronounced letters taken out? "What *Damm* could withstand this orthographic deluge?"[89]

Behind the humorous façade was a very serious point. As absurd as it was, Damm's proposal was an excellent metaphor for what rationalists were trying to do across the board: abolish contingency, remove mystery, and achieve a pure, universal, timeless form of knowledge, free from all history, religion, and culture. Meanwhile the letter *h* was an excellent metaphor for the problem with that attempt: the stubborn reality that language, like knowledge as a whole, is cheerfully contingent, sublimely mysterious, and very much a product of history, religion, and culture. The silent *h*—like the Spirit of God who brings all language into being, in fact—was mysterious, inaudible, arbitrary, blowing wherever it wanted, and blissfully free from rationalist control. That was why Damm wanted to expunge it. "He wants to preach crucifixion against an innocent breath," Hamann remarked.[90] But the rationalist project was doomed to failure. "It is the spirit that quickens; the letter is flesh, and your dictionaries are straw."[91]

If that sounds like a rather postmodernist argument, both in form and in content, that is because it is. Hamann anticipated Nietzsche, Heidegger, and Derrida in several important ways; his playfulness with language, his metacritique of Kant, his linguistic philosophy, and his demonstration that reason cannot provide the grounding for itself were all decades ahead of their time.[92] (Peter Leithart puts it nicely, "It takes a prophet to contribute to debates two hundred years before they start.")[93] But Hamann's way forward is very different from the postmodernists'. They would reject all metanarratives and move toward nihilism; he rejected all metanarratives except one, and embraced Christianity. They thought the alternative to self-illumination was darkness. He thought the alternative was illumination from somewhere—or Someone—else.

In the aftermath of the Enlightenment, that essential choice remains. "The fundamental option comes down to one or another form of secular postmodernity or a postsecular theology," writes the Hamann scholar John Betz. "One can take the road of faith, which, as an inspired tradition attests, leads to ever greater enlightenment; or one can take the road of postmodern unbelief, which leads to nihilism."[94] For Hamann, the choice between Christ and the void was not difficult. "All the colours of the most beautiful world grow pale," he explained, "as soon as you extinguish that light, the firstborn of creation."[95]

The WEIRDER Prophets

It presumably goes without saying that the vast majority of Christians in 1776 were not reading Hamann or metacritiquing the Enlightenment. Nor, in the main, were they arguing for religious freedom, campaigning for abolition, or writing hymns and sermons about grace. Most of them were doing what ordinary Christians have done in every generation: working, eating, sleeping, raising their families, praying, loving, dying. Many were unaware of the debates raging all around them on matters of grace and truth, freedom and faith. Plenty of others were actively opposed to religious liberty (especially in the southern half of Europe) or the abolition of slavery (especially on the western side of the Atlantic). In that sense, the Christians we have considered in this chapter are no more representative of the Western church in 1776 than the founding fathers, the *philosophes*, and the Lunar Men are representative of everybody else.

But the reason for considering them is not that they are representative; it is that they are instructive. Whether they meant to or not—and Hamann clearly did, while Toplady probably didn't—they cultivated Christian ways of thinking, acting, and feeling that were extremely well suited to the WEIRDER world that was dawning around them. An individual experience of grace, it turned out, would prove particularly appealing to people in the age of Industrialization and Romanticism. Calls for personal and religious freedom would only grow louder as the world became more Western, Rich, and Democratic. Hamann's vision of Christian truth, more self-consciously, met the challenge of an Educated, Ex-Christian culture head on. It would take decades for some of these individuals to be vindicated by events. But that is often the way things go. A prophet is not without honor, except in his own century.

Fortunately for us, that means that their emphases have only grown in relevance over the last two hundred and fifty years.

Opportunities

Possibilities for a Postsecular World

Is there a thing of which it is said,
"See, this is new"?
It has been already
in the ages before us.
ECCLESIASTES 1:10

And the Word became flesh and dwelt among us,
and we have seen his glory, glory as of the only Son
from the Father, full of grace and truth.
JOHN 1:14

THE WEST IS NOT AS POST-CHRISTIAN as it seems. We saw that in chapter 6. No doubt, there are places on earth—the more conservative areas of the United States, for instance—where it can feel like the wider culture is currently rejecting Christianity at an unprecedented rate. But the Protestant paganism that characterizes the WEIRDER world is still, despite itself, irreducibly Christian. Imagine a cryogenically frozen Viking waking up in twenty-first century Scandinavia, or Asterix and Obelix encountering German social democracy or French *laïcité*, or one of Mahine's Polynesian ancestors being transported to contemporary New Zealand. As "secular" as those places might feel to believers, their values would seem deeply Christian to anyone who had not experienced them before.

Jürgen Habermas, perhaps our greatest living philosopher, puts it like this:

> For the normative self-understanding of modernity, Christianity has functioned as more than just a precursor or catalyst. Universalistic egalitarianism, from which sprang the ideals of freedom and a collective life in solidarity, the autonomous conduct of life and emancipation, the individual morality of conscience, human rights and democracy, is *the direct legacy of the Judaic ethic of justice and the Christian ethic of love.* This legacy, substantially unchanged, has been the subject of a continual critical reappropriation and reinterpretation. Up to this very day there is no alternative to it.[1]

As such, for Habermas, the world we are entering is not so much post-Christian as postsecular. Secular reason will always have its place, he argues, but it cannot ground itself (as we saw at the end of chapter 10), and that is a major problem. It can proclaim the goodness of science and choice and liberal democracy until it is blue in the face—but it cannot explain *why* we should develop particular technologies, choose particular goods, conceive of morality in a particular way, or be motivated to act in solidarity with others. It cannot even ask these questions, let alone answer them. To offer *whys* as well as *hows*, *ends* as well as *means*, you need faith: a worldview, a set of moral commitments, a religion, grounded in something beyond secular reason. The title of one recent work in which Habermas makes this case says it all: *An Awareness of What Is Missing—Faith and Reason in a Post-Secular Age.*[2] Reports of Christianity's death, it seems, have been greatly exaggerated.

Nevertheless, it is undoubtedly the case that living in that postsecular age presents plenty of challenges for orthodox believers. Whatever we call it—postsecularism, post-Christianity, Protestant paganism, or something else entirely—society is still WEIRDER. People are still skeptical toward Christianity, and in some cases (one thinks of sexual ethics in particular) downright hostile. The pagan gods are still here, in varying levels of disguise, most notably Mammon, Aphrodite, Apollo, Ares, Gaia, and Dionysus. Renouncing them all to follow Christ is still costly. Many people are still more committed to money, sex, and power than Father, Son, and Spirit (and the transformations we have traced in this book have made money, sex, and power more available to Western people than ever before). It is still harder for a rich person to enter the kingdom than for a camel to pass through the eye of a needle. The church still has many flaws, and the cultural influence of Christianity has made those flaws more, not less, unattractive to everybody else. And the sheer extent of that cultural influence makes people feel like they have already tried following Jesus and found it wanting, rather than finding it difficult and leaving it untried.[3] As any salesperson will tell you, it is hard to convince people to go for something new, but far harder if they think they have gone for it already and it didn't work.

Compounding those external cultural challenges is an internal, psychological one that is as unsettling as it is unspoken: many Christians feel like they are losing. In some Western countries, this is a question of sheer numbers. The percentage of people in church on Sundays has fallen substantially in many WEIRDER nations since the Second World War, even as it has risen substantially in parts of the Majority World over the same period.[*] But even in areas where levels of churchgoing remain strong, there is a widely held perception that Christian convictions have become increasingly marginal in public life. In some cases, they undoubtedly have. The American culture wars, which have now gone global through the influence of social media, provide plenty of examples.[4]

That decline in numbers and/or acceptability has met with varied responses from the WEIRDER church. Some of those responses—repentance, prayer, a renewed commitment to discipleship—are clearly positive. Others—fear, hostility, and the pursuit of influence or power by

---

[*] Unsurprisingly, there is plenty of debate about why this decline has happened, and why some nations (particularly the United States) appear to be such outliers. Is it the result of education, whereby religious skepticism rises with the progress of science, technology, and rationality? (No.) It is the result of prosperity, which causes people to depend on personal wealth or state welfare to protect them in troubled times, rather than their community and/or God? (Partly.) Is it the result of demography, as improvements in healthcare and contraception lead to smaller families, which in turn cause lower levels of religious commitment? (Probably.) Is it driven by the privatization of postwar life in general, whereby people abandon community participation across the board—clubs, unions, churches, sports teams, pubs, societies, and so forth—in favor of leisure activities that take place in private homes or anonymous third spaces? (Definitely.) Is it something else?

compromising morally or theologically—are obviously negative. Some observers remain optimistic and argue that things are not as bad as they seem; just look at growing church X, famous Christian Y, or thriving movement Z. Others think they are a good deal worse; did you hear about the Christian who got fired for saying a, doing b, or posting c? Some think the church needs a radical change of approach: her mission should be broader or narrower, her congregations should be larger or smaller, her voice on controversial subjects should be louder or quieter, her services should be more or less familiar to the surrounding culture, her teaching methods should be more traditional or innovative, she should adopt this new model that is working in India or Iran or Indonesia or Indiana or whatever. Others think the challenge is not really a methodological one at all, and that the church should essentially hunker down, get used to life on the margins, faithfully continue doing what she has always done, be prepared to suffer for what she believes, pray, and trust the God who brings life to the dead that he will do something new.

In that environment, the church of 1776 does not offer us a silver bullet. There is no strategy identified in the late eighteenth century that would transform the fortunes of the church today, if only we had the courage to implement it. Having said that, each of the three responses we considered in the previous chapter—the celebration of grace, the pursuit of freedom, and a postsecular vision of Christian truth—has the potential to strengthen the church as she seeks to reach and love the WEIRDER world around her. At the very least, the ways in which eighteenth-century Christians saw God do new things then, from revival and modern missions to religious freedom and abolitionism, should reassure those hoping that God will do a new thing now. Everything is unprecedented once.

Free Grace

In the final scene of Lin-Manuel Miranda's musical, Eliza Hamilton asks the question that haunts the post-Christian West. In the fifty years since her husband died, Eliza has given her life to preserving his legacy and to philanthropic activities, which include campaigning against slavery, establishing a school, fundraising for public works, and founding an orphanage. Her humanitarian resumé is extraordinarily impressive for a nineteenth-century woman, or indeed anybody. Yet as *Hamilton* closes, and she reflects on all that her workaholic, legacy-obsessed husband would have achieved if he had only lived longer, she wonders whether even her extensive catalogue of good works has been sufficient. Poignantly, she asks twice: Have I done enough?

It is a revealing question, especially since it says more about the anxieties of Broadway musical writers—and audiences—than the real Eliza Hamilton.[5] How many good works are "enough"? Enough to what? By whose standard? How would we know? There is nothing new about these questions; they are perennials of the human experience. But there are a number of features of the WEIRDER world that make them louder and more troubling. That, in turn, draws people toward the uniquely satisfying answer to them provided in Christianity: the grace of God.

One of those features is the sheer level of privilege that most WEIRDER people have experienced. If you live in grinding poverty, facing the daily threat of war and disease, and desperately trying to eke enough out of the ground or the workshop to feed your family until you die at the age of thirty, there is very little time to worry about whether you have "done enough" to justify your place on earth, let alone your place in history. But if you are healthy, educated, safe, and rich, with bountiful opportunities and many decades in which to pursue them, the question of legacy looms large (which you can see if you spend any time around high-net-worth individuals, or even graduates in their forties). Have I made the best use of the gifts I was given? Will I leave the world a better place than I found it? Did I make a mark? Have I done enough? Will they tell my story? The pressure of privilege is very real. With great power comes great responsibility, and as Spiderman knows very well, that responsibility can become a burden. The more privileged you are, the more tempting it is to seek justification by works.

Another feature is the WEIRDER obsession with identity. In most cultures, the question of identity is answered by society as a whole: you belong to this land, this people, this religion, this village, this extended family. Identity is not chosen, it is given. But for reasons we traced in chapter 8, WEIRDER people see selfhood quite differently. We take it for granted that life involves working out who we are, and then projecting our chosen identity out into the world. And that task falls to us as individuals. Who we "are" is constructed by our own actions and choices—economically, sexually, professionally, religiously, socially, creatively—and it is our responsibility to ensure that other people accept, recognize, and validate our chosen identity (which explains the prominence of identity in political discussions, to say nothing of the amount of yelling on social media).[6] That is why people say things like "I'm just trying to work out who I am," "You can be anyone you want," "If you don't accept this, then you don't accept *me*," or (tragically) "I don't know who I am anymore." Our very selves are constructions rather than gifts, secured and maintained by works and not grace. It can be exhausting.

For a third example, consider the ways in which we gain (or lose) status in the modern West.[7] Historically, in settled societies, the status of individuals and families was largely predetermined by birth. Rigid social hierarchies have been a fact of life for millennia: some people are born into nobility and honor, some into peasantry and mundanity, some into slavery and shame, and once your lot has been allocated, there is precious little chance of changing it. WEIRDER people, by contrast, think like egalitarian meritocrats. Everybody is equal, at least in theory. Status is achieved rather than inherited, earned rather than granted. People can rise as high (or fall as low) as they deserve. Not only that, but anybody can be anything if they put their minds to it; the only thing people need to realize their dreams of success, power, and fame is to pursue them with sufficient passion. The problem with this account is not just that it is clearly false. It is also that, in emphasizing effort over talent and works over grace, it means that people have nobody to blame but themselves when their hopes do not materialize. A fourteenth-century farmer who finds himself near the bottom of the social hierarchy can put it down to the cards he was dealt in life. A twenty-first century Westerner of equivalent status will feel like they have no such excuse. The implications, from stimulant usage to mental health conditions to suicide rates, are all around us.[8]

The point here is not that we should be nostalgic for a simpler time, when our station in life, occupation, and role in society were all settled for us at birth. That world is gone, and few of us would like it back. The point is that for all its many benefits—life expectancy, wealth, safety, education, health, choice, and the rest—the WEIRDER world is one that amplifies our cries for grace. The pressure of privilege, the construction of identity, and the pursuit of status make us restless by minimizing the givenness of things and exaggerating the power of achievement. They relentlessly confront us with Eliza Hamilton's question (or is it Lin-Manuel Miranda's?): Have I done enough? We could mention other factors too: the minute-by-minute comparisons we experience on social media, for example, or the prevalence of cancel culture, with its unattainable moral standards and dearth of grace. Anyone who thinks that justification by works is an exclusively religious phenomenon just needs to spend a few minutes on Twitter.

Those cries for grace are a marvelous opportunity for the contemporary church, because they are answered, uniquely, and fulsomely, in the Christian gospel. Grace has always been one of Christianity's most striking features. The claim that God in Christ takes the sin and death of the world upon himself, in order that he might freely and incongruously give his righteousness and life to those who do not deserve it, is without parallel in any other system of belief, religious or otherwise.[9] In a world powered by works and measured by achievement, there is something deeply refreshing about the unmerited, transforming favor of God, given without regard to the worth of the recipient. Rebellious wastrels return home to red-carpet welcomes; work-shy vineyard workers receive far more than they deserved; tax collectors and sinners enter ahead of Pharisees and Bible teachers; last-minute converts enter paradise on the same terms as everybody else. The message is entirely pitched at those whose works do *not* measure up. As preachers never tire of pointing out, there is a chasm of difference between the last words of the Buddha ("Strive with earnestness!") and the dying words of Christ ("It is finished!").[10]

The message of grace turns WEIRDER ways of thinking about privilege, identity, and status upside down. Those who have been given much, whether we call it "privilege" or "blessing," are still called to use their gifts for the benefit of others—"freely you have received, freely give," and so on—but their love and generosity are the results (or "fruits") of divine favor, not the means of securing it. Identity, likewise, is given rather than constructed; the believer becomes a new creation through union with Christ, and their new behavior flows from their new identity, not the other way around. Human ways of apportioning status are exploded by the cross, where the Lord of glory dies the shameful death of a slave before rising to the place of highest honor and sharing it with all who trust him. Where, then, is boasting? What do you have that you did not receive?

In each of these ways, and many others, the grace of God in Christ enables (and indeed requires) the believer to change the question that the

WEIRDER world so often asks. For the Christian, the focus is not on the individual, and the question is not: "Have I done enough?" After all, anyone with a modicum of self-awareness will cheerfully admit that the answer is no. The focus, rather, is on Christ, and the question is: "Has he?"

True Freedom

Christianity is liberating or it is nothing. That gives the contemporary church an advantage, a challenge, and an opportunity.

According to the fourth chapter of Luke's Gospel, Jesus launched his public ministry by claiming to fulfill Isaiah's promises of good news to the poor, freedom for the captives, and liberty for the oppressed. John presents Christ as the Son who sets people free, and free indeed. Paul articulates his gospel as a message of redemption: from slavery, fear, sin, death, law, judgment, the cosmic powers, and the present evil age. The defining moment of the entire Hebrew Bible is the exodus from Egypt, the ultimate story of liberation from slavery. The sacraments that the church has practiced ever since deliberately evoke that story, from the Passover meal (Eucharist) to the Red Sea crossing (baptism). There are calls for the forgiveness of debts and for deliverance from evil at the heart of the Lord's Prayer, drawing on the Jewish freedom festivals of Passover, Yom Kippur, and Jubilee. Christian eschatology revolves around the promise of freedom from captivity for the whole world. And Christian ethics are fundamentally redemptive: the church is to receive God's freedom, refuse to fall back again into slavery, and extend that liberty to others. For the Lord is the Spirit, and where the Spirit of the Lord is, there is freedom.[11]

That vision still resonates with the instincts of WEIRDER people, not least because (as we saw in chapter 6) those instincts have been forged on the anvil of Christianity. Freedom is one of the few abstractions to be celebrated across the political spectrum. Granted, people conceptualize it quite differently. On the right, it is generally seen individually, with oppression most likely to come from the interference, taxation, and overreach of the all-powerful state; on the left, it is generally seen corporately, with oppression baked into the structures of society through historical injustices. But virtually everyone agrees that freedom for all oppressed people is a goal worth pursuing. Our villains are all tyrants (Hitler, Stalin, Mao, Pol Pot). Our saints, both on the right (Lincoln, Churchill, Reagan) and the left (Tubman,

King, Mandela), are lauded for having delivered people from the menace of tyranny. Our fairytales are stories of liberation. The ethical impulse of the contemporary West is redemptive in nature—good news for the poor, freedom for the captives, liberty for the oppressed, and release for those in darkness—and that chimes with the Christian gospel in all kinds of ways. That is the advantage.

The challenge is obvious: Christians have often failed to live up to that vision, especially when money and power are available. The church of 1776 brings that into sharp focus. As American dissenters were calling for religious liberty, Spanish inquisitors were cracking down on Enlightenment sympathizers. As Lemuel Haynes and Granville Sharp were arguing that slavery was incompatible with Scripture, plenty of their brothers and sisters were busy arguing (and practicing) the exact opposite. As Olaudah Equiano was sharing the gospel on a ship in the West Indies, many other professing Christians were on ships in both the West and East Indies for rather more nefarious reasons. Wheat and tares grow together.

Variations on that theme have been played out in every generation since. There were Christians on both sides at Fort Sumter, Stalingrad, Selma, and Soweto. For all the worshipers who went from church on Sundays to join civil rights marches in the 1960s, there were also worshipers who went from church on Sundays to fire tear gas and water cannons in their faces. To this day, many Christians care far more about religious liberty when they are a beleaguered minority than a moral majority, and while this may be quite natural, it smacks of hypocrisy nonetheless. All of us are less likely to notice oppression if we benefit from it than if we suffer from it.[†] So living out the manifesto of Christ in Luke 4 takes more than simply affirming it, or applying it to situations in which we have something to gain and very little to lose. It means honestly assessing ourselves in light of it, in dialogue with the people Jesus and Isaiah were talking about—oppressed people, prisoners, those with disabilities, the disenfranchised, the enslaved, refugees, minorities, those in poverty—before repenting of the ways in which

---

[†]   In the justly famous words of Upton Sinclair, "It is difficult to get a man to understand something, when his salary depends upon his not understanding it!" *I, Candidate for Governor: And How I Got Licked* (1935; repr., Berkeley: University of California Press, 1994), 109. The number of situations to which this applies in the contemporary church, tragically, are too numerous to mention.

we have fallen short of it, and renewing our commitment to an ethic of liberation. Free people free people.

And this brings us to the opportunity. The Christian vision of freedom is far larger, more holistic, and more genuinely liberating than its WEIRDER equivalent. In the modern understanding, oppression is fundamentally external to the person. People are constrained by things outside of them—whether guns or governments, laws or circumstances—and the goal is to set people free from those constraints so that they can choose what they want for themselves. But in the ancient understanding, from the Torah to Aristotle to Paul's letters, that is only half the picture. Human beings can also be imprisoned by things within themselves: sinful desires, foolish cravings, untrained passions. The goal of freedom is not unconstrained choices as such; our choices might well be destructive, and the very things from which we need to be freed. Slavery comes from the flesh as well as the powers, from the self as well as the other. So genuine liberty is not just a matter of freedom *from* things that might restrict our autonomy but freedom *to* choose those things that cause us to flourish, and become what we were originally created to be. In order to be truly free, we need to be liberated from captivity to *sin*—our lusts, pride, greed, envy, and so on—as well as captivity to human oppressors or economic circumstances. That is what Jesus came to bring.

Those contrasting visions of slavery and freedom are juxtaposed neatly in Suzanne Collins's *The Hunger Games*.[12] In an intriguing move, Collins creates a world in which the two great dystopias of twentieth-century fiction, Aldous Huxley's *Brave New World* and George Orwell's *1984*, exist side by side in the same universe. The residents of District 12, including the protagonist Katniss Everdeen, are oppressed in the *1984* sense that is most familiar to WEIRDER people: physical coercion, omnipresent surveillance, electrified fences, draconian laws, material deprivation. The residents of the Capitol, by contrast, are in bondage to their carnal passions running amok, like the people in *Brave New World*. Their vacuous pastimes, absurd makeup, obscene practices (like vomiting up meals so that they can eat more), obsession with entertainment, and inane conversation all bear witness to the invisible chains of unconstrained desire, the combined effect of which is to make their lives emptier, less meaningful, and in many ways more pitiable than those of Katniss, Peeta, and their friends. Those in the

Districts need freedom from the dreaded other. Those in the Capitol need freedom from the deadened self.

The opportunity for the church, then, is to present the WEIRDER world with the Christian vision of liberty in all its fullness: spiritual and physical, freedom *from* and freedom *to*, confronting the flesh within and the powers without. At her worst, the church has missed the mark on both of these. She has sometimes slipped into gnosticism (with insufficient concern for physical oppression, economic circumstances, imperial realities, and Orwellian despotic powers), and sometimes slid into materialism (with insufficient attention given to true spirituality, and the need to fight against the Huxleyan tendency to trivialize, despoil, and consume). But at her best, she has battled both Orwell's and Huxley's dystopias, contending against the tyranny of the other and the tyranny of the self, and embodying a freedom that truly liberates captives, whatever their chains may be.

That vision will sound compelling to many. But it will also sound puzzling, especially to those for whom the freedom to do whatever you desire matters far more than the freedom to desire the right things. Many today, like citizens of the Capitol in *The Hunger Games* or the World State in *Brave New World*, will be surprised by the language of freedom in this sort of context, because they are free to do whatever they want and have never been enslaved to anyone. The Judeans said the exact same thing to Jesus in the eighth chapter of John's Gospel. But Jesus's reply captured the issue perfectly. "Truly, truly, I say to you, everyone who practices sin is a slave to sin," he explained. "So if the Son sets you free, you will be free indeed" (John 8:34, 36).

Gracious Truth

The year 2016 is often seen as a turning point. That was the year that "post-truth" entered the vernacular, as political campaigns on both sides of the Atlantic started trafficking in palpable falsehoods (or "alternative facts"), as opposed to the disputed narratives, misleading statistics, and exaggerated promises that usually characterize political debate.[‡] Suddenly bookstores and newspaper op-ed sections were awash with laments about the end of

---

‡   The notorious phrase "alternative facts" was actually coined in January 2017. Interestingly, within four days of Kellyanne Conway using it, George Orwell's *1984* had become the number one bestseller on Amazon.

truth in public life and proposals for how to get it back. A flurry of similar TV dramas came out whose premises revolved around "fake news." Serious discussions took place about whether democratic norms can be maintained in a society when a large number of its citizens reject basic claims about matters of fact. The Oxford Dictionaries named "post-truth" their word of the year.

"Post-truth" discourse did not originate in 2016, obviously; that was simply the year that the populist right successfully weaponized it to politically defeat the elite left. In 2004, the American author Ralph Keyes published a book with the prophetic title *The Post-Truth Era: Dishonesty and Deception in Everyday Life*. A generation before that, Hannah Arendt traced the genealogy of political "defactualization" to advertising and the rise of the consumer society, in her *Lying in Politics: Reflections on the Pentagon Papers*.[13] A generation before that, George Orwell wrote the novel whose imagery ("memory hole," "thought police," "doublethink") still dominates the discussion. The first use of the term "fake news" was fifty years earlier, in the 1890s. And it was two decades before that, way back in 1873, that Friedrich Nietzsche had made this eerie statement in his essay on truth, lies, and metaphor:

> What then is truth? A movable host of metaphors, metonymies, and anthropomorphisms: in short, a sum of human relations which have been poetically and rhetorically intensified, transferred, and embellished, and which, after long usage, seem to a people to be fixed, canonical, and binding. *Truths are illusions which we have forgotten are illusions*—they are metaphors that have become worn out and have been drained of sensuous force, coins which have lost their embossing and are now considered as metal and no longer as coins.[14]

Admittedly, most people who use the term "post-truth" today are not going anything like this far. The contemporary phenomenon would be better described as "post-trust": the erosion of public confidence in certain institutions, particularly in academia and the legacy media, to serve as credible arbiters of public knowledge. Yet we should also acknowledge the philosophical and theological roots of the problem. If Johann Georg Hamann was right—if the attempt to ground reason in itself turned out to be an elaborate failure, and if no such ultimate grounding is even possible without divine revelation—then post-Christianity will lead to post-truth eventually, and Nietzsche is merely stating the obvious. We would expect to find WEIRDER societies struggling to disentangle truth claims from power claims, useful truths from noble lies, objective reality from "living my truth," and eventually fact from fiction.

We touched on an illuminating example in chapter 6. Yuval Noah Harari's book *Sapiens* has sold over twenty million copies. Its earnestly scientific account of human development, and impeccable endorsements from Barack Obama, Bill Gates, and all the top newspapers, make it seem like the polar opposite of a post-truth narrative. But one of its central arguments is that we all agree on things that are false, and that affirming things that are false is in fact vital in establishing healthy and prosperous societies. We know that human rights do not really exist. We know that people are not really equal. Those ideas are myths that we have created, largely through the "imagined order" of Christianity. Yet we affirm them even when we reject Christianity. And we are right to do so, because myths like these—widely held but factually incorrect—enable large numbers of human beings to cooperate effectively, build a better world, and pursue life, freedom, and happiness.[15] In a subsequent book, Harari goes further, explaining that we are "a post-truth species, whose power depends on creating and believing fictions."[16] Falsehoods facilitate cohesion and liberty, and that's just the way it is. The untruth will set you free.

No doubt, there are people who are happy to live with that level of cognitive dissonance, if only because it means they can pick and choose their moral absolutes.[17] There may even be people who think Harari's suggested responses—a blend of bourgeois life hacks, decaffeinated Buddhism, and resignation—are equal to the task of engaging with a post-truth world.[18] But to many others, that kind of dissociation between what one claims to believe and what one actually believes will seem absurd or even dangerous, with side effects ranging from cynicism and apathy to emptiness and despair. It is hard to promote or proscribe certain behavior if you think your moral framework is merely a useful fiction. It is hard to be hopeful about the world, or motivated to change it, without committing to some account of reality that you are convinced is essentially true. It is even harder to make sacrifices or campaign for justice on the basis of beliefs you acknowledge to be essentially false. For plenty of people today, especially the oppressed or disenfranchised, a post-truth world is an unaffordable luxury.

The Christian vision, in which truth is personally embodied by God himself, could not be more different. The contrast is dramatized in one of history's most memorable confrontations. On one side you have Jesus Christ, claiming not just to witness to the truth but to actually *be* the truth, and claiming that everyone who is of the truth listens to his voice. On the other you have Pontius Pilate, asking "What is truth?" and then disappearing outside without waiting for an answer. One reveals utter integrity, the love of God speaking truth to power and being ready to suffer the consequences; the other offers an imperial smirk, the nonchalant shrug of a man who will be paid and be powerful regardless of what he thinks is "true." In Christ, divine veracity is enfleshed; in Pilate, human cynicism is exposed. It is somehow fitting that the former dies, and has been visually represented ever since, beneath words written—but not really believed as true—by the latter (John 18:28–40; 19:19–22).

It took several centuries, but Christ's approach to truth eventually prevailed over Pilate's. It came to be believed by millions (and eventually billions) of people that there is one God, Creator of heaven and earth, who has created human beings in his image; that his Son, who shares his divine nature, became human, was crucified under Pontius Pilate, rose from the dead in accordance with the Scriptures, and ascended into heaven; and that his Spirit continues to give life to his people and guide them into all the truth. Consequently, it is possible to know what is true, not just about God, but about creation, humanity, history, and the future. Creation is coherent, created with purpose by an all-loving God. Every human being possesses inestimable value simply by bearing God's image. History is heading somewhere under divine guidance rather than going round and round in circles. The future will be better than the present, culminating in the renewal of all things and the final encounter with the love that moves the sun and other stars. And the implications of those four truth claims are indelibly stamped on the WEIRDER world. Historically they were known as knowledge, dignity, providence, and hope. Today we call them science, human rights, meaning, and progress.§

§ It is interesting that Francis Bacon, the man often credited for the rise of empirical science and thus indirectly the Industrial Revolution (see chapter 7), is also the man who famously used the confrontation between Pilate and Christ to launch his essay on truth: "'What is truth?' said

None of this proves that the Christian account of reality is actually true. That has to be established in other ways. Indeed it might be complete nonsense, which we only go along with because we find it more appealing than the animist, polytheist, Islamic, or nihilist alternatives. But it does mean, I suggest, that we should *want* it to be true. If the central tenets of Christianity correspond to reality—if God is love, creation is good, humans are image bearers, sin is forgivable, Christ is risen, death is temporary, and justice is coming—then our commitment to human rights and equality reflect divine warrant rather than wish fulfilment, and the world is an immeasurably more hopeful and more meaningful place than it is if they do not.[19] We should all want that. And when people want things to be true, as Blaise Pascal pointed out four centuries ago, they are halfway there already:

> Men despise religion. They hate it and are afraid it may be true. The cure for this is first to show that religion is not contrary to reason, but worthy of reverence and respect. Next make it attractive: make good men wish it were true. Then show that it is.[20]

Renewal

This leaves dozens of questions unanswered, as all books do. How exactly do you show that Christianity is true in a culture like ours? How do you help believers, let alone everybody else, embrace the full range of Christian truth revealed in Scripture rather than just the bits that WEIRDER people find palatable? What does a comprehensive vision of true freedom look like? How does it work when it comes to everyday issues like money, sex, and power? How can the church best express the grace of God in Christ, and the joy that goes with it, in her corporate worship, liturgy, and prayer? These are all good questions, even if we do not have space to get into them here. Fortunately, most Christian

---

jesting Pilate, and would not stay for an answer." Bacon's *Of Truth* goes on to argue that it is "the sovereign good of human nature" to inquire, know, and believe what is true, on the basis that "the first creature of God in the works of the days was the light of the sense, the last was the light of reason, and his Sabbath work ever since is the illumination of his spirit." As such, "it is heaven upon earth to have a man's mind move in charity, rest in providence, and turn upon the poles of truth." Indeed. See Francis Bacon, *Of Truth*, Bartleby (website), accessed January 3, 2023, https://www.bartleby.com/.

resources today address at least one of them in some form. I have written books on each of them myself.[21]

But that still leaves the question I raised at the start of this chapter: Does the church need a radical change of approach to adjust to an unprecedented world or a renewed commitment to the doctrines, practices, and experiences that have sustained the church in the past?

Generally speaking, I lean toward the latter. WEIRDER people, even those in the church, are natural Pelagians. We think success comes through trying, not trusting; we want things to work, and if they do not, we experiment with something else; we are more likely than our ancestors were to venerate strategies, steps, and solutions, and less likely than they were to honor mysteries, mystics, and martyrs; and we hate the idea of "losing," whatever that is. So if the church is declining in numbers or moving to the margins of society, our instinct is to assume that we are missing something, and so we seek to rectify it by a change of tactics. That generates plenty of innovation, no doubt, but it also causes striving and a good deal of anxiety. Pelagianism always does.

By contrast, when you read people who have thought seriously about the deeper historical and cultural forces that have shaped the modern West, you find a rather different picture emerging.[22] Fidelity scores higher than novelty. Loss of influence is not a cause for panic. The doctrines, experiences, and practices that the church needs today are much the same as the ones she needed in the eighteenth century, and the tenth, and the second. We are responsible for obedience not outcomes, faithfulness not fruit; if we do not see the results we used to by praying, worshiping, reading Scripture, serving the poor, preaching the gospel, sharing the sacraments, and loving one another, we carry on with those things regardless and walk by faith not by sight. Genuine revival, when it comes, is at God's initiative rather than ours. In the meantime, we wait, rejoicing always, praying without ceasing, giving thanks in all circumstances, and resolving not to be anxious about tomorrow, for we have no idea what tomorrow will bring.

In the end, for all the ways in which 1776 remade the world, there is nothing new under the sun. That is not to say that we have no need of breakthrough, transformation, or revival. It is simply to say that when those things happen, as they surely will, they will not come from under the sun but from the One enthroned above it, who is committed to making all things new. The words of Augustus Toplady, written at the start of 1776, still hold true: "Providence, unerring providence, governs all events. And grace, unchangeable grace, is faithful to its purpose. May we live by faith on both."[23]

Acknowledgments

THIS IS THE MOST FUN I have ever had writing a book, and it has made me grateful for many things.

One is the time and space to research and write it in the first place. Thank you to Steve and Deb Tibbert, the Trustees and Elders at King's Church London, and everyone who made it possible for me to have a sabbatical in the summer of 2022, without which I might never have finished. Thanks to Andy, Alex, and all at Urban Ground in Eastbourne, where much of the writing was actually done. I am very grateful to Geoff and Jess Youngs for letting us stay in their beautiful home. Thank you also to the indispensable friends and family who help look after our children when I am buried in books: Mark and Julia Evetts, Jenny Owen, Richard and Jenny James, and many others.

In some ways, the most precious resource when you are writing is encouragement. I am so thankful for those who expressed an interest in the project, asked clarifying questions, and deepened my resolve to work on it at crucial times: Nathan Gamester over fish and chips in Eastbourne, Tom Holland in a Brixton pub, Jez Field in a Seaford curry house, Jen Wilkin in a roundtable discussion in Texas, Collin Hansen and Jeremy Treat in an unintended Holiday Inn bar in Washington DC, Joel Virgo at Brown's in Brighton, Brannon McAllister and the Council of The Gospel Coalition in the Museum of the Bible, Matt Anderson at a Fort Worth barbecue, Dave Holden on a beach in Cyprus, and Justin Taylor at Crossway before this all started. Rob Milton gave me a vital source from Augustus Toplady, and Oli Stevens gave me a slightly less vital bobblehead of George Washington to watch over me as I studied.

Erik Wolgemuth, my agent, heard a garbled version of my idea while he was locked down in Denver and has been a fount of encouragement, diligence, and helpful suggestions ever since. Rachel, my wife, has been far more interested in and supportive of the project than I deserved, especially given the amount of time I have spent talking about it. And Samuel James and Kevin Emmert have been through the whole manuscript with a plethora of fine-tooth combs, sharpening and correcting it in all sorts of ways, for which I am extremely grateful (and somewhat in awe). Any remaining errors are, needless to say, entirely my fault.

Endnotes

Chapter 1: Roots

1. Eric Hobsbawm, *The Age of Revolution: Europe, 1789–1848* (London: Abacus, 1962), 13.
2. William Faulkner, *Requiem for a Nun* (London: Vintage, 2015), 85.
3. John Simpson, *Strange Places, Questionable People* (London: Pan Macmillan, 1999), 131.
4. Interview with Christopher Benson, "Faithful Presence," *Christianity Today*, May 14, 2010, https://www.christianitytoday.com/.
5. James Baldwin, as quoted in *I Am Not Your Negro*, directed by Raoul Peck, (Artemis Productions, 2016).
6. This paragraph and some of what follows in the remainder of this chapter was first published in Andrew Wilson, "1776: The Origin Story of the Post-Christian West," *Think Theology* (blog), February 25, 2021, https://thinktheology.co.uk/.
7. The acronym WEIRD was first coined by Joseph Henrich, Steven Heine, and Ara Norenzayan, "The Weirdest People in the World?," *Behavioral and Brain Sciences* 33 (2010), 61–83. For a peer-reviewed article in a brain science journal, it has a surprisingly arresting first line: "In the tropical forests of New Guinea, the Etoro believe that for a boy to achieve manhood he must ingest the semen of his elders." It has since been followed up in much greater detail by Joseph Henrich, *The WEIRDest People in the World: How the West Became Psychologically Peculiar and Particularly Prosperous* (London: Allen Lane, 2020), of which more in chap. 2.
8. *Parks and Recreation*, season 6, episode 1, "London," directed by Dean Holland, aired September 26, 2013, on NBC.
9. Thomas Paine, *The American Crisis (No. 1)* (Boston: 1776).
10. William Heath, *Memoirs of Major-General Heath. Containing Anecdotes, Details of Skirmishes, Battles, and Other Military Events, During the American War* (Boston: Thomas and Andrews, 1798), 60 (September 15, 1776).
11. Lemuel Haynes, *Liberty Further Extended, or Free Thoughts on the Illegality of Slave-Keeping*; see Ruth Bogin, "'Liberty Further Extended': A 1776 Antislavery Manuscript by Lemuel Haynes," *The William and Mary Quarterly* 40, no. 1 (1983), 95.
12. Abigail Adams to John Adams, March 31, 1776; see John Adams and Abigail Adams, *The Adams Papers: Adams Family Correspondence*, vol. 1, *December 1761–May 1776*, ed. Lyman H. Butterfield (Cambridge: Harvard University Press, 1963), 369–71.
13. Edmund Burke to Richard Champion, May 30, 1776; see Edmund Burke, *Correspondence of the Right Honourable Edmund Burke*, 4 vols. (London: Rivington, 1844), 2:107.

14. Luke Tyerman, *The Life and Times of the Rev. John Wesley*, 3 vols. (London: Hodder and Stoughton, 1872), 3:234–35.

15. Thomas Paine, *Common Sense: Addressed to the Inhabitants of America* (Philadelphia: Bradford, 1776), 161.

16. James Boswell, *The Life of Samuel Johnson* (1791; repr., London: Penguin, 2008), 510.

17. Jeremy Bentham, *A Fragment on Government* (London: Payne, Elmsly, and Brooke, 1776), ii.

18. Adam Smith, *The Wealth of Nations*, 2 vols., ed. Andrew Skinner (1776; repr., London: Penguin, 1999), 2:32.

19. Horace Walpole to Anne, Countess of Upper Ossory, August 16, 1776; see Horace Walpole, *Letters Addressed to the Countess of Ossory, From the Year 1769 to 1797, by Horace Walpole*, ed. Robert Vernon Smith, 2 vols. (London: Bentley, 1848).

20. Virginia Declaration of Rights (June 29, 1776), art. 16, National Archives (website), accessed December 20, 2022, https://www.archives.gov/.

21. The Declaration of Independence, National Archives (website), accessed December 20, 2022, https://www.archives.gov/founding-docs/declaration-transcript.

22. The term "postsecular" is drawn from the German philosopher Jürgen Habermas; see chap. 11.

23. George Orwell, *Nineteen Eighty-Four* (1949; repr., London: Penguin, 1954), 127.

Chapter 2: Quirks

1. Tara Westover, *Educated: A Memoir* (London: Penguin, 2018).

2. Charles Taylor, *A Secular Age* (Cambridge, MA: Belknap Press of Harvard University Press, 2007), chap. 6.

3. That the assumptions in this paragraph are generated by the influence of Christian theology is impossible to substantiate here, but for excellent recent presentations of the case, see, e.g., Larry Siedentop, *Inventing the Individual: The Origins of Western Liberalism* (London: Penguin, 2015); Nick Spencer, *The Evolution of the West: How Christianity Has Shaped Our Values* (London: SPCK, 2016); Christian Smith, *Atheist Overreach: What Atheism Can't Deliver* (Oxford: Oxford University Press, 2019); Tom Holland, *Dominion: The Making of the Western Mind* (London: Little Brown, 2019).

4. Nobody saw this more clearly (and critically) than Friedrich Nietzsche, *Beyond Good and Evil* (1886; repr., London: Penguin, 2003).

5. Roger Scruton, "Dancing Properly," in *Confessions of a Heretic: Selected Essays* (London: Notting Hill Editions, 2016), 50–64.

6. Jonathan Haidt, *The Righteous Mind: Why Good People Are Divided by Politics and Religion* (London: Penguin, 2012), 111–79.

7. Shinobu Kitayama, "Perceiving an Object and its Context in Different Cultures: A Cultural Look at New Look," *Psychological Science* 14, no. 3 (2003): 201–6.

8. Greg Lukianoff and Jonathan Haidt, *The Coddling of the American Mind: How Good Intentions and Bad Ideas are Setting Up a Generation for Failure* (London: Penguin, 2018).

9. See Joseph Henrich, *The WEIRDest People in the World: How the West Became Psychologically Peculiar and Particularly Prosperous* (London: Allen Lane, 2020), 21–58, 193–232, for the supporting experiments, data, and charts.

10. Henrich, WEIRDEST People in the World, 41.

11. The next two paragraphs originally appeared in Andrew Wilson, "1776 and the Origin Story of the Post-Christian West," The Gospel Coalition (website), May 31, 2021, https://www.thegospelcoalition.org/.

12. White House Press Release: "Remarks by The First Lady at 'Hamilton at the White House' Student Workshop," American Presidency Project (website), March 14, 2016, https://www.presidency.ucsb.edu/.

13. The next two paragraphs originally appeared in Andrew Wilson, "It's Hamilton's World. We're Just Living in It," *Christianity Today*, February 14, 2022, https://www.christianitytoday.com/.

14. Lin-Manuel Miranda, "Yorktown," in *Hamilton: An American Musical* (New York: Grand Central, 2016).

15. Miranda, "A Winter's Ball," in *Hamilton*.

16. Miranda, "Alexander Hamilton," in *Hamilton*.

17. Miranda, "Hurricane," in *Hamilton*.

18. Miranda, "Burn," in *Hamilton*.

19. See Owen Strachan, "Keep Your Eyes on the Trees: An Essay on *1917*, the Most Profound Film Since *Tree of Life*," Providence (website), May 7, 2020, https://providencemag.com/.

20. *1917*, directed by Sam Mendes (DreamWorks, 2019).

21. William Blake, *Memorandum*, K 437; see Peter Ackroyd, *Blake* (London: Vintage, 1999), 257–67. The code relates to the prosecution record.

22. Hilary Mantel, *Bring Up the Bodies* (London: Fourth Estate, 2012), 140–41.

23. This case is made superbly by Holland in *Dominion*.

24. Charles Taylor, *Sources of the Self: The Making of the Modern Identity* (Cambridge, MA: Harvard University Press, 1989).

25. Philip Rieff, *The Triumph of the Therapeutic: Uses of Faith after Freud* (1966; repr., Chicago: University of Chicago Press, 1987).

26. Robert N. Bellah et al., *Habits of the Heart: Individualism and Commitment in American Life* (1985; repr., Berkeley: University of California Press, 2008).

27. The majority opinion in *Planned Parenthood v. Casey*, 1992.

28. For a much fuller version of this story, see Carl Trueman, *The Rise and Triumph of the Modern Self: Cultural Amnesia, Expressive Individualism, and the Road to Sexual Revolution* (Wheaton, IL: Crossway, 2020).

29. Marilynne Robinson, *The Givenness of Things: Essays* (London: Virago Press, 2015).

30. The question, then, is how best to help those with gender dysphoria. See Preston Sprinkle, *Embodied: Transgender Identities, the Church, and What the Bible Has to Say* (Colorado Springs: David C. Cook, 2021).

31. Slavoj Žižek, "There Is Nothing Inherently Revolutionary in Transgenderism," The Radical Revolution, June 22, 2020, YouTube video, www.youtube.com/.

32. Alan Jacobs, "On Cultural Socialism and Metaphysical Capitalism," *The Homebound Symphony* (blog), February 14, 2019, https://blog.ayjay.org/.

33. Zygmunt Bauman, *Liquid Modernity* (Cambridge: Polity; Oxford: Blackwell, 2000); see also Umberto Eco, *Chronicles of a Liquid Society* (London: Vintage, 2017).

Chapter 3: Maps

1. See Peter Moore's outstanding *Endeavour: The Ship and the Attitude That Changed the World* (London: Vintage, 2019); also Nicholas Thomas, *Discoveries: The Voyages of Captain Cook* (London: Penguin, 2018).

2. Joseph Banks on May 29, 1769; see Joseph Banks, *Journal of the Right Honourable Sir Joseph Banks*, ed. Joseph Hooker (London: Macmillan, 1896), 93.

3. Banks on July 14, 1770; see Banks, *Journal*, 287.

4. Banks on May 15, 1770; see "April–June 1770," Captain Cook Society (website), https://www.captaincooksociety.com/.

5. James Cook on April 30, 1770; see James Cook, *Captain Cook's Journal during His First Voyage round the World Made in H. M. Bark "Endeavour," 1768–71* [. . .], ed. W. J. L. Wharton (London, Elliott Stock, 1893), accessed online at Gutenberg Project Australia (website), https://gutenberg.net.au/; cf. J. C. Beaglehole, *The Journals of Captain James Cook*, 4 vols. (Cambridge: Cambridge University Press, 1955–1967).

6. Cook on January 16, 1769; see Cook, *Cook's First Voyage*.

7. E.g., Dinesh D'Souza, *What's So Great about America* (Washington DC: Regnery, 2002), chap. 2.

8. Jared Diamond, *Guns, Germs, and Steel: A Short History of Everybody for the Last 13,000 Years* (1997; repr., London: Vintage, 2017), 14. Anyone familiar with Diamond's book will quickly see how much it has informed parts of this chapter.

9. Niall Ferguson, *Civilization: The Six Killer Apps of Western Power* (London: Penguin, 2012), 10.

10. Ian Morris, *Why the West Rules—for Now: The Patterns of History, and What They Reveal about the Future* (London: Profile, 2010), 11.

11. Samuel Johnson, *The History of Rasselas, Prince of Abyssinia* (London, 1759). Rasselas, of course, is a fictional character created by Samuel Johnson.

12. Cook to John Walker, November 20, 1772; see Beaglehole, *Journals*, 2:689.

13. Cook on February 6, 1775; see James Cook, *A Voyage towards the South Pole and round the World* [. . .], vol. 2 (London: Strahan and Cadell, 1777), accessed online at Gutenberg Project Australia (website), accessed December 21, 2022, https://www.gutenberg.org/.

14. Cook on January 6, 1774; see James Cook, *A Voyage towards the South Pole and round the World* [. . .], vol. 1 (London: Strahan and Cadell, 1777), accessed online at Gutenberg Project Australia (website), December 21, 2022, https://www.gutenberg.org/.

15. Cook on February 6, 1775; see Cook, *Voyage towards the South Pole and round the World*, vol. 2.

16. Georg Forster, *A Voyage around the World, in His Britannic Majesty's Sloop, Resolution* [. . .], 2 vols. (London, 1777), 1:587.

17. Forster, *Voyage*, 1:593–95. Forster speculated (wrongly) that the catastrophe might have been a volcanic eruption.

18. Quoted and translated in Thomas, *Discoveries*, 224.

19. As David Graeber and David Wengrow have recently shown, these groups of hunter-gatherers and foragers were far more varied in their social, economic, and political structures than is often assumed; the idea that they were all mobile, egalitarian, nomadic bands does not reflect the archaeological or biogeographical evidence. See David Graeber and David Wengrow, *The Dawn of Everything: A New History of Humanity* (London: Allen Lane, 2021).

20. Thomas Hobbes, *Leviathan*, ed. Richard Tuck (Cambridge: Cambridge University Press, 1996), 86–90.

21. Cook on August 23, 1770; see Cook, *Cook's First Voyage*.

22. Clearly, farming was not a sufficient condition for these technologies, which took thousands of years to emerge (to say nothing of those groups that started farming and then abandoned it). But it was almost certainly a necessary one.

23. See David W. Anthony, *The Horse, the Wheel and Language: How Bronze-Age Riders from the Eurasian Steppes Shaped the Modern World* (Princeton: Princeton University Press, 2007).

24. See Kyle Harper, *Plagues upon the Earth: Disease and the Course of Human History* (Princeton: Princeton University Press, 2021), pt. 2.

25. George Orwell, *Animal Farm* (London: Penguin, 1951), 114.

26. The data in this table is drawn from Diamond, *Guns, Germs, and Steel*, 95–96, 120–21, 135, 153–61.

27. Said al-Andalusi, *Categories of Nations* (1068), quoted in Bernard Lewis, *The Muslim Discovery of Europe* (New York: Norton, 2001), 68.

28. Diamond, *Guns, Germs, and Steel*; Tim Marshall, *Prisoners of Geography: Ten Maps That Tell You Everything You Need to Know about Global Politics* (London: Elliott and Thompson, 2015); Victor Lieberman, *Strange Parallels: Southeast Asia in Global Context, c. 80–1830*, 2 vols. (Cambridge: Cambridge University Press, 2003–2010); David Landes, *The Wealth and Poverty of Nations: Why Some Are So Rich and Some Are So Poor* (New York: Norton, 1998); Kenneth Pomeranz, *The Great Divergence: China, Europe and the Making of the Modern World Economy* (Princeton: Princeton University Press, 2000); Morris, *Why the West Rules*.

29. From Cook's letter to the Navy Board, April 2, 1776, accessed online at Trove, https://nla.gov.au/nla.obj-568199552/view.

30. The numbers here are hotly debated by historians, but nobody doubts that Zheng's ships were very large in comparison to European equivalents.

31. For a good recent summary of Zheng He's voyages, see David Abulafia, *The Boundless Sea: A Human History of the Oceans* (London: Penguin, 2020), 251–71; cf. Michael Wood, *The Story of China: A Portrait of a Civilisation and its People* (London: Simon and Schuster, 2020).

32. Cook, *Journals*, 3:769. The comment comes from the surgeon William Anderson on December 28, 1776.

33. The Qianlong emperor's letter to George III, 1793; see E. Backhouse and J. O. P. Bland, *Annals and Memoirs of the Court of Peking* (Boston: Houghton Mifflin, 1914), 322–31.

34. For the sources, see the outstanding epilogue in Moore, *Endeavour*, 339–53.

35. John Barrow, *A Voyage to Cochinchina, in the Years 1792 and 1793* (London: Cadell and Davies, 1806), 64.

Chapter 4: Patriots

1. There had been plenty of democracies before, of course, from classical Athens and ancient India to Central Africa and Mesoamerica. But none of them were on anything like a national scale, and none had the defining characteristics of modern democracies (competitive elections, episodic popular participation, state bureaucracies responsible for day-to-day matters, and so forth). See David Stasavage, *The Decline and Rise of Democracy: A Global History from Antiquity to Today* (Princeton: Princeton University Press, 2020), who calls them "early democracies."

2. For the moniker see Eric Hobsbawm, *The Age of Revolution: Europe, 1789–1848* (London: Abacus, 1962).

3. Antoine Marie Cerisier, *Observations Impartiales d'un Vrai Hollandois à ses Compatriotes* (Arnhem: Nyhof, 1779), 15.

4. Alexander Radishchev, "Ode to Liberty" (1790), later incorporated into his *A Journey from St. Petersburg to Moscow*, trans. Leo Wiener (Cambridge, MA: Harvard University Press, 1958). Radishchev was sentenced to death by Catherine the Great for

writing it; after recanting his work and begging her forgiveness, this sentence was commuted to exile in Siberia.

5. John Adams to James Lloyd, March 6, 1815, accessed online at Founders Online, National Archives, https://founders.archives.gov/documents/Adams/99-02-02-6427.

6. Richard Price, *Observations on the Importance of the American Revolution and the Means of Making It a Benefit to the World* (London: Cadell, 1785), 123.

7. Horace Walpole to Horace Mann, May 9, 1779, in Horace Walpole, *The Letters of Horace Walpole, Earl of Orford*, 9 vols., ed Peter Cunningham (London: Bohn, 1861), 7:198.

8. Vincente Rocafuerte et al., *Ideas Necesarias á Todo Pueblo Americano Independiente* (Philadelphia: Huntington, 1821), 3.

9. Jonathan Israel, *The Expanding Blaze: How the American Revolution Ignited the World* (Princeton: Princeton University Press, 2017), 221.

10. Price, *Observations*, 1–2.

11. Price, *Observations*, 6.

12. George Washington to John Cadwalader or Thomas Mifflin, January 1, 1777, in Philander Chase ed., *The Papers of George Washington* (Charlottesville: University Press of Virginia, 1997), 7:510–11.

13. General Orders, July 4, 1776, in Chase, *The Papers of George Washington*, 5:197.

14. For evidence that the flag in question was the Grand Union rather than the Union Jack, see Byron DeLear, "Revisiting the Flag at Prospect Hill: Grand Union or Just British?," *Raven: A Journal of Vexillology* 21 (2014): 19–70.

15. George Washington to Joseph Reed, January 4, 1776, in Chase, *The Papers of George Washington*, 3:23–27.

16. For the arrival in Cambridge on New Year's Day, see Allen French, *The First Year of the American Revolution* (Boston: Houghton Mifflin, 1934), 630.

17. George III's speech to parliament, October 27, 1775.

18. Nathanael Greene to Samuel Ward, January 4, 1776, accessed online at Northern Illinois University Digital Library, https://digital.lib.niu.edu/islandora/object/niu-amarch%3A104907.

19. Washington to Reed, December 15, 1775, cited in Rick Atkinson, *The British Are Coming: The War for America 1775–1777* (London: Collins, 2019), 186.

20. A subsequent investigation revealed that of the thirteen hundred structures destroyed, the British were responsible for just fifty-one (and only nineteen in the attack of January 1). At the time, however, the burning of Norfolk was seen as a totemic example of British brutality.

21. Washington to Reed, January 31, 1776, in Chase, *The Papers of George Washington*, 3:225–29.

22. Carter Braxton to Landon Carter, April 14, 1776: "It is a true saying of a Wit— We must hang together or separately." Accessed online at Maine Historical Society, https://www.mainememory.net/artifact/102148.

23. Benjamin Franklin and James Wilson to Jasper Yeates, July 4, 1776, accessed online at Founders Online, National Archives, https://founders.archives.gov/documents/Franklin/01-22-02-0293.

24. Dumas Malone, *Jefferson the Virginian* (Boston: Little Brown, 1948), 229.

25. John Hancock to George Washington, July 4, 1776: "I flatter myself things will now take a different turn, as the contest to keep possession of power is now at an end, and a new mode of government, equal to the exigencies of our affairs will be adopted,

agreeable to the recommendation of Congress to the United Colonies." Chase, *The Papers of George Washington*, 5:203–4.

26. General Orders, July 4, 1776; George Washington to John Hancock, July 4, 1776, in Chase, *The Papers of George Washington*, 5:197, 199.

27. Samuel Blachley Webb on July 9, 1776; see Worthington Ford, ed., *Correspondence and Journals of Samuel Blachley Webb*, 3 vols., ed. Worthington Ford (New York: Wickersham, 1893), 1:153.

28. Frank Moore, *Diary of the American Revolution*, 2 vols. (New York: Scribner, 1860), 1:271.

29. Worthington Ford, ed., *Journals of the Continental Congress, 1774–1789*, 34 vols. (Washington, 1904–1937), 5:517–18.

30. Charles Lee to George Washington, January 5, 1776, in Chase, *The Papers of George Washington*, 3:30–31.

31. General Orders, July 2, 1776, in Chase, *The Papers of George Washington*, 5:179–82.

32. Lee to Washington, February 19, 1776, in see Chase, *The Papers of George Washington*, 3:339–41.

33. Daniel McCurtin, "Journal of the Times at the Siege of Boston," in *Papers Relating Chiefly to the Maryland Line During the Revolution*, ed. Thomas Balch (Philadelphia: Seventy-Six Society, 1857), 40.

34. See Chase, *The Papers of George Washington*, 5:208–9.

35. Newark Committee of Correspondence to George Washington, July 4, 1776, in Chase, *The Papers of George Washington*, 5:207–8.

36. William Livingston to Washington, July 4, 1776, in Chase, *The Papers of George Washington*, 5:204–5.

37. Washington to Artemas Ward, July 4, 1776, in Chase, *The Papers of George Washington*, 5:210.

38. James Clinton to Washington, July 4, 1776, in Chase, *The Papers of George Washington*, 5:197–99.

39. Joseph Reed to John Adams, July 4, 1776, accessed online at Founders Online, National Archives, https://founders.archives.gov/documents/Adams/06-04-02-0146.

40. William Heath, *Memoirs of Major-General Heath. Containing Anecdotes, Details of Skirmishes, Battles, and Other Military Events, during the American War* (Boston: Thomas and Andrews, 1798), 60 (September 15, 1776).

41. George Washington to John Hancock, September 25, 1776, in Chase, *The Papers of George Washington*, 6:393–401.

42. See Washington Irving, *The Life of George Washington*, 5 vols. (New York: Putnam, 1855–1859), 2:424.

43. George Washington to John Washington, November 6–19, 1776, in Chase, *The Papers of George Washington*, 7:102–6.

44. Washington to Hancock, November 30, 1776, in Chase, *The Papers of George Washington*, 7:232–34.

45. John Jacob, *A Biographical Sketch of the Life of the Late Captain Michael Cresap* (Cincinnati: Dodge, 1866), 12.

46. Patrick Henry to Thomas Jefferson, December 19, 1776, cited in Arthur Lefkowitz, *The Long Retreat: The Calamitous American Defense of New Jersey, 1776* (New Brunswick: Rutgers University Press, 1998), 54.

47. Lefkowitz, *The Long Retreat*, 67.

48. David Hackett Fischer, *Washington's Crossing* (Oxford: Oxford University Press, 2004), 155.

49. Fischer, *Washington's Crossing*, 172–81.

50. Thomas Paine, *The American Crisis (No. 1)* (Boston: 1776).

51. Continental Congress instructions to Benjamin Franklin, Silas Deane and Arthur Lee, September 24 to October 22, 1776, accessed online at Founders Online, National Archives, https://founders.archives.gov/documents/Franklin /01-22-02-0371.

52. American Commissioners to the Comte de Vergennes, December 23, 1776, accessed online at Founders Online, National Archives, https://founders.archives.gov /documents/Franklin/01-23-02-0038.

53. William Wilcox ed., *The Papers of Benjamin Franklin*, vol. 23, *October 27, 1776 through April 30, 1777* (New Haven, CT: Yale University Press, 1983), 113ff.

54. American Commissioners to the Comte de Vergennes, January 5, 1777, in Wilcox, *The Papers of Benjamin Franklin*, 23:120–24.

55. The King's Answer to the American Commissioners, January 13, 1777; American Commissioners to Gérard, January 14, 1777, in Wilcox, *The Papers of Benjamin Franklin*, 23:164–66, 180–82.

56. American Commissioners to Vergennes, December 4, 1777; see Walter Isaacson, *Benjamin Franklin: An American Life* (New York: Simon and Schuster, 2003), 343.

57. James Grant to Carl von Donop, December 17, 1776, quoted in David Bonk, *Trenton and Princeton 1776–1777: Washington Crosses the Delaware* (New York: Bloomsbury, 2012), 44.

58. Fischer, *Washington's Crossing*, 206–20.

59. Washington to Hancock, December 27, 1776, in Chase, *The Papers of George Washington*, 7:454–61.

60. Washington to William Maxwell, December 28, 1776, in Chase, *The Papers of George Washington*, 7:472–73.

61. Sadly there is no primary evidence that Cornwallis actually said this, but it is frequently quoted in his biographies; see Fischer, *Washington's Crossing*, 530.

62. Johann Ewald's diary, January 3, 1776; see Johann von Ewald, *Diary of the American War: A Hessian Journal*, trans and ed. Joseph Tustin (New Haven, CT: Yale University Press, 1979), 51.

63. James McPherson in Fischer, *Washington's Crossing*, ix.

64. George Corner, *The Autobiography of Benjamin Rush* (Princeton: American Philosophical Society: 1948), 124.

65. General Orders, August 12, 1776, in Chase, *The Papers of George Washington*, 5:672–75 (and frequently).

66. "The men who wrote the Constitution sought by every evasion, and almost by subterfuge, to keep recognition of slavery out of the basic form of the new government. They founded their hopes on the prohibition of the slave trade, being sure that without continual additions from abroad, this tropical people would not long survive, and thus the problem of slavery would disappear in death. They miscalculated." W. E. B. Du Bois, *Black Reconstruction: An Essay toward a History of the Part Which Black Folk Played in the Attempt to Reconstruct Democracy in America, 1860–1880* (New York: Harcourt, 1935), 4. On Jefferson's inconsistencies, see Thomas S. Kidd, *Thomas Jefferson: A Biography of Spirit and Flesh* (New Haven, CT: Yale University Press, 2022).

67. Alexander Hamilton at the Constitutional Convention, June 21 and 26, 1787; see Alexander Hamilton, *The Works of Alexander Hamilton*, 7 vols., ed. John Hamilton (New York: Trow, 1850), 2:440; Robert Yates et al., *Secret Proceedings and Debates of the Convention Assembled at Philadelphia, in the year 1787, for the Purpose of Forming the Constitution of the United States of America* (Albany: Websters and Skinners, 1821), 170–71.

68. Washington to the Marquis de Lafayette, May 10, 1786, accessed online at Founders Online, National Archives, https://founders.archives.gov/documents/Washington /04-04-02-0051.

69. John Adams to John Taylor, December 17, 1814, accessed online at Founders Online, National Archives, https://founders.archives.gov/documents/Adams/99-02-02-6370.

70. John Adams, *A Defence of the Constitutions of Government of the United States of America* (London: Dilly and Stockdale, 1787–1788); this represents a change from his earlier *Thoughts on Government* (Philadelphia: Dunlap, 1776), in which it was the aristocracy's job to mediate between the ruler and the people. See the excellent analysis of Gordon S. Wood, *Revolutionary Characters: What Made the Founders Different* (New York: Penguin, 2006), 175–202.

71. Jefferson to William Short, January 3, 1793, Founders Online, National Archives, accessed December 19, 2022, https://founders.archives.gov/documents/Jefferson /01-25-02-0016.

72. John Adams to Samuel Adams, October 18, 1790, Founders Online, National Archives, accessed December 19, 2022, https://founders.archives.gov/documents /Adams/06-20-02-0254.

73. Samuel Adams to John Adams, November 25, 1790; see Founders Online, National Archives, accessed December 19, 2022, https://founders.archives.gov/documents /Adams/06-20-02-0257; emphasis original.

74. C. Bradley Thompson, *America's Revolutionary Mind: A Moral History of the American Revolution and the Declaration That Defined It* (New York: Encounter, 2019), 33.

75. John Locke, *Two Treatises on Civil Government* (1689; repr., London: Routledge, 1884), 266.

76. John Adams to Jonathan Sewell, February 1760, Founders Online, National Archives, accessed December 20, 2022, https://founders.archives.gov/documents/Adams/06 -01-02-0030.

77. Jefferson to John Trumbull, February 15, 1789, Founders Online, National Archives, accessed December 19, 2022, https://founders.archives.gov/documents/Jefferson/01 -14-02-0321.

78. Locke, *Two Treatises*, 193–4, 240, 244. The obvious difference is the shift from the right to possessions and property (in Locke) to the right to pursue happiness (in the Declaration).

79. *Rhode Island Colonial Records*, 1:112 (March 16–19, 1641).

80. For an excellent overview, see James T. Kloppenberg, *Toward Democracy: The Struggle for Self-Rule in European and American Thought* (Oxford: Oxford University Press, 2016), 61–93.

81. Benjamin Rush to Walter Jones, July 30, 1776, in Lyman Henry Butterfield, ed., *The Letters of Benjamin Rush*, 2 vols. (Princeton: Princeton University Press, 1951), 1:108. A week earlier, Rush had written to Charles Lee contrasting "the proprietary gentry" of Pennsylvania with the "honest men" who had now taken their seats. Rush's position on this would evolve over the next few months, partly as a result of his friendship with Adams, and partly in response to the unicameral Pennsylvania Constitution in September.

82. Jefferson to Roger Weightman, June 24, 1826, Library of Congress (website), accessed December 20, 2022, https://www.loc.gov/exhibits/declara/rcwltr.html.

83. Jean-Jacques Rousseau, *The Social Contract*, trans. Henry Tozer (New York : Scribner, 1895), 100.

84. Jean Meslier, *Le Testament*, 3 vols. (Amsterdam: Meijer, 1862), 1:19.

85. An extreme example of this oversimplification is Seth David Radwell, *American Schism: How the Two Enlightenments Hold the Secret to Healing our Nation* (Austin: Greenleaf, 2021), drawn from the (hardly oversimple, but often overdrawn) distinction in Jonathan Israel's work. For a more nuanced account see Joseph Ellis, *Founding Brothers* (New York: Vintage, 2000), 13–16, 206–48.

86. Thomas Paine, *Common Sense: Addressed to the Inhabitants of America* (Philadelphia: Bradford, 1776), 161.

87. John Adams to Abigail Adams, March 19, 177, Massachusetts Historical Society (website), accessed December 20, 2022, https://www.masshist.org/digitaladams /archive/doc?id=L17760319ja.

88. John Adams, *Diary and Autobiography of John Adams*, vol. 3, *Diary, 1782–1804; Autobiography, Part One (to October 1776)*, ed. L. H. Butterfield (Cambridge, MA: Harvard University Press, 1961), 331.

89. William Cobbett, *The Parliamentary History of England from the Earliest Period to the Year 1803*, 36 vols. (London: Hansard, 1806–1820), 18:1286–98.

90. Richard Price, *Observations on the Nature of Civil Liberty* (London: Dilly and Cadell, 1776), 7–8.

91. Constitution of Pennsylvania (September 28, 1776), sec. 6, *The Avalon Project*, Yale Law School Lillian Goldman Law Library (website), accessed December 20, 2022, https://avalon.law.yale.edu/18th_century/pa08.asp.

92. John Cartwright, *Take Your Choice! Representation and Respect, Imposition and Contempt; Annual Parliaments and Liberty, Long Parliaments and Slavery* (London: Almon, 1776), 21.

93. Constitution of New Jersey (July 2, 1776), art. 4; see https://www.state.nj.us/state /archives/docconst76.html. This still excluded all married women, however, and was later rescinded.

94. For an interesting discussion of whether "hypocrisy" is quite the right word here (Kidd thinks it is not in Jefferson's case), see Kidd, *Thomas Jefferson*, 1–2, and throughout. Several founding fathers had their own complicated histories with slavery; see, e.g., Ron Chernow, *Washington: A Life* (New York: Penguin, 2010); Isaacson, *Benjamin Franklin*; David McCullough, *John Adams* (New York: Touchstone, 2001); Ron Chernow, *Alexander Hamilton* (New York: Penguin, 2004); Annette Gordon-Reed, *The Hemingses of Monticello* (New York: Norton, 2008).

95. Washington to Phyllis Wheatley, February 28, 1776, in Chase, *The Papers of George Washington*, 3:387.

96. Thomas Jefferson, *Notes on the State of Virginia* (London: Stockdale, 1787), 234.

97. Thomas Day, *Fragment of an Original Letter on the Slavery of the Negroes, Written in the Year 1776* (London: Stockdale, 1784), 7.

98. Day, *Fragment of an Original Letter*, 10.

99. Virginia Declaration of Rights (June 29, 1776), art. 12, National Archives (website), accessed December 20, 2022, https://www.archives.gov/founding-docs/virginia -declaration-of-rights.

100. Virginia Declaration of Rights (June 29, 1776), art. 16.

101. This way of framing things is drawn from Acemoglu and Robinson, *The Narrow Corridor*.

102. Thucydides, *History of the Peloponnesian War*, trans. Thomas Hobbes (London: Bohn, 1843), 187–99 (2:34–46).

103. Robert Burns, "Is There for Honest Poverty," in *Poems and Songs* (Edinburgh: Nimmo, 1868), 295–96.

Chapter 5: Lights

1. Denis Diderot to Sophie Volland, October 20, 1760; Diderot to Sophie Volland, September 22, 1761; see Denis Diderot, *Oeuvres Complètes*, 20 vols. (Paris: Garnier Frères, 1875–1877), 18:506–20, 19:49–53.

2. Diderot to Sophie Volland, May 10, 1759, in Diderot, *Oeuvres Complètes*, 18:353–55.

3. L'Abbé Morellet, *Mémoires* (Paris: Librairie Française, 1821), 128–29.

4. Jean-Jacques Rousseau, *The Confessions of Jean-Jacques Rousseau*, trans. J. M. Cohen (London: Penguin, 1953), 374 and frequently (Cohen translates it with the less pejorative "circle").

5. Voltaire to M. de Farges, February 25, 1776, Whitman College (website), accessed December 21, 2022, https://www.whitman.edu/VSA/letters/2.25.1776.html.

6. David Hume to William Strahan, February 11, 1776, in David Hume, *Letters of David Hume to William Strahan*, ed. Birkbeck Hill (Oxford: Clarendon, 1888), 311–14.

7. *Morning Chronicle*, February 13, 1776, in Justin Lovill, ed., *1776: A London Chronicle or How to Divert Oneself While Losing an Empire* (Padstow: Bunbury, 2019), 244.

8. The first person to use *Aufklärung* in the sense of a historical movement was G. W. F. Hegel in his *Lectures on the History of Philosophy* (1833). For the English usage, see James Schmidt, "Inventing the Enlightenment: Anti-Jacobins, British Hegelians and the Oxford English Dictionary," *Journal of the History of Ideas* 64, no. 3 (July 2003), 421–33.

9. For an excellent short history, see Jonathan Israel, *Democratic Enlightenment: Philosophy, Revolution and Human Rights, 1750–1790* (Oxford: Oxford University Press, 2011), 56–92.

10. Denis Diderot, "Encyclopédie," in Denis Diderot and Jean-Baptiste le Rond d'Alembert, eds., *Encyclopédie ou Dictionnaire Raisonné des Sciences, des Arts et des Métiers*, 35 vols. (Paris: 1751–1772), 5:635–49.

11. Jean-Baptiste le Rond d'Alembert, "Discours Préliminaire des Editeurs," in *Encyclopédie*, 1:xx.

12. d'Alembert, "Discours Préliminaire des Editeurs," xxiv.

13. Gotthold Ephraim Lessing, *The Education of the Human Race*, trans. F. W. Robertson (London: King, 1872), 88.

14. Immanuel Kant, "An Answer to the Question: What Is Enlightenment?" in *Political Writings*, 2nd ed., trans. H. B. Nisbet, ed. Hans Reiss (Cambridge: Cambridge University Press, 1991), 54; emphasis original.

15. *Monty Python's Life of Brian*, directed by Terry Jones (HandMade Films, 1979).

16. Israel, *Democratic Enlightenment*, 648–83, despite his sharp separation between "moderate" and "radical" Enlighteners in the 1770s, demonstrates their essential unity when the philosophic movement was threatened (for example, during the trial of Delisle de Sales in 1776–1777).

17. Carl Sagan, *Cosmos* (New York: Random House, 1980), 335.

18. William Camden, "Certaine Poemes, or Poesies, Epigrammes, Rhythmes, and Epitaphs of the English Nation in Former Times," in *Remaines of a Greater Worke*

(London, 1605), 2. The English term "middle age" was introduced by John Foxe's *Actes and Monuments*, 2 vols. (London: Day, 1570), 1:215, passim.

19. See, e.g., Ronald Numbers, ed., *Galileo Goes to Jail, and Other Myths about Science and Religion* (Cambridge, MA: Harvard University Press, 2010).

20. Thomas Reid, "Inquiry into the Human Mind," in *The Works of Thomas Reid, with an Account of His Life and Writings*, 4 vols., ed. Dugald Stewart (Charlestown: Etheridge, 1813), 1:181.

21. Alexander Pope, "Epitaph: Intended for Sir Isaac Newton" (1730); see Susan Ratcliffe, *Oxford Treasury of Sayings and Quotations* (Oxford: Oxford University Press, 2011), 398. The echoes of Genesis are significant here. Light comes as the creative power of the word and brings order out of chaos, which is what scientists are primarily there to do.

22. Jean-Antoine Nollet, *L'Art des Expériences*, 3 vols. (Paris: 1770), 1:xx–xxi.

23. This interpretation follows Diderot's "Explication du frontispice de l'Encyclopédie"; slightly modified for clarity.

24. The term "enlightened despot," or "enlightened absolutist," is usually applied to Frederick the Great of Prussia (r. 1740–1786), Joseph II of Austria (1765–1790) and Catherine the Great of Russia (1762–1796), although it also applies variously to Charles III of Spain (1759–1788), Leopold, Grand Duke of Tuscany (1765–1790), Gustav III of Sweden (1771–1792), and others; see Ritchie Robertson, *The Enlightenment: The Pursuit of Happiness, 1680–1790* (London: Allen Lane, 2020).

25. Newton dated the letter February 5, 1675, but this was incorrect, since it comes in response to a letter Hooke wrote in January 1676; see the Newton Project (website), accessed December 21, 2022, https://www.newtonproject.ox.ac.uk/view/texts/normalized/OTHE00101.

26. See James Gleick, *Isaac Newton* (London: Harper Perennial, 2003), 3: "Isaac Newton said he had seen further by standing on the shoulders of giants, but he did not believe it." It is a pithy and arresting first line, although given the subsequent argument it may be Gleick, rather than Newton, who does not quite believe what he is writing.

27. Seb Falk, *The Light Ages: A Medieval Journey of Discovery* (London: Allen Lane, 2020); cf. Matthew Gabriele and David Perry, *The Bright Ages: A New History of Medieval Europe* (New York: Harper, 2021); James Hannam, *God's Philosophers: How the Medieval World Laid the Foundations of Modern Science* (London: Icon, 2009).

28. "Bernard of Chartres used to compare us to [puny] dwarfs perched on the shoulders of giants. He pointed out that we see more and farther than our predecessors, not because we have keener vision or greater height, but because we are lifted up and borne aloft on their gigantic stature." John of Salisbury, *The Metalogicon of John of Salisbury: A Twelfth-Century Defense of the Verbal and Logical Arts of the Trivium*, trans. Daniel McGarry (Berkeley: University of California Press, 1955), 167.

29. See Michael Wood, *The Story of China: A Portrait of a Civilisation and its People* (London: Simon and Schuster, 2020), 116–17, 196–201.

30. Eric Hobsbawm, "Barbarism: A User's Guide," in his *On History* (London: Abacus, 1998), 336.

31. Caitlin Hutchison, "University of Edinburgh Renames David Hume Tower over 'Racist' Views," *The Herald*, September 13, 2020, https://www.heraldscotland.com/.

32. David Hume, "Of National Characters" (1748); see Hume, *Political Essays*, ed. Knud Haakonssen (Cambridge: Cambridge University Press, 1994), 86.

33. The evidence for Williams's attendance at Cambridge is debated. Most of what we know about him, including this, comes from the polygenist and defender of slavery

Edward Long, *The History of Jamaica, or General Survey of the Antient and Modern State of That Island: With Reflections on Its Situation Settlements, Inhabitants, Climate, Products, Commerce, Laws, and Government*, 3 vols. (London: T. Lowndes, 1774).

34. Voltaire, *Essai sur les Moeurs et l'Esprit des Nations* (1756), in Voltaire, *Oeuvres Complètes*, 52 vols. (Paris: Garnier, 1877–1885), 12:357.

35. Voltaire, "Septième Lettre d'Amabed" (1769), in *Oeuvres Complètes*, 21:462.

36. Immanuel Kant, "Observations on the Feeling of the Beautiful and Sublime" (1764), in Emmanuel Chukwudi Eze, *Race and the Enlightenment: A Reader* (Oxford: Blackwell, 1997), 55–56.

37. Kant, "Observations," in Eze, *Race and the Enlightenment*, 57.

38. There are exceptions, of course. The Marquis de Condorcet (1743–1794) held views on race, slavery, women, economics, politics, education, and God that twenty-first century people tend to agree with; we could also mention Diderot, among others. Whether these counterexamples exonerate the whole, or even constitute a (good) "Radical Enlightenment" whose reputation need not be damned by association with the (bad) "Moderate Enlightenment," is an entirely different question, however; see chap. 4.

39. See John Gray, *Seven Types of Atheism* (London: Allen Lane, 2018), 57: "Much of the Enlightenment was an attempt to demonstrate the superiority of one section of humankind—that of Europe and its colonial outposts—over all the rest. Evangelists for the Enlightenment will say this was a departure from the 'true' Enlightenment, which is innocent of all evil. Just as religious believers will tell you that 'true' Christianity played no part in the Inquisition, secular humanists insist that the Enlightenment had no responsibility for the rise of modern racism. This is demonstrably false. Modern racist ideology is an Enlightenment project."

40. See, for example, Peter Gay, *The Enlightenment: An Interpretation*, 2 vols. (New York: Knopf, 1966); Robertson, *The Enlightenment*.

41. See Joyce Appleby, *Shores of Knowledge: New World Discoveries and the Scientific Imagination* (New York: Norton, 2013), 147.

42. William Withering, *A Botanical Arrangement of all the Vegetables Naturally Growing in Great Britain*, 2 vols. (Birmingham: Swinney, 1776).

43. Johann Georg Siegesbeck, *Epicrisis in Clar. Linnaei Nuperrime Evulgatum Systema Plantarum Sexuale, et huic Superstructam Methodum Botanicam* (St. Petersburg, 1737).

44. Comte de Buffon, *Histoire Naturelle*, 10 vols. (Paris: Hacquart, 1801), 4:90.

45. Erasmus Darwin to William Withering, May 13, 1775, in Jenny Uglow, *The Lunar Men: The Friends Who Made the Future, 1730–1810* (London: Faber, 2002), 276–79.

46. Erasmus Darwin, *Zoonomia*, 2 vols. (1794; repr., London: Johnson, 1801), 2:240.

47. John Whitehurst, *An Inquiry into the Original State and Formation of the Earth: Deduced from Facts and the Laws of Nature. To Which Is Added an Appendix, Containing Some General Observations on the Strata in Derbyshire* (London: Cooper, 1778).

48. Josiah Wedgwood to Thomas Bentley, October 24, 1778, in Uglow, *The Lunar Men*, 301.

49. For a good recent account, see Urs App, *The Birth of Orientalism* (Philadelphia: University of Pennsylvania Press, 2010), 363–439.

50. Edmund Burke, ed., *Annual Register: Or a View of the History, Politicks, and Literature, for the Year 1762* (London: Dodsley, 1763), 103.

51. William Jones, *Lettre à Monsieur A*** du P***, Dans Laquelle est Compris L'Examen de sa Traduction des Livres Attribués à Zoroastre* (London: Elmsly, 1771). Jones was

only twenty-four at the time, but he would go on to learn twenty-eight languages, and is best known today for suggesting that all Indo-European languages come from the same root, effectively launching comparative linguistics. In an anonymous pamphlet, Jones argued that Anquetil-Duperron had been hoodwinked: his modern Persian was poor, his "holy book" was boring and repetitive, he was something of a scoundrel, and he had simply been tricked into believing that he was holding genuine Zoroastrian texts rather than rhapsodic, fanciful nonsense. In the end, Anquetil-Duperron's text (though not his translation) would be vindicated, but at the time, most people agreed with Jones. The minority who believed the book was authentic were led by Johann Friedrich Kleuker, who translated it into German, and Edward Gibbon, who cited it in his *History of the Decline and Fall of the Roman Empire*—both of which were published in 1776. See Johann Friedrich Kleuker, *Zend-Avesta, Zoroasters Lebendiges Wort*, 3 vols. (Riga: Hartknoch, 1776–1777); Edward Gibbon, *The History of the Decline and Fall of the Roman Empire*, 6 vols. (London: Strahan and Cadell, 1776–1789), 1:205.

52. The term "Axial Age" was coined by Karl Jaspers in 1949. For a recent assessment, see Robert Bellah and Hans Joas, eds., *The Axial Age and Its Consequences* (Cambridge, MA: Belknap Press, 2012).

53. Abraham Hyacinthe Anquetil-Duperron, *Zend-Avesta, Ouvrage de Zorastre: Contenant les Idées Théologiques, Physiques & Morales de ce Législateur, les Cérémonies du Culte Religieux qu'il a Établi, & Plusieurs Traits Importans Relatifs à l'Ancienne Histoire des Perses*, 3 vols. (Paris: Tilliard, 1771), 1:2:7.

54. Anne Robert Jacques Turgot, "Plan de deux Discours sur l'Histoire Universelle," in *Oeuvres de Turgot et Documents le Concernant*, 5 vols., ed. Gustav Schelle (Paris: Alcan, 1913), 1:278–87; William Robertson, *The History of America* (London: Strahan and Cadell, 1777); Guillaume-Thomas Raynal, *Histoire Philosophique et Politique, Des Établissements et du Commerce des Européens dans les deux Indes*, 5 vols. (Geneva: Pellet, 1780).

55. Edward Gibbon, *Memoirs of My Life* (1796; repr., London: Penguin, 2006), February 17, 1776.

56. Horace Walpole to Edward Gibbon, February 14, 1776, Yale University Lewis Walpole Library (website), accessed December 21, 2022, https://libsvcs-1.its.yale.edu/hw correspondence/page.asp?vol=41&page=334.

57. Gibbon, *Decline and Fall*, 1:29.

58. E.g., Gibbon, *Decline and Fall*, chap. 52.

59. Anquetil-Duperron, *Zend-Avesta*, 1:1:vi–vii.

60. For an excellent summary, see Robertson, *The Enlightenment*, 293–301.

61. Gabriel Bonnot de Mably, *De la Législation, ou Principes des Loix* (Amsterdam, 1776).

62. Adam Smith, *The Wealth of Nations*, 2 vols., ed. Andrew Skinner (1776; repr., London: Penguin, 1999), 2:367.

63. Mably, *Principes des Loix*, 299.

64. Mably, *Principes des Loix*, 299–300.

65. See Leigh Whaley, "Networks, Patronage and Women of Science during the Italian Enlightenment," in *Early Modern Women* 11, no. 1 (2016), 187–96.

66. Jérôme de Lalande, *Bibliographie Astronomique avec l'histoire de l'Astronomie* (Paris: Imprimerie de la République, 1802), 687.

67. John Morgan, *Journal of Dr. John Morgan of Philadelphia from the City of Rome to the City of London 1764* (Philadelphia: J. R. Lippincott, 1907), July 20, 1764.

68. See Voltaire to Laura Bassi, November 23, 1744, in Alberto Elena, "In lode della filosofessa di Bologna: An Introduction to Laura Bassi," *Isis* 82, no. 3 (1991), 510–18.
69. Luigi Simeoni, *Storia della Università di Bologna*, vol. 2 (Bologna: Nicola Zanichelli, 1947), 95.
70. Johann Gottfried Herder, *Briefe zur Beförderung der Humanität* (Riga: Hartknoch, 1793), no. 79.
71. Immanuel Kant, *Notes and Fragments*, trans. Curtis Bowman, Paul Guyer, and Frederick Rauscher, ed. Paul Guyer (Cambridge: Cambridge University Press, 2005), 181–84; cf. 73, on the question of dates.
72. Madame de Staël, *De L'Allemagne* (1813; repr., Paris: Charpentier, 1844), 452.
73. The best summary I know of is Roger Scruton, *Kant: A Very Short Introduction* (Oxford: Oxford University Press, 2001).
74. Immanuel Kant, *Critique of Pure Reason*, trans. Mary Gregor (Cambridge: Cambridge University Press, 1998), 193–94 (A51, B75).
75. Jane Austen, *Northanger Abbey* (London: Penguin, 2011), chap. 22; cf. Deirdre Shauna Lynch, "'Young Ladies Are Delicate Plants': Jane Austen and Greenhouse Romanticism," *English Literary History* 77, no. 3 (2010): 689–729.

Chapter 6: Skeptics

1. David Hume, *Philosophical Essays concerning Human Understanding* (London: Millar, 1748), 182.
2. William Mure, ed., *Selections from the Family Papers Preserved at Caldwell*, 3 vols. (Glasgow: Maitland Club, 1854), 2:177–78.
3. Charles Ryskamp and Frederick Pottle, eds., *Boswell: The Ominous Years, 1774–1776* (New York: McGraw Hill, 1963), 201.
4. Charles Weis and Frederick Pottle, eds., *Boswell in Extremes, 1776–1778* (New York: McGraw Hill, 1970), 11–13.
5. Joseph Black to Adam Smith, August 26, 1776, Econlib (website), accessed December 21, 2022, https://www.econlib.org/book-chapters/chapter-letter-from-adam-smith-l-l-d-to-william-strahan-esq/.
6. David Hume, *The Life of David Hume, Written by Himself* (London: Strahan and Cadell, 1777), 62.
7. Adam Smith to Andreas Holt, October 26, 1780, University of Glasgow (website), accessed December 21, 2022, https://www.gla.ac.uk/myglasgow/library/files/special/exhibns/scottish/adamsmith.html.
8. James Boswell, *The Life of Samuel Johnson* (1791; repr., London: Penguin, 2008), 585.
9. Thomas Jefferson to Benjamin Franklin, June 21, 1776, Founders Online, National Archives, accessed December 21, 2022, https://founders.archives.gov/documents/Jefferson/01-01-02-0168.
10. For a reconstruction of the draft and how it became the final version, see Julian P. Boyd, *The Declaration of Independence: The Evolution of the Text as Shown in Facsimiles of Various Drafts by Its Author, Thomas Jefferson* (Princeton: Princeton University Press, 1945). For a shorter account see Isaacson, *Benjamin Franklin*, 309–13.
11. There is plenty of literature on the meaning of "self-evident" in the Declaration and how it differs from other eighteenth-century (and twenty-first-century) uses; a good survey is provided in C. Bradley Thompson, *America's Revolutionary Mind: A Moral History of the American Revolution and the Declaration That Defined It* (New York: Encounter, 2019), 69–95.

12. Quoted in Charles Taylor, *A Secular Age* (Cambridge, MA: Belknap Press of Harvard University Press, 2007), 596.

13. Friedrich Nietzsche, *On the Genealogy of Morals*, trans. Michael A. Scarpitti (London: Penguin, 2013).

14. Yuval Noah Harari, *Sapiens: A Brief History of Humankind* (London: Vintage, 2011), 123. For a fuller argument, see Nicholas Wolterstorff, *Justice: Rights and Wrongs* (Princeton: Princeton University Press, 2008).

15. Thomas S. Kidd, *Thomas Jefferson: A Biography of Spirit and Flesh* (New Haven, CT: Yale University Press, 2022), 50–56, shows how Jefferson reworked George Mason's wording in the Virginia Declaration of Rights to make it more explicit that these rights derive from their Creator.

16. John Locke, *Two Treatises on Civil Government* (1689; repr., London: Routledge, 1884), 193–94; cf. Algernon Sidney, *Discourses concerning Government* (London: Millar, 1763), 17–18: "Nothing can be more evident, than that if many had been created, they had been all equal, unless God had given a preference to one."

17. Locke, *Two Treatises*, 193; at least part of Locke's motive in quoting Hooker here was to embarrass his Tory opponents by citing one of the Church of England's most influential theologians.

18. Richard Hooker, *Of the Laws of Ecclesiastical Polity*, ed. Arthur Stephen McGrade (1597; repr., Cambridge: Cambridge University Press, 1989), 80 (quoting *Code* 3.28.11 and Matt. 22:37–40); cf. Alan Cromartie, "Theology and Politics in Richard Hooker's Thought," *History of Political Thought* 21, no. 1 (2000): 41–66.

19. The same is true of Algernon Sidney, who derived his statement about equality from the stories of Adam and Abraham in Genesis (*Discourses concerning Government*, 17–18). We could make a similar case for the development of individual rights and the rule of law; see, e.g., Larry Siedentop, *Inventing the Individual: The Origins of Western Liberalism* (London: Penguin, 2015), esp. 192–251; Nick Spencer, *The Evolution of the West: How Christianity Has Shaped Our Values* (London: SPCK, 2016), 38–50, 125–37; more pungently, Christian Smith, *Atheist Overreach: What Atheism Can't Deliver* (Oxford: Oxford University Press, 2019), 45–86.

20. Tom Holland, *Dominion: The Making of the Western Mind* (London: Little Brown, 2019), 524.

21. See Holland, *Dominion*, 470–98.

22. Voltaire to Diderot, December 8, 1776, Electronic Enlightenment (website), accessed December 21, 2022, see https://doi.org/10.13051/ee:doc/voltfrVF1280082a1c.

23. Voltaire to Diderot, June 1749, in Voltaire, *Oeuvres Complètes*, 52 vols. (Paris: Garnier, 1877–1885), 37:22–23.

24. Diderot to Voltaire, September 29, 1762, in Voltaire, *Oeuvres Complètes*, 42:253.

25. Roland Mortier, *Diderot en Allemagne, 1750–1850* (Geneva: Slatkine, 1986), 34–35; Diderot to Étienne Damilaville, 1766.

26. Norman Torrey, "Voltaire's Reaction to Diderot," *Proceedings of the Modern Language Association* 50, no. 4 (1935): 1118.

27. Peter Gay, *The Enlightenment: The Rise of Modern Paganism*, 2 vols. (New York: Knopf, 1966), 1:64; Lester Crocker, *The Embattled Philosopher: A Biography of Denis Diderot* (East Lansing: Michigan State College Press, 1954), 318.

28. Denis Diderot, "Entretien d'un philosophe avec la Maréchale de ***" (1776), in *Oeuvres Complètes*, 20 vols. (Paris: Garnier Frères, 1875–1877), 2:507–28.

29. Voltaire, "Epître à L'auteur du Livre des Trois Imposteurs" (1769), in *Oeuvres Complètes*, 52 vols. (Paris: Garnier, 1877–1885), 10:402–5.

30. Voltaire, "Sermon des Cinquantes" (1762), in *Oeuvres Complètes*, 24:437–54.

31. See especially Jonathan Israel, *Radical Enlightenment: Philosophy and the Making of Modernity, 1650–1750* (Oxford: Oxford University Press, 2002); Israel, *Democratic Enlightenment: Philosophy, Revolution and Human Rights, 1750-1790* (Oxford: Oxford University Press, 2012); Israel, *The Expanding Blaze: How the American Revolution Ignited the World* (Princeton: Princeton University Press, 2017); cf. Philipp Blom, *Wicked Company: Freethinkers and Friendship in Pre-Revolutionary Paris* (London: Weidenfeld and Nicolson, 2011).

32. See especially Anthony La Vopa, "A New Intellectual History? Jonathan Israel's Enlightenment," *The Historical Journal* 52, no. 3 (2009): 717–38; cf. Steffen Ducheyne, ed., *Reassessing the Radical Enlightenment* (Milton Park, Abingdon, UK: Routledge, 2017); Michael Bentley, "He Was Right All Along," *The Critic* (March 2020); Ritchie Robertson, "Pick Your Teams," *Times Literary Supplement* (June 2020).

33. This case is made with some panache in Holland, *Dominion*, especially 371–89.

34. *120 Days of Sodom* was sold in 2014 for $7 million, which compares to $7.57 million for *The Canterbury Tales* in 1998 and $8.14 million for the *Declaration of Independence* in 2000.

35. Several of these events are historically (as well as morally) controversial, due to the difficulty of establishing exactly what happened in each case and how consensual it was. For a good biography, see Neil Schaeffer, *The Marquis de Sade: A Life* (1998; repr., Cambridge, MA: Harvard University Press, 2000).

36. Marquis de Sade, *The Misfortunes of Virtue and Other Early Tales*, trans. David Coward (Oxford: Oxford University Press, 1992), 152, 154, 157.

37. Marquis de Sade, *Justine, or, The Misfortunes of Virtue*, trans. John Phillips (Oxford: Oxford University Press, 2012), 142.

38. Sade, *Justine*, 84.

39. Marquis de Sade, *Juliette*, trans. Austryn Wainhouse (New York: Grove Press, 1968), 178.

40. Sade, *Juliette*, 177.

41. Sade, *Juliette*, 143.

42. Sade, *Juliette*, 732.

43. Quoted in Simone de Beauvoir, "Must We Burn Sade?," in *The Marquis de Sade: An Essay*, trans. Paul Dinnage (1962; repr., London: New English Library, 1972), 41.

44. Immanuel Kant, *Religion Within the Boundaries of Mere Reason*, trans. Allen Wood (Cambridge: Cambridge University Press, 1998); Jean-Jacques Rousseau, *The Social Contract*, trans. Henry Tozer (New York: Scribner, 1895), bk. 4, chap. 8.

45. On Jefferson's complicated religious journey see Kidd, *Thomas Jefferson*, esp. 149–70.

46. For a fascinating analysis see John Gray, *Seven Types of Atheism* (London: Allen Lane, 2018), whose survey includes numerous figures from 1776 (Sade, Hume, Voltaire, Mesmer, and Kant in particular) in starring roles.

47. Diderot to Sophie Volland, October 30, 1759, in Denis Diderot, *Oeuvres Complètes*, 20 vols. (Paris: Garnier Frères, 1875–1877), 18:419.

48. Taylor, *A Secular Age*, 1–29, 539–93.

49. See, for example, Spencer, *The Evolution of the West*, 94–109; David Bentley Hart, *Atheist Delusions: The Christian Revolution and Its Fashionable Enemies* (New Haven, CT: Yale University Press, 2009), 56–98; Rodney Stark, *For the Glory of God: How Monotheism Led to Reformations, Science, Witch-Hunts, and the End of Slavery* (Princeton: Princeton University Press, 2003), 121–97; Alec Ryrie, *Unbelievers: An Emotional History of Doubt* (Cambridge, MA: Harvard University Press, 2019).

50. Gay, *Rise of Modern Paganism*, 8–9.

51. Diderot, "Grecs, philosophie des," in Denis Diderot and Jean-Baptiste le Rond d'Alembert, eds., *Encyclopédie ou Dictionnaire Raisonné des Sciences, des Arts et des Métiers*, 35 vols. (Paris: 1751–1772), 7:904–12; Edward Gibbon, *The History of the Decline and Fall of the Roman Empire*, 6 vols. (London: Strahan and Cadell, 1776–1789), vol. 1, chap. 2; Kant, *Critique of Pure Reason*, 107 (Bx); Hume, *Essays*, 1:133; Yvon, "Barbares," in *Encyclopédie*, 2:68–69.

52. Voltaire, *Essai sur les Moeurs et l'Esprit des Nations* (1756), in Voltaire, *Oeuvres Complètes*, vol. 12, chap. 24.

53. Lucretius, *De Rerum Natura*, trans. William Leonard (New York: Dutton, 1916), 1:151–60.

54. Gibbon, *Decline and Fall*, chap. 3.

55. David Hume, *Four Dissertations* (London: Millar, 1757), 60.

56. Hume, *Four Dissertations*, 62.

57. Hume, *Four Dissertations*, 61.

58. "There was always room for one more god in the ancient system; but to say this is not to say that the state religion of old Rome was 'tolerant.' If pagans did not preach compulsion, that was only because there was nothing to compel—the belief system shared by all peoples of their empire was polytheistic, with local variations only in the names of particular deities and the specifics of particular practices. . . . Christianity, as an artificial community that defied kinship on the basis of belief, attracted a more heterogenous membership and in doing so threatened the established order." H. A. Drake, *Constantine and the Bishops: The Politics of Intolerance* (Baltimore: John Hopkins University Press, 2000), 453. Cf. J. A. North, *Roman Religion* (Cambridge: Cambridge University Press, 2000), 63; Hart, *Atheist Delusions*, 183–98; Steven Smith, *Pagans and Christians in the City: Culture Wars from the Tiber to the Potomac* (Grand Rapids, MI: Eerdmans, 2018), 130–57.

59. Gay, *Rise of Modern Paganism*, 401.

60. For a good summary, see Smith, *Pagans and Christians*, 102–29.

61. Abraham Joshua Heschel, *God in Search of Man: A Philosophy of Judaism* (New York: Farrar, Straus and Giroux, 1955), 91; cf. Jan Assmann, *The Price of Monotheism*, trans. Robert Savage (Stanford, CA: Stanford University Press, 2010), 39; Robert Louis Wilken, *The Christians as the Romans Saw Them* (New Haven, CT: Yale University Press, 2003), 91; James O'Donnell, *Pagans: The End of Traditional Religion and the Rise of Christianity* (New York: Ecco, 2015), 67: "The gods . . . were mainly the mightiest part of the world itself, not beings that somehow stood outside it all."

62. Peter Jones, *One or Two: Seeing a World of Difference* (Enumclaw, WA: Winepress, 2010).

63. Heschel, *God in Search of Man*, 91.

64. Chantal Delsol, *La Fin de la Chrétienté* (Paris: Cerf, 2021).

65. Chantal Delsol, "The End of Christianity," *Hungarian Conservative* 1, no. 3 (2021), https://www.hungarianconservative.com/.

66. Ritchie Robertson, *The Enlightenment: The Pursuit of Happiness, 1680-1790* (London: Allen Lane, 2020), 1–9, and throughout.

67. Hume, *Four Dissertations*, 25–27; emphasis added.

68. Smith, *Pagans and Christians*, 193–216.

69. Jacques Maritain, *Three Reformers: Luther, Descartes, Rousseau* (New York: Scribner, 1950), 30.

70. See Brad Gregory, *The Unintended Reformation: How a Religious Revolution Secularized Society* (Cambridge, MA: Harvard University Press, 2015).

71. Taylor, *A Secular Age*, 29–45, drawing on Max Weber's concept of *Entzauberung* ("disenchantment").

72. Although see the important critique of Jason Josephson-Storm, *The Myth of Disenchantment: Magic, Modernity, and the Birth of the Human Sciences* (Chicago: University of Chicago Press, 2017). Josephson-Storm argues that beliefs in magic, spiritualism, and pseudosciences like alchemy and mesmerism have always been present in the West, including among leading scientists, and that we have witnessed de-Christianization rather than disenchantment as such.

73. Taylor, *A Secular Age*, 77.

74. Taylor, *A Secular Age*, 290.

75. For Taylor's own summary of the first half of his book, see *A Secular Age*, 375.

76. Michel de Montaigne, *Essays*, rev ed., trans. M. A. Screech (London: Penguin, 2013), 167.

77. Ryrie, *Unbelievers*, 182.

78. Tara Burton, *Strange Rites: New Religions for a Godless World* (New York: Public Affairs, 2020), calls this large and growing group of people the "Remixed"; polls and surveys often refer to them as the "Nones."

79. Gibbon, *Decline and Fall*, 1242.

80. David Hume, *Dialogues concerning Natural Religion* (London, 1779), 186.

81. Hume, *Dialogues*, 244–50.

82. Hume, *Dialogues*, 121.

83. Hume, *Dialogues*, 225–26.

84. Jeremy Bentham, *A Fragment on Government* (Oxford: Clarendon, 1891), 93.

85. Bentham, *A Fragment on Government*, 93.

86. Alexis de Tocqueville, *Democracy in America*, trans. Harvey Mansfield and Debra Winthrop (Chicago: University of Chicago Press, 2000), 406.

87. Tocqueville, *Democracy in America*, 511–14. For an excellent discussion of this phenomenon in nineteenth-century America, see Benjamin Storey and Jenna Silber Storey, *Why We Are Restless: On the Modern Quest for Contentment* (Princeton: Princeton University Press, 2021), 140–75.

88. T. S. Eliot, *The Idea of a Christian Society* (London: Faber, 1939), 13.

89. See the fascinating essay of David Bentley Hart, "No Turning Back: Peter Sloterdijk's 'After God,'" *Commonweal* 148, no. 7 (July/August 2021), https://www.commonwealmagazine.org/.

Chapter 7: Machines

1. Madison Smartt Bell, *Lavoisier in the Year One: The Birth of a New Science in an Age of Revolution* (New York: Norton, 2005), 13–14.

2. Robert Krulwich, "Who's the Guy with the Big Head on 77th Street?," *National Geographic*, June 24, 2016, https://www.nationalgeographic.com/.

3. J. L. Lagrange, *Notice sur la vie et les ouvrages de M. le comte J.-L. Lagrange, par M. Delambre. Mémoires extraits des recueils de l'Académie de Turin*, vol. 1 of *Oeuvres de Lagrange*, ed. J. A. Serret and Gaston Darboux (Paris: Gauthier-Villars, 1867), xl.

4. See Asa Briggs, *Victorian Cities* (Berkeley: University of California Press, 1993), 88.

5. Alexis de Tocqueville, *Journeys to England and Ireland* (1835; repr., New York: Transaction, 2003), 106–8.

6. Hippolyte Taine, *Notes on England* (New York: Holt and Williams, 1872), 274.

7. Henry Colman, *European Life and Manners, In Familiar Letters to Friends*, 2 vols. (Boston: Little and Brown, 1849), 1:95–97.

8. Charles Napier, *The Life and Opinions of Charles Napier*, 4 vols. (London: John Murray, 1857), 2:57.

9. Fredrika Bremer, *The Homes of the New World: Impressions of America*, trans. Mary Howitt, 2 vols. (New York: 1858), 1:605.

10. Friedrich Engels, *The Condition of the Working Class in England in 1844* (London: Swan Sonnenschein, 1892), 53.

11. Engels, *Condition of the Working Class*, 277.

12. De Tocqueville, *Journeys to England and Ireland*, 107.

13. See Simon Garfield, *The Last Journey of William Huskisson* (London: Faber, 2003).

14. Most historians who talk about an "Industrial Revolution" would regard it as starting in Britain somewhere between the 1760s (T. S. Ashton) and the 1780s (Eric Hobsbawm), although it would be decades before it felt like an industrial society to most of its inhabitants. For a defense of the concept, see Tim Blanning, *The Pursuit of Glory: Europe 1648–1815* (2007; repr., London: Penguin, 2008), 125–41.

15. The first official gathering was on New Year's Eve 1775; the "Lunar Society" name emerged in 1776. For a magnificent overview of the group, see Uglow, *The Lunar Men*.

16. Darwin to Matthew Boulton, July 29, 1767, Revolutionary Players (website), accessed December 21, 2022, https://www.revolutionaryplayers.org.uk/letter-from-erasmus -darwin-to-matthew-boulton-17670729/.

17. It was revised and published separately two years later as James Keir, *A Treatise on the Various Kinds of Permanently Elastic Fluids, or Gases* (London: Cadell and Elmsley, 1779).

18. Joseph Priestley, *Experiments and Observations on Different Kinds of Air*, 6 vols. (London: Johnson, 1774–1777), 1:87–91.

19. Benjamin Franklin to Joseph Priestley, April 10, 1774.

20. Joseph Priestley, *Directions for Impregnating Water with Fixed Air* (London: Johnson, 1772).

21. Priestley, *Experiments and Observations*, 2:293–303.

22. For a more rigorous, less cheeky way of making this point, see Jan de Vries and Ad van der Woude, *The First Modern Economy: Success, Failure and Perseverance of the Dutch Economy, 1500–1815* (Cambridge: Cambridge University Press, 1997), 665–710; Margaret Jacob, *The First Knowledge Economy: Human Capital and the European Economy, 1750–1850* (Cambridge: Cambridge University Press, 2014), 136–219.

23. The literature here is vast. Works I have found helpful include Eric Jones, *The European Miracle: Environments, Economies and Geopolitics in the History of Europe and Asia* (Cambridge: Cambridge University Press, 2003); David Landes, *The Wealth and Poverty of Nations: Why Some Are so Rich and Some Are so Poor* (New York: Norton, 1998); David Abernethy, *The Dynamics of Global Dominance: European Overseas Empires, 1415–1980* (New Haven, CT: Yale University Press, 2000); Eric Hobsbawm, *Industry and Empire* (London: Penguin, 1999); Kenneth Pomeranz, *The Great Divergence: China, Europe and the Making of the Modern World Economy* (Princeton: Princeton University Press, 2000); Joel Mokyr, *The Gifts of Athena: Historical Origins of the Knowledge Economy* (Princeton: Princeton University Press, 2002); Christopher Bayly, *The Birth of the Modern World, 1780–1914* (Oxford: Blackwell, 2004); Gregory Clark, *A Farewell to Alms: A Brief Economic History of the World* (Princeton: Princeton University Press, 2007); Ronald Findlay and Kevin O'Rourke, *Power and*

Plenty: Trade, War, and the World Economy in the Second Millennium (Princeton: Princeton University Press, 2007); Blanning, *Pursuit of Glory*; Robert Allen, *The Industrial Revolution in Global Perspective* (Cambridge: Cambridge University Press, 2009); Max Weber, *The Protestant Ethic and the Spirit of Capitalism* (Oxford: Oxford University Press, 2010); Prasannan Parthasarathi, *Why Europe Grew Rich and Asia Did Not* (Cambridge: Cambridge University Press, 2011); Jean-Laurent Rosenthal and Bin Wong, *Before and Beyond Divergence: The Politics of Economic Change in China and Europe* (Cambridge, MA: Harvard University Press, 2011); William Rosen, *The Most Powerful Idea in the World: A Story of Steam, Industry and Invention* (London: Pimlico, 2011); Immanuel Wallerstein, *The Modern World-System III: The Second Era of Great Expansion of the Capitalist World Economy 1730–1840s* (Berkeley: University of California Press, 2011); Ferguson, *Civilization*; Daron Acemoglu and James Robinson, *Why Nations Fail: The Origins of Power, Prosperity and Poverty* (New York: Crown, 2012); Emma Griffin, *Liberty's Dawn: A People's History of the Industrial Revolution* (New Haven, CT: Yale University Press, 2013); Peer Vries, *Escaping Poverty: The Origins of Modern Economic Growth* (Vienna: Vienna University Press, 2013); Jacob, *First Knowledge Economy*; Roger Osborne, *Iron, Steam and Money: The Making of the Industrial Revolution* (London: Pimlico, 2014); Sven Beckert, *Empire of Cotton: A New History of Global Capitalism* (London: Penguin, 2015); Philip Hoffman, *Why Did Europe Conquer the World?* (Princeton: Princeton University Press, 2015); Deirdre McCloskey, *Bourgeois Equality: How Ideas, Not Capital or Institutions, Enriched the World* (Chicago: University of Chicago Press, 2016); Priya Satia, *Empire of Guns: The Violent Making of the Industrial Revolution* (Richmond: Duckworth, 2018); Walter Scheidel, *Escape from Rome: The Failure of Empire and the Road to Prosperity* (Princeton: Princeton University Press, 2019); Padraic Scanlan, *Slave Empire: How Slavery Built Modern Britain* (London: Robinson, 2020).

24. Allen, *Industrial Revolution in Global Perspective*, 275 (he means northern England rather than northern Britain).

25. François Rabelais, *The Life of Gargantua and of Pantagruel*, trans. Floyd Gray (New York: Appleton-Century-Crofts, 1966), 15.

26. In reality, this "pull" is of course a "push" from the atmospheric pressure outside the cylinder.

27. Osborne, *Iron, Steam and Money*, 88–89.

28. Marten Triewald (1734), quoted in Osborne, *Iron, Steam and Money*, 39.

29. *Monthly Chronicle*, August 7, 1729, quoted in Osborne, *Iron, Steam and Money*, 103.

30. This phrase is taken from Ernest Hemingway, *The Sun Also Rises* (New York: Scribner, 1956), 136.

31. Robert Hart, "Reminiscences of James Watt," in *Transactions of the Glasgow Archaeological Society* 1, no. 1 (1859), 4.

32. John Robison, quoted in Ben Russell, *James Watt: Making the World Anew* (London: Reaktion, 2014), 76.

33. Boulton to Watt, quoted in James Muirhead, *The Life of James Watt* (New York: Appleton, 1859), 207.

34. Boulton to Watt, quoted in Muirhead, *Life of James Watt*, 87.

35. Boulton to Watt, October 28, 1783, in Uglow, *The Lunar Men*, 369.

36. Boswell, *Life of Johnson*, 510.

37. H. W. Dickinson and Rhys Jenkins, *James Watt and the Steam Engine* (Oxford: Clarendon, 1927), 129.

38. Nicolas-Joseph Cugnot's *fardier à vapeur* (1770) was the first full-size self-powered vehicle, but it could hardly be described as a "working locomotive," and was quickly abandoned. The engineer William Murdoch, who worked for Boulton and Watt, had built several smaller locomotives from 1784 onward that could move around inside, but not with high-pressure steam, and nothing of the scale of *Puffing Devil*.

39. Davies Gilbert, quoted in H. W. Dickinson and Arthur Titley, *Richard Trevithick: The Engineer and the Man* (Cambridge: Cambridge University Press, 1934), 48.

40. Lord Sheffield speaking in the House of Commons, cited in Blanning, *The Pursuit of Glory*, 131.

41. Carlo Castone Della Torre Di Rezzonico Comasco, *Viaggio in Inghilterra* (Venice: Tipografia di Alvisopoli, 1824), trans. in Malcolm Dick, "Discourses for the New Industrial World: Industrialisation and the Education of the Public in Late Eighteenth Century Britain," *History of Education* 37, no. 4 (2008), 567–84, at 572.

42. Elizabeth Montagu to Matthew Boulton, October 31, 1771, in Uglow, *The Lunar Men*, 211–12.

43. James Keir, Memorandum on Matthew Boulton, December 3, 1809, in Uglow, *The Lunar Men*, 210.

44. Erasmus Darwin, "The Economy of Vegetation [. . .]," 1:259–63, accessed at Project Gutenberg, December 21, 2022, https://www.gutenberg.org/cache/epub/9612/pg9612.html.

45. Kenneth Morgan, ed., *An American Quaker in the British Isles: The Travel Journals of Jabez Maud Fisher, 1775–1779* (Oxford: Oxford University Press, 1992), 253.

46. Georg Christoph Lichtenberg to Johann Andreas Scerhagen, October 16, 1775, trans. in Margaret Mare and W. H. Quarrell, *Lichtenberg's Visits to England as Described in His Letters and Diaries* (Oxford: Clarendon Press, 1938), 97.

47. Adam Smith, *The Wealth of Nations*, 2 vols., ed. Andrew Skinner (1776; repr., London: Penguin, 1999), 1:109.

48. Josiah Wedgwood to Thomas Bentley, July 22, 1772.

49. R. S. Fitton and Alfred P. Wadworth, *The Strutts and the Arkwrights, 1758–1830: A Study of the Early Factory System* (New York: Barnes and Noble, 1958).

50. See Tristram Hunt, *The Radical Potter: Josiah Wedgwood and the Transformation of Britain* (London: Allen Lane, 2021).

51. Wedgwood to Bentley, after September 8, 1767, in Uglow, *The Lunar Men*, 88.

52. G. J. Barker-Benfield, *The Culture of Sensibility: Sex and Society in Eighteenth Century Britain* (Chicago: University of Chicago Press, 1992), 212.

53. Wedgwood to Bentley, May 31, 1767, in Uglow, *The Lunar Men*, 218–19.

54. Wedgwood to Bentley, August 23, 1772, in Uglow, *The Lunar Men*, 201.

55. A. N. Whitehead, *Science and the Modern World* (New York: Free Press, 1967), 141: "The greatest invention of the nineteenth century was the invention of the method of invention."

56. I am deliberately avoiding the technical debate about the distinction between invention and innovation, whether they are fundamentally different, and which should be seen as more important and/or more difficult; see, e.g., Matt Ridley, *How Innovation Works* (London: Fourth Estate, 2020).

57. George Washington to Thomas Jefferson, September 26, 1785, Founders Online, National Archives, accessed December 21, 2022, https://founders.archives.gov/documents/Washington/04-03-02-0251.

58. Donald Hopkins, *The Greatest Killer: Smallpox in History* (Chicago: University of Chicago Press, 2002), 80–81; Patrick John Pead, *Benjamin Jesty, the Grandfather of Vaccination* (Newcastle: Cambridge Scholars Press, 2020), 55.

59. See Jacob, *First Knowledge Economy*, 136–84, on what she calls "the puzzle of French retardation"; cf. Blanning, *Pursuit of Glory*, 3–39, 125–41.

60. Studies of persistence effects in Europe have regularly shown that Protestantism is associated with high literacy, small gender gaps, long work hours, high incomes, low preference for leisure, high tax revenues, and urbanization. See Sascha Becker, Steven Pfaff, and Jared Rubin, "Causes and Consequences of the Protestant Reformation," *Explorations in Economic History* 62 (2016): 1–25.

61. Clive Field, "Counting Religion in England and Wales: the Long Eighteenth Century, c. 1680–c. 1840," *Journal of Ecclesiastical History* 63, no. 4 (October 2012): 693–720.

62. Francis Bacon, *In Praise of Knowledge* (1592), accessed at Bartleby (website), accessed December 21, 2022, https://www.bartleby.com/library/prose/485.html.

63. Robert Boyle, *Some Considerations Touching the Usefulnesse of Experimental Naturall Philosophy*, 2 vols. (Oxford: Davis, 1663), second part, 3–4.

64. Thomas Sprat, *The History of the Royal Society of London, for the Improving of Natural Knowledge* (London: Martyn, 1667), 397.

65. Francis Bacon, *The New Organon*, trans. Michael Silverthorne (Cambridge: Cambridge University Press, 2000), 66. See Joel Mokyr, *A Culture of Growth* (Princeton: Princeton University Press, 2016), 70–98.

66. James Watt to William Small, April 28, 1769, in Uglow, *The Lunar Men*, 244.

67. See Ridley, *How Innovation Works*.

68. Johann Wolfgang von Goethe, *Prometheus* (1772–1774); Lord Byron, *Prometheus* (1816); Percy Bysshe Shelley, *Prometheus Unbound* (1820). The Romantic fascination with the character is bound up with his defiance of the gods, and his determination to forge his own fate.

69. Mary Shelley and Karen Swallow Prior, *Frankenstein: A Guide to Reading and Reflecting* (Nashville: B&H, 2021), 67.

70. For a vivid description of nineteenth-century Chicago (and Manchester), for example, see Ben Wilson, *Metropolis: A History of Humankind's Greatest Invention* (London: Jonathan Cape, 2020), 209–33.

71. Hilaire Belloc, *The Modern Traveller* (1898), accessed at Project Gutenberg (website), accessed December 21, 2022, https://www.gutenberg.org/files/61521/61521-h/61521-h.htm

72. For a trenchant, intelligent recent critique of the impact of industrialization, see Jake Meador, *What Are Christians For? Life Together at the End of the World* (Downers Grove, IL: InterVarsity Press, 2022), 49–77.

Chapter 8: Lovers

1. See Margaret Drabble, "Romanticism," in *The Oxford Companion to English Literature*, 5th ed., ed. Margaret Drabble (Oxford: Oxford University Press, 1985), 842; Tim Blanning, *The Romantic Revolution* (London: Phoenix, 2010), 3; Michael Ferber, *Romanticism: A Very Short Introduction* (Oxford: Oxford University Press, 2010), 12–13.

2. Frederick C. Beiser, *Enlightenment, Revolution and Romanticism: The Genesis of Modern German Political Thought 1790–1800* (Cambridge, MA: Harvard University Press, 1992), 410.

3. Isaiah Berlin, *The Roots of Romanticism: The A. W. Mellon Lectures in the Fine Arts 1965*, ed. Henry Hardy (London: Pimlico, 2000), 5.

4. Berlin, *Roots of Romanticism*, 1.

5. Berlin, *Roots of Romanticism*, 1.

6. Berlin, *Roots of Romanticism*, 16–18.

7. G. W. F. Hegel, *Aesthetics: Lectures on Fine Art*, trans. T. M. Knox, 2 vols. (Oxford: Clarendon, 1975), 1:519.

8. Adrian Williams, *Portrait of Liszt: By Himself and His Contemporaries* (Oxford: Clarendon, 1990), 351.

9. William Blake, *Milton: A Poem* (London: Blake, 1811), 44.

10. Jean-Jacques Rousseau, *The Confessions of Jean-Jacques Rousseau*, trans. J. M. Cohen (London: Penguin, 1953), 17.

11. See Blanning, *Romantic Revolution*, 31–36.

12. William Wordsworth and Samuel Taylor Coleridge, *Lyrical Ballads: 1798 and 1802* (Oxford: Oxford University Press, 2013), 98.

13. I owe this point to Carl Trueman, speaking at Westminster Theological Seminary in 2014.

14. Clive James, "Casanova Comes Again," *New Yorker*, August 25 and September 1, 1997.

15. Ian Kelly, *Casanova: Actor, Lover, Priest, Spy* (London: Hodder and Stoughton, 2008), 317–22.

16. See Kelly, *Casanova*, 124–36.

17. See Ian Keable-Elliott, *The Century of Deception: The Birth of the Hoax in Eighteenth-Century England* (London: Westbourne, 2021).

18. Simon Sebag Montefiore, *Catherine the Great and Potemkin* (London: Weidenfeld and Nicolson, 2000), 229–32.

19. Kelly, *Casanova*, 120.

20. Kelly, *Casanova*, 127.

21. Bruce Duncan, *Lovers, Parricides, and Highwaymen: Aspects of Sturm und Drang Drama* (Rochester, NY: Camden House, 1999), 121; Sigrid Damm, *Cornelia Goethe* (Frankfurt am Main: Insel, 1992), 230.

22. There is ongoing debate about whether music and the visual arts should be included within the *Sturm und Drang*, but all agree that it was primarily a literary movement.

23. Johann Wolfgang von Goethe, *From My Life: Poetry and Truth*, vol. 4 of *Goethe's Collected Works*, trans. Robert Heitner (New York: Suhrkamp, 1987), 384. Goethe went on to say that their abilities brought "joy and good" when used well, but "vexation and evil" when used badly.

24. Quoted and translated in Duncan, *Lovers, Parricides, and Highwaymen*, 1.

25. Nicholas Boyle, *Goethe: The Poet and the Age*, vol. 1, *The Poetry of Desire (1749–1790)* (Oxford: Clarendon, 1991), 154.

26. The name was suggested to Klinger by Christoph Kaufmann; the play was originally called *Wirrwarr* ("Confusion").

27. Edward Harris, "Friedrich Maximilian Klinger," in *German Writers in the Age of Goethe: Sturm und Drang to Classicism*, ed. James Hardin and Christoph Schweitzer (Detroit: Gale, 1990), 125; Duncan, *Lovers, Parricides, and Highwaymen*, 179.

28. Edward Harris, "J. M. R. Lenz," in Hardin and Schweitzer, eds., *German Writers in the Age of Goethe*, 174.

29. Johann Gottfried Herder, *Selected Early Works, 1764–1767*, trans. Ernest Menze with Michael Palma (University Park: Pennsylvania State University Press, 1992), 202–3; emphasis original.

30. John Simons, "Friedrich Schiller," in Hardin and Schweitzer, eds., *German Writers in the Age of Goethe*, 239.

31. Johann Heinrich Merck to Christoph Martin Wieland, July 9, 1777, quoted and translated in Roy Pascal, *The German Sturm und Drang* (Manchester: Manchester University Press, 1953), 88.

32. Quoted and translated in Blanning, *Romantic Revolution*, 34.

33. Johann Wolfgang von Goethe, *The Sufferings of Young Werther*, trans. Bayard Quincy Morgan (New York: Frederick Ungar, 1957), 22.

34. Johann Gottfried Herder to Caroline Flachsland, January 9, 1773, quoted and translated in Blanning, *Romantic Revolution*, 112.

35. Friedrich Schiller, *On the Aesthetic Education of Man, in a Series of Letters*, ed. and trans. Elizabeth Mary Wilkinson and L. A. Willoughby (Oxford: Clarendon, 1982), 9, 107.

36. See Andrea Wulf, *Magnificent Rebels: The First Romantics and the Invention of the Self* (London: John Murray, 2022).

37. Kyle Harper, *From Shame to Sin: The Christian Transformation of Sexual Morality in Late Antiquity* (Cambridge, MA: Harvard University Press, 2013).

38. Kevin White, *The First Sexual Revolution: The Emergence of Male Heterosexuality in Modern America* (New York: New York University Press, 1993).

39. Faramerz Dabhoiwala, *The Origins of Sex: A History of the First Sexual Revolution* (London: Penguin, 2012).

40. For what follows see Dabhoiwala, *Origins of Sex*, 37–78.

41. Peter Laslett and Karla Oosterveen, "Long-Term Trends in Bastardy in England: A Study of the Illegitimacy Figures in the Parish Registers and in the Reports of the Registrar General, 1591–1960," *Population Studies* 27, no. 2 (1973): 255–86, esp. 267.

42. Bentham's arguments were compiled in his "Offences Against One's Self: Paederasty" (1785).

43. See Dabhoiwala, *Origins of Sex*, 282–348.

44. Chevalier d'Éon to Pierre Beaumarchais, January 7, 1776; see Justin Lovill, ed., *1776: A London Chronicle or How to Divert Oneself While Losing an Empire* (Padstow: Bunbury, 2019), 194.

45. *The Morning Post and Daily Advertiser*, November 11, 1775.

46. Beaumarchais to d'Éon, January 18, 1776; d'Éon to Beaumarchais, January 30, 1776; see Lovill, *1776*, 212, 226.

47. As such, d'Éon was more intersex than transgender in the modern sense. For a full biography, see Gary Kates, *Monsieur d'Éon Is a Woman: A Tale of Political Intrigue and Sexual Masquerade* (New York: Basic Books, 1995).

48. For a rollercoaster account of the trial and her life, see Catherine Ostler, *The Duchess Countess: The Woman Who Scandalised a Nation* (London: Simon and Schuster, 2021).

49. Quoted in Matthew Kinservik, *Sex, Scandal, and Celebrity in Eighteenth-Century London* (New York: Palgrave Macmillan, 2007), 2.

50. Hannah More, "The Works of Hannah More," in *The Eclectic Review XII* (London: Jackson and Walford, 1834), 453–54.

51. Prince Hoare, ed., *Memoirs of Granville Sharp Esq, Composed From His Own Manuscripts* (London: Colburn, 1820), 151. Sharp's original, typically for the period, identifies Lord Sandwich and Martha (W)ray as Lord S***** and Miss W*****.

52. Fred R. Shapiro, *The Yale Book of Quotations* (New Haven, CT: Yale University Press, 2006), 281. Coincidentally, Foote was also the playwright who helped expose

the Duchess of Kingston's bigamy; he was subsequently accused (and acquitted) of sexual assault himself.

53. The obvious comparison here would be with the Profumo affair (1961–1963), in which Harold Macmillan's Secretary for War had an affair with a young model and lied about it, leading to his resignation and the fall of the Conservative government. See Richard Davenport-Hines, *An English Affair: Sex, Class and Power in the Age of Profumo* (London: Harper, 2013).

54. Smith, *Wealth of Nations*, 2:381–82.

55. William Blake, *Songs of Experience* (1789; repr., London: Blake, 1794); cf. Peter Ackroyd, *Blake* (London: Vintage, 1999), 43–55, 141–43.

56. Leo Damrosch, *Jean-Jacques Rousseau: Restless Genius* (New York: Houghton Mifflin, 2005), 479–80.

57. Jacques-Henri Bernardin de Saint Pierre, *La Vie et Les Ouvrages de Jean-Jacques Rousseau*, ed. Maurice Souriau (Paris: Cornély, 1907), 49.

58. Olivier de Corancez, *De J. J. Rousseau* (Paris: Desenne et Maradan, 1798), 22, 40.

59. William Wordsworth, *The Poetical Works of William Wordsworth* (1826; repr., London: Moxon, 1847), 144–45; Wordsworth, *The Prelude*, ed. James Engell and Michael Raymond (Oxford: Oxford University Press, 2016), pt. 12, line 218.

60. Robert Wokler, *Rousseau: A Very Short Introduction* (Oxford: Oxford University Press, 2001), 135.

61. Jean-Jacques Rousseau, *The Reveries of the Solitary Walker*, trans. Anon (London: Robinson, 1796), walk 1.

62. Rousseau, *Reveries*, walk 1; emphasis added. This last phrase, taken from an English translation in 1796, is a puzzling rendition of Rousseau's "en songeant au prix qu'avait mérité mon coeur"; we would more naturally take this to mean "in thinking of the prize my heart deserved."

63. Rousseau to Malesherbes, January 4, 1762; see Jean-Jacques Rousseau, *The Collected Writings of Rousseau*, vol. 5, *The Confessions and Correspondence, Including the Letters to Malesherbes*, trans. Christopher Kelly (Hanover: University Press of New England, 1995), 573.

64. Rousseau, *Reveries*, walk 4.

65. It is a testament to the influence of Rousseau and his contemporaries that the line given to Polonius in *Hamlet* 1:3, "to thine own self be true," is interpreted as if it means roughly what Rousseau meant by it, as opposed to what Shakespeare (let alone Polonius) meant by it. See William Shakespeare, *Hamlet, Prince of Denmark* (Cambridge: Cambridge University Press, 2003), 110.

66. Robert N. Bellah et al., *Habits of the Heart: Individualism and Commitment in American Life* (1985; repr., Berkeley: University of California Press, 2008).

67. Philip Rieff, *The Triumph of the Therapeutic: Uses of Faith after Freud* (1966; repr., Chicago: University of Chicago Press, 1987), 239.

68. Charles Taylor, *A Secular Age* (Cambridge, MA: Belknap, 2007), 475. See also his *Sources of the Self*, in which he shows that although we modern people are united in our commitments to universal justice, beneficence, equality, freedom, self-rule, and the avoidance of death and suffering, we have reached those commitments by very different routes: (1) "the original theistic grounding for these standards," (2) "a naturalism of disengaged reason, which in our day takes scientistic forms," and (3) "a third family of views which finds its sources in Romantic expressivism or in one of the modernist successor visions." See Taylor, *Sources of the Self: The Making of the Modern Identity* (Cambridge, MA: Harvard University Press, 1989), 495.

69. For a compelling account of this process see Carl R. Trueman, *The Rise and Triumph of the Modern Self: Cultural Amnesia, Expressive Individualism, and the Road to Sexual Revolution* (Wheaton, IL: Crossway, 2020).

70. Rousseau, *Reveries*, walk 6.

71. Rousseau, *Reveries*, walk 2.

72. Donna Tartt, *The Goldfinch* (London: Little, Brown, 2013), 852.

73. Tartt, *The Goldfinch*, 852–53; emphasis added.

Chapter 9: Profits

1. For these terms, see, respectively, Angus Deaton, *The Great Escape: Health, Wealth and the Origins of Inequality* (Princeton: Princeton University Press, 2013); Samuel Huntington, *The Clash of Civilizations and the Remaking of the World Order* (New York: Simon and Schuster, 1996); Deirdre McCloskey, *Bourgeois Equality: How Ideas, Not Capital or Institutions, Enriched the World* (Chicago: University of Chicago Press, 2016); Erik Jones, *The European Miracle: Environments, Economies and Geopolitics in the History of Europe and Asia* (Cambridge: Cambridge University Press, 2003).

2. The explanation for this is the greater levels of inequality in farming societies when compared to bands of hunter-gatherers (so Thomas Jefferson was far richer than the average caveman/cavewoman, but the majority of his global contemporaries were not). For evidence and analysis, see Gregory Clark, *A Farewell to Alms: A Brief Economic History of the World* (Princeton: Princeton University Press, 2007), 19–189.

3. McCloskey, *Bourgeois Equality*, 5–8, 33.

4. Stephen Pinker, *Enlightenment Now: The Case for Reason, Science, Humanism and Progress* (London: Penguin, 2018); Ian Morris, *The Measure of Civilization: How Social Development Decides the Fate of Nations* (Princeton: Princeton University Press, 2013).

5. For the explanation, see Ian Morris, *Why the West Rules—for Now: The Patterns of History, and What They Reveal about the Future* (London: Profile, 2010), 135–71; for the data, see Morris, *Measure of Civilization*.

6. John Rae, *Life of Adam Smith* (London: Macmillan, 1895), 5.

7. For a good recent biography, see Jesse Norman, *Adam Smith: What He Thought and Why It Matters* (London: Penguin, 2018).

8. According to Boswell, April 13, 1776; see Charles Ryskamp and Frederick Pottle, eds., *Boswell: The Ominous Years, 1774–1776* (New York: McGraw Hill, 1963), 337.

9. Quoted in Tim Blanning, *Pursuit of Glory: Europe 1648–1815* (2007; repr., London: Penguin, 2008), 187. See, e.g., Francois Quesnay, *Tableau Economique, et Maximes Générales du Gouvernement Economique* (Versailles, 1758); Victor de Riquetti de Mirabeau, *Philosophie Rurale, ou Economie Générale et Politique de l'Agriculture* (Amsterdam, 1764); Anne Robert Jacques Turgot, *Réflexions sur la Formation et la Distribution des Richesses* (1788); cf. Benjamin Franklin to Cadwalader Evans, February 20, 1768): "The true source of riches is husbandry. Agriculture is truly productive of new wealth; manufactures only change forms. . . . Riches are not increased by manufacturing." Founders Online, National Archive, accessed January 3, 2023, https://founders.archives.gov/documents/Franklin/01-15-02-0029.

10. This had been around in England since the Tudors. As one writer had put it in 1549, "We must always take heed that we buy no more from strangers than we sell them, for so should we impoverish ourselves and enrich them." See Thomas Smith, *A Discourse of the Common Weal of This Realm of England* (London: Marshe, 1581);

cf. Jacob Viner, "English Theories of Foreign Trade Before Adam Smith," *Journal of Political Economy* 38, no. 3 (1930): 249–301. It also provided much of the underlying rationale for domestic protectionism, the insufferable behavior of the East India Company, and the grotesqueries of the Atlantic triangular trade.

11. Adam Smith, *The Wealth of Nations*, 2 vols., ed. Andrew Skinner (1776; repr., London: Penguin, 1999), 2:5–247 (on the mercantile system), 2:247–75 (on the agricultural system).

12. Smith, *Wealth of Nations*, 2:32; emphasis added.

13. Smith, *Wealth of Nations*, 2:274.

14. Smith, *Wealth of Nations*, 2:245.

15. For twenty key works that present all these arguments, see Jones, *European Miracle*; David Landes, *The Wealth and Poverty of Nations: Why Some Are so Rich and Some Are so Poor* (New York: Norton, 1998); David Abernethy, *The Dynamics of Global Dominance: European Overseas Empires, 1415–1980* (New Haven, CT: Yale University Press, 2000); Kenneth Pomeranz, *The Great Divergence: China, Europe and the Making of the Modern World Economy* (Princeton: Princeton University Press, 2000); Joel Mokyr, *The Gifts of Athena: Historical Origins of the Knowledge Economy* (Princeton: Princeton University Press, 2002); Christopher Bayly, *The Birth of the Modern World, 1780–1914* (Oxford: Blackwell, 2004); Clark, *Farewell to Alms*; Ronald Findlay and Kevin O'Rourke, *Power and Plenty: Trade, War, and the World Economy in the Second Millennium* (Princeton: Princeton University Press, 2007); Robert Allen, *The Industrial Revolution in Global Perspective* (Cambridge: Cambridge University Press, 2009); Prasannan Parthasarathi, *Why Europe Grew Rich and Asia Did Not* (Cambridge: Cambridge University Press, 2011); Jean-Laurent Rosenthal and Bin Wong, *Before and Beyond Divergence: The Politics of Economic Change in China and Europe* (Cambridge, MA: Harvard University Press, 2011); Immanuel Wallerstein, *The Modern World-System III: The Second Era of Great Expansion of the Capitalist World Economy 1730–1840s* (Berkeley: University of California Press, 2011); Niall Ferguson, *Civilization: The Six Killer Apps of Western Power* (London: Penguin, 2012); Daron Acemoglu and James Robinson, *Why Nations Fail: The Origins of Power, Prosperity and Poverty* (New York: Crown, 2012); Peer Vries, *Escaping Poverty: The Origins of Modern Economic Growth* (Vienna: Vienna University Press, 2013); Sven Beckert, *Empire of Cotton: A New History of Global Capitalism* (London: Penguin, 2015); Philip Hoffman, *Why Did Europe Conquer the World?* (Princeton: Princeton University Press, 2015); McCloskey, *Bourgeois Equality*; Walter Scheidel, *Escape from Rome: The Failure of Empire and the Road to Prosperity* (Princeton: Princeton University Press, 2019).

16. Smith, *Wealth of Nations*, 1:174; emphasis added.

17. Smith, *Wealth of Nations*, 1:197, 380.

18. Smith, *Wealth of Nations*, 1:517.

19. Smith, *Wealth of Nations*, 1:176.

20. Acemoglu and Robinson, *Why Nations Fail*, 7–44.

21. Ferguson, *Civilization*, 96–140.

22. Bolívar argued that tolerance was "the most grievous error," federalism was too "complicated" and "weak" to work, his fellow citizens were "not yet able to exercise their rights themselves in the fullest measure," and that "America can only be ruled by an able despotism. . . . Can we place laws above heroes and principles above men?" See Simón Bolívar, "The Cartagena Manifesto" (December 15, 1812), in Gerald Fitzgerald, ed., *The Political Thought of Bolivar: Selected Writings* (The Hague:

Nijhoff, 1977), 10–18; Simon Bolívar to Francisco de Paula Santander, July 8, 1826, quoted in John Lynch, "Bolívar and the Caudillos," *Hispanic American Historical Review* 63, no. 1 (1983), 3–35.

23. The Glorious Revolution was particularly significant, because by (1) limiting the power of the Crown, and preventing the monarchy from arbitrarily changing or abolishing people's rights, it (2) made property far securer than it had been previously, which (3) increased incentives to invest, which (4) caused private capital markets to flourish and (5) gave the state access to far more borrowing (because investors were more certain of getting their money back), all of which (6) lowered transaction costs and (7) engendered growth in industry and trade. The classic statement is Douglass North and Barry Weingast, "Constitutions and Commitment: The Evolution of Institutions Governing Public Choice in Seventeenth-Century England," *The Journal of Economic History* 49, no. 4 (1989): 803–32.

24. In a subsequent work, Acemoglu and Robinson answer this question by pointing to the interaction between hierarchical Roman state machinery and democratic Germanic tribal societies in Western Europe in the centuries following the fall of Rome. See Daron Acemoglu and James Robinson, *The Narrow Corridor: How Nations Struggle for Liberty* (London: Penguin, 2020), 152–265.

25. Clark, *Farewell to Alms*, 146–48.

26. See William T. Rowe, *China's Last Empire: The Great Qing* (Cambridge, MA: Belknap, 2009), 122–48; McCloskey, *Bourgeois Equality*, 85–86, 129–38; Carol Shiue and Wolfgang Keller, "Markets in China and Europe on the Eve of the Industrial Revolution," *American Economic Review* 97, no. 4 (2007): 1189–1216; cf. Loreb Brandt, Debin Ma, and Thomas Rawski, "From Divergence to Convergence: Re-evaluating the History Behind China's Economic Boom," *Journal of Economic Literature* 52, no. 1 (2014): 56–64.

27. William Dalrymple, *The Anarchy: The Relentless Rise of the East India Company* (London: Bloomsbury, 2019), 14, estimates the income of the Mughal Emperor in the early seventeenth century to be £10 billion in today's terms. The most visible symbol of this wealth today is, of course, the Taj Mahal.

28. Guillaume-Thomas Raynal, *A Philosophical and Political History of the Settlements and Trade of the Europeans in the East and West Indies*, trans. J. O. Justamond, 6 vols. (London: Strahan and Cadell, 1798 [1776]); Inquisition edict, Seville, March 23, 1776.

29. Guillaume-Thomas Raynal, *Histoire Philosophique et Politique, Des Établissements et du Commerce des Européens dans les Deux Indes*, 5 vols. (Geneva: Pellet, 1780), 4:703–5.

30. Jan Pieterszoon Coen to the Council of Seventeen, December 27, 1614, quoted and translated in Findlay and O'Rourke, *Power and Plenty*, 178.

31. Dalrymple, *Anarchy*, 215–22.

32. Raynal, *Histoire des Deux Indes*, 1:385. A calmer but in many ways more damning appraisal of the British was given by the Mughal historian Ghulam Hussain Khan: "The English have a custom of coming for a number of years, and then of going away to pay a visit to their native country, without any of them showing an inclination to fix themselves in this land. And as they join to that custom another one of theirs, which every one holds as a divine obligation: that of scraping together as much money as they can in this country, and carrying these immense sums to the Kingdom of England; so it should not be surprising that these two customs, blended together, should be ever undermining and ruining this country, and should become an eternal bar to it ever flourishing again." Syed Ghulam Hussain

Tabatabai Khan, *Seir Mutaqherin; or Review of Modern Times: Being an History of India*, vol. 3 (Calcutta: 1790), 194–95.

33. Bayly, *Birth of the Modern World*, 52–55.

34. Jan De Vries, "The Industrial Revolution and the Industrious Revolution," *Journal of Economic History* 54 (1994): 249–70.

35. Beckert, *Empire of Cotton*, 63–73.

36. Beckert, *Empire of Cotton*, 119.

37. Beckert, *Empire of Cotton*, 46, 75.

38. E.g., Joel Mokyr, *A Culture of Growth* (Princeton: Princeton University Press, 2016); Landes, *Wealth and Poverty of Nations*; McCloskey, *Bourgeois Equality*; Niall Ferguson, *Civilisation: The Six Killer Apps of Western Power* (London: Penguin, 2012); William Rosen, *The Most Powerful Idea in the World: A Story of Steam, Industry and Invention* (London: Pimlico, 2011).

39. Diderot, "Chinois, Philosophie des," in *Encyclopédie ou Dictionnaire Raisonné des Sciences, des Arts et des Métiers*, 35 vols. (Paris: 1751–1772), vol. 3.

40. The intensity of year-round rice cultivation, when compared to the seasonal flurries and lulls of the wheat harvest, means that East Asians have probably been working harder than Europeans for ten thousand years; see Malcolm Gladwell, *Outliers: The Story of Success* (2008; repr., London: Penguin, 2009), 232–39. And not just in manual labor: the rigor of the Chinese examination system at the time was unparalleled, and a source of endless fascination to European observers, who published dozens of books on it during the Qing period. Many of the *philosophes* were ardent Sinophiles for exactly this reason, with Voltaire marveling in his *Essai sur les Moeurs* at the severe exams and the effective government they produced (in *Oeuvres Complètes*, 52 vols. [Paris: Garnier, 1877–1885], 13:162).

41. Ibrahim Müteferrika, *Traité de la Tactique*, trans. Charles Réviczki (Vienna: Trattnern, 1769).

42. Joseph Henrich, *The WEIRDest People in the World: How the West Became Psychologically Peculiar and Particularly Prosperous* (London: Allen Lane, 2020), 21.

43. Larry Siedentop, *Inventing the Individual: The Origins of Western Liberalism* (London: Penguin, 2015), 265–77.

44. Tom Holland, *Dominion: The Making of the Western Mind* (London: Little Brown, 2019), 185–205.

45. A. N. Whitehead, *Science and the Modern World* (New York: Free Press, 1967), 12.

46. Yuval Noah Harari, *Sapiens: A Brief History of Humankind* (London: Vintage, 2011), 275–306.

47. Mokyr, *Culture of Growth*, 287–320.

48. Eltjo Buringh and Jan Luiten Van Zanden, "Charting the 'Rise of the West': Manuscripts and Printed Books in Europe, A Long-Term Perspective from the Sixth through Eighteenth Centuries," *Journal of Economic History* 69, no. 2 (2009), 409–45.

49. McCloskey, *Bourgeois Equality*, 316–25.

50. James Boswell, *The Life of Samuel Johnson* (1791; repr., London: Penguin, 2008), 529.

51. David Hume, "Of the Rise and Progress of the Arts and Sciences," in Hume, *Essays and Treatises on Several Subjects*, 2 vols. (London: Cadell, 1768), 1:129–32.

52. Hume, *Essays*, 1:133.

53. Montesquieu, *The Spirit of the Laws*, trans. and ed. Anne M. Cohler, Basia Carolyn Miller and Harold Samuel Stone (Cambridge: Cambridge University Press, 1989), 283.

54. Hoffman, *Why Did Europe Conquer the World?*

55. Joel Mokyr, *The Lever of Riches: Technological Creativity and Economic Progress* (Oxford: Oxford University Press, 1990), 237. Oft-cited examples include the abolition of the Ming treasure voyages and the Ottoman sultan's decision to destroy the Istanbul observatory in 1580 (ironically, in the same year that the King of Denmark built one for Tycho Brahe).

56. He makes this case with considerable brio in Scheidel, *Escape from Rome*, 491–502.

57. Scheidel, *Escape from Rome*, 15.

58. David Cosandey, *Le Secret de l'Occident: Vers un Théorie Générale du Progès Scientifique* (Paris: Flammarion, 2008), 533–69.

59. On why Rome was such a dramatic exception to this general rule, see Scheidel, *Escape from Rome*, 51–123.

60. In his excellent chapter on the Republic of Letters, Joel Mokyr quotes the Talmudic wisdom that *kin'at sofrim tarbeh chochma*: "The jealousy of the learned shall increase wisdom." Mokyr, *Culture of Growth*, 180.

61. Bernard Mandeville, "The Grumbling Hive, or Knaves Turn'd Honest" (1705), later published in *The Fable of the Bees* (London: Roberts, 1714).

Chapter 10: Christians

1. David Hempton, *The Church in the Long Eighteenth Century* (London: Tauris, 2011), 139.

2. Peter Berger, *The Sacred Canopy: Elements of a Sociological Theory of Religion* (New York: Anchor, 1967), 129.

3. Hempton, *Church in the Long Eighteenth Century*, 139.

4. See, e.g., Hempton, *Church in the Long Eighteenth Century*; David Sorkin, *The Religious Enlightenment: Protestants, Jews, and Catholics from London to Vienna* (Princeton: Princeton University Press, 2008).

5. Augustus Toplady, "Reflections for the Beginning of the Year 1776," in *The Works of Augustus M. Toplady*, 6 vols. (London: Baynes, 1825), 3:450–51. I am very grateful to Rob Milton for the reference.

6. Augustus Toplady, "Let Your Moderation Be Known to All," in *Works*, 3:306.

7. Toplady, "Let Your Moderation Be Known to All," in *Works*, 3:305.

8. Toplady, "Let Your Moderation Be Known to All," in *Works*, 3:306.

9. Toplady, "Let Your Moderation Be Known to All," in *Works*, 3:308.

10. Toplady to Rev. Mr. B. P. of New York, September 6, 1773; see *The Works of Augustus Toplady, A New Edition Complete in One Volume* (London: Cornish, 1853), 669.

11. John Wesley to George Merryweather, June 24, 1770; see Luke Tyerman, *The Life and Times of the Rev. John Wesley*, 3 vols. (London: Hodder and Stoughton, 1872), 3:83.

12. First published in full in *The Gospel Magazine* (March 1776), 131–32.

13. Augustus Toplady, *Psalms and Hymns for Public and Private Worship* (London: Dilly, 1776).

14. John Wesley, *A Collection of Hymns for the Use of the People Called Methodists* (London: Paramore, 1780), preface dated October 20, 1779.

15. John Newton and William Cowper, *Olney Hymns* (1779; repr., Glasgow: Collins, 1829), 304.

16. Newton and Cowper, *Olney Hymns*, 58. For the recording and performance statistics, see Tony Reinke, *Newton on the Christian Life: To Live Is Christ* (Wheaton, IL: Crossway, 2015), 38; Jonathan Aitken, *John Newton: From Disgrace to Amazing Grace* (Wheaton, IL: Crossway, 2007), 224.

17. Aitken, *John Newton*, 235.

18. Newton and Cowper, *Olney Hymns*, 50.

19. Newton and Cowper, *Olney Hymns*, 118.

20. Newton and Cowper, *Olney Hymns*, 165.

21. Newton and Cowper, *Olney Hymns*, 183.

22. James Brewster, ed., *Life of the Reverend John Newton, in a Series of Letters Written by Himself to the Rev. Dr. Haweis* (Edinburgh: Anderson and Bryce, 1824), 180.

23. Brewster, *Life of the Reverend John Newton*, 180–81.

24. Quoted in Aitken, *John Newton*, 347.

25. *The Works of the Rev. John Newton: From the Last London Edition*, 6 vols. (New York: Williams and Whiting, 1810), 2:442.

26. Two slightly different outlines of the sermon, which was preached in a friend's home, have survived; for this amalgamation see Reinke, *Newton on the Christian Life*, 268.

27. On the likelihood of rape, see William Phipps, *Amazing Grace in John Newton: Slave-Ship Captain, Hymnwriter, and Abolitionist* (Macon, GA: Mercer University Press, 2001), 33.

28. Josiah Pratt, ed., *Eclectic Notes: Or Notes of Discussions on Religious Topics at the Meetings of the Eclectic Society* (London: Nisbet, 1856), 272.

29. See the preface to Newton and Cowper, *Olney Hymns*, 47–51.

30. John Newton to Alexander Clunie, July 26, 1766, in John Newton, "A Series of Religious Letters Written to Alexander Clunie, from the Year 1761, to the Death of Mr. Clunie in 1770," Grace Gems (website), accessed January 3, 2023, https://www .gracegems.org/Newton/christian_correspondent.htm.

31. Henry Venn to John Brasier, December 2, 1776, in *The Life and a Selection from the Letters of the Late Henry Venn*, ed. Henry Venn (London: Hatchard, 1839), 218.

32. See Roy Hattersley, *John Wesley: A Brand from the Burning* (London: Abacus, 2004), 126–55.

33. John Berridge, *Sion's Songs, or Hymns Composed for the Use of Them That Love and Follow the Lord Jesus Christ in Sincerity* (London: Vallance and Conder, 1785), 202.

34. Newton and Cowper, *Olney Hymns*, 344.

35. This claim has been challenged, most notably by Vincent Carretta, on the grounds that Equiano's baptismal records suggest he was born in South Carolina. The view taken here, following most interpreters, is that Equiano's version of events is correct.

36. Olaudah Equiano, *The Interesting Narrative and Other Writings*, ed. Vincent Carretta (London: Penguin, 2003), 59–61.

37. Equiano, *The Interesting Narrative*, 188–92.

38. Equiano, *The Interesting Narrative*, 184, quoting Robert Robinson's "Come Thou Fount of Every Blessing" (1758).

39. Erik Gøbel, *The Danish Slave Trade and Its Abolition* (Leiden: Brill, 2016), 25.

40. Hempton, *Church in the Long Eighteenth Century*, 82–86.

41. Friedrich Martin's diary, May 4, 1738, in Jon F. Sensbach, *Rebecca's Revival: Creating Black Christianity in the Atlantic World* (Cambridge: Harvard University Press, 2005), 46.

42. Sensbach, *Rebecca's Revival*, 188–89.

43. Sensbach, *Rebecca's Revival*, 127–28.

44. Hearing of December 22, 1738; see Sensbach, *Rebecca's Revival*, 120–21.

45. Count Zinzendorf's address to slaves, February 15, 1739, quoted in Christian G. A. Oldendorp, *History of the Mission of the Evangelical Brethren on the Caribbean Islands of St. Thomas, St. Croix and St. John*, trans. Arnold Highfield and Vladimir Barac, ed. Johann Jakob Bossart (Ann Arbor: Karoma, 1987), 361–63.

46. Lemuel Haynes, *Liberty Further Extended, or Free Thoughts on the Illegality of Slave-Keeping*; see Ruth Bogin, "'Liberty Further Extended': A 1776 Antislavery Manuscript by Lemuel Haynes," *The William and Mary Quarterly* 40, no. 1 (1983), 95.

47. Indeed, as Haynes was writing these words, Equiano was sailing from the Caribbean to London, having just been threatened with re-enslavement; see Equiano, *The Interesting Narrative*, 210–19.

48. Samuel Hopkins, *A Dialogue concerning the Slavery of the Africans [. . .]* (Norwich: Spooner, 1776).

49. Jonathan Sassi, "'This Whole Country Have Their Hands Full of Blood This Day': Transcription and Introduction of an Antislavery Sermon Manuscript Attributed to the Reverend Samuel Hopkins," *Proceedings of the American Antiquarian Society* 112, no. 1 (2002): 66–67.

50. John Wesley, *Thoughts on Slavery* (London: Hawes, 1774), 24.

51. Wesley, *Thoughts on Slavery*, 27–28.

52. Maurice Jackson, *Let This Voice Be Heard: Anthony Benezet, Father of Atlantic Abolitionism* (Philadelphia: University of Pennsylvania Press, 2009), 154.

53. Granville Sharp, *The Just Limitation of Slavery in the Laws of God* (London: White, 1776), 20–21, 38–39, 49.

54. John Witherspoon, *The Dominion of Providence over the Passions of Men* (Philadelphia, 1777), 33.

55. Madison's amendments to the Declaration of Rights, May 29–June 12, 1776, in *The Papers of James Madison*, 17 vols., ed. William Hutchinson and William Rachal (Chicago: University of Chicago Press, 1962–1991), 1:174–75.

56. Virginia Declaration of Rights (June 29, 1776), art. 16, National Archives (website), accessed January 3, 2023, https://www.archives.gov/founding-docs/virginia-declaration-of-rights; emphasis added.

57. Constitution of Pennsylvania (September 28, 1776), sec. 6, *The Avalon Project*, Yale Law School Lillian Goldman Law Library (website), accessed January 3, 2023, https://avalon.law.yale.edu/18th_century/pa08.asp.

58. See Thomas Kidd, *God of Liberty: A Religious History of the American Revolution* (New York: Basic Books, 2010), 37–55.

59. Thomas Jefferson, *Autobiography*, January 6, 1821, *The Avalon Project*, Yale Law School Lillian Goldman Law Library (website), accessed January 3, 2023, https://avalon.law.yale.edu/19th_century/jeffauto.asp.

60. Thomas Jefferson, *The Papers of Thomas Jefferson*, vol. 1, *1760–1776*, ed. Julian Boyd, Mina R. Bryan, Lyman H. Butterfield (Princeton: Princeton University Press, 1950), 525–29.

61. Haynes, *Liberty Further Extended*.

62. Hendrik Kraemer, quoted in James O'Flaherty, "Some Major Emphases of Hamann's Theology," *Harvard Theological Review* 51, no. 1 (1958): 39.

63. Although, see Johann Georg Hamann, *Writings on Philosophy and Language*, trans. Kenneth Haynes (Cambridge: Cambridge University Press, 2007); Hamann, *London Writings: The Spiritual and Theological Journal of Johann Georg Hamann*, trans. John Kleinig, ed Gene Edward Veith (Evansville, IN: Ballast, 2021). For the languages, see

John Betz, *After Enlightenment: The Post-Secular Vision of J. G. Hamann* (Oxford: Blackwell, 2012), 91.

64. Johann Wolfgang von Goethe to Charlotte von Stein, September 17, 1784; Oswald Bayer, ed., *Johann Georg Hamann: "Der hellste Kopf seiner Zeit"* (Tübingen: Attempto Verlag, 1998), cited and translated in Betz, *After Enlightenment*, 2.

65. Friedrich Schlegel, quoted and translated in Betz, *After Enlightenment*, 1.

66. Both quoted and translated in Isaiah Berlin, *The Magus of the North: J. G. Hamann and the Origins of Modern Irrationalism* (London: Fontana, 1994), 3.

67. Quoted and translated in Berlin, *The Magus of the North*, 2.

68. G. W. F. Hegel, "Hamanns Schriften," *Jahrbücher für wissenschaftliche Kritik* (1828); the epithet is quoted and translated in Betz, *After Enlightenment*, 312.

69. Søren Kierkegaard, *The Concept of Anxiety: A Simple Psychologically Orienting Deliberation on the Dogmatic Issue of Hereditary Sin*, ed. and trans. Reidar Thomte (Princeton: Princeton University Press, 1980), 178, 198.

70. See Immanuel Kant, *Correspondence*, trans. Arnulf Zweig (Cambridge: Cambridge University Press, 1999), 577.

71. Isaiah Berlin, much the most well-known interpreter of Hamann in the second half of the twentieth century, admitted to not being very interested in this vision: "Hamann's theology and his religious metaphysics I find I am neither drawn to nor competent to discuss, except in so far as they are part and parcel of the rest of what he wrote." Berlin, *Magus of the North*, xv. Consequently, Berlin reads (and critiques) Hamann as essentially an irrationalist, a view that has been widely rejected in more recent scholarship; see, e.g., Oswald Bayer, *A Contemporary in Dissent: Johann Georg Hamann as a Radical Enlightener* (Grand Rapids, MI: Eerdmans, 2012); Betz, *After Enlightenment*; cf. Kenneth Haynes's introduction in Hamann, *Writings on Philosophy and Language*, xvi: "The fundamental divide between Hamann and Jacobi makes clear how inadequate it is to regard Hamann as a philosopher of irrationalism or an advocate of faith as opposed to reason."

72. Johann Georg Hamann, *Londoner Schriften*, ed. Oswald Bayer and Bernd Weissenborn (Munich: Beck, 1993), 338–39; for all translated sections of this work hereafter, see Betz, *After Enlightenment*, 30–62.

73. Hamann, *Londoner Schriften*, 343–44.

74. See Hamann, *London Writings*.

75. Hamann, *Londoner Schriften*, 345–46.

76. Hamann, *Londoner Schriften*, 373.

77. Hamann, "Aesthetica in Nuce," in *Writings on Philosophy and Language*, 77.

78. Hamann, "Metacritique on the Purism of Reason," in *Writings on Philosophy and Language*, 209–10.

79. Johann Georg Hamann, *Briefwechsel*, 6 vols., ed. Walther Ziesemer and Arthur Henkel (Wiesbaden: Insel, 1955–1975), 1:394, translated in Betz, *After Enlightenment*, 43.

80. See Betz, *After Enlightenment*, 47–53.

81. Johann Georg Hamann, "Socratic Memorabilia," in *Sämtliche Werke*, 6 vols., ed. Josef Nadler (Vienna: Herder, 1949–1957), 2:73, translated in Betz, *After Enlightenment*, 78.

82. Hamann to Immanuel Kant, July 27, 1759. Hamann makes much of the fact that the German *Glaube*, like the New Testament *pistis*, can be translated either "belief" or "faith."

83. Hamann, "Socratic Memorablia," in *Sämtliche Werke*, 2:73, translated in Betz, *After Enlightenment*, 82.

84. Hamann, *Londoner Schriften*, 131.

85. Hamann, "Metacritique," 213.

86. See his comments on Kant: "The first purification of reason consisted in the partly misunderstood, partly failed attempt to make reason independent of all tradition and custom and belief in them. The second is even more transcendent and comes to nothing less than independence from experience and its everyday induction. . . . The third, highest, and, as it were, empirical purism is therefore concerned with language." Hamann, "Metacritique," 207–8.

87. Johann Georg Hamann, "New Apology of the Letter H," in *Writings on Philosophy and Language*, 146–63.

88. Christian Tobias Damm, *Betrachtungen über die Religion* (Berlin: n.p., 1773), 232–34, quoted and translated in Hamann, "New Apology," 147.

89. Hamann, "New Apology," 151.

90. Hamann, "New Apology," 148.

91. Hamann, "New Apology," 163.

92. For demonstration and analysis, see Betz, *After Enlightenment*, 312–40.

93. Peter Leithart in his endorsement of Bayer, *Contemporary in Dissent*.

94. Betz, *After Enlightenment*, 317–19.

95. Hamann, "Aesthetica in Nuce," 78.

Chapter 11: Opportunities

1. Jürgen Habermas, "A Conversation about God and the World: Interview with Eduardo Mendieta," in *Religion and Rationality: Essays on Reason, God, and Modernity*, ed. Eduardo Mendieta (Cambridge, MA: MIT Press, 2002), 148–49; emphasis added. For some helpful reflections on this theme in Habermas's later work, see Gene Edward Veith Jr., *Post-Christian: A Guide to Contemporary Thought and Culture* (Wheaton, IL: Crossway, 2020), 289–95.

2. Jürgen Habermas et al, *An Awareness of What Is Missing: Faith and Reason in a Post-Secular Age*, trans. Ciaran Cronin (Cambridge: Polity, 2010). Habermas's proposal for a way forward still leaves something missing, however; see Stanley Fish, "Does Reason Know What It Is Missing?," *New York Times*, April 12, 2010, https://www.nytimes.com/.

3. G. K. Chesterton, *What's Wrong with the World?* (London: Cassell, 1913), 39.

4. Helen Lewis, "The World Is Trapped in America's Culture War," *The Atlantic*, October 27, 2020, https://www.theatlantic.com/.

5. See Ron Chernow, *Alexander Hamilton* (New York: Penguin, 2004), epilogue.

6. See Charles Taylor, *Sources of the Self: The Making of the Modern Identity* (Cambridge, MA: Harvard University Press, 1989).

7. For a fascinating recent survey, see Will Storr, *The Status Game: On Social Position and How We Use It* (London: William Collins, 2021).

8. On the connection between status, health outcomes, and suicide, see Storr, *Status Game*, 13–19.

9. John Barclay makes an excellent case for seeing the incongruity of grace (*charis*) as the defining feature of Paul's understanding of it, in contrast to the ways in which his Jewish, Greek, and Roman contemporaries understood *charis*. See John M. G. Barclay, *Paul and the Gift* (Grand Rapids, MI: Eerdmans, 2015).

10. The best translation of *appamādena sampādethā* is still debated; for a more Pauline version ("Work out your salvation with diligence") see T. W. Rhys Davids, *Buddhist Suttas* (Oxford: Clarendon, 1881), 114. For the dying words of Jesus, see John 19:30.

11. Matt. 6:9–13; Luke 4:16–21; John 8:36; Acts 13:38–39; Rom. 3:24; 6:15–23; 7:1–6; 8:1–4, 18–25; 1 Cor. 10:1–4; 2 Cor. 3:17; Gal. 1:3–5; 4:21–31; 5:1–15; etc.

12. Suzanne Collins, *The Hunger Games* (New York: Scholastic, 2008). The next two paragraphs are adapted from Andrew Wilson, "Hunger Games and Dystopia," *First Things*, April 3, 2013, https://www.firstthings.com/.

13. Hannah Arendt, "Lying in Politics: Reflections on the Pentagon Papers," in *Crises of the Republic: Lying in Politics; Civil Disobedience; On Violence; Thoughts on Politics and Revolution* (New York: Harcourt, 1972), 1–48.

14. Friedrich Nietzsche, *Philosophy and Truth: Selections from Nietzsche's Notebooks of the Early 1870s*, trans. Daniel Breazeale (Atlantic Highlands, NJ: Humanities Press, 1979), 84; emphasis original.

15. Yuval Noah Harari, *Sapiens: A Brief History of Humankind* (London: Vintage, 2011), 121–26.

16. Yuval Noah Harari, *21 Lessons for the 21st Century* (London: Vintage, 2018), 271–75.

17. For a good example, see Mari Ruti: "Although I believe that values are socially constructed rather than God given . . . I do not believe that gender inequality is any more defensible than racial inequality, despite repeated efforts to pass it off as culture-specific 'custom' rather than an instance of injustice." Mari Ruti, *The Call of Character: Living a Life Worth Living* (New York: Columbia University Press, 2014), 36. It is hard to see how this at all coherent; see Timothy Keller, *Making Sense of God: An Invitation to the Skeptical* (New York: Viking, 2016), 168–69.

18. Harari, *21 Lessons*, chap. 17. For a fascinating profile, see Ian Parker, "Yuval Noah Harari's History of Everyone, Ever," *New Yorker*, February 10, 2020, https://www.newyorker.com/.

19. See Luc Ferry: "I grant you that amongst the available doctrines of salvation, nothing can compete with Christianity—provided, that is, that you are a believer. If one is not a believer—and one cannot force oneself to believe, nor pretend to believe—then we must learn to think differently about the ultimate question posed by all doctrines of salvation. . . . I find the Christian proposition infinitely more tempting—except for the fact that I do not believe it. But were it to be true I would certainly be a taker." Luc Ferry, *A Brief History of Thought: A Philosophical Guide to Living*, trans. Theo Cuffe (New York: Harper Perennial, 2011), 261, 263.

20. Blaise Pascal, *Pensées*, trans. A. J. Krailsheimer (London: Penguin, 1995), 4.

21. See, respectively, my *If God, Then What? Wondering Aloud about Truth, Origins and Redemption* (Nottingham, UK: Inter-Varsity Press, 2012); *Unbreakable: What the Son of God Said about the Word of God* (Leyland, UK: 10 Publishing, 2014); *Echoes of Exodus: Tracing Themes of Redemption through Scripture* (Wheaton, IL: Crossway, 2018), with Alastair J. Roberts; *1 Corinthians For You* (Charlotte, NC: The Good Book Company, 2021); *Spirit and Sacrament: An Invitation to Eucharismatic Worship* (Grand Rapids, MI: Zondervan, 2018).

22. Fifteen people whose insights I have found particularly helpful here are Hannah Anderson, Anthony Bradley, Andy Crouch, Ross Douthat, David Bentley Hart, Alan Jacobs, Tim Keller, Peter Leithart, Jake Meador, Mark Sayers, Jamie Smith, Charles Taylor, Carl Trueman, Tom Wright, Christopher Watkin.

23. Augustus Toplady, "Reflections for the Beginning of the Year 1776," in *The Works of Augustus M. Toplady*, 6 vols. (London: Baynes, 1825), 3:451.

Select Bibliography

Many of the primary sources I have cited are letters that are freely available online, most notably the comprehensive collection at www.founders.archives.gov. Among the published works that I have consulted, the following have been particularly helpful.

Primary Sources

Adams, John. *Autobiography, Part One to October 1776.* Edited by L. H. Butterfield. Cambridge, MA: Harvard University Press, 1961.

Adams, John. *A Defence of the Constitutions of Government of the United States of America.* London: Dilly and Stockdale, 1787–1788.

Adams, John. *Thoughts on Government.* Philadelphia: Dunlap, 1776.

Anquetil-Duperron, Abraham Hyacinthe. *Zend-Avesta, Ouvrage de Zorastre: Contenant les Idées Théologiques, Physiques & Morales de ce Législateur, les Cérémonies du Culte Religieux qu'il a Établi, & Plusieurs Traits Importans Relatifs à l'Ancienne Histoire des Perses.* 3 Vols. Paris: Tilliard, 1771.

Bacon, Francis. *The New Organon.* Translated by Michael Silverthorne. Cambridge: Cambridge University Press, 2000.

Barrow, John. *A Voyage to Cochinchina in the years 1792 and 1793.* London: Cadell, 1806.

Beaglehole, J. C. *The "Endeavour" Journal of Joseph Banks, 1768–1771.* 2 Vols. Sydney: New South Wales Library, 1962.

Beaglehole, J. C. *The Journals of Captain James Cook.* 4 Vols. Cambridge: Cambridge University Press, 1955–1967.

Bentham, Jeremy. *An Answer to the Declaration of the American Congress.* London: Cadell, 1776.

Bentham, Jeremy. *A Fragment on Government.* London: Payne, Elmsly, and Brooke, 1776.

Berridge, John. *Sion's Songs, or Hymns Composed for the Use of Them That Love and Follow the Lord Jesus Christ in Sincerity.* London: Vallance and Conder, 1785.

Blake, William. *Songs of Experience.* London: Blake, 1794. First published 1789.

Boswell, James. *The Life of Samuel Johnson.* London: Penguin, 2008. First published 1791.

Boyle, Robert. *Some Considerations Touching the Usefulnesse of Experimental Naturall Philosophy.* 2 Vols. Oxford: Hall, 1663.

Burke, Edmund, ed. *Annual Register: Or a View of the History, Politicks, and Literature, for the Year 1762.* London: Dodsley, 1763.

Cartwright, John. *Take Your Choice! Representation and Respect, Imposition and Contempt; Annual Parliaments and Liberty, Long Parliaments and Slavery.* London: Almon, 1776.

Casanova, Giacomo. *The Memoirs of Jacques Casanova de Seingalt.* 12 Vols. Translated by Arthur Machen. New York: Putnam, 1894.

Cerisier, Antoine Marie. *Observations Impartiales d'un Vrai Hollandois à ses Compatriotes.* Arnhem: Nyhof, 1779.

De Corancez, Olivier. *De J. J. Rousseau.* Paris: Desenne et Maradan, 1798.

Corner, George. *The Autobiography of Benjamin Rush.* Princeton: American Philosophical Society: 1948.

Erasmus Darwin, *Zoonomia.* 2 Vols. London: Johnson, 1801.

Day, Thomas. *Fragment of an Original Letter on the Slavery of the Negroes, Written in the Year 1776.* London: Stockdale, 1784.

Diderot, Denis, and Jean-Baptiste le Rond d'Alembert, eds. *Encyclopédie ou Dictionnaire Raisonné des Sciences, des Arts et des Métiers.* 35 Vols. Paris: 1751–1772.

Diderot, Denis. *Oeuvres Complètes.* 20 Vols. Paris: Garnier Frères, 1875–1877.

Engels, Friedrich. *The Condition of the Working Class in England in 1844.* London: Swan Sonnenschein, 1892.

Equiano, Olaudah. *The Interesting Narrative and Other Writings.* Edited by Vincent Carretta. London: Penguin, 2003.

Von Ewald, Johann. *Diary of the American War: A Hessian Journal.* Translated and edited by Tustin, Joseph. New Haven, CT: Yale University Press, 1979.

Eze, Emmanuel Chukwudi. *Race and the Enlightenment: A Reader.* Oxford: Blackwell, 1997.

Ford, Worthington, ed. *Correspondence and Journals of Samuel Blachley Webb.* 3 Vols. New York: Wickersham Press, 1893.

Forster, Georg. *A Voyage around the World, in His Britannic Majesty's Sloop, Resolution* [. . .]. 2 Vols. London, 1777.

Gibbon, Edward. *The History of the Decline and Fall of the Roman Empire.* 6 Vols. London: Strahan and Cadell, 1776–1789.

Gibbon, Edward. *Memoirs of My Life.* London: Penguin, 2006. First Published 1796.

Von Goethe, Johann Wolfgang. *From My Life: Poetry and Truth.* Vol. 4 of *Goethe's Collected Works.* Translated by Robert Heitner. New York: Suhrkamp, 1987.

Von Goethe, Johann Wolfgang. *The Sufferings of Young Werther.* Translated by Bayard Quincy Morgan. New York: Frederick Ungar, 1957.

Hamann, Johann Georg. *Briefwechsel.* 6 Vols. Edited by Walther Ziesemer and Arthur Henkel. Wiesbaden: Insel, 1955–1975.

Hamann, Johann Georg. *London Writings: The Spiritual and Theological Journal of Johann Georg Hamann.* Translated by John Kleinig. Edited by Gene Edward Veith. Evansville, IN: Ballast Press, 2021.

Hamann, Johann Georg. *Sämtliche Werke.* Edited by Josef Nadler. Vienna: Herder, 1949–1957.

Hamann, Johann Georg. *Writings on Philosophy and Language.* Translated by Kenneth Haynes. Cambridge: Cambridge University Press, 2007.

Hamilton, Alexander. *The Works of Alexander Hamilton.* 7 Vols. Edited by John Hamilton. New York: Trow, 1850.

Haynes, Lemuel. *Liberty Further Extended, or Free Thoughts on the Illegality of Slave-Keeping.* In Ruth Bogin, "'Liberty Further Extended': A 1776 Antislavery Manuscript by Lemuel Haynes," *The William and Mary Quarterly* 40, no. 1 (1983): 85–105.

Hegel, G. W. F. *Aesthetics: Lectures on Fine Art.* 2 Vols. Translated by T. M. Knox. Oxford: Clarendon, 1975.

Herder, Johann Gottfried. *Selected Early Works, 1764–1767.* Translated by Ernest Menze with Michael Palma. University Park: Pennsylvania State University Press, 1992.

Hoare, Prince, ed. *Memoirs of Granville Sharp Esq, Composed From His Own Manuscripts.* London: Colburn, 1820.

Hopkins, Samuel. *A Dialogue concerning the Slavery of the Africans* [. . .]. Norwich: Spooner, 1776.

Hooker, Richard. *Of the Laws of Ecclesiastical Polity*. Edited by Arthur Stephen McGrade. Cambridge: Cambridge University Press, 1989. First published 1597.

Hume, David. *Dialogues concerning Natural Religion*. London, 1779.

Hume, David. *Essays and Treatises on Several Subjects*. 2 Vols. London: Cadell, 1768.

Hume, David. *Four Dissertations*. London: Millar, 1757.

Hume, David. *The Life of David Hume, Written by Himself.* London: Strahan and Cadell, 1777.

Hume, David. *Philosophical Essays concerning Human Understanding*. London: Millar, 1748.

Hume, David. *Political Essays*. Edited by Knud Haakonssen. Cambridge: Cambridge University Press, 1994.

Jefferson, Thomas. *Notes on the State of Virginia*. London: Stockdale, 1787.

Jefferson, Thomas. *The Papers of Thomas Jefferson*. 20 Vols. Edited by Julian Boyd. Princeton: Princeton University Press, 1943–1980.

Jones, William. *Lettre a Monsieur A*** du P***, Dans Laquelle est Compris L'Examen de sa Traduction des Livres Attribués à Zoroastre*. London: Elmsly, 1771.

Kant, Immanuel. *Political Writings*. 2nd Edition. Translated by H. B. Nisbet. Edited by Hans Reiss. Cambridge: Cambridge University Press, 1991.

Kant, Immanuel. *Critique of Pure Reason*. Translated and edited by Paul Guyer and Allen Wood. Cambridge: Cambridge University Press, 1998.

Kant, Immanuel. *Correspondence*. Translated by Arnulf Zweig. Cambridge: Cambridge University Press, 1999.

Kant, Immanuel. *Notes and Fragments*. Translated by Curtis Bowman, Paul Guyer, and Frederick Rauscher. Edited by Paul Guyer. Cambridge: Cambridge University Press, 2005.

Keir, James. *A Treatise on the Various Kinds of Permanently Elastic Fluids, or Gases*. London: Cadell and Elmsley, 1779.

Kleuker, Johann Friedrich. *Zend-Avesta, Zoroasters Lebendiges Wort*. 3 Vols. Riga: Hartknoch, 1776–1777.

De Lalande, Jérôme. *Bibliographie Astronomique avec l'histoire de l'Astronomie*. Paris: Imprimerie de la République, 1802.

Lessing, Gotthold Ephraim. *The Education of the Human Race*. Translated by F. W. Robertson. London: King, 1872.

Locke, John. *Two Treatises on Civil Government*. London: Routledge, 1884. First published 1689.

Long, Edward. *The History of Jamaica, or General Survey of the Antient and Modern State of That Island: With Reflections on Its Situation Settlements, Inhabitants, Climate, Products, Commerce, Laws, and Government*. 3 Vols. London: T. Lowndes, 1774.

Lovill, Justin, ed. *1776: A London Chronicle*. Padstow: Bunbury, 2019.

Lucretius, *De Rerum Natura*. Translated by William Leonard. New York: Dutton, 1916.

De Mably, Gabriel Bonnot. *De la Législation, ou Principes des Loix*. Amsterdam, 1776.

Madison, James. *The Papers of James Madison*. 17 Vols. Edited by William Hutchinson and William Rachal. Chicago: University of Chicago Press, 1962–1991.

Mandeville, Bernard. *The Fable of the Bees*. London: Tonson, 1714.

Mare, Margaret, and W. H. Quarrell. *Lichtenberg's Visits to England as Described in His Letters and Diaries*. Oxford: Clarendon Press, 1938.

Meslier, Jean. *Le Testament*. 3 Vols. Amsterdam: Meijer, 1864.

De Montaigne, Michel. *Essays*. Revised Edition. Translated by M. A. Screech. London: Penguin, 2013.

Montesquieu, Charles Louis de Secondat. *The Spirit of the Laws*. Translated and edited by Anne M. Cohler, Basia Carolyn Miller, and Harold Samuel Stone. Cambridge: Cambridge University Press, 1989.

Morgan, Kenneth, ed. *An American Quaker in the British Isles: The Travel Journals of Jabez Maud Fisher, 1775–1779*. Oxford: Oxford University Press, 1992.

Müteferrika, Ibrahim. *Traité de la Tactique*. Translated by Charles Réviczki. Vienna: Trattnern, 1769.

Newton, John, and William Cowper. *Olney Hymns*. Glasgow: Collins, 1829. First published 1779.

Newton, John. *The Works of the Rev. John Newton: From the Last London Edition*. 6 Vols. New York: Williams and Whiting, 1810.

Nietzsche, Friedrich. *On the Genealogy of Morals*. Translated by Michael A. Scarpitti. London: Penguin, 2013.

Nietzsche, Friedrich. *Philosophy and Truth: Selections from Nietzsche's Notebooks of the Early 1870s*. Translated by Daniel Breazeale. Atlantic Highlands, NJ: Humanities Press, 1979.

Nollet, Jean-Antoine. *L'Art des Expériences*. 3 Vols. Paris: 1770.

O'Flaherty, James. *Hamann's Socratic Memorabilia: A Translation and Commentary*. Baltimore: Johns Hopkins Press, 1967.

Paine, Thomas. *Common Sense: Addressed to the Inhabitants of America*. Philadelphia: Bradford, 1776.

Pascal, Blaise. *Pensées*. Translated by A. J. Krailsheimer. London: Penguin, 1995.

Price, Richard. *Observations on the Importance of the American Revolution and the Means of Making It a Benefit to the World*. London: Cadell, 1785.

Price, Richard. *Observations on the Nature of Civil Liberty*. London: Dilly and Cadell, 1776.

Priestley, Joseph. *Directions for Impregnating Water with Fixed Air*. London: Johnson, 1772.

Priestley, Joseph. *Experiments and Observations on Different Kinds of Air*. 6 Vols. London: Johnson, 1774–1777.

Radishchev, Alexander. *A Journey from St. Petersburg to Moscow*. Translated by Leo Wiener. Cambridge, MA: Harvard University Press, 1958.

Raynal, Guillaume-Thomas. *Histoire Philosophique et Politique, Des Établissements et du Commerce des Européens dans les deux Indes*. 5 Vols. Geneva: Pellet, 1780.

Guillaume-Thomas, Raynal. *A Philosophical and Political History of the Settlements and Trade of the Europeans in the East and West Indies*. 6 Vols. Translated by J. O. Justamond. London: Strahan and Cadell, 1776.

Robertson, William. *The History of America*. London: Strahan and Cadell, 1777.

Rocafuerte, Vincente, et al. *Ideas Necesarias á Todo Pueblo Americano Independiente*. Philadelphia: Huntingdon, 1821.

Rousseau, Jean-Jacques. *The Confessions of Jean-Jacques Rousseau*. Translated by J. M. Cohen. London: Penguin, 1953.

Rousseau, Jean-Jacques. *The Reveries of the Solitary Walker*. Translated by Anon. London: Robinson, 1796.

Ryskamp, Charles and Frederick Pottle, ed. *Boswell: The Ominous Years, 1774–1776*. New York: McGraw Hill, 1963.

De Sade, Marquis. *Juliette*. Translated by Austryn Wainhouse. New York: Grove Press, 1968.

De Sade, Marquis. *Justine, or, The Misfortunes of Virtue*. Translated by John Phillips. Oxford: Oxford University Press, 2012.

De Sade, Marquis. *The Misfortunes of Virtue and Other Early Tales*. Translated by David Coward. Oxford: Oxford University Press, 1992.

Schiller, Friedrich. *On the Aesthetic Education of Man, in a Series of Letters*. Translated and edited by Elizabeth Mary Wilkinson and L. A. Willoughby. Oxford: Clarendon, 1982.

Sharp, Granville. *The Just Limitation of Slavery in the Laws of God*. London: White, 1776.

Shelley, Mary, and Karen Swallow Prior. *Frankenstein: A Guide to Reading and Reflecting*. Nashville: B&H, 2021. First published 1818. Reprinted with new material.

Sprat, Thomas. *The History of the Royal Society of London, for the Improving of Natural Knowledge*. London: Martyn, 1667.

Sidney, Algernon. *Discourses concerning Government*. London: Millar, 1763.

Smith, Adam. *The Wealth of Nations*. 2 Vols. Ed. Andrew Skinner. London: Penguin, 1999. First published 1776.

De Staël, Madame. *De L'Allemagne*. Paris: Charpentier, 1844. First published 1813.

De Tocqueville, Alexis. *Democracy in America*. Translated by Harvey Mansfield and Debra Winthrop. Chicago: University of Chicago Press, 2000.

Toplady, Augustus. *The Works of Augustus M. Toplady*. 6 Vols. London: Baynes, 1825.

Toplady, Augustus. *Psalms and Hymns for Public and Private Worship*. London: Dilly, 1776.

Voltaire. *Oeuvres Complètes*. 52 Vols. Paris: Garnier Frères, 1877–1885.

Weis, Charles, and Frederick Pottle, eds. *Boswell in Extremes, 1776–1778*. New York: McGraw Hill, 1970.

Wesley, John. *A Collection of Hymns for the Use of the People Called Methodists*. London: Paramore, 1780.

Wesley, John. *Thoughts on Slavery*. London: Hawes, 1774.

Whitehurst, John. *An Inquiry into the Original State and Formation of the Earth: Deduced from Facts and the Laws of Nature. To Which Is Added an Appendix, Containing Some General Observations on the Strata in Derbyshire*. London: Cooper, 1778.

Witherspoon, John. *The Dominion of Providence over the Passions of Men.* Philadelphia, 1777.

Wordsworth, William. *The Poetical Works of William Wordsworth.* London: Moxon, 1847. First published 1826.

Wordsworth, William, and Samuel Taylor Coleridge. *Lyrical Ballads: 1798 and 1802.* Oxford: Oxford University Press, 2013.

Secondary Sources

Abernethy, David. *The Dynamics of Global Dominance: European Overseas Empires, 1415–1980.* New Haven, CT: Yale University Press, 2000.

Abulafia, David. *The Boundless Sea: A Human History of the Oceans.* London: Penguin, 2020.

Acemoglu, Daron, and James Robinson. *The Narrow Corridor: How Nations Struggle for Liberty.* London: Penguin, 2020.

Acemoglu, Daron, and James Robinson. *Why Nations Fail: The Origins of Power, Prosperity and Poverty.* New York: Crown, 2012.

Ackroyd, Peter. *Blake.* London: Vintage, 1999.

Aitken, Jonathan. *John Newton: From Disgrace to Amazing Grace.* Wheaton, IL: Crossway, 2007.

Allen, Robert. *The Industrial Revolution in Global Perspective.* Cambridge: Cambridge University Press, 2009.

Anthony, David. *The Horse, the Wheel and Language: How Bronze-Age Riders from the Eurasian Steppes Shaped the Modern World.* Princeton: Princeton University Press, 2007.

Appleby, Joyce. *Shores of Knowledge: New World Discoveries and the Scientific Imagination.* New York: Norton, 2013.

Assmann, Jan. *The Price of Monotheism.* Translated by Robert Savage. Stanford: Stanford University Press, 2010.

Atkinson, Rick. *The British Are Coming: The War for America 1775–1777.* London: Collins, 2019.

Barclay, John M. G. *Paul and the Gift.* Grand Rapids, MI: Eerdmans, 2015.

Barker-Benfield, G. J. *The Culture of Sensibility: Sex and Society in Eighteenth-Century Britain.* Chicago: University of Chicago Press, 1992.

Bayer, Oswald. *A Contemporary in Dissent: Johann Georg Hamann as a Radical Enlightener.* Grand Rapids, MI: Eerdmans, 2012.

Bayly, Christopher. *The Birth of the Modern World, 1780–1914*. Oxford: Blackwell, 2004.

Beckert, Sven. *Empire of Cotton: A New History of Global Capitalism*. London: Penguin, 2015.

Beiser, Frederick. *Enlightenment, Revolution, and Romanticism: The Genesis of Modern German Political Thought 1790–1800*. Cambridge, MA: Harvard University Press, 1992.

Bell, Madison Smartt. *Lavoisier in the Year One: The Birth of a New Science in an Age of Revolution*. New York: Norton, 2005.

Bellah, Robert, et al, *Habits of the Heart: Individualism and Commitment in American Life*. Berkeley: University of California Press, 2008. First published 1985.

Berger, Peter. *The Sacred Canopy: Elements of a Sociological Theory of Religion*. New York: Anchor, 1967.

Berlin, Isaiah. *The Magus of the North: J. G. Hamann and the Origins of Modern Irrationalism*. London: Fontana, 1994.

Berlin, Isaiah. *The Roots of Romanticism: The A. W. Mellon Lectures in the Fine Arts 1965*. Edited by Henry Hardy. London: Pimlico, 2000.

Betz, John. *After Enlightenment: The Post-Secular Vision of J. G. Hamann*. Oxford: Blackwell, 2012.

Blanning, Tim. *The Pursuit of Glory: Europe 1648–1815*. London: Penguin, 2008. First published 2007.

Blanning, Tim. *The Romantic Revolution*. London: Phoenix, 2010.

Blom, Philipp. *Wicked Company: Freethinkers and Friendship in Pre-Revolutionary Paris*. London: Weidenfeld and Nicolson, 2011.

Boyd, Julian. *The Declaration of Independence: The Evolution of the Text as Shown in Facsimiles of Various Drafts by Its Author, Thomas Jefferson*. Princeton: Princeton University Press, 1945.

Boyle, Nicholas. *Goethe: The Poet and the Age*. Oxford: Clarendon, 1991.

Brewster, James, ed. *Life of the Reverend John Newton, in a Series of Letters Written by Himself to the Rev. Dr. Haweis*. Edinburgh: Anderson and Bryce, 1824.

Burnard, Trevor. *Mastery, Tyranny, and Desire: Thomas Thistlewood and His Slaves in the Anglo-Jamaican World*. Chapel Hill: University of North Carolina Press, 2004.

Bundock, Michael. *The Fortunes of Francis Barber: The True Story of the Jamaican Slave Who Became Samuel Johnson's Heir*. New Haven, CT: Yale University Press, 2015.

Burton, Tara. *Strange Rites: New Religions for a Godless World.* New York: Public Affairs, 2020.

Chernow, Ron. *Washington: A Life.* New York: Penguin, 2010.

Chernow, Ron. *Alexander Hamilton.* New York: Penguin, 2004.

Clark, Gregory. *A Farewell to Alms: A Brief Economic History of the World.* Princeton: Princeton University Press, 2007.

Collins, Suzanne. *The Hunger Games.* New York: Scholastic, 2008.

Cosandey, David. *Le Secret de l'Occident: Vers un Théorie Générale du Progès Scientifique.* Paris: Flammarion, 2008.

Crocker, Lester. *The Embattled Philosopher: A Biography of Denis Diderot.* East Lansing: Michigan State College Press, 1954.

Dabhoiwala, Faramerz. *The Origins of Sex: A History of the First Sexual Revolution.* London: Penguin, 2012.

Dalrymple, William. *The Anarchy: The Relentless Rise of the East India Company.* London: Bloomsbury, 2019.

Damrosch, Leo. *Jean-Jacques Rousseau: Restless Genius.* New York: Houghton Mifflin, 2005.

Damrosch, Leo. *The Club: Johnson, Boswell, and the Friends Who Shaped an Age.* New Haven: Yale University Press, 2019.

Darwin, John. *After Tamerlane: The Rise and Fall of Global Empires, 1400–2000.* London: Penguin, 2008.

Deaton, Angus. *The Great Escape: Health, Wealth and the Origins of Inequality.* Princeton: Princeton University Press, 2013.

Delsol, Chantal. *La Fin de la Chrétienté.* Paris: Cerf, 2021.

Diamond, Jared. *Guns, Germs, and Steel: A Short History of Everybody for the Last 13,000 Years.* London: Vintage, 2017. First published 1997.

Dickinson, H. W., and Arthur Titley. *Richard Trevithick: The Engineer and the Man.* Cambridge: Cambridge University Press, 1934.

Dickinson, H. W., and Rhys Jenkins. *James Watt and the Steam Engine.* Oxford: Clarendon, 1927.

Drabble, Margaret. "Romanticism." In *The Oxford Companion to English Literature.* 5th Edition. Edited by Margaret Drabble. Oxford: Oxford University Press, 1985.

Drake, H. A. *Constantine and the Bishops: The Politics of Intolerance.* Baltimore: John Hopkins University Press, 2000.

Ducheyne, Steffen, ed. *Reassessing the Radical Enlightenment.* Milton Park, Abingdon, UK: Routledge, 2017.

Duncan, Bruce. *Lovers, Parricides, and Highwaymen: Aspects of Sturm und Drang Drama.* Rochester, NY: Camden House, 1999.

Dunn, John. *Democracy: A History.* London: Penguin, 2006.

Ellis, Joseph. *Founding Brothers.* New York: Vintage, 2000.

Falk, Seb. *The Light Ages: A Medieval Journey of Discovery.* London: Allen Lane, 2020.

Ferber, Michael. *Romanticism: A Very Short Introduction.* Oxford: Oxford University Press, 2010.

Ferguson, Niall. *Civilisation: The Six Killer Apps of Western Power.* London: Penguin, 2012.

Ferry, Luc. *A Brief History of Thought: A Philosophical Guide to Living.* Translated by Theo Cuffe. New York: Harper Perennial, 2011.

Findlay, Ronald, and Kevin O'Rourke. *Power and Plenty: Trade, War, and the World Economy in the Second Millennium.* Princeton: Princeton University Press, 2007.

Fischer, David Hackett. *Washington's Crossing.* Oxford: Oxford University Press, 2004.

Gabriele, Matthew, and David Perry. *The Bright Ages: A New History of Medieval Europe.* New York: Harper, 2021.

Garfield, Simon. *The Last Journey of William Huskisson.* London: Faber, 2003.

Gatrell, Vic. *The First Bohemians: Life and Art in London's Golden Age.* London: Penguin, 2014.

Gay, Peter. *The Enlightenment: An Interpretation.* 2 Vols. New York: Knopf, 1966.

Gleick, James. *Isaac Newton.* London: Harper Perennial, 2003.

Gordon-Reed, Annette. *The Hemingses of Monticello.* New York: Norton, 2008.

Graeber, David, and David Wengrow. *The Dawn of Everything: A New History of Humanity.* London: Allen Lane, 2021.

Gray, John. *Seven Types of Atheism.* London: Penguin, 2018.

Gregory, Brad. *The Unintended Reformation: How a Religious Revolution Secularized Society.* Cambridge, MA: Harvard University Press, 2015.

Griffin, Emma. *Liberty's Dawn: A People's History of the Industrial Revolution.* New Haven, CT: Yale University Press, 2013.

Habermas, Jürgen, et al. *An Awareness of What Is Missing: Faith and Reason in a Post-Secular Age.* Translated by Ciaran Cronin. Cambridge: Polity Press, 2010.

Haidt, Jonathan. *The Righteous Mind: Why Good People Are Divided by Politics and Religion*. London: Penguin, 2012.

Hannam, James. *God's Philosophers: How the Medieval World Laid the Foundations of Modern Science*. London: Icon, 2009.

Harari, Yuval Noah. *21 Lessons for the 21st Century*. London: Vintage, 2018.

Harari, Yuval Noah. *Sapiens: A Brief History of Humankind*. London: Vintage, 2011.

Hardin, James, and Christoph Schweitzer, eds. *German Writers in the Age of Goethe: Sturm und Drang to Classicism*. Detroit: Gale, 1990.

Harper, Kyle. *From Shame to Sin: The Christian Transformation of Sexual Morality in Late Antiquity*. Cambridge, MA: Harvard University Press, 2013.

Harper, Kyle. *Plagues upon the Earth: Disease and the Course of Human History*. Princeton: Princeton University Press, 2021.

Hart, David Bentley. *Atheist Delusions: The Christian Revolution and Its Fashionable Enemies*. New Haven, CT: Yale University Press, 2009.

Hattersley, Roy. *John Wesley: A Brand from the Burning*. London: Abacus, 2004.

Hempton, David. *The Church in the Long Eighteenth Century*. London: Tauris, 2011.

Henrich, Joseph. *The WEIRDest People in the World: How the West Became Psychologically Peculiar and Particularly Prosperous*. London: Allen Lane, 2020.

Heschel, Abraham Joshua. *God in Search of Man: A Philosophy of Judaism*. New York: Farrar, Straus and Giroux, 1955.

Hobsbawm, Eric. *The Age of Revolution: Europe, 1789–1848*. London: Abacus, 1962.

Hobsbawm, Eric. *Industry and Empire*. London: Penguin, 1999.

Hoffman, Philip. *Why Did Europe Conquer the World?* Princeton: Princeton University Press, 2015.

Holland, Tom, *Dominion: The Making of the Western Mind*. London: Little Brown, 2019.

Hopkins, Donald. *The Greatest Killer: Smallpox in History*. Chicago: University of Chicago Press, 2002.

Hunt, Tristram. *The Radical Potter: Josiah Wedgwood and the Transformation of Britain*. London: Allen Lane, 2021.

Irving, Washington. *The Life of George Washington*. 5 Vols. New York: Putnam, 1855–1859.

Isaacson, Walter. *Benjamin Franklin: An American Life.* New York: Simon and Schuster, 2003.

Isakhan, Benjamin, and Stephen Stockwell, eds. *The Secret History of Democracy.* New York: Palgrave Macmillan, 2011.

Israel, Jonathan. *Democratic Enlightenment: Philosophy, Revolution, and Human Rights 1750–1790.* Oxford: Oxford University Press, 2012.

Israel, Jonathan. *The Expanding Blaze: How the American Revolution Ignited the World.* Princeton: Princeton University Press, 2017.

Israel, Jonathan. *Radical Enlightenment: Philosophy and the Making of Modernity, 1650–1750.* Oxford: Oxford University Press, 2002.

Jackson, Maurice. *Let This Voice Be Heard: Anthony Benezet, Father of Atlantic Abolitionism.* Philadelphia: University of Pennsylvania Press, 2009.

Jacob, Margaret. *The First Knowledge Economy: Human Capital and the European Economy, 1750–1850.* Cambridge: Cambridge University Press, 2014.

Jenkins, Philip. *Fertility and Faith: The Demographic Revolution and the Transformation of World Religions.* Waco, TX: Baylor University Press, 2020.

Jones, Eric. *The European Miracle: Environments, Economies and Geopolitics in the History of Europe and Asia.* Cambridge: Cambridge University Press, 2003.

Jones, Peter. *One or Two: Seeing a World of Difference.* Enumclaw, WA: Winepress, 2010.

Josephson-Storm, Jason. *The Myth of Disenchantment: Magic, Modernity, and the Birth of the Human Sciences.* Chicago: University of Chicago Press, 2017.

Kates, Gary. *Monsieur d'Éon Is a Woman: A Tale of Political Intrigue and Sexual Masquerade.* New York: Basic Books, 1995.

Keable-Elliott, Ian. *The Century of Deception: The Birth of the Hoax in Eighteenth-Century England.* London: Westbourne Press, 2021.

Keller, Timothy. *Making Sense of God: An Invitation to the Skeptical.* New York: Viking, 2016.

Kelly, Ian. *Casanova: Actor, Lover, Priest, Spy.* London: Hodder and Stoughton, 2008.

Ghulam Hussain Tabatabai Khan, Syed. *Seir Mutaqherin; or Review of Modern Times: Being an History of India.* 3 Vols. Calcutta: 1790.

Kidd, Thomas S. *God of Liberty: A Religious History of the American Revolution.* New York: Basic Books, 2010.

Kidd, Thomas S. *Thomas Jefferson: A Biography of Spirit and Flesh.* New Haven, CT: Yale University Press, 2022.

Kinservik, Matthew. *Sex, Scandal, and Celebrity in Eighteenth-Century London.* New York: Palgrave Macmillan, 2007.

Kloppenberg, James. *Toward Democracy: The Struggle for Self-Rule in European and American Thought.* Oxford: Oxford University Press, 2016.

Landes, David. *The Wealth and Poverty of Nations: Why Some Are So Rich and Some Are So Poor.* New York: Norton, 1998.

Lefkowitz, Arthur. *The Long Retreat: The Calamitous American Defense of New Jersey, 1776.* New Brunswick: Rutgers University Press, 1998.

Lewis, David. *The Voyaging Stars: Secrets of the Pacific Island Navigators.* New York: Norton, 1978.

Lieberman, Victor. *Strange Parallels: Southeast Asia in Global Context, c. 800–1830.* 2 Vols. Cambridge: Cambridge University Press, 2003–2010.

Lukianoff, Greg, and Jonathan Haidt. *The Coddling of the American Mind: How Good Intentions and Bad Ideas are Setting Up a Generation for Failure.* London: Penguin, 2018.

McCloskey, Deirdre. *Bourgeois Equality: How Ideas, Not Capital or Institutions, Enriched the World.* Chicago: University of Chicago Press, 2016.

McCullough, David. *1776: America and Britain at War.* New York: Penguin, 2005.

McCullough, David. *John Adams.* New York: Touchstone, 2001.

MacCulloch, Diarmaid. *A History of Christianity: The First Three Thousand Years.* London: Penguin, 2010.

Meador, Jake. *What Are Christians For? Life Together at the End of the World.* Downers Grove, IL: InterVarsity Press, 2022.

Mishra, Pankaj. *From the Ruins of Empire: The Revolt Against the West and the Remaking of Asia.* London: Penguin, 2013.

Mokyr, Joel. *The Gifts of Athena: Historical Origins of the Knowledge Economy.* Princeton: Princeton University Press, 2002.

Mokyr, Joel. *The Lever of Riches: Technological Creativity and Economic Progress.* Oxford: Oxford University Press, 1990.

Montefiore, Simon Sebag. *Catherine the Great and Potemkin.* London: Weidenfeld and Nicolson, 2000.

Morris, Ian. *The Measure of Civilization: How Social Development Decides the Fate of Nations.* Princeton: Princeton University Press, 2013.

Morris, Ian. *Why the West Rules—for Now: The Patterns of History, and What They Reveal about the Future.* London: Profile, 2010.

Peter Moore, *Endeavour: The Ship and the Attitude that Changed the World.* London: Vintage, 2019.

Muirhead, James. *The Life of James Watt.* New York: Appleton, 1859.

Norman, Jesse. *Adam Smith: What He Thought and Why It Matters.* London: Penguin, 2018.

North, Douglass, and Barry Weingast. "Constitutions and Commitment: The Evolution of Institutions Governing Public Choice in Seventeenth-Century England," *The Journal of Economic History* 49, no. 4 (1989): 803–32.

North, J. A. *Roman Religion.* Cambridge: Cambridge University Press, 2000.

O'Donnell, James. *Pagans: The End of Traditional Religion and the Rise of Christianity.* New York: Ecco, 2015.

Osborne, Roger. *Iron, Steam and Money: The Making of the Industrial Revolution.* London: Pimlico, 2014.

Osborne, Roger. *Of the People, by the People: A New History of Democracy.* London: Pimlico, 2011.

Ostler, Catherine. *The Duchess Countess: The Woman Who Scandalised a Nation.* London: Simon and Schuster, 2021.

Paine, Lincoln. *Sea and Civilisation.* London: Vintage, 2013.

Parthasarathi, Prasannan. *Why Europe Grew Rich and Asia Did Not.* Cambridge: Cambridge University Press, 2011.

Pascal, Roy. *The German Sturm und Drang.* Manchester: Manchester University Press, 1953.

Pead, Patrick John. *Benjamin Jesty, the Grandfather of Vaccination.* Newcastle: Cambridge Scholars Press, 2020.

Phipps, William. *Amazing Grace in John Newton: Slave-Ship Captain, Hymnwriter, and Abolitionist.* Mercer: Mercer University Press, 2001.

Pinker, Stephen. *Enlightenment Now: The Case for Reason, Science, Humanism and Progress.* London: Penguin, 2018.

Pomeranz, Kenneth. *The Great Divergence: China, Europe, and the Making of the Modern World Economy.* Princeton: Princeton University Press, 2000.

Rae, John. *Life of Adam Smith.* London: Macmillan, 1895.

Reinke, Tony. *Newton on the Christian Life: To Live Is Christ.* Wheaton, IL: Crossway, 2015.

Rieff, Philip. *The Triumph of the Therapeutic: Uses of Faith after Freud.* Chicago: University of Chicago Press, 1987.

Robertson, Ritchie. *The Enlightenment: The Pursuit of Happiness, 1680–1790.* London: Allen Lane, 2020.

Rosen, William. *The Most Powerful Idea in the World: A Story of Steam, Industry and Invention.* London: Pimlico, 2011.

Rosenthal, Jean-Laurent, and Bin Wong. *Before and Beyond Divergence: The Politics of Economic Change in China and Europe.* Cambridge, MA: Harvard University Press, 2011.

Rowe, William. *China's Last Empire: The Great Qing.* Cambridge: Harvard University Press, 2009.

Russell, Ben. *James Watt: Making the World Anew.* London: Reaktion, 2014.

Ryrie, Alec. *Unbelievers: An Emotional History of Doubt.* Cambridge: Harvard University Press, 2019.

De Saint Pierre, Jacques-Henri Bernardin. *La Vie et Les Ouvrages de Jean-Jacques Rousseau.* Edited by Maurice Souriau. Paris: Cornély, 1907.

Satia, Priya. *Empire of Guns: The Violent Making of the Industrial Revolution.* Richmond: Duckworth, 2018.

Scanlan, Padraic. *Slave Empire: How Slavery Built Modern Britain.* London: Robinson, 2020.

Schaeffer, Neil. *The Marquis de Sade: A Life.* Cambridge, MA: Harvard University Press, 2000. First Published 1998.

Scheidel, Walter. *Escape from Rome: The Failure of Empire and the Road to Prosperity.* Princeton: Princeton University Press, 2019.

Scott, David. *Leviathan: The Rise of Britain as a World Power.* London: Collins, 2014.

Scruton, Roger. *Kant: A Very Short Introduction.* Oxford: Oxford University Press, 2001.

Sensbach, Jon F. *Rebecca's Revival: Creating Black Christianity in the Atlantic World.* Cambridge, MA: Harvard University Press, 2005.

Siedentop, Larry. *Inventing the Individual: The Origins of Western Liberalism.* London: Penguin, 2015.

Smith, Christian. *Atheist Overreach: What Atheism Can't Deliver.* Oxford: Oxford University Press, 2019.

Smith, Steven. *Pagans and Christians in the City: Culture Wars from the Tiber to the Potomac.* Grand Rapids: Eerdmans, 2018.

Sorkin, David. *The Religious Enlightenment: Protestants, Jews, and Catholics from London to Vienna.* Princeton: Princeton University Press, 2008.

Spencer, Nick. *The Evolution of the West: How Christianity Has Shaped Our Values.* London: SPCK, 2016.

Stark, Rodney. *For the Glory of God: How Monotheism Led to Reformations, Science, Witch-Hunts, and the End of Slavery.* Princeton: Princeton University Press, 2003.

Stasavage, David. *The Decline and Rise of Democracy: A Global History from Antiquity to Today.* Princeton: Princeton University Press, 2020.

Storey, Benjamin, and Jenna Silber Storey. *Why We Are Restless: On the Modern Quest for Contentment.* Princeton: Princeton University Press, 2021.

Storr, Will. *The Status Game: On Social Position and How We Use It.* London: William Collins, 2021.

Tartt, Donna. *The Goldfinch.* London: Little, Brown, 2013.

Taylor, Charles. *A Secular Age.* Cambridge, MA: Belknap Press of Harvard University Press, 2007.

Taylor, Charles. *Sources of the Self: The Making of the Modern Identity.* Cambridge, MA: Harvard University Press, 1989.

Thomas, Nicholas. *Discoveries: The Voyages of Captain Cook.* London: Penguin, 2018.

Thompson, Bradley. *America's Revolutionary Mind: A Moral History of the American Revolution and the Declaration That Defined It.* New York: Encounter, 2019.

Trueman, Carl R. *The Rise and Triumph of the Modern Self: Cultural Amnesia, Expressive Individualism, and the Road to Sexual Revolution.* Wheaton, IL: Crossway, 2020.

Turchin, Peter "A Theory for Formation of Large Empires." *Journal of Global History* 4 (2009): 191–217.

Tyerman, Luke. *The Life and Times of the Rev. John Wesley.* 3 Vols. London: Hodder and Stoughton, 1872.

Uglow, Jenny. *The Lunar Men: The Friends Who Made the Future, 1730–1810.* London: Faber, 2002.

Veith, Gene. *Post-Christian: A Guide to Contemporary Thought and Culture.* Wheaton, IL: Crossway, 2020.

Vries, Peer. *Escaping Poverty: The Origins of Modern Economic Growth.* Vienna: Vienna University Press, 2013.

De Vries, Jan. "The Industrial Revolution and the Industrious Revolution." *Journal of Economic History* 54 (1994): 249–70.

De Vries, Jan, and Ad van der Woude. *The First Modern Economy: Success, Failure, and Perseverance of the Dutch Economy, 1500–1815.* Cambridge: Cambridge University Press, 1997.

Wallerstein, Immanuel. *The Modern World-System III: The Second Era of Great Expansion of the Capitalist World Economy 1730–1840s.* Berkeley: University of California Press, 2011.

Watkin, Christopher. *Biblical Critical Theory: How the Bible's Unfolding Story Makes Sense of Modern Life and Culture.* Grand Rapids, MI: Zondervan, 2022.

Weber, Max. *The Protestant Ethic and the Spirit of Capitalism.* Oxford: Oxford University Press, 2010.

White, Jerry. *London in the Eighteenth Century: A Great and Monstrous Thing.* London: Bodley Head, 2012.

White, Kevin. *The First Sexual Revolution: The Emergence of Male Heterosexuality in Modern America.* New York: New York University Press, 1993.

Whitehead, A. N. *Science and the Modern World.* New York: Free Press, 1967.

Wilken, Robert Louis. *The Christians as the Romans Saw Them.* New Haven, CT: Yale University Press, 2003.

Wilson, Ben. *Metropolis: A History of Humankind's Greatest Invention.* London: Jonathan Cape, 2020.

Wokler, Robert. *Rousseau: A Very Short Introduction.* Oxford: Oxford University Press, 2001.

Wolterstorff, Nicholas. *Justice: Rights and Wrongs.* Princeton: Princeton University Press, 2008.

Wood, Gordon. *Revolutionary Characters: What Made the Founders Different.* New York: Penguin, 2006.

Wood, Michael. *The Story of China: A Portrait of a Civilisation and Its People.* London: Simon and Schuster, 2020.

Wulf, Andrea. *Magnificent Rebels: The First Romantics and the Invention of the Self.* London: John Murray, 2022.

Index